story and art by

RYOMA KITADA

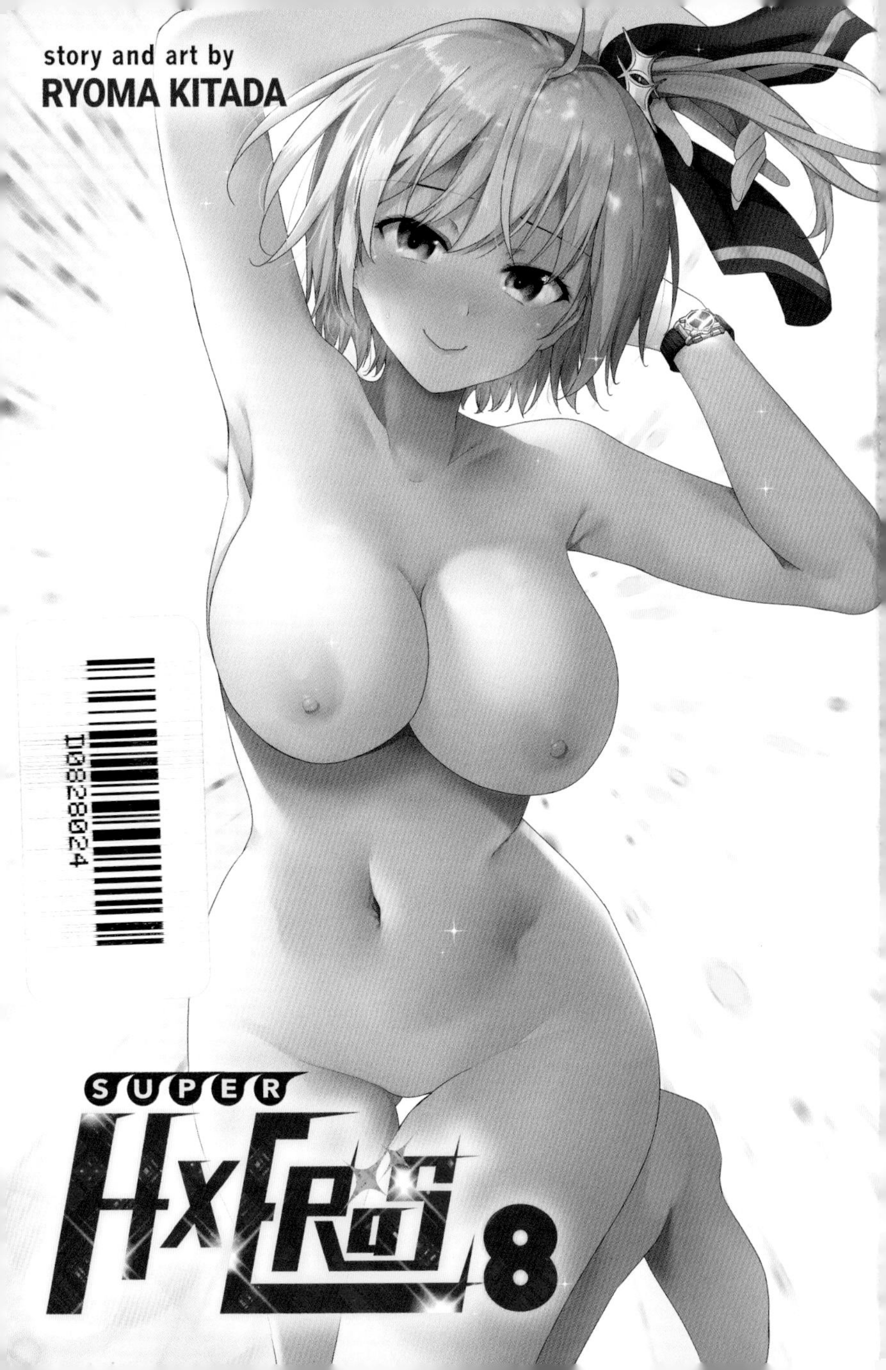

SUPER HxEROS 8

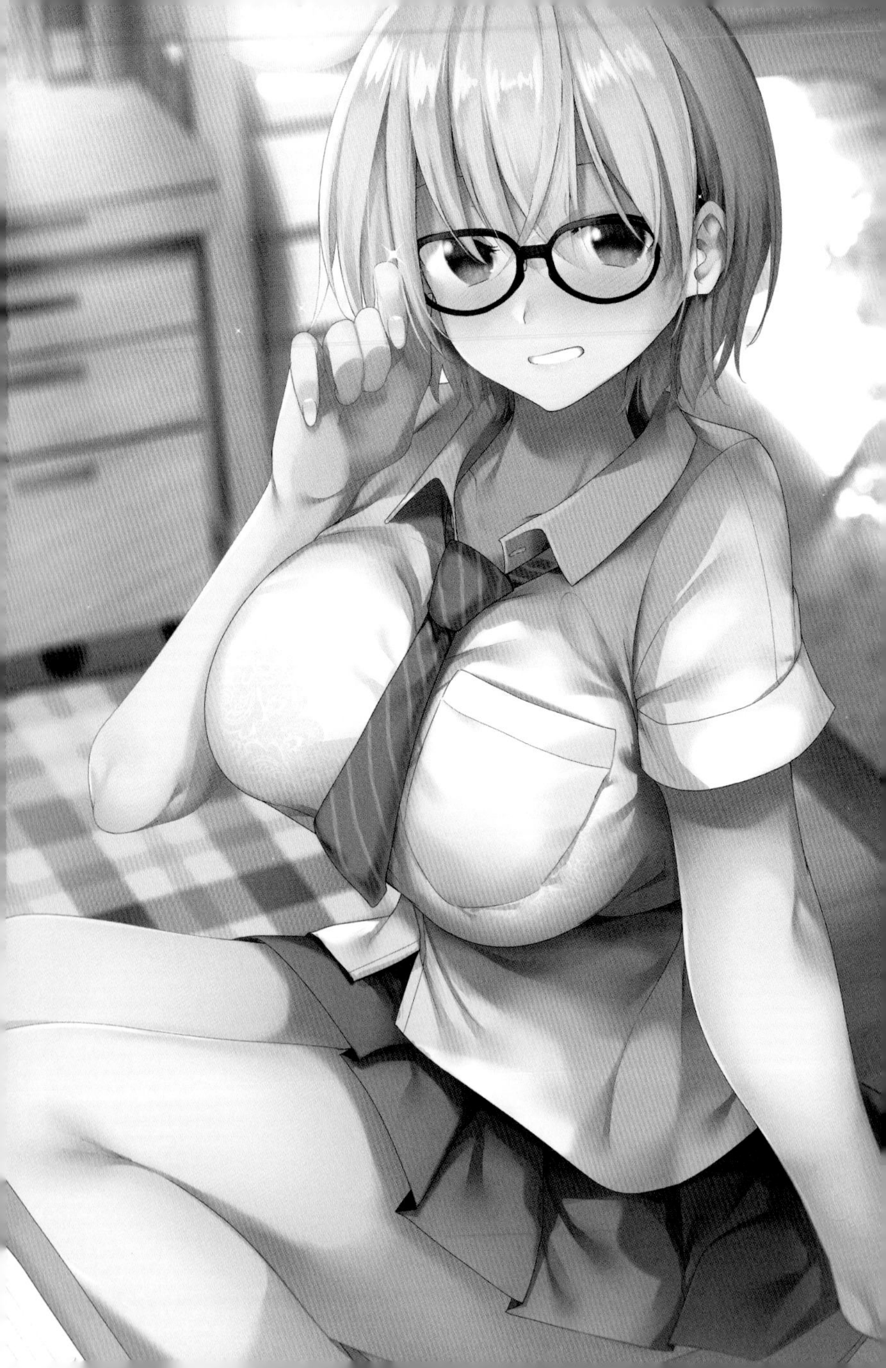

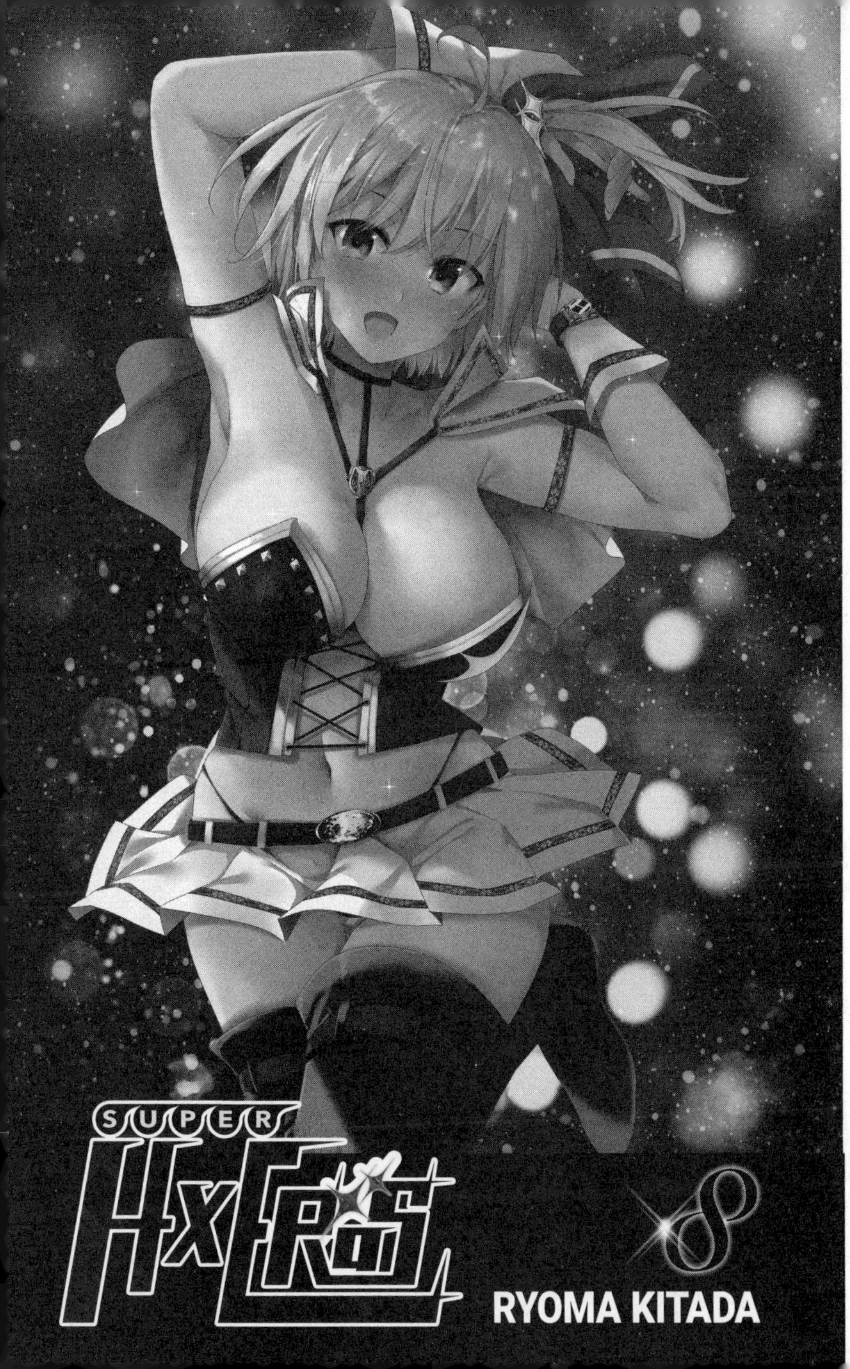
SUPER
HxEros
8
RYOMA KITADA

HXEROS Characters

HXEROS: A team of heroes that use the power of eros and H-Energy to fight the alien Kiseichuu.

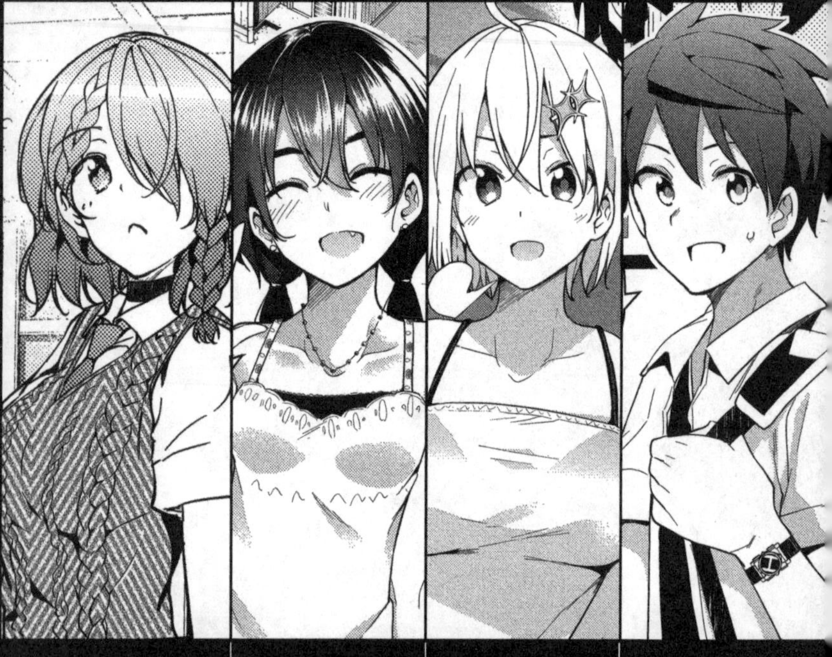

Maihime Shirayuki

HXE White

A sweet, clumsy girl who looks normal on the outside but is a total horndog on the inside.

Momoka Momozono

HXE Pink

Tired of always being in her sister's shadow, she took up the superhero mantle. Has caught onto Retto's feelings for Kirara.

Kirara Hoshino

HXE Yellow

Extremely adverse to sex and sexual innuendo due to a traumatic attack when she was young. After remembering Retto proposed marriage to her when they were kids, promised him an eventual answer.

Retto Enjo

HXE Red

Became a hero to avenge his childhood friend, Kirara, after a Kiseichuu attack traumatized her as a child. Coincidentally, also in love with her.

Story

Retto and the gang corner the Kiseichuu queen, but a mysterious girl with a black HXEROS device spirits her away. Soon after, a new student resembling said mystery girl joins Retto's class: Yoitsuki Shou. But after growing close to her, Retto and Kirara are convinced they are not one and the same. Then, when the HXEROS head to Okinawa on a school trip, Shou and Retto end up alone together during a test of courage, and a small origami crane tumbles out of her bag, hinting at a connection to the mystery girl...

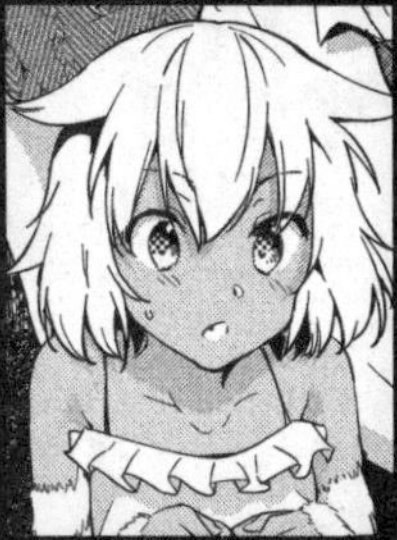

Chacha

Shunned Kiseichuu Princess. Has the ability to amplify H-Energy.

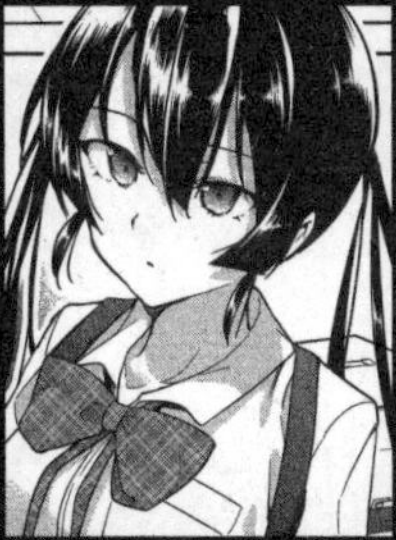

Yoitsuki Shou

New student in Retto's class. Cursed to have "sexy accidents" visited upon herself and everyone around her.

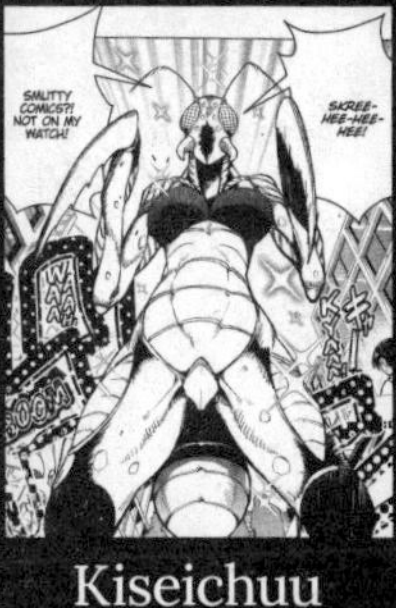
SMUTTY COMICS?! NOT ON MY WATCH!
SKREE-HEE-HEE-HEE!

Kiseichuu

Evil aliens who seek to destroy humanity by draining their H-Energy, the source of human sexual desire.

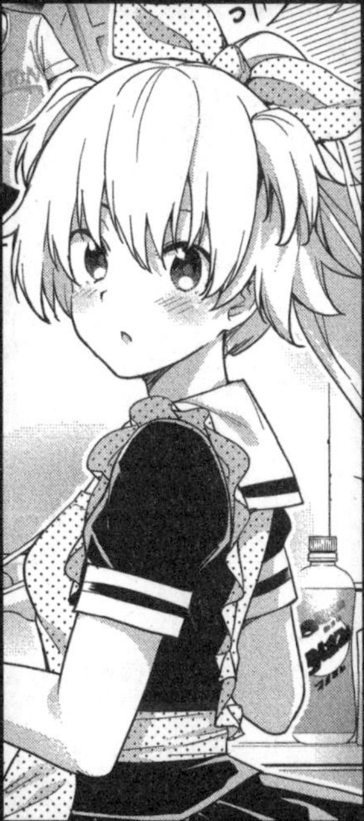

Sora Tenkuji

HXE Blue

Loves to draw hentai manga. Responsible for designing the XERO Suits.

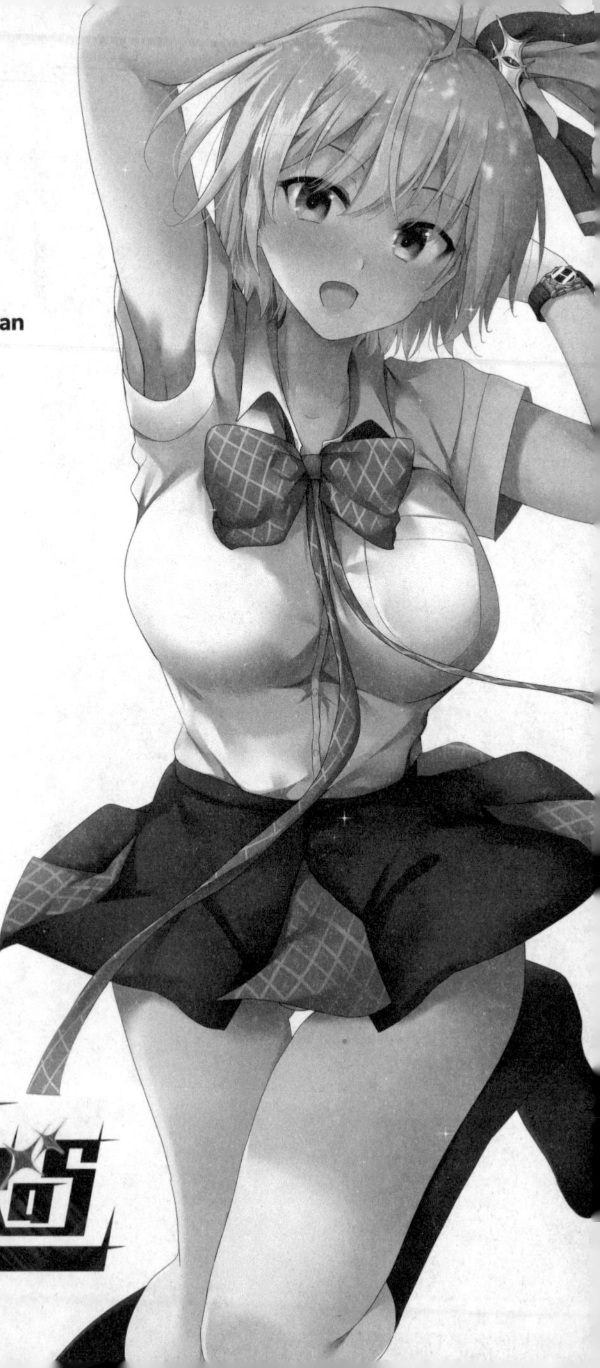

SUPER HXEROS

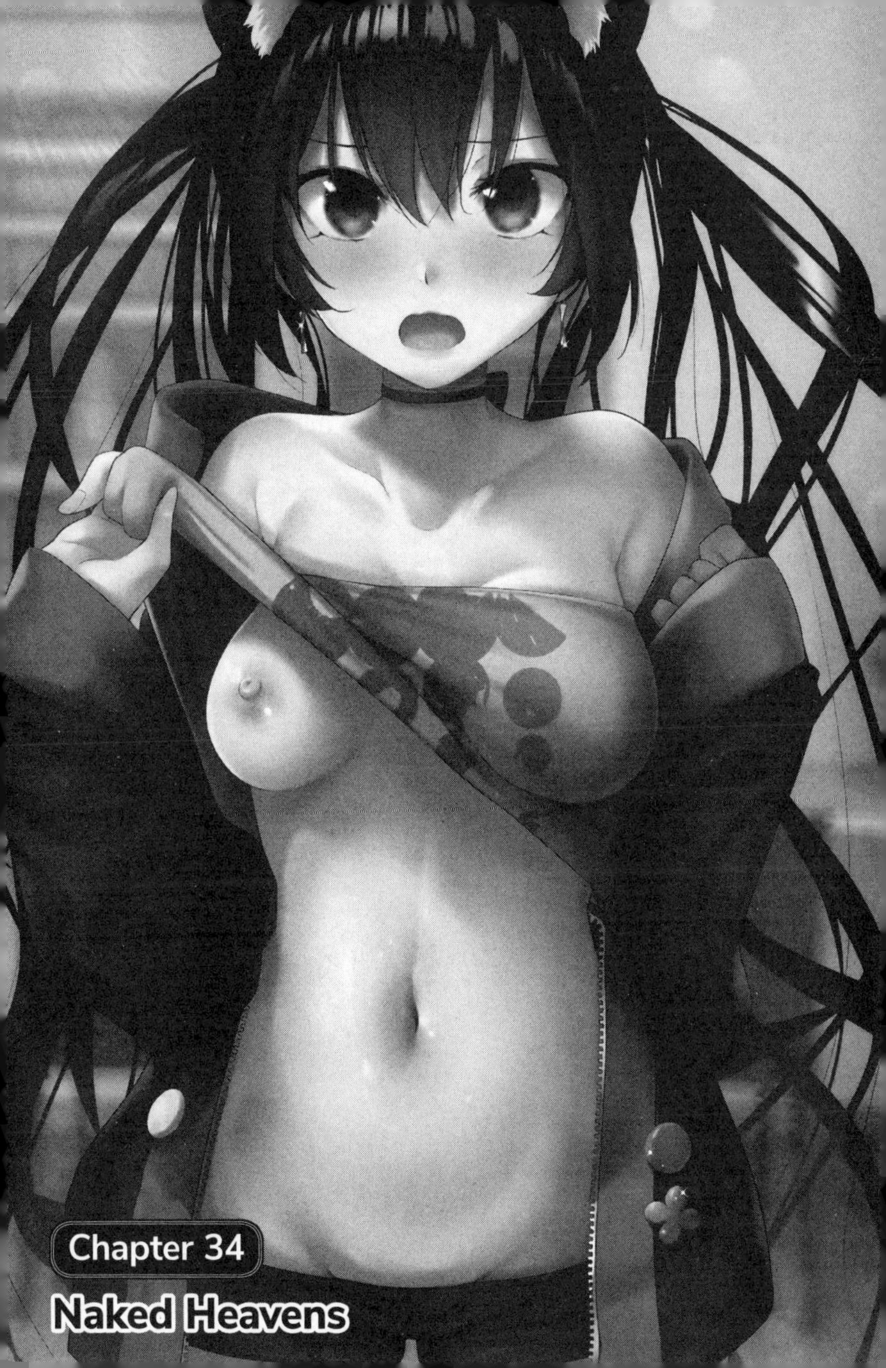

Chapter 34
Naked Heavens

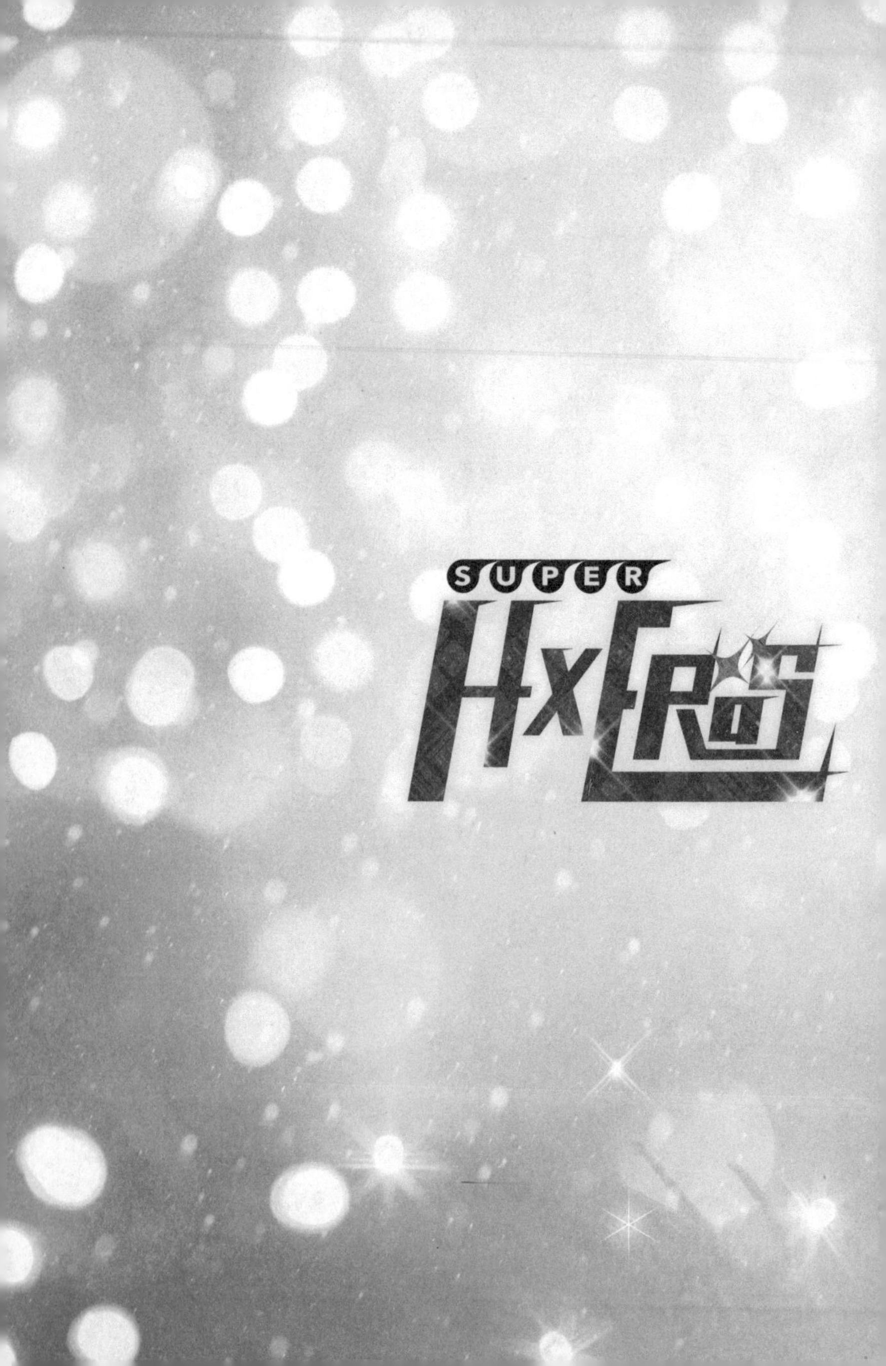
SUPER
HxEROS

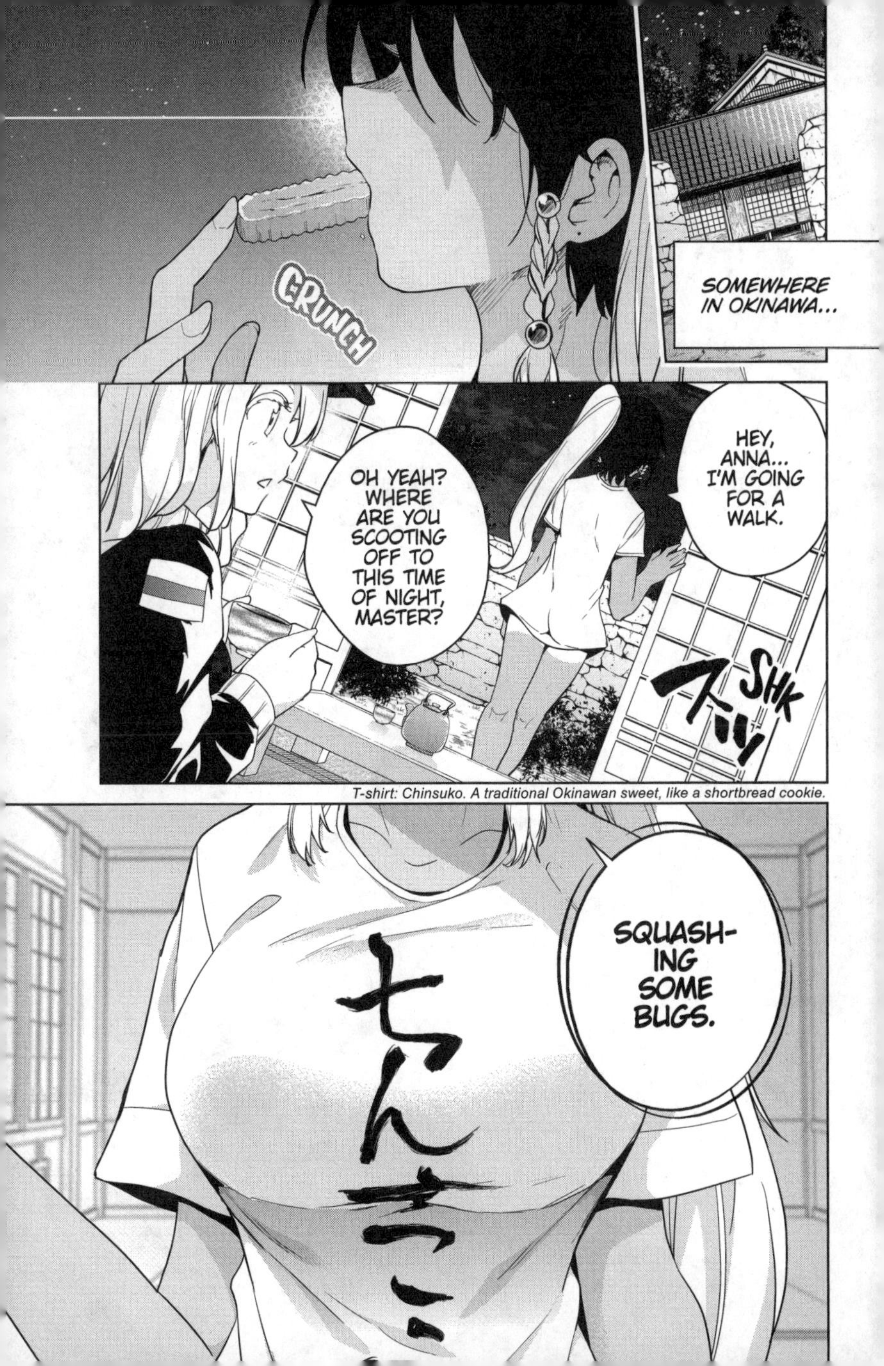
SOMEWHERE IN OKINAWA...
GRUNCH
HEY, ANNA... I'M GOING FOR A WALK.
OH YEAH? WHERE ARE YOU SCOOTING OFF TO THIS TIME OF NIGHT, MASTER?
SHK
SQUASHING SOME BUGS.

T-shirt: Chinsuko. A traditional Okinawan sweet, like a shortbread cookie.

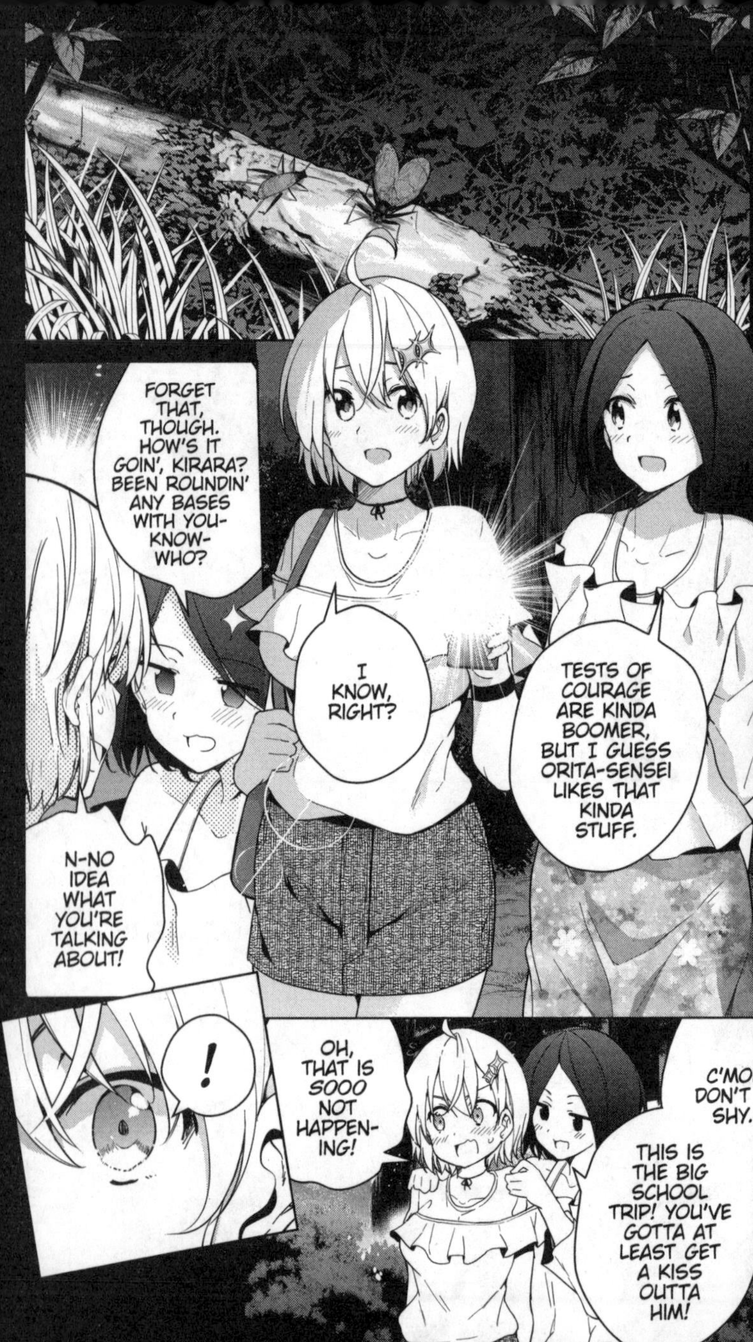
TESTS OF COURAGE ARE KINDA BOOMER, BUT I GUESS ORITA-SENSEI LIKES THAT KINDA STUFF.
I KNOW, RIGHT?
FORGET THAT, THOUGH. HOW'S IT GOIN', KIRARA? BEEN ROUNDIN' ANY BASES WITH YOU-KNOW-WHO?
N-NO IDEA WHAT YOU'RE TALKING ABOUT!
C'MON, DON'T BE SHY...
THIS IS THE BIG SCHOOL TRIP! YOU'VE GOTTA AT LEAST GET A KISS OUTTA HIM!
OH, THAT IS SOOO NOT HAPPENING!
!

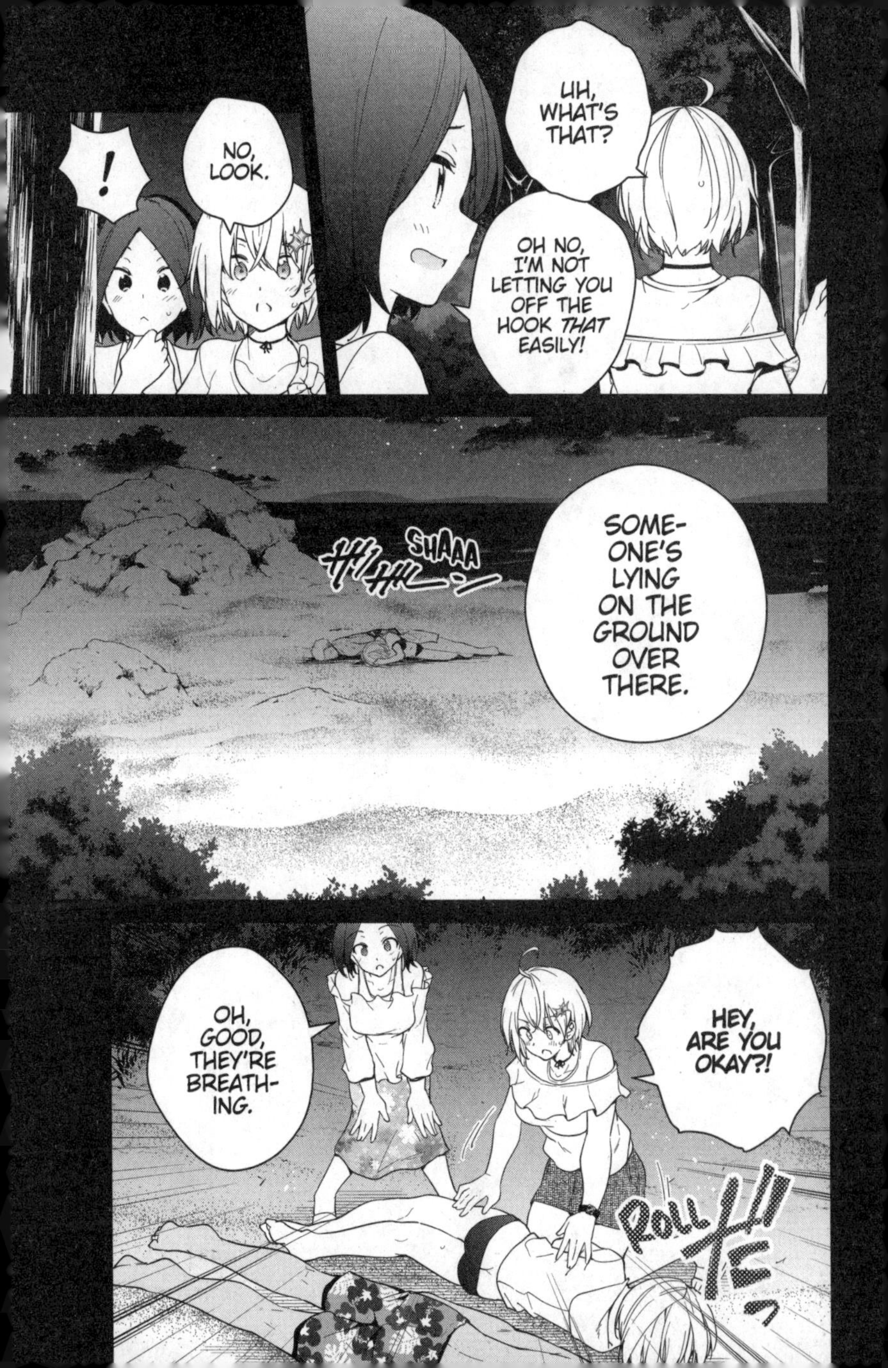
UH, WHAT'S THAT?
OH NO, I'M NOT LETTING YOU OFF THE HOOK *THAT* EASILY!
NO, LOOK.
!
SOME-ONE'S LYING ON THE GROUND OVER THERE.
SHAAA
HEY, ARE YOU OKAY?!
OH, GOOD, THEY'RE BREATH-ING.
ROLL

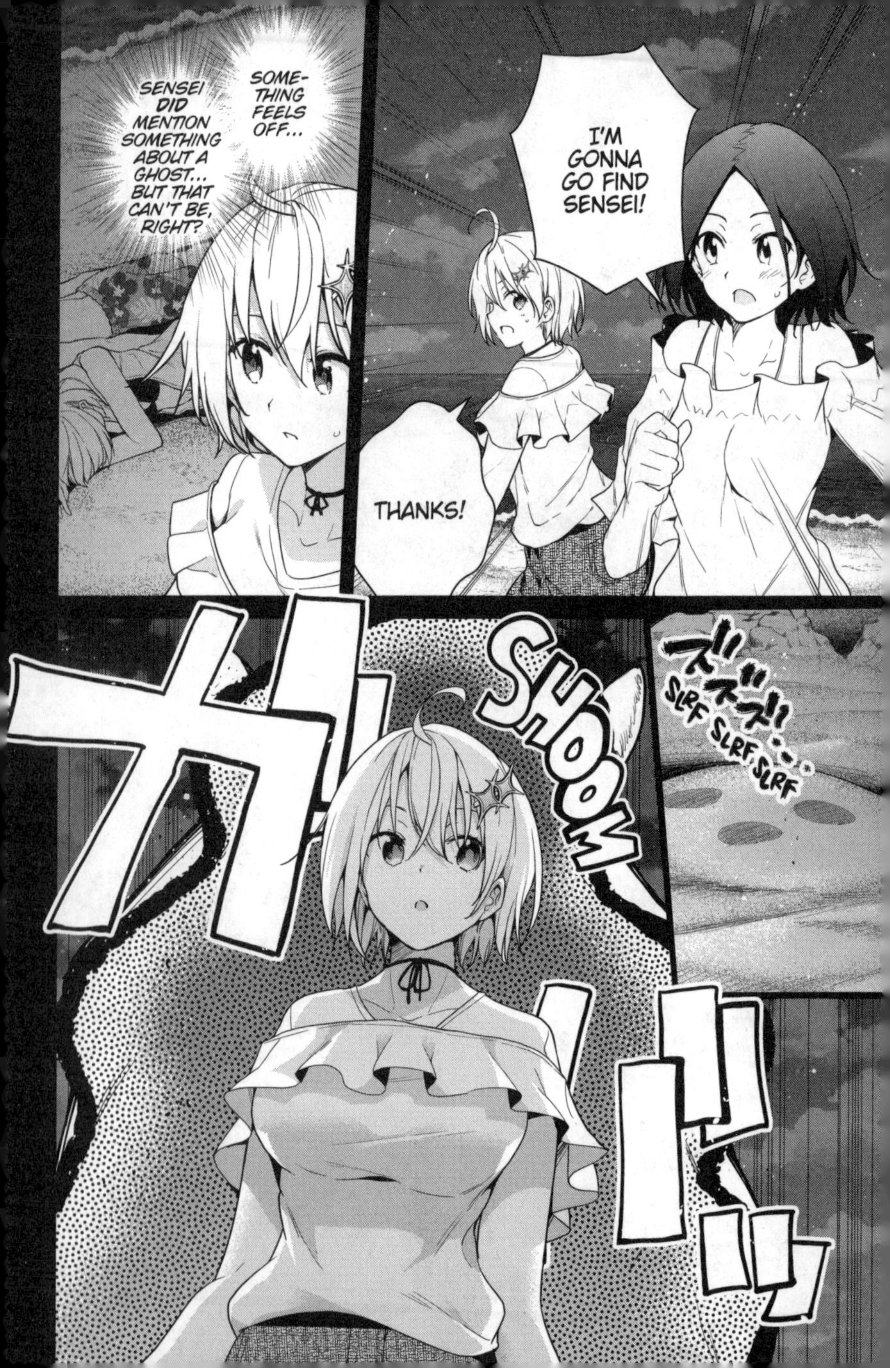
I'M GONNA GO FIND SENSEI!
THANKS!
SOMETHING FEELS OFF...
SENSEI DID MENTION SOMETHING ABOUT A GHOST... BUT THAT CAN'T BE, RIGHT?
ズズズ…
SLRF SLRF SLRF
SHOOM

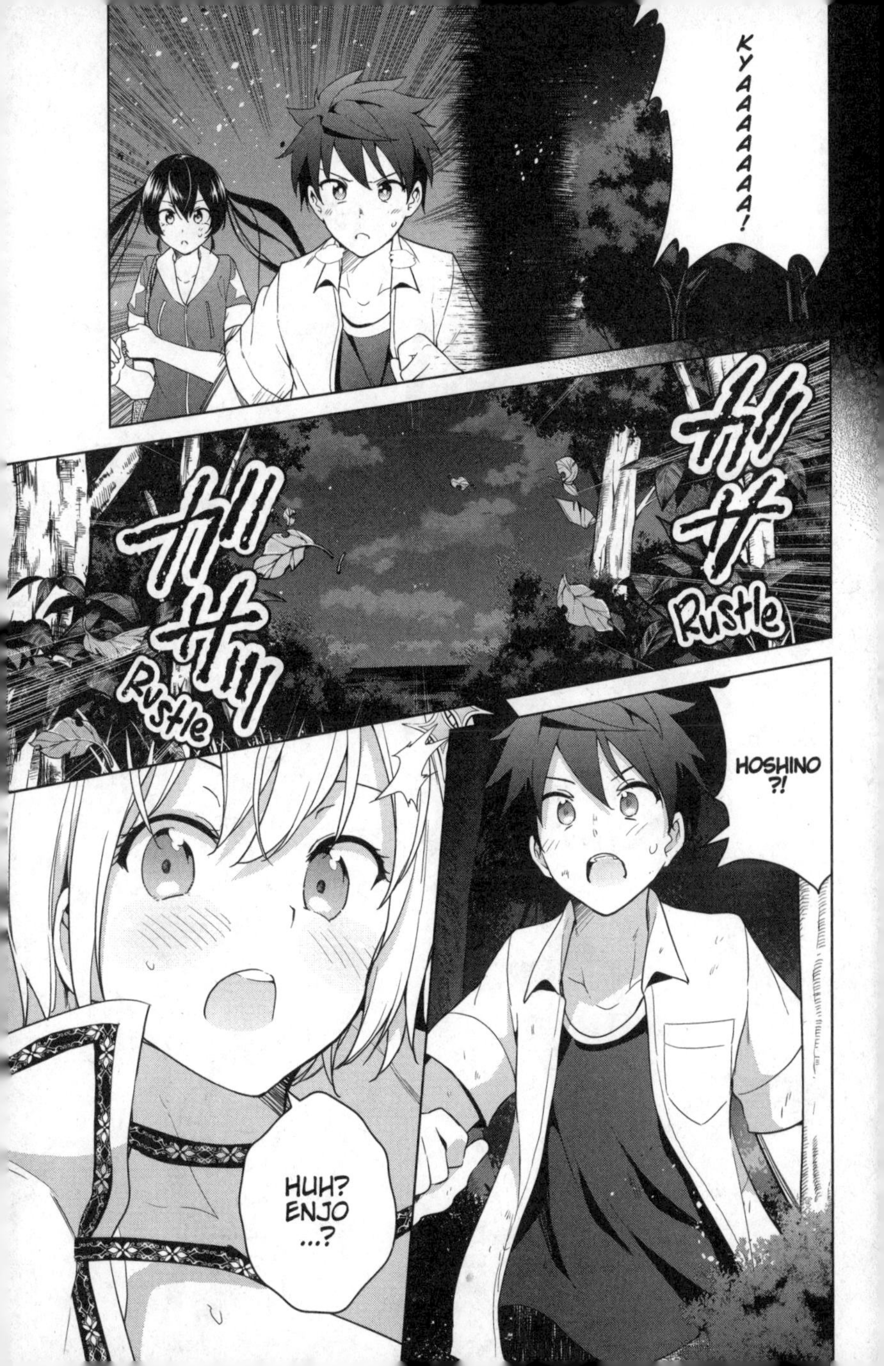
KYAAAAAAA!
Rustle
Rustle
HOSHINO ?!
HUH? ENJO ...?

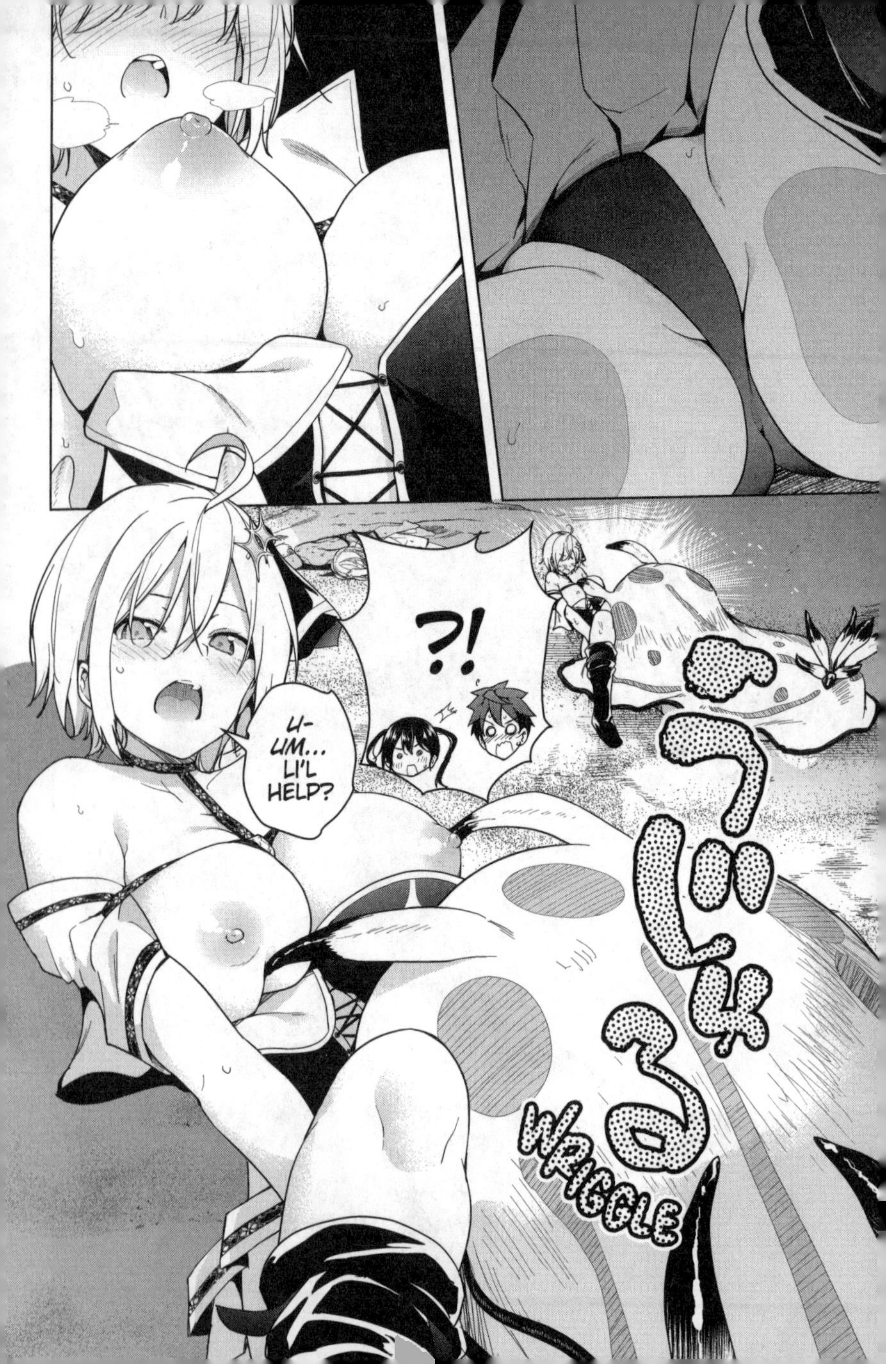
?!
うじゅる
WRIGGLE
U-UM... LI'L HELP?

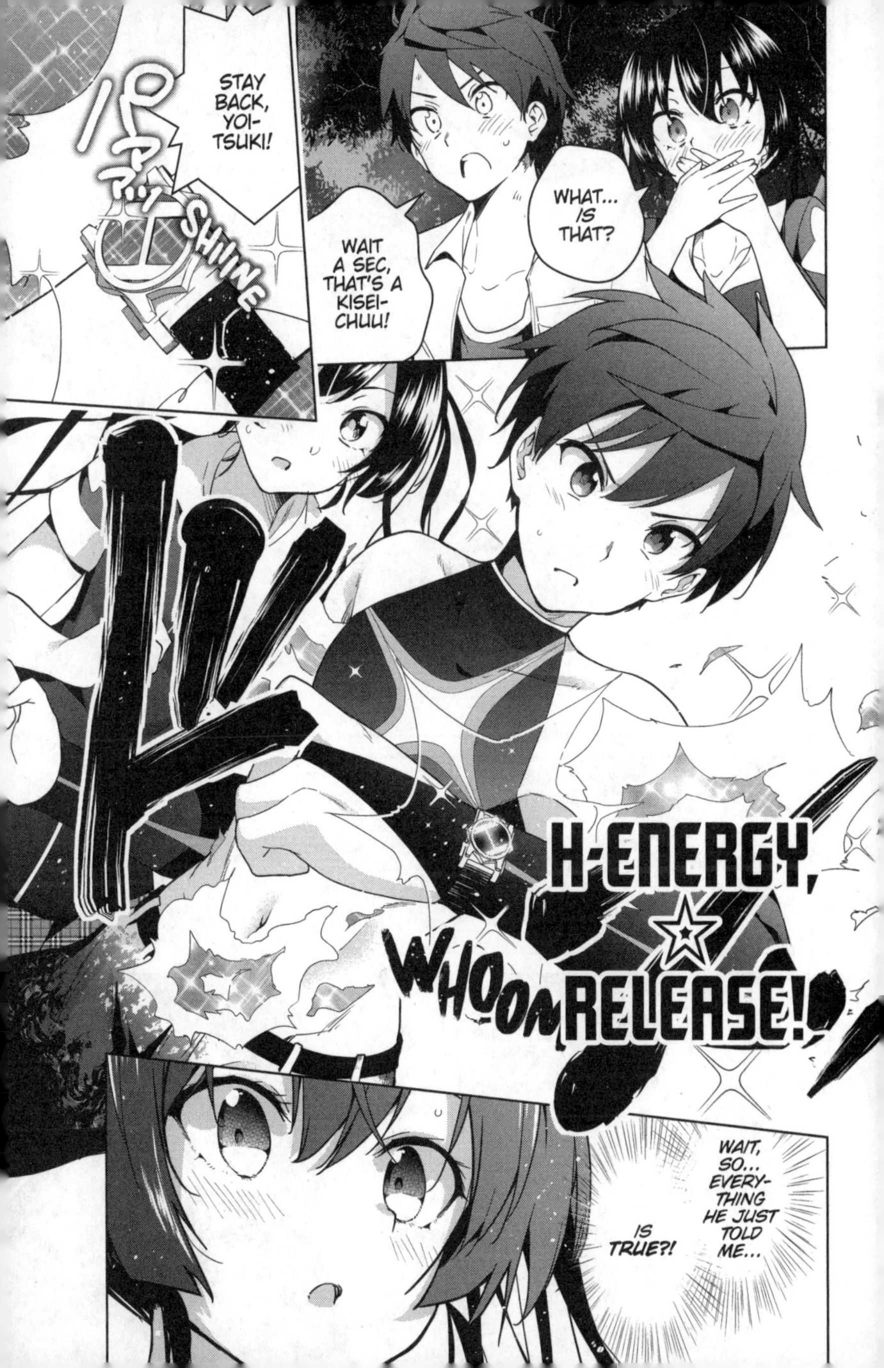
WHAT... IS THAT?
WAIT A SEC, THAT'S A KISEI-CHUU!
STAY BACK, YOI-TSUKI!
SHINE
H-ENERGY, ☆ RELEASE!
WHOOM
WAIT, SO... EVERY-THING HE JUST TOLD ME...
IS TRUE?!

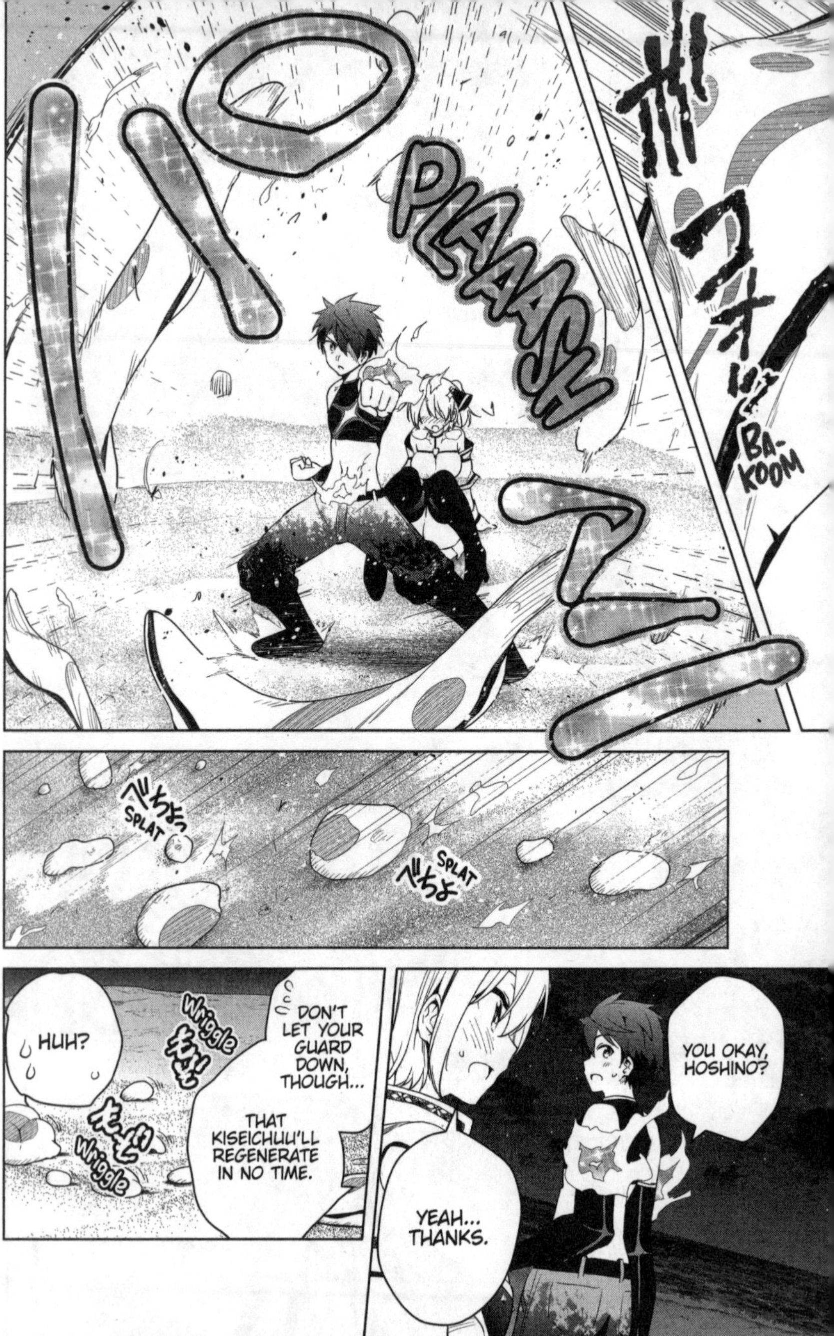
BA-KOOM
PIAAASH
べちょっ SPLAT
べちょ SPLAT
YOU OKAY, HOSHINO?
YEAH... THANKS.
DON'T LET YOUR GUARD DOWN, THOUGH...
wriggle
THAT KISEICHUU'LL REGENERATE IN NO TIME.
HUH?
wriggle

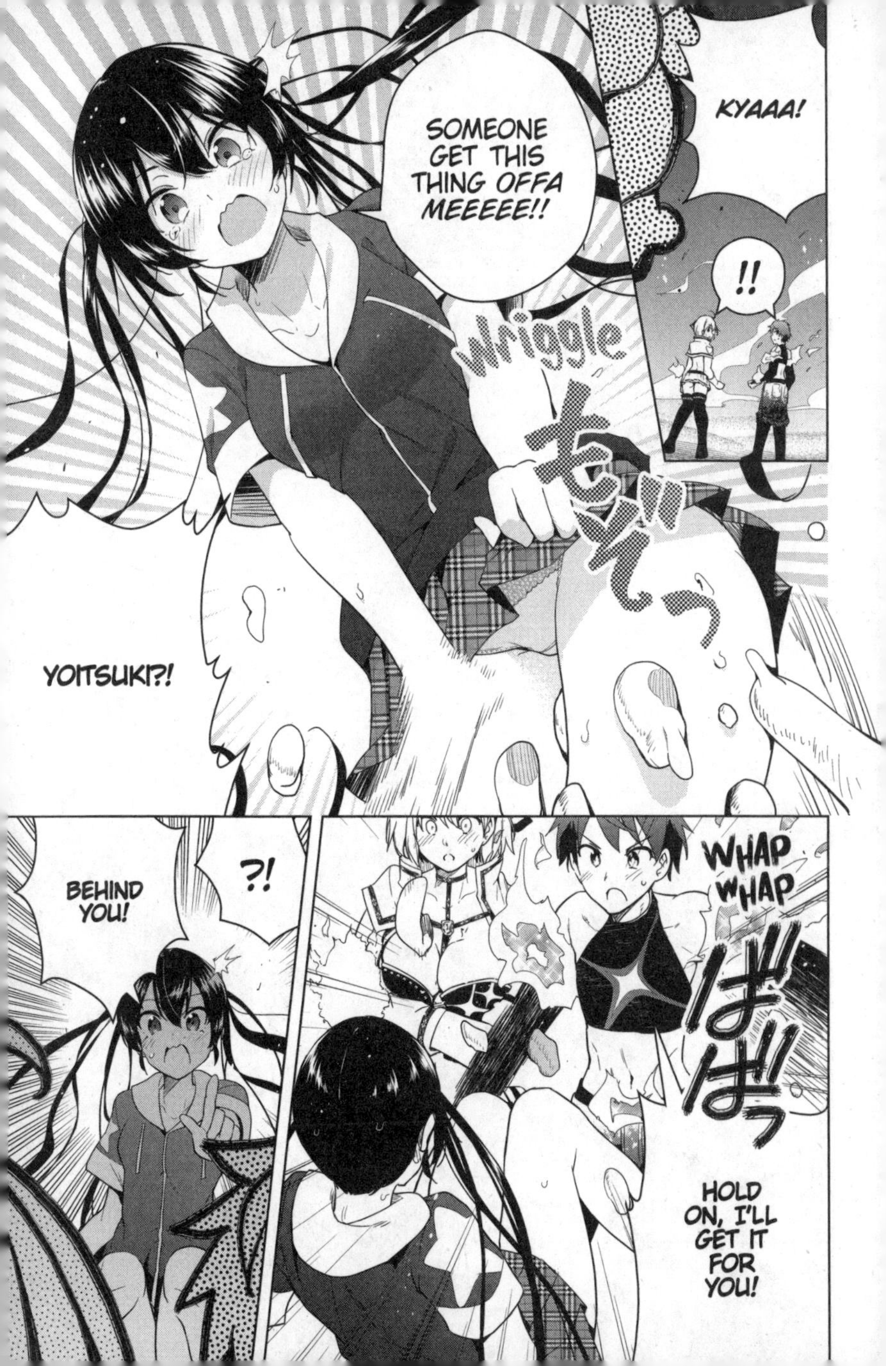
KYAAA!
!!
SOMEONE GET THIS THING OFFA MEEEEE!!
Wriggle
YOITSUKI?!
WHAP WHAP
HOLD ON, I'LL GET IT FOR YOU!
?!
BEHIND YOU!

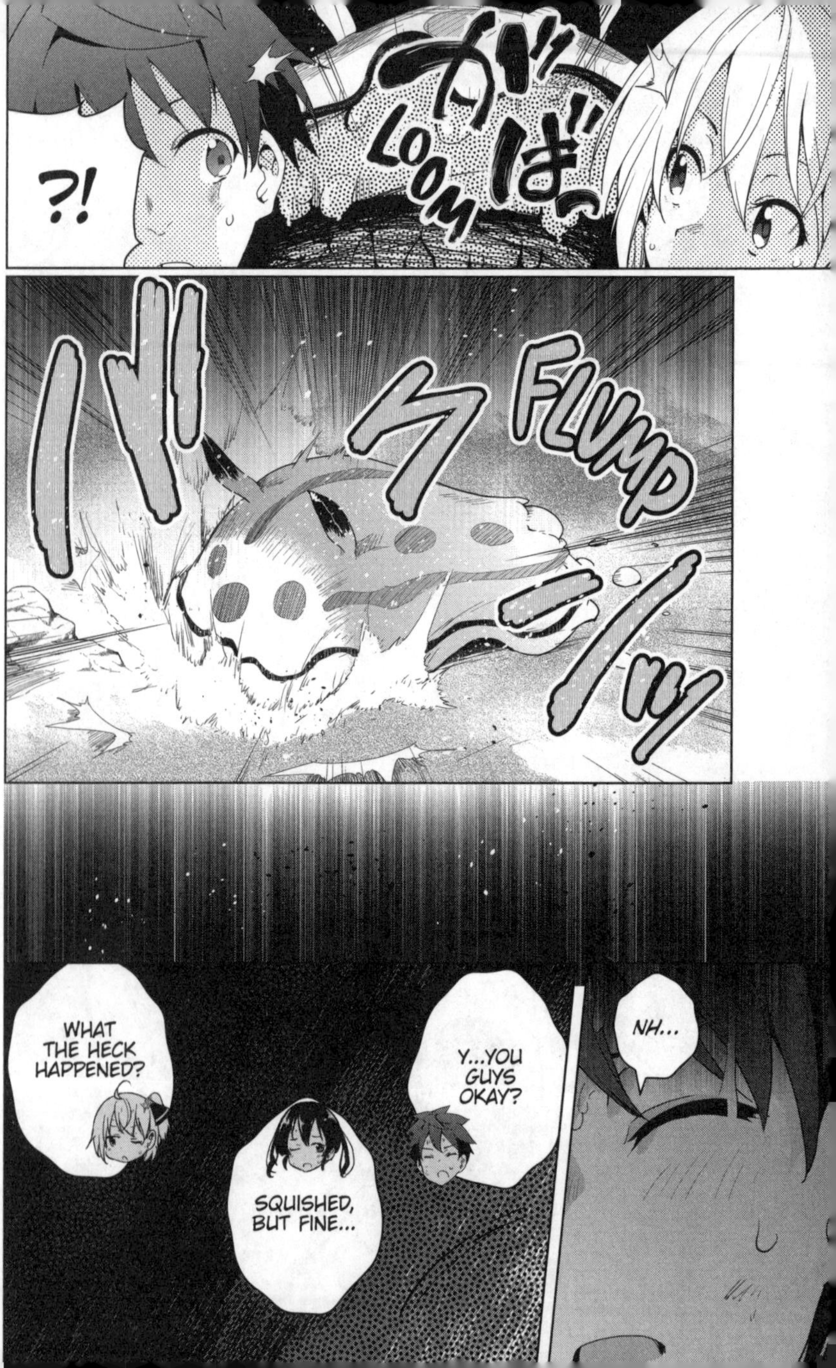
がばっ
LOOM
?!
FLUMP
NH...
Y...YOU GUYS OKAY?
WHAT THE HECK HAPPENED?
SQUISHED, BUT FINE...

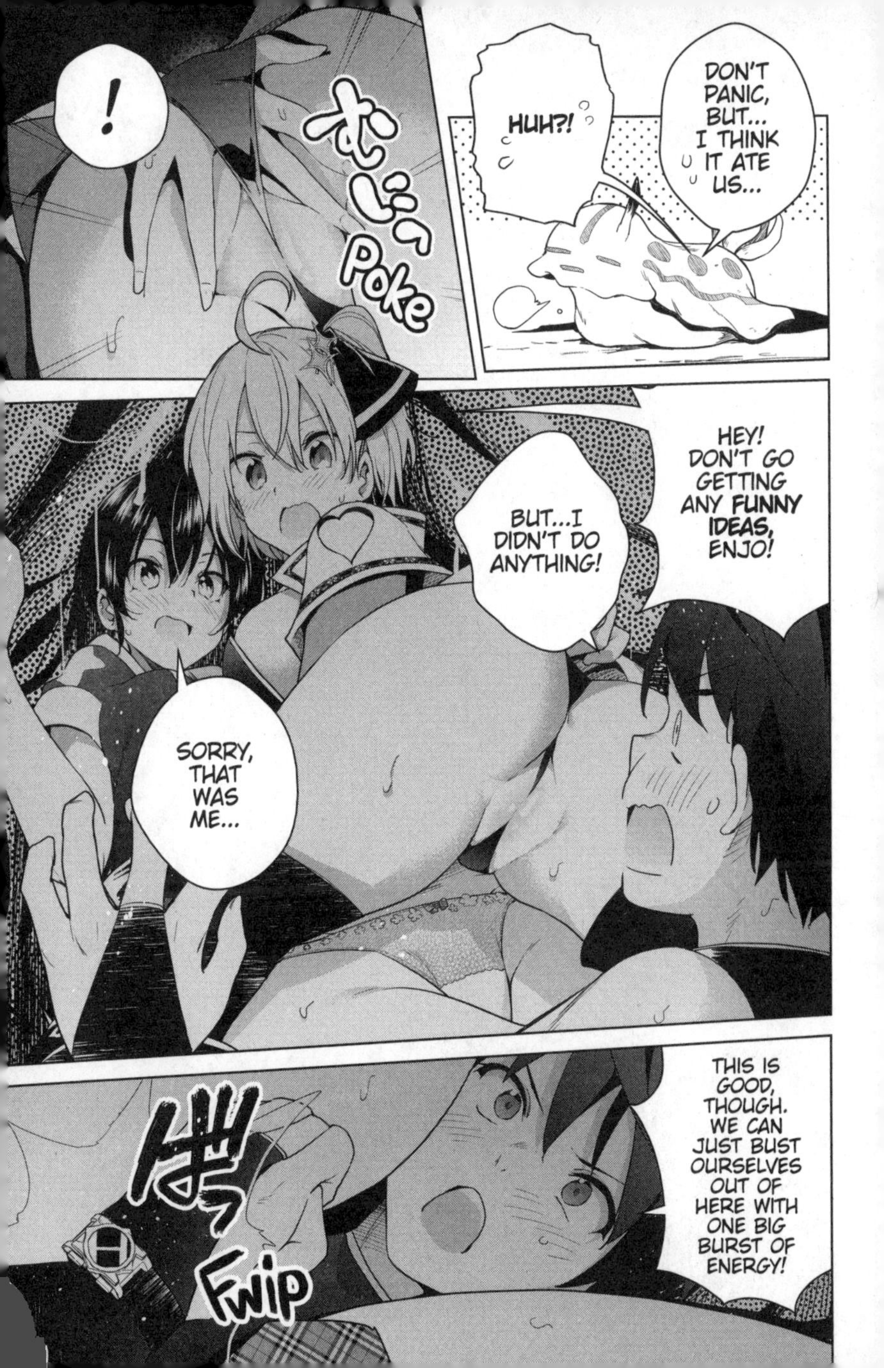

DON'T PANIC, BUT... I THINK IT ATE US...
HUH?!
!
むにっ
Poke
HEY! DON'T GO GETTING ANY **FUNNY IDEAS**, ENJO!
BUT...I DIDN'T DO ANYTHING!
SORRY, THAT WAS ME...
THIS IS GOOD, THOUGH. WE CAN JUST BUST OURSELVES OUT OF HERE WITH ONE BIG BURST OF ENERGY!
ぱっ
Fwip

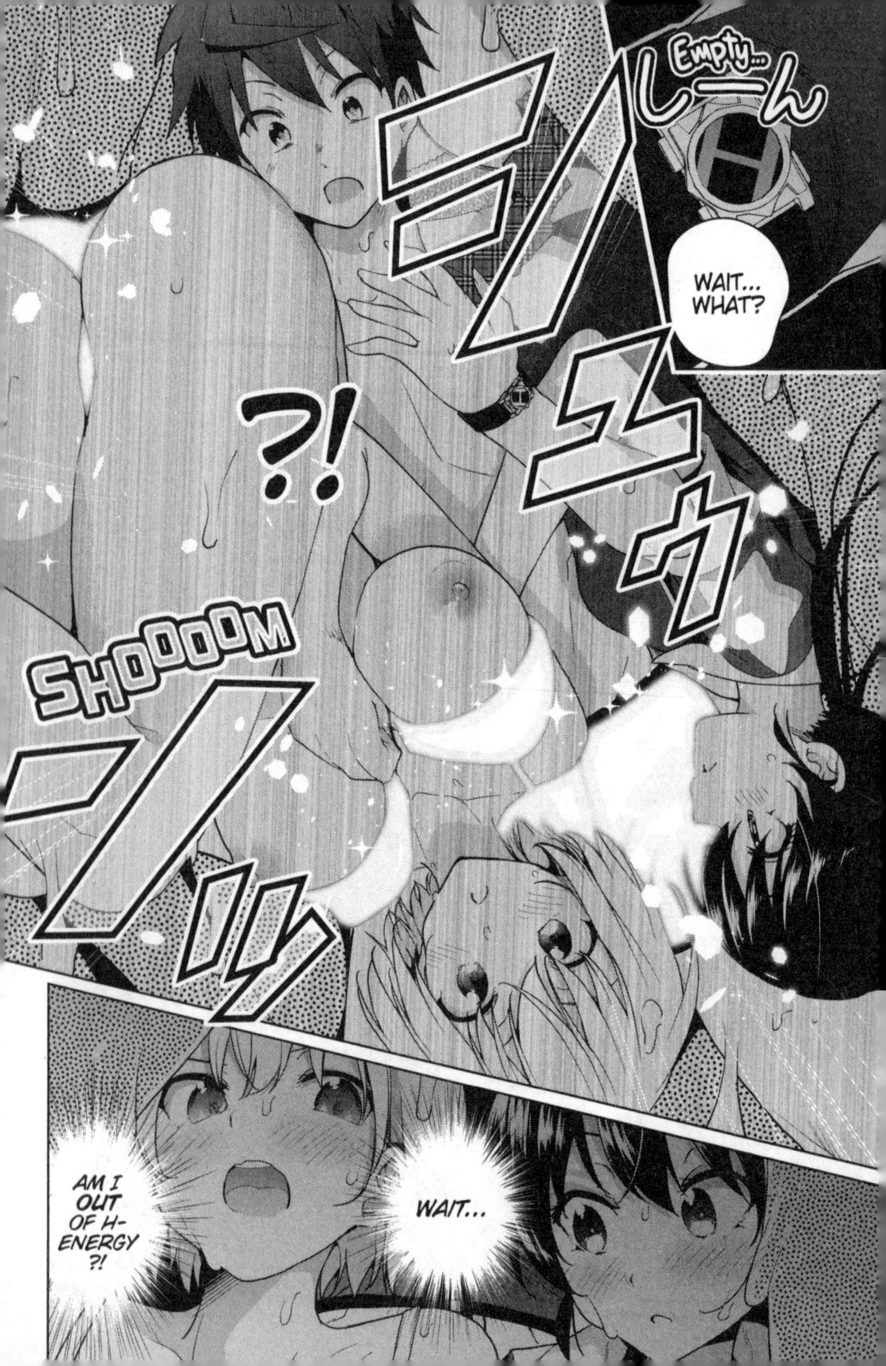
Empty...
しーん
WAIT... WHAT?
?!
SHOOOOOM
WAIT...
AM I OUT OF H-ENERGY ?!

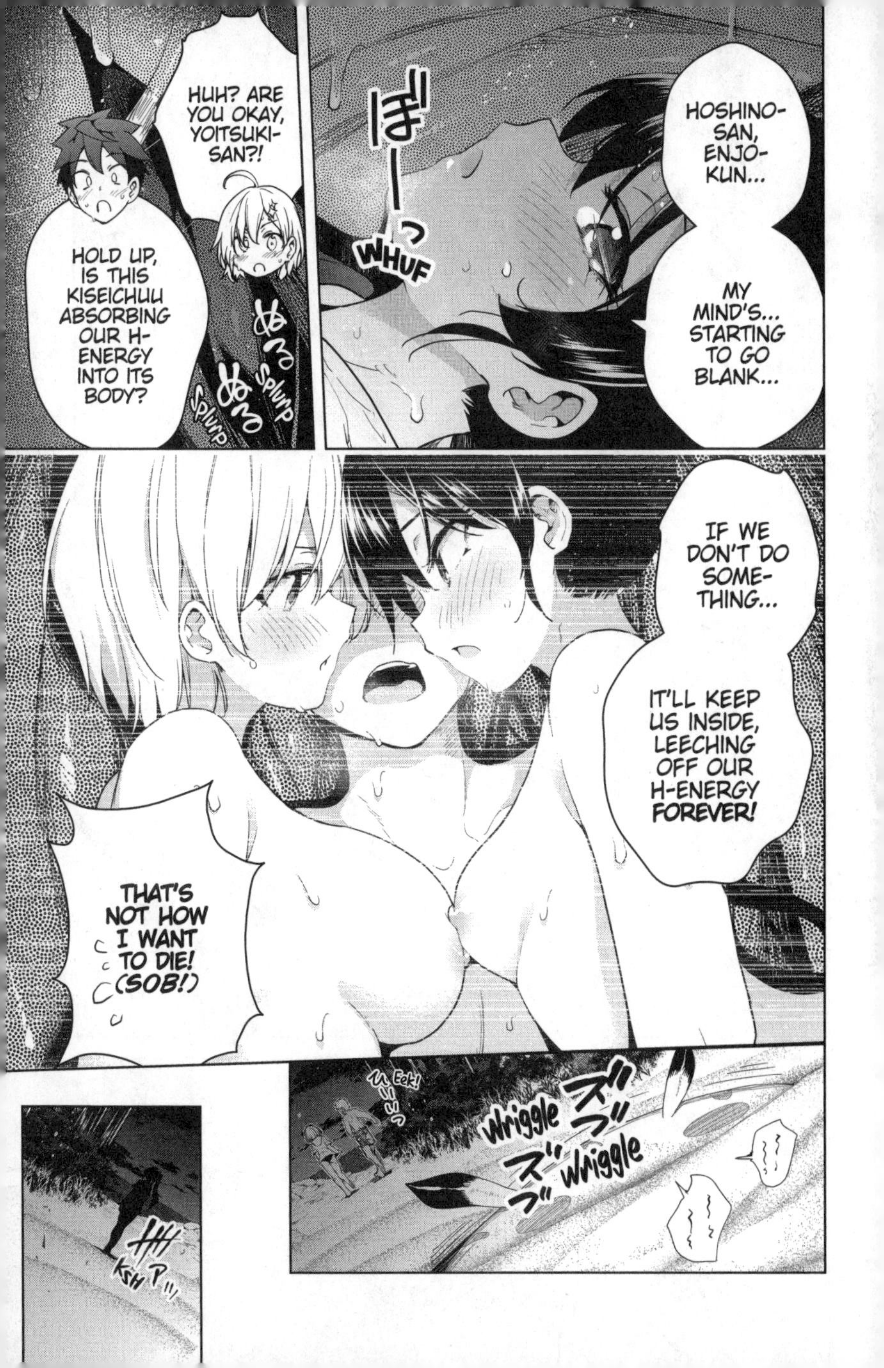
HOSHINO-SAN, ENJO-KUN...
MY MIND'S... STARTING TO GO BLANK...
ぼーっ
WHUF
HUH? ARE YOU OKAY, YOITSUKI-SAN?!
HOLD UP, IS THIS KISEICHUU ABSORBING OUR H-ENERGY INTO ITS BODY?
Splurp
Splurp
IF WE DON'T DO SOME-THING...
IT'LL KEEP US INSIDE, LEECHING OFF OUR H-ENERGY FOREVER!
THAT'S NOT HOW I WANT TO DIE! (SOB!)
Eek!
Wriggle
Wriggle
KSH P

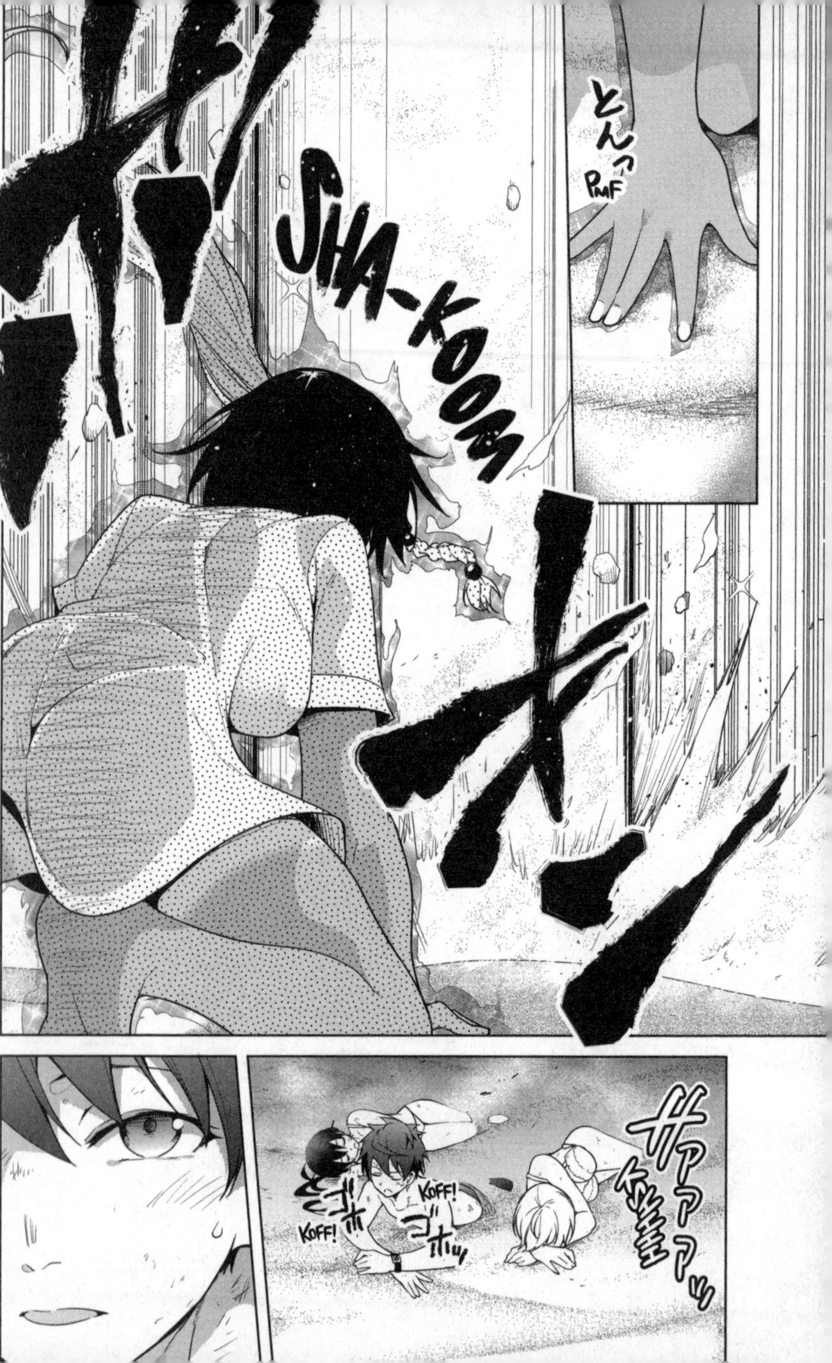
とんっ
PMF
SHA-KOOM
サァァァッ
KSSSH
ゴホ
KOFF!
ゴホッ
KOFF!

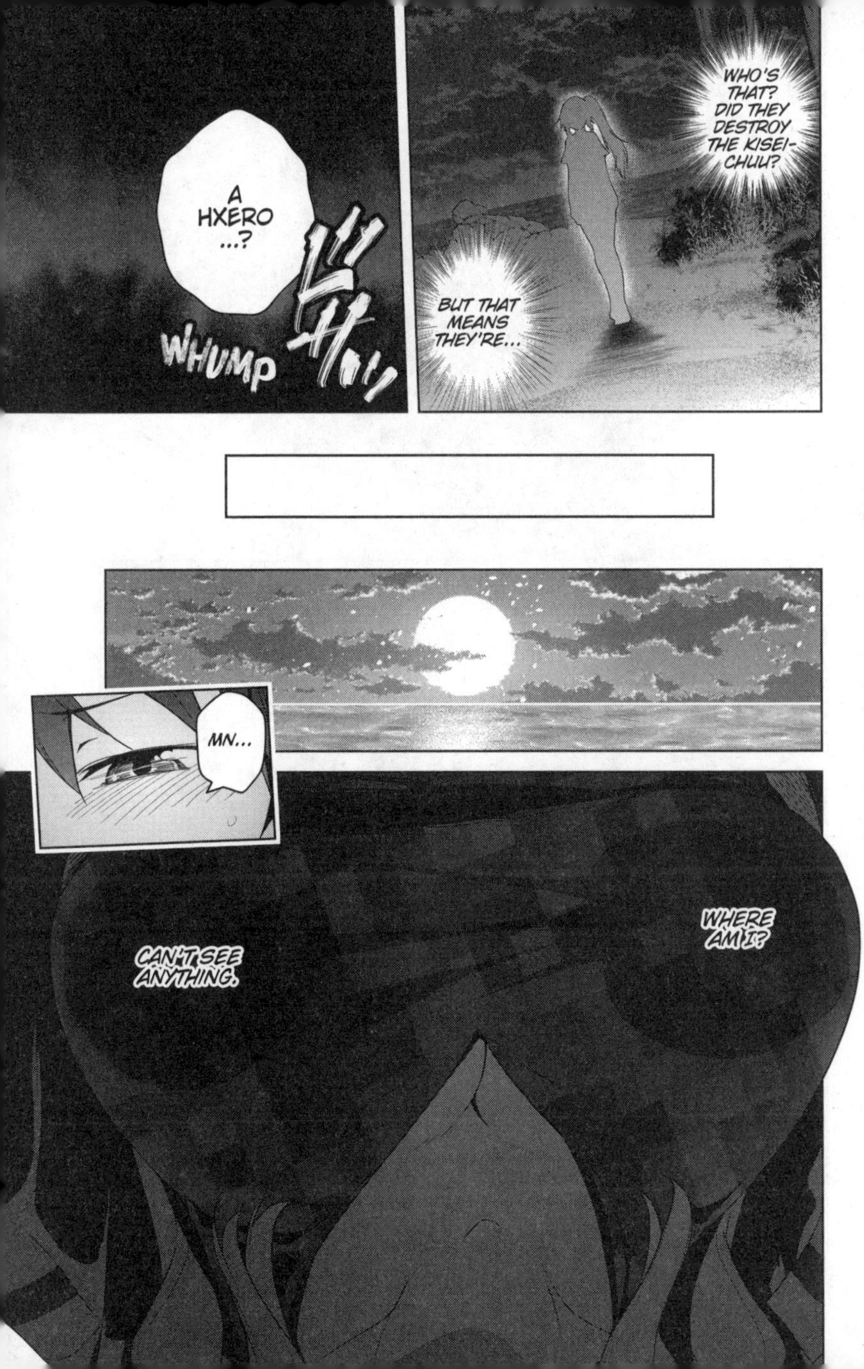
WHO'S THAT? DID THEY DESTROY THE KISEI-CHUU?
BUT THAT MEANS THEY'RE...
A HXERO ...?
WHUMP
MN...
WHERE AM I?
CAN'T SEE ANYTHING.

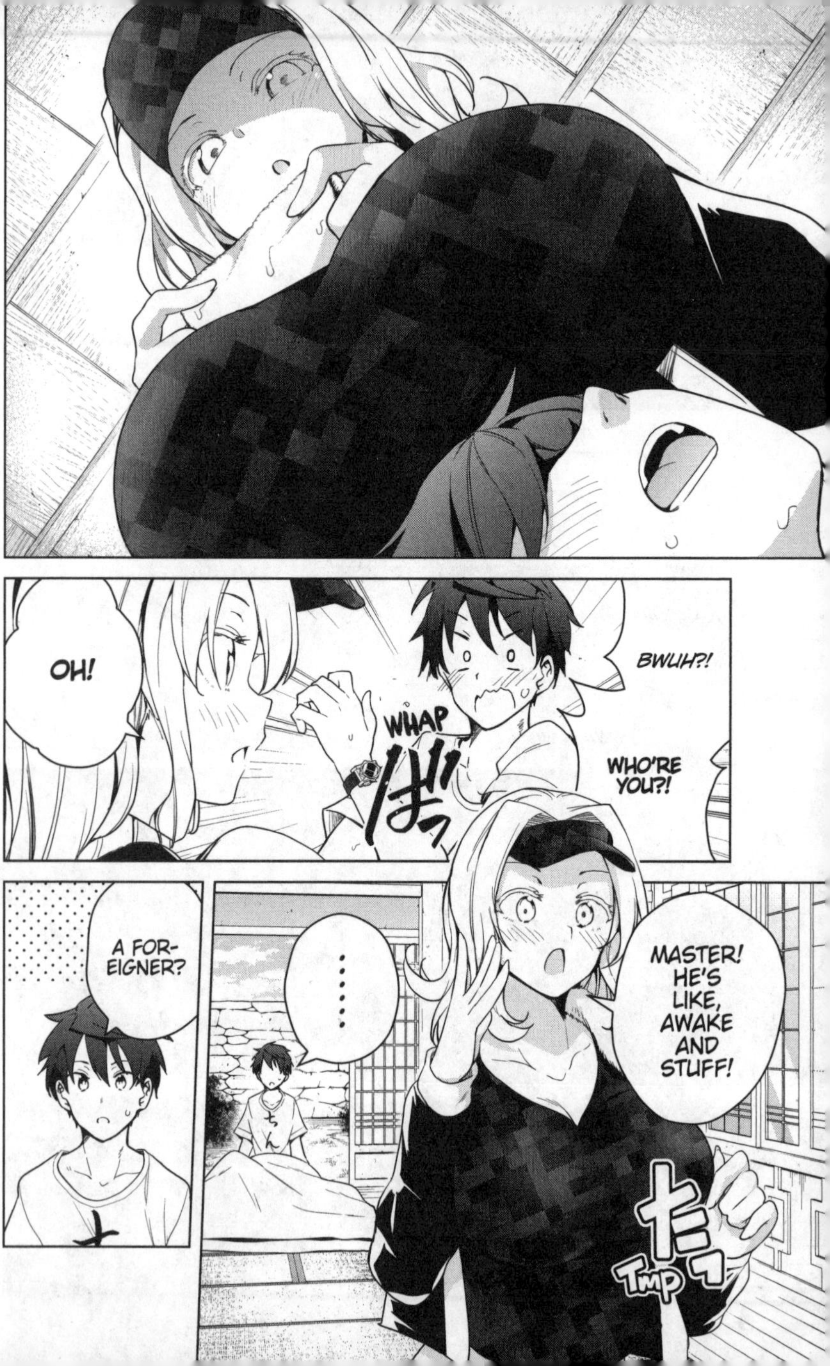
BWUH?!
WHO'RE YOU?!
WHAP
ぱっ
OH!
MASTER! HE'S LIKE, AWAKE AND STUFF!
たっ
Tmp
......
A FOR-EIGNER?

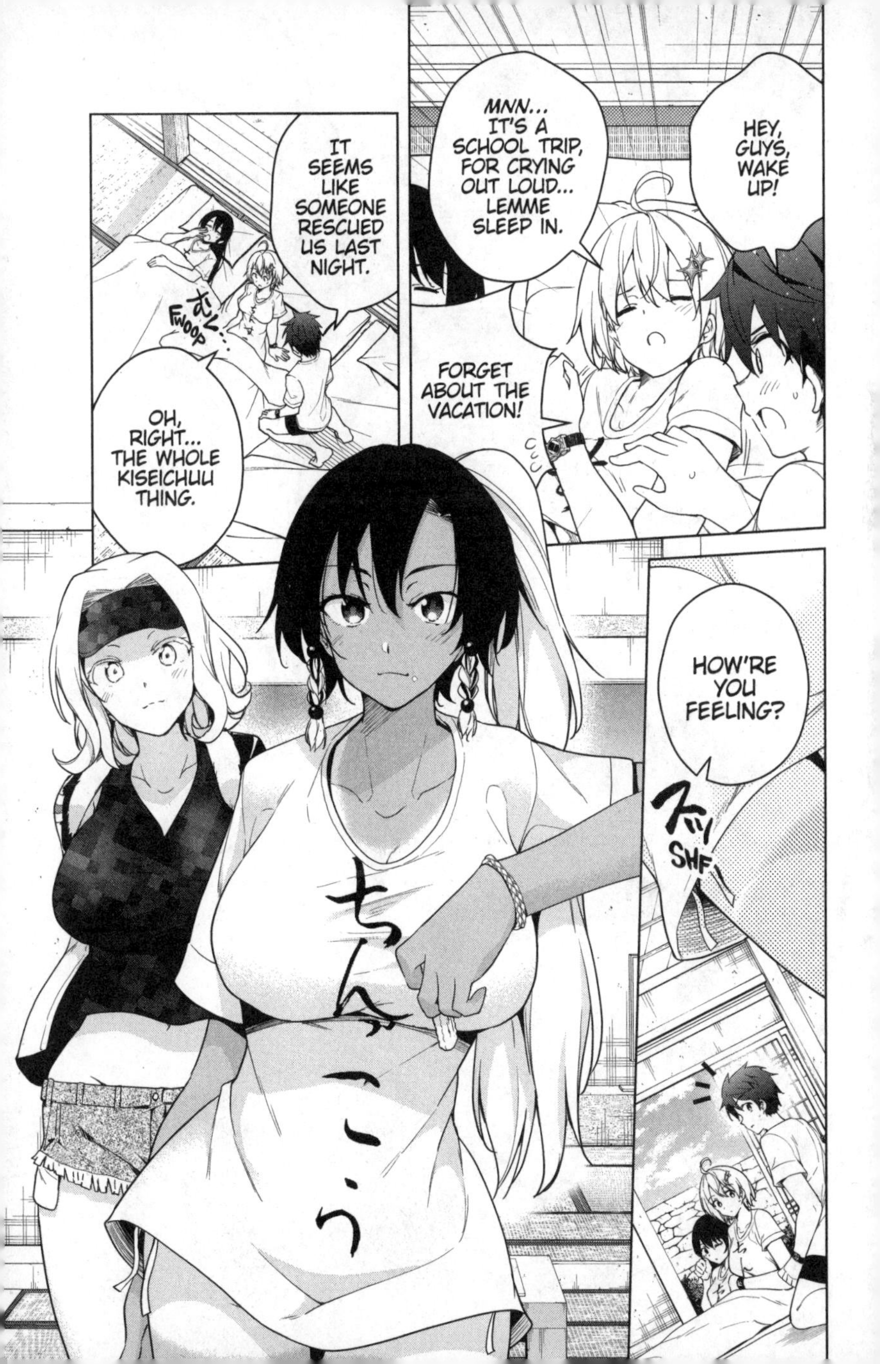
HEY, GUYS, WAKE UP!
MNN... IT'S A SCHOOL TRIP, FOR CRYING OUT LOUD... LEMME SLEEP IN.
FORGET ABOUT THE VACATION!
IT SEEMS LIKE SOMEONE RESCUED US LAST NIGHT.
むく FWOOP
OH, RIGHT... THE WHOLE KISEICHUU THING.
HOW'RE YOU FEELING?
スッ SHF

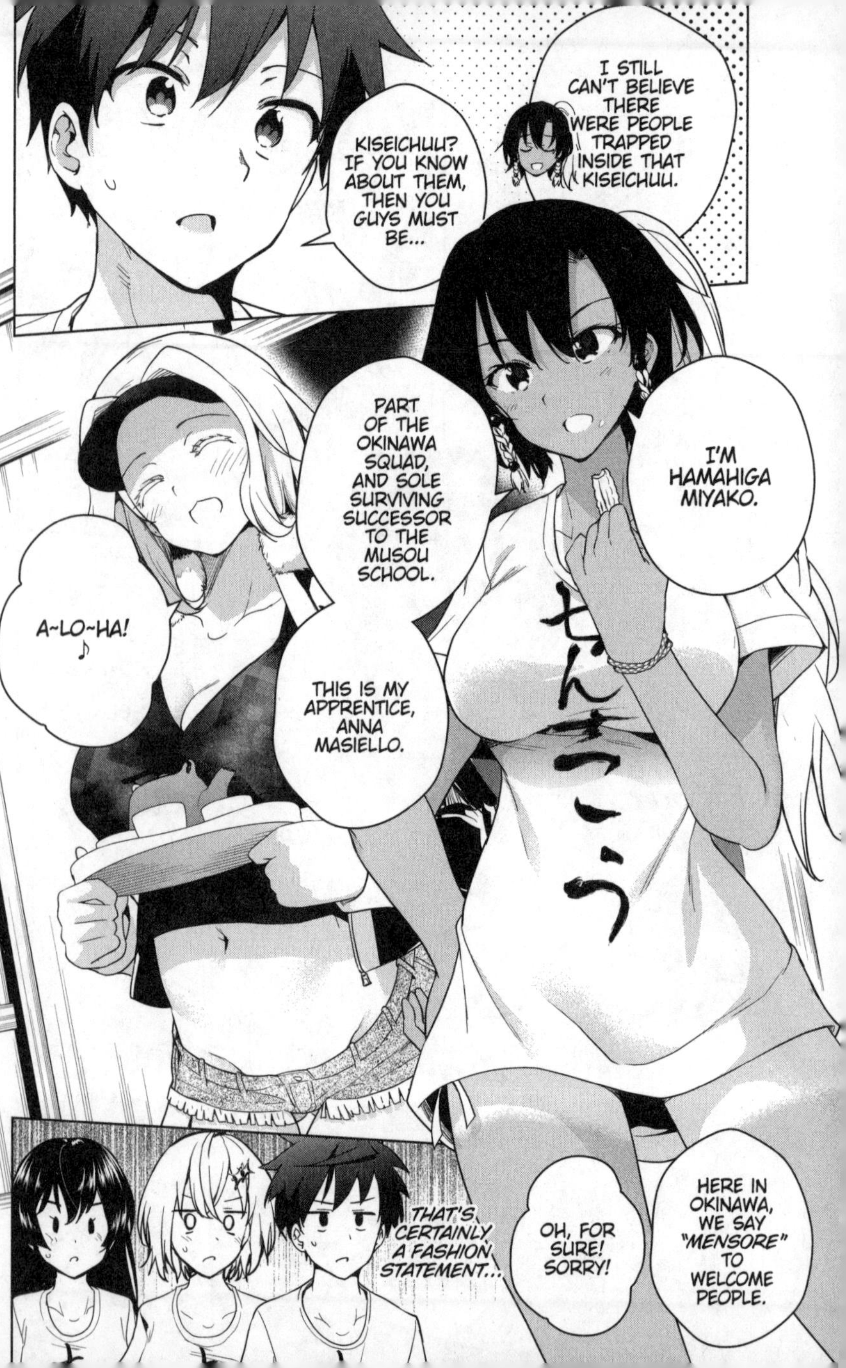
I STILL CAN'T BELIEVE THERE WERE PEOPLE TRAPPED INSIDE THAT KISEICHUU.
KISEICHUU? IF YOU KNOW ABOUT THEM, THEN YOU GUYS MUST BE...
I'M HAMAHIGA MIYAKO.
PART OF THE OKINAWA SQUAD, AND SOLE SURVIVING SUCCESSOR TO THE MUSOU SCHOOL.
THIS IS MY APPRENTICE, ANNA MASIELLO.
A~LO~HA! ♪
HERE IN OKINAWA, WE SAY "MENSORE" TO WELCOME PEOPLE.
OH, FOR SURE! SORRY!
THAT'S CERTAINLY A FASHION STATEMENT...

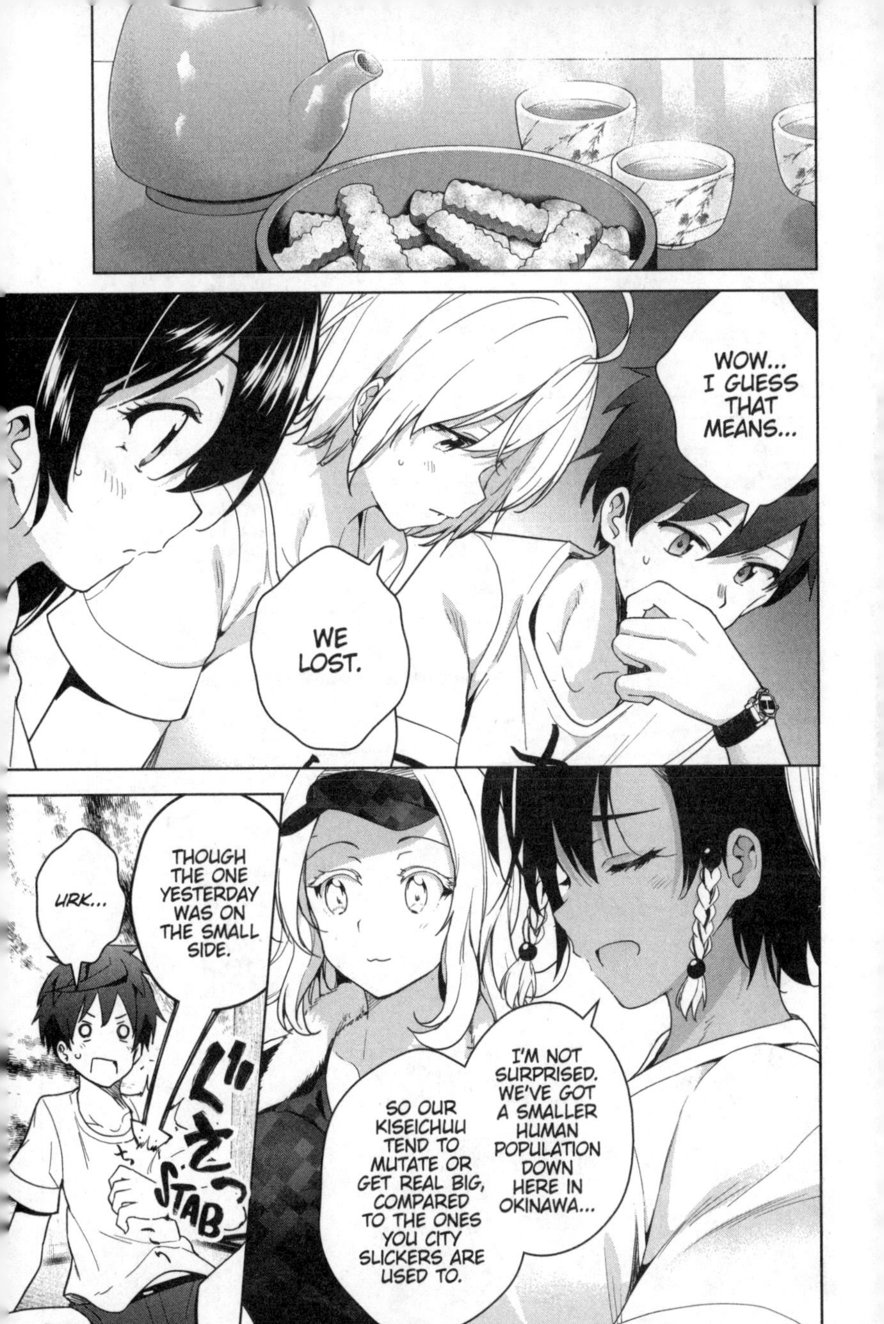
WOW... I GUESS THAT MEANS...
WE LOST.
I'M NOT SURPRISED. WE'VE GOT A SMALLER HUMAN POPULATION DOWN HERE IN OKINAWA...
SO OUR KISEICHUU TEND TO MUTATE OR GET REAL BIG, COMPARED TO THE ONES YOU CITY SLICKERS ARE USED TO.
THOUGH THE ONE YESTERDAY WAS ON THE SMALL SIDE.
URK...
ぐさっ
STAB

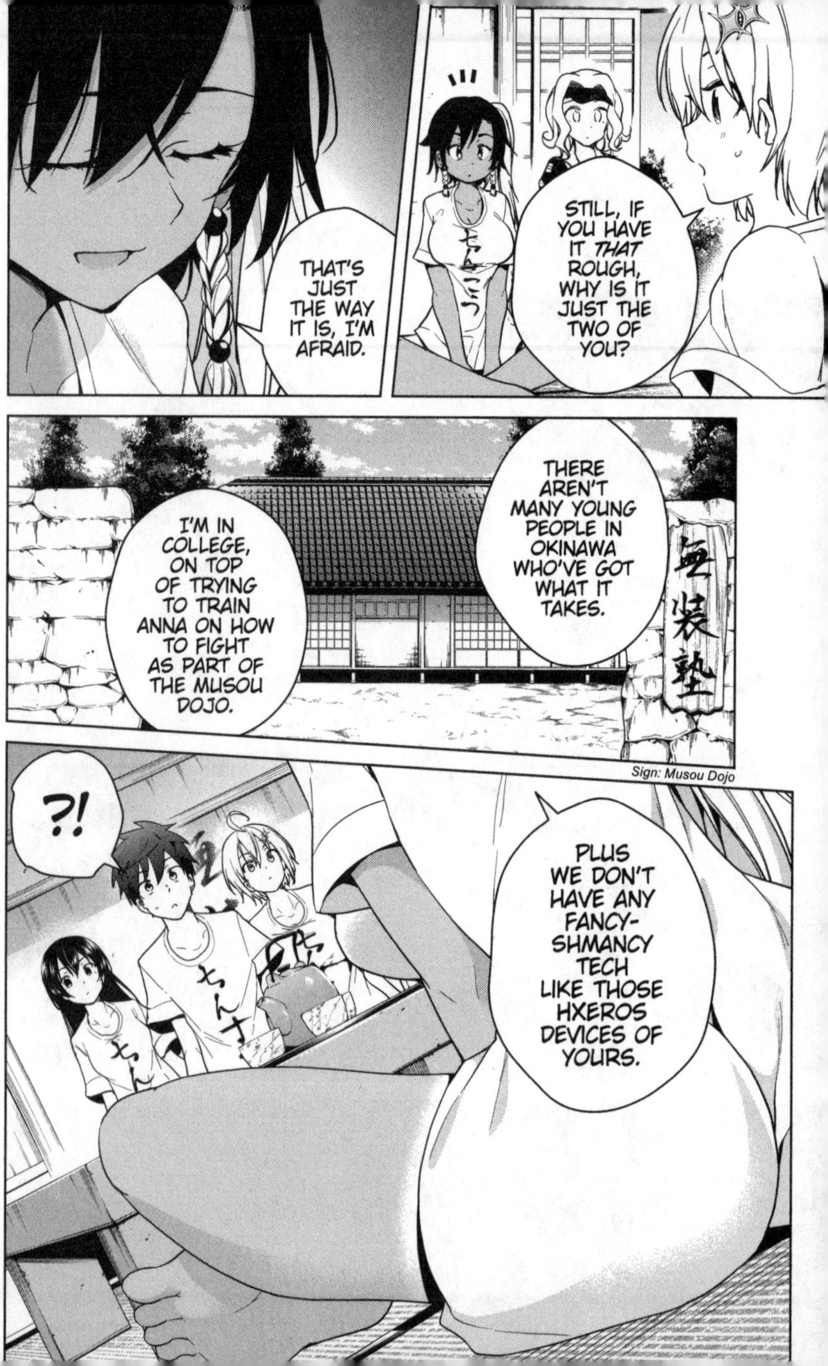
STILL, IF YOU HAVE IT *THAT* ROUGH, WHY IS IT JUST THE TWO OF YOU?
THAT'S JUST THE WAY IT IS, I'M AFRAID.
THERE AREN'T MANY YOUNG PEOPLE IN OKINAWA WHO'VE GOT WHAT IT TAKES.
I'M IN COLLEGE, ON TOP OF TRYING TO TRAIN ANNA ON HOW TO FIGHT AS PART OF THE MUSOU DOJO.
PLUS WE DON'T HAVE ANY FANCY-SHMANCY TECH LIKE THOSE HXEROS DEVICES OF YOURS.
?!
Sign: Musou Dojo

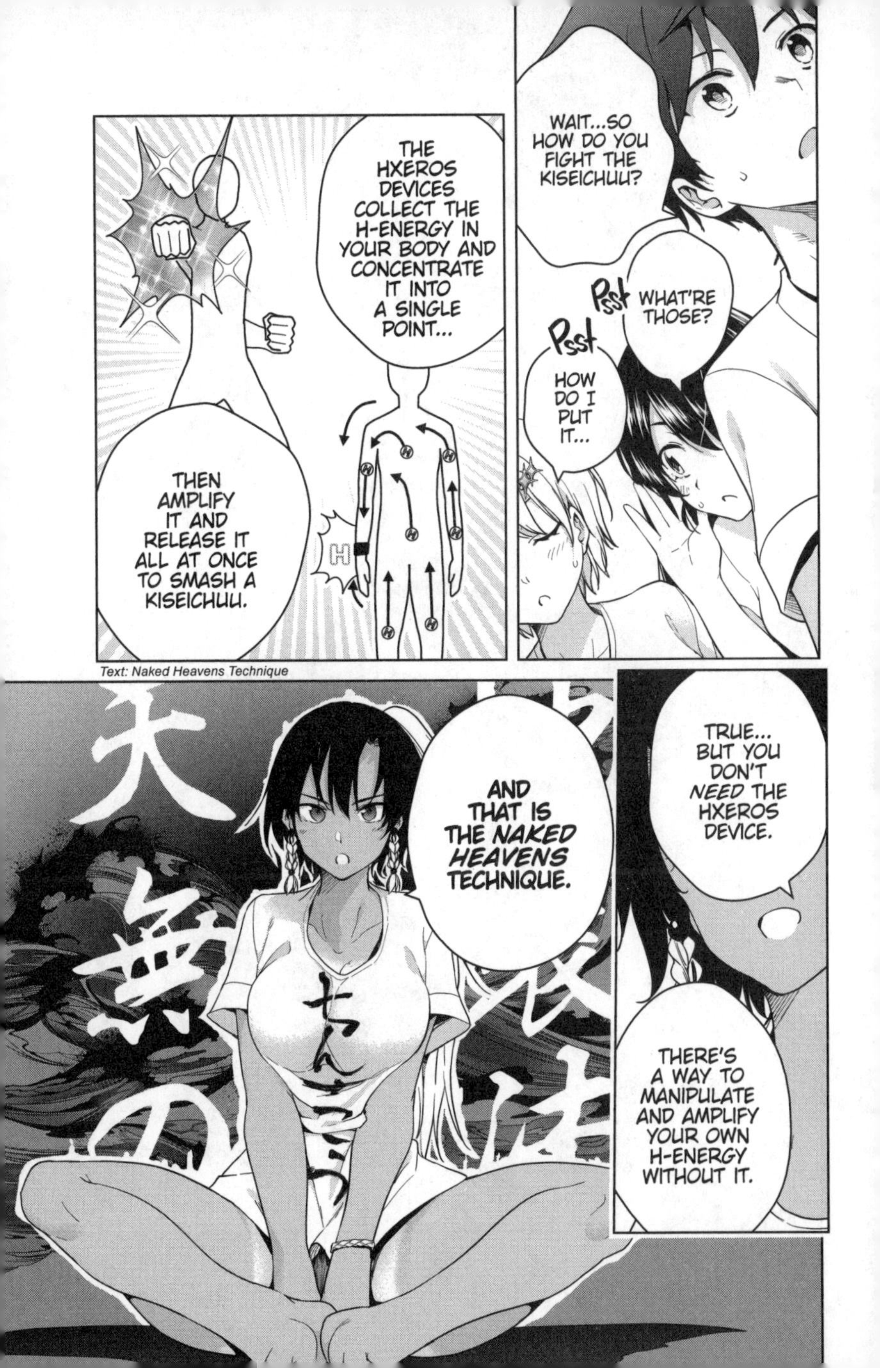
WAIT...SO HOW DO YOU FIGHT THE KISEICHUU?
Psst
WHAT'RE THOSE?
Psst
HOW DO I PUT IT...
THE HXEROS DEVICES COLLECT THE H-ENERGY IN YOUR BODY AND CONCENTRATE IT INTO A SINGLE POINT...
H
THEN AMPLIFY IT AND RELEASE IT ALL AT ONCE TO SMASH A KISEICHUU.
TRUE... BUT YOU DON'T *NEED* THE HXEROS DEVICE.
THERE'S A WAY TO MANIPULATE AND AMPLIFY YOUR OWN H-ENERGY WITHOUT IT.
AND THAT IS THE *NAKED HEAVENS* TECHNIQUE.
Text: Naked Heavens Technique

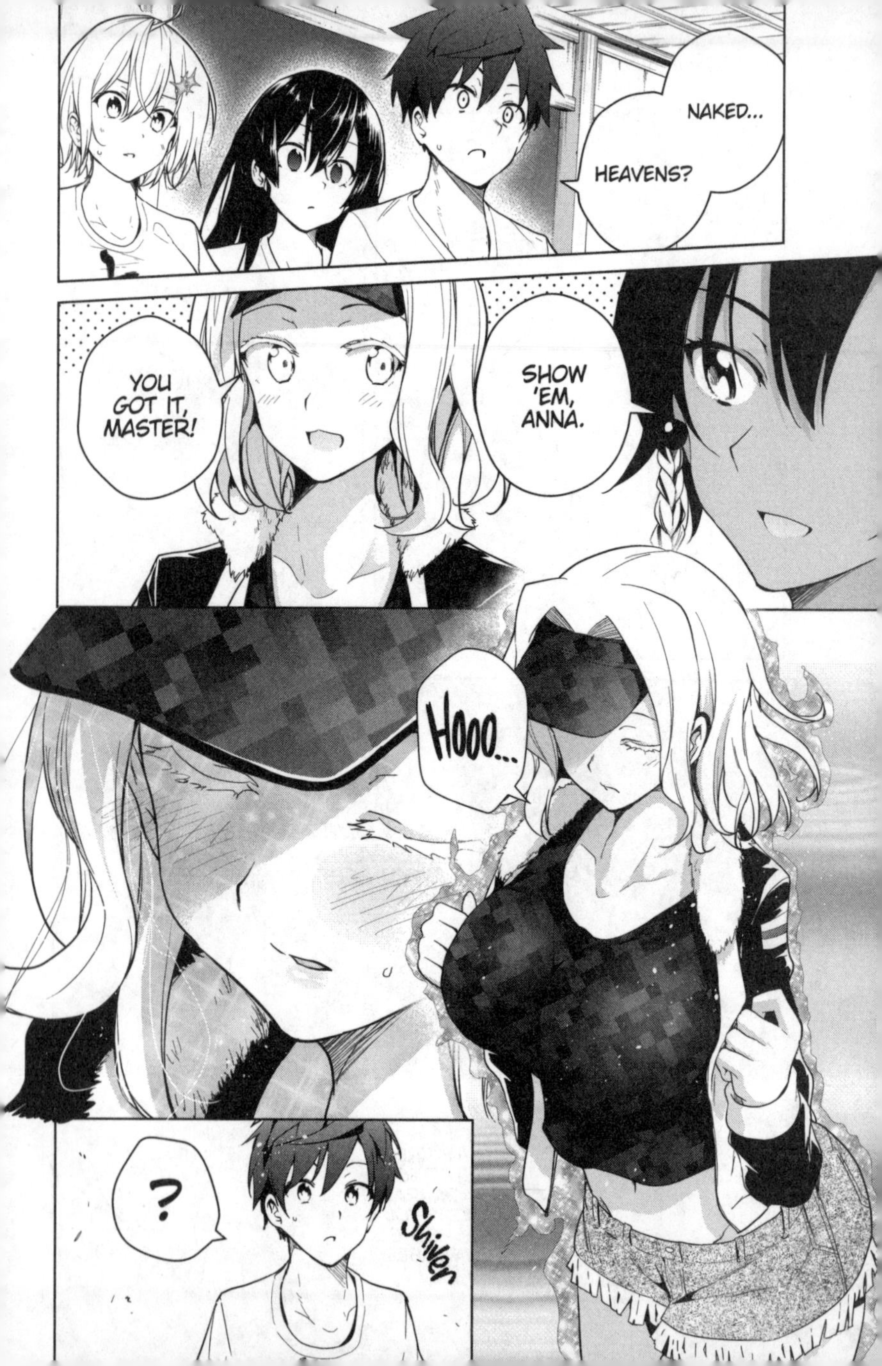
NAKED... HEAVENS?
SHOW 'EM, ANNA.
YOU GOT IT, MASTER!
Hooo...
?
Shiver

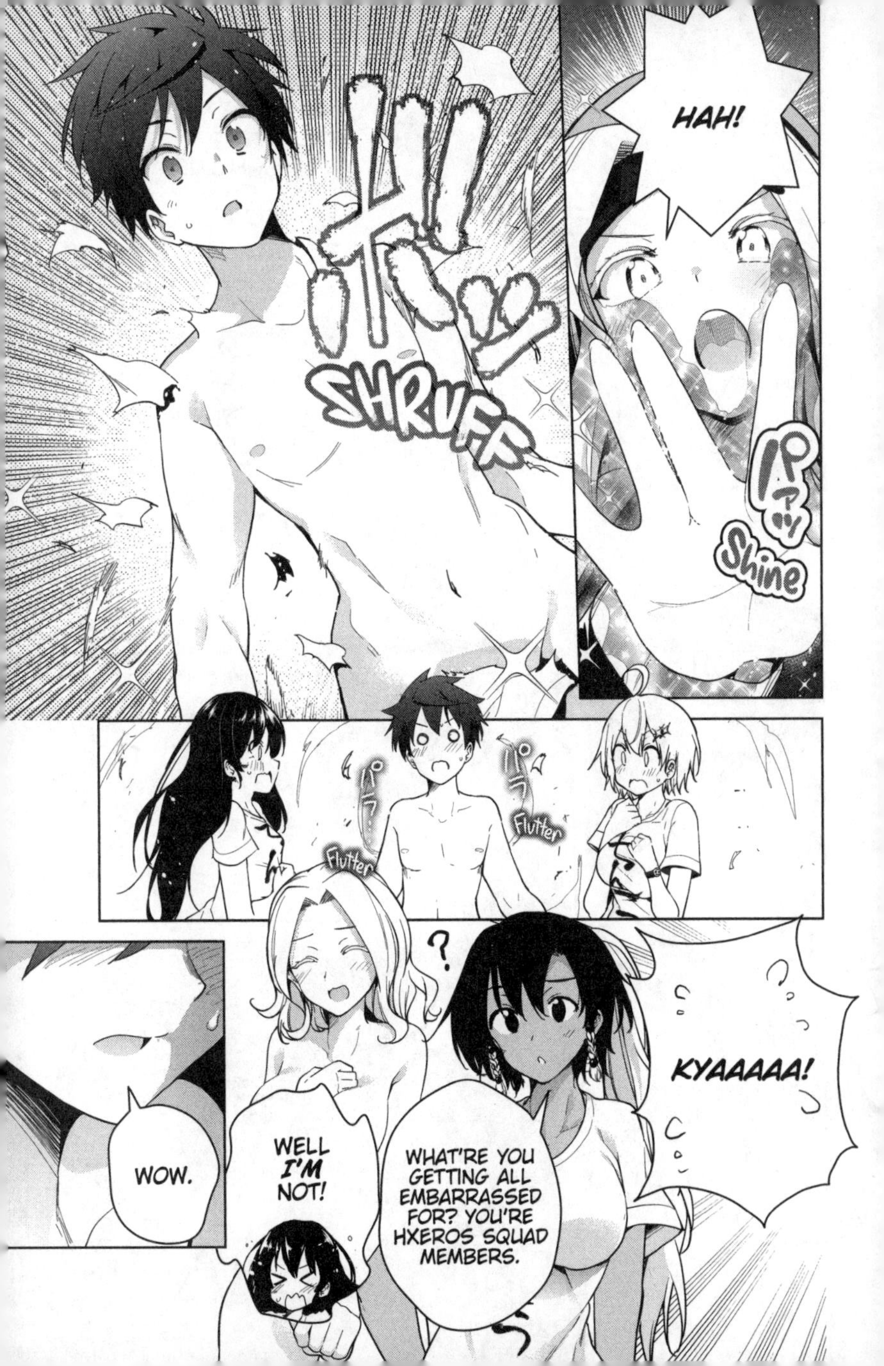
HAH!
Shine
SHRUFF
Flutter
Flutter
KYAAAAA!
?
WHAT'RE YOU GETTING ALL EMBARRASSED FOR? YOU'RE HXEROS SQUAD MEMBERS.
WELL *I'M* NOT!
WOW.

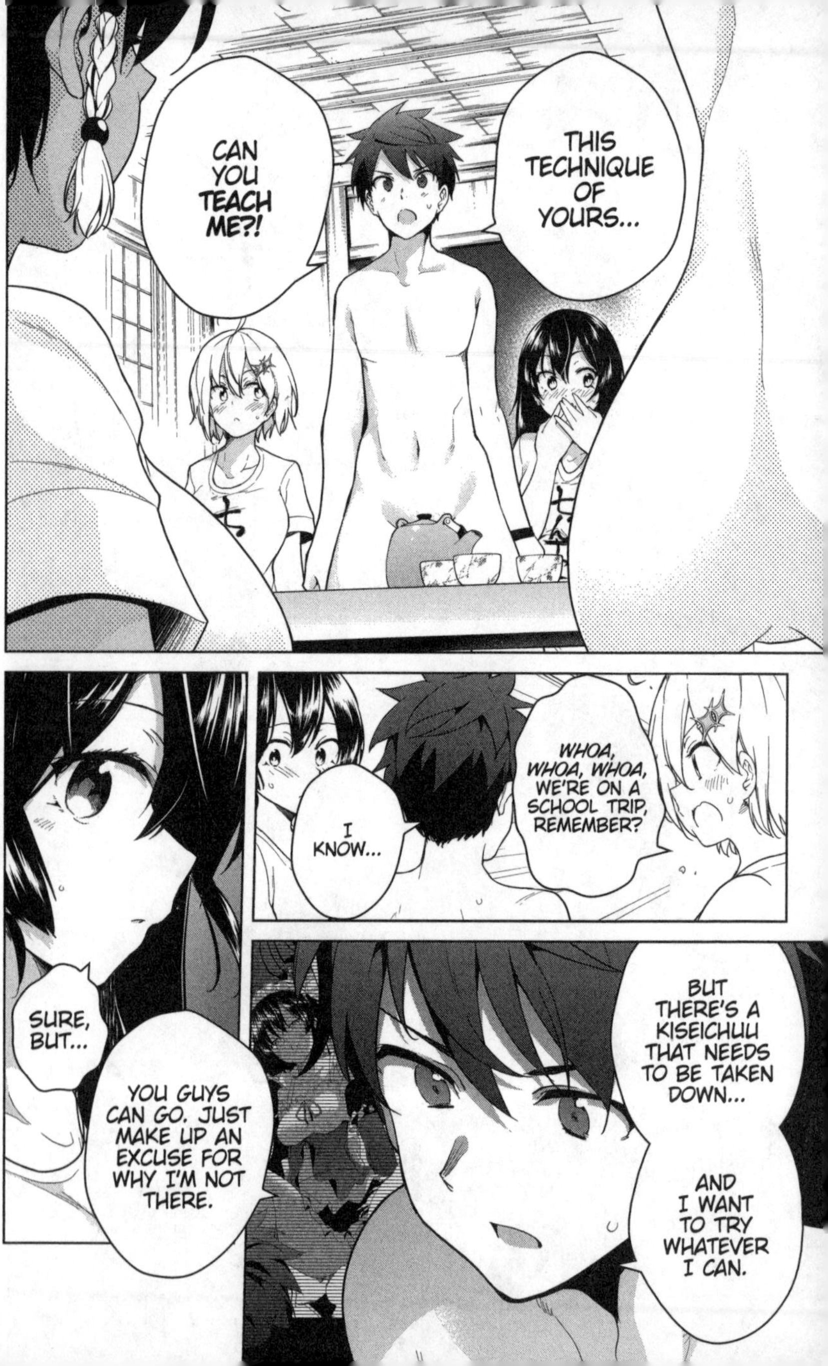
THIS TECHNIQUE OF YOURS...
CAN YOU TEACH ME?!
WHOA, WHOA, WHOA, WE'RE ON A SCHOOL TRIP, REMEMBER?
I KNOW...
BUT THERE'S A KISEICHUU THAT NEEDS TO BE TAKEN DOWN...
YOU GUYS CAN GO. JUST MAKE UP AN EXCUSE FOR WHY I'M NOT THERE.
AND I WANT TO TRY WHATEVER I CAN.
SURE, BUT...

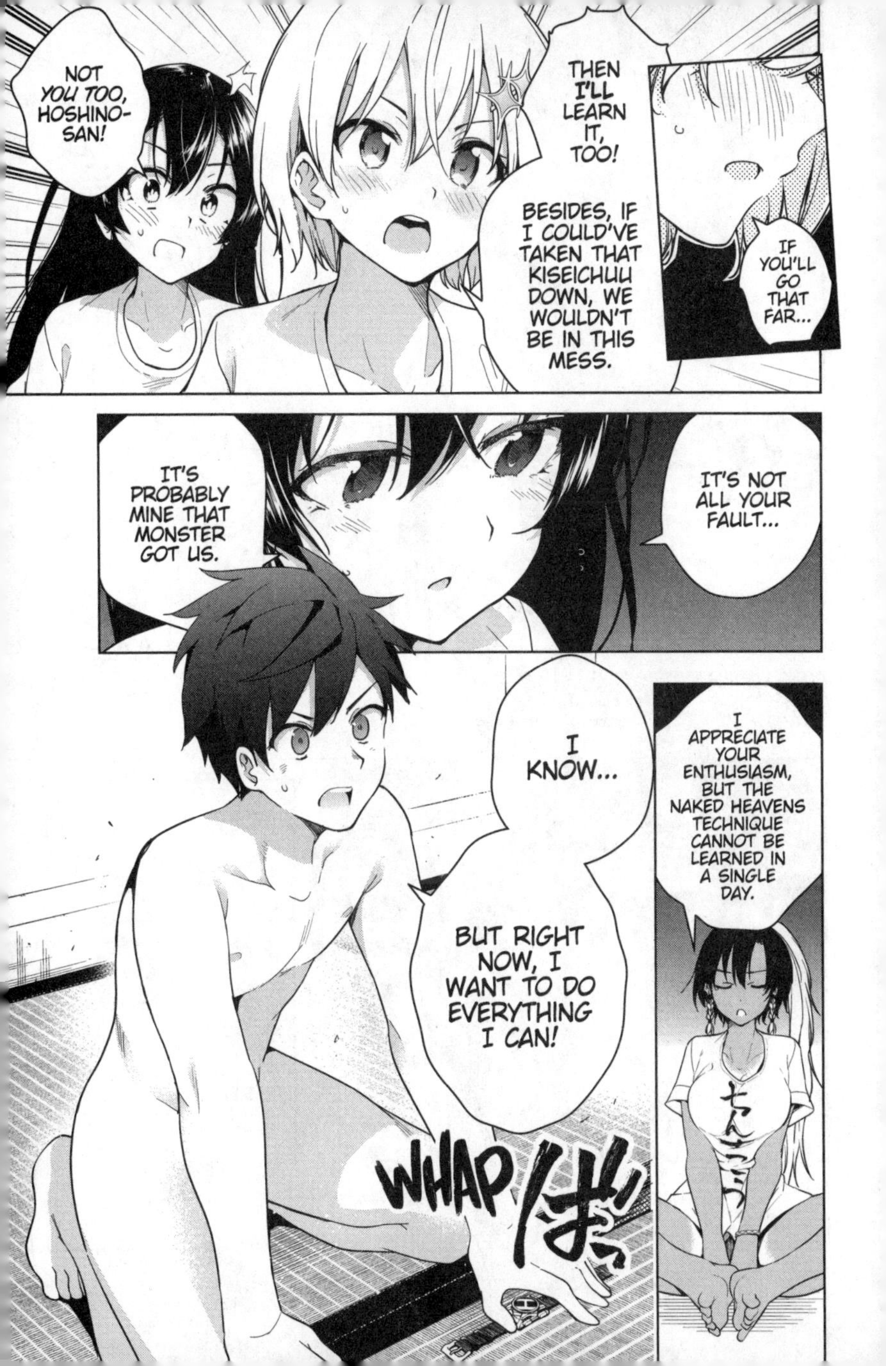
IF YOU'LL GO THAT FAR...
THEN I'LL LEARN IT, TOO!
BESIDES, IF I COULD'VE TAKEN THAT KISEICHUU DOWN, WE WOULDN'T BE IN THIS MESS.
NOT YOU TOO, HOSHINO-SAN!
IT'S NOT ALL YOUR FAULT...
IT'S PROBABLY MINE THAT MONSTER GOT US.
I APPRECIATE YOUR ENTHUSIASM, BUT THE NAKED HEAVENS TECHNIQUE CANNOT BE LEARNED IN A SINGLE DAY.
I KNOW...
BUT RIGHT NOW, I WANT TO DO EVERYTHING I CAN!
WHAP

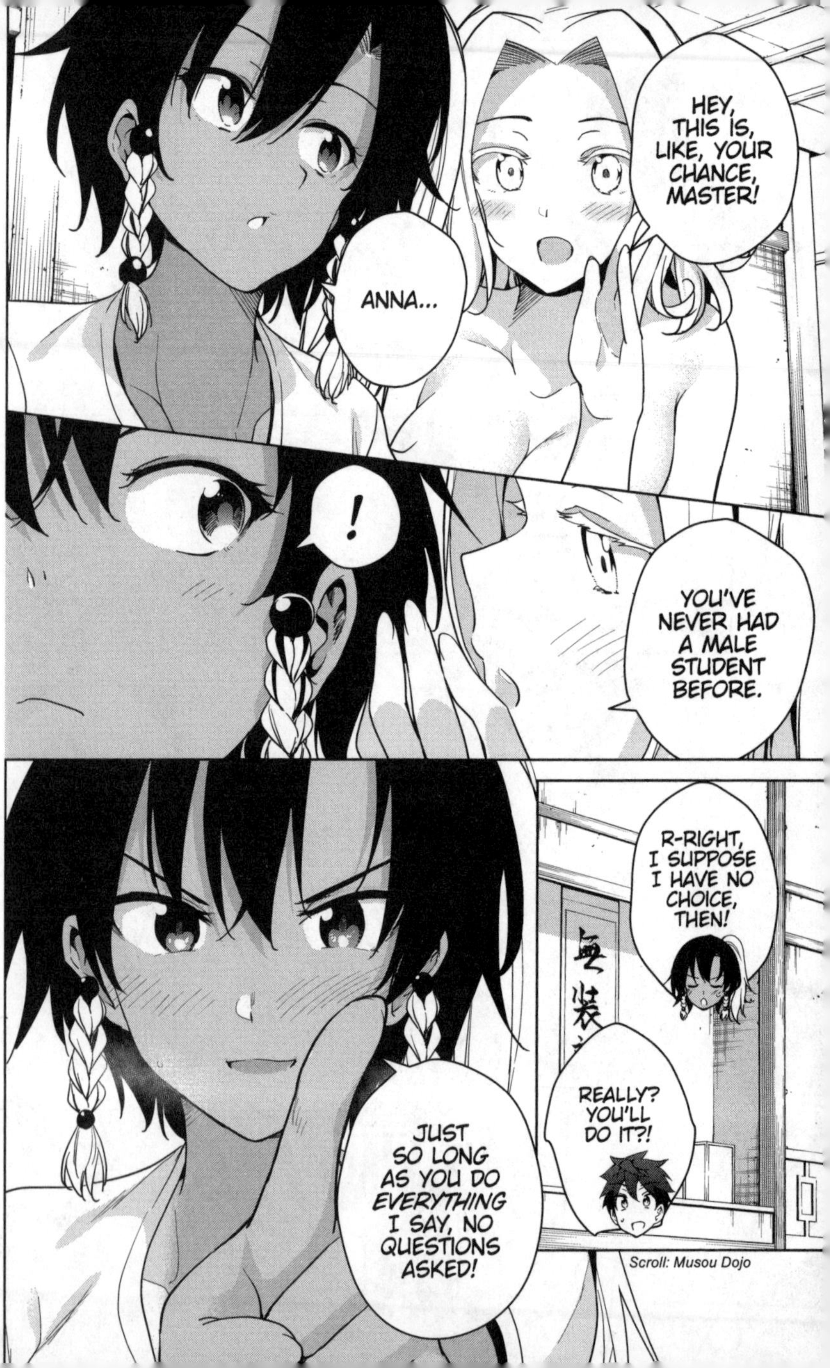
HEY, THIS IS, LIKE, YOUR CHANCE, MASTER!
ANNA...
YOU'VE NEVER HAD A MALE STUDENT BEFORE.
!
R-RIGHT, I SUPPOSE I HAVE NO CHOICE, THEN!
REALLY? YOU'LL DO IT?!
JUST SO LONG AS YOU DO *EVERYTHING* I SAY, NO QUESTIONS ASKED!
Scroll: Musou Dojo

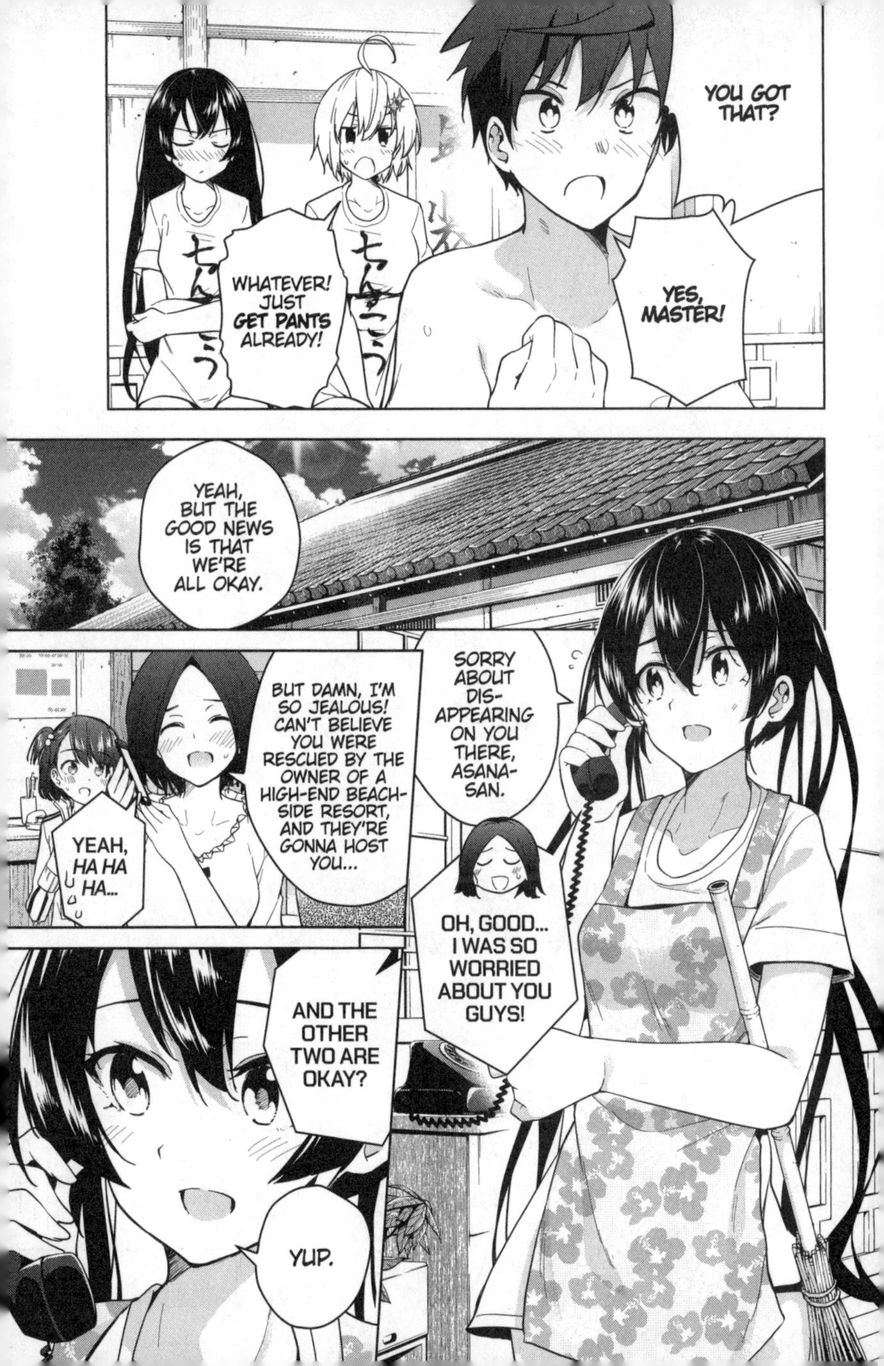
YOU GOT THAT?
YES, MASTER!
WHATEVER! JUST GET PANTS ALREADY!
YEAH, BUT THE GOOD NEWS IS THAT WE'RE ALL OKAY.
SORRY ABOUT DIS-APPEARING ON YOU THERE, ASANA-SAN.
OH, GOOD... I WAS SO WORRIED ABOUT YOU GUYS!
BUT DAMN, I'M SO JEALOUS! CAN'T BELIEVE YOU WERE RESCUED BY THE OWNER OF A HIGH-END BEACH-SIDE RESORT, AND THEY'RE GONNA HOST YOU...
YEAH, HA HA HA...
AND THE OTHER TWO ARE OKAY?
YUP.

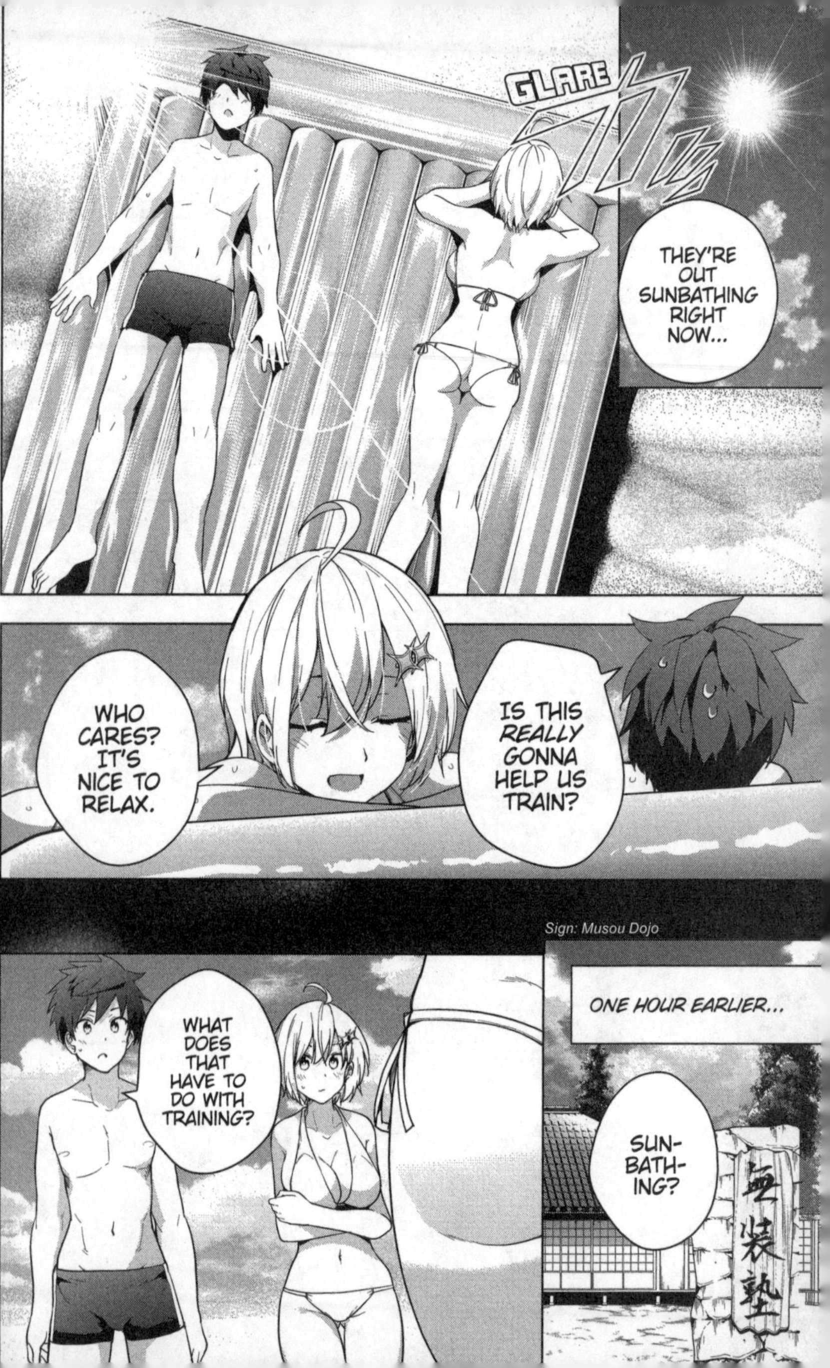
GLARE
THEY'RE OUT SUNBATHING RIGHT NOW...
IS THIS *REALLY* GONNA HELP US TRAIN?
WHO CARES? IT'S NICE TO RELAX.
Sign: Musou Dojo
ONE HOUR EARLIER...
SUN-BATH-ING?
WHAT DOES THAT HAVE TO DO WITH TRAINING?

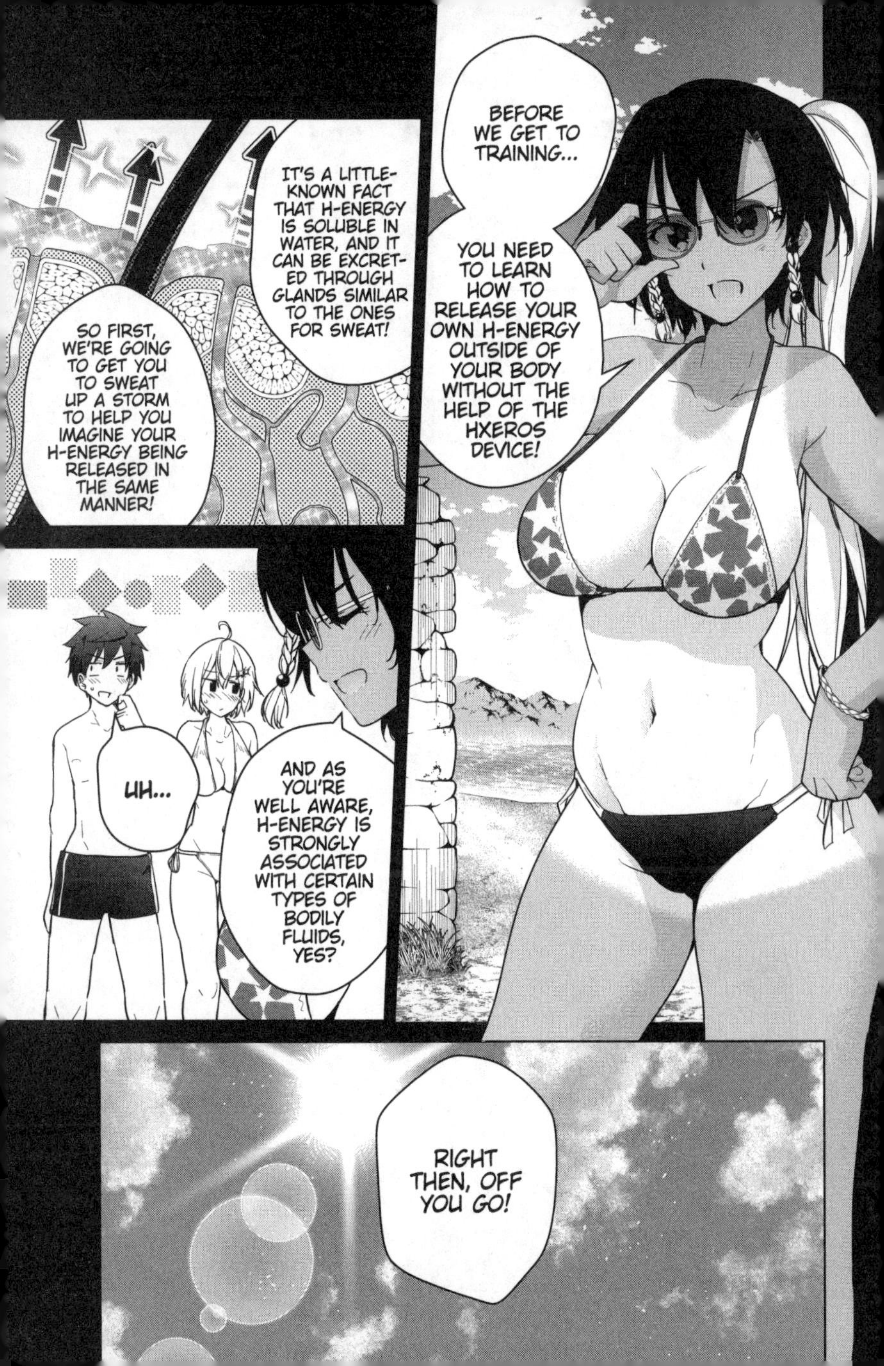
BEFORE WE GET TO TRAINING...
YOU NEED TO LEARN HOW TO RELEASE YOUR OWN H-ENERGY OUTSIDE OF YOUR BODY WITHOUT THE HELP OF THE HXEROS DEVICE!
IT'S A LITTLE-KNOWN FACT THAT H-ENERGY IS SOLUBLE IN WATER, AND IT CAN BE EXCRETED THROUGH GLANDS SIMILAR TO THE ONES FOR SWEAT!
SO FIRST, WE'RE GOING TO GET YOU TO SWEAT UP A STORM TO HELP YOU IMAGINE YOUR H-ENERGY BEING RELEASED IN THE SAME MANNER!
AND AS YOU'RE WELL AWARE, H-ENERGY IS STRONGLY ASSOCIATED WITH CERTAIN TYPES OF BODILY FLUIDS, YES?
UH...
RIGHT THEN, OFF YOU GO!

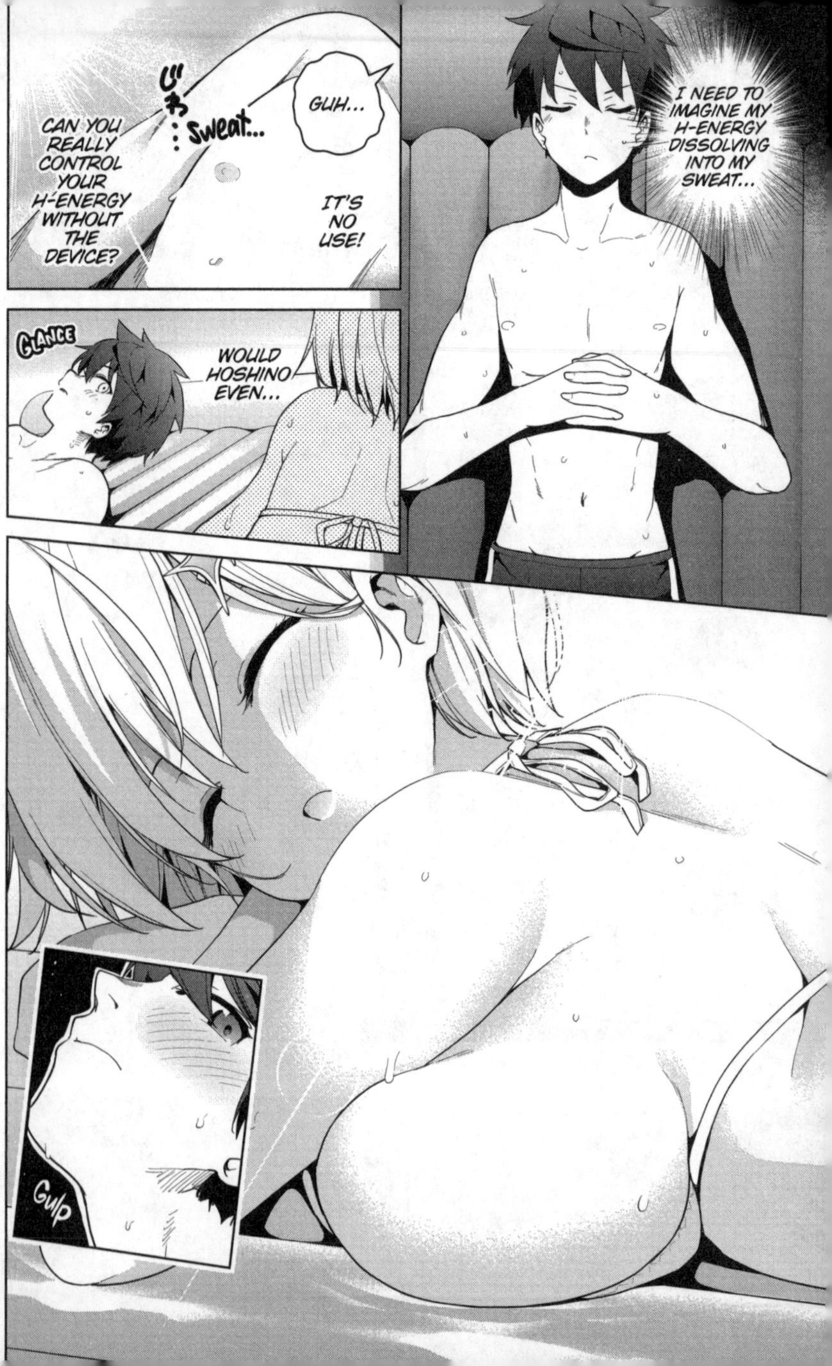
I NEED TO IMAGINE MY H-ENERGY DISSOLVING INTO MY SWEAT...
じわ・・・
Sweat...
CAN YOU REALLY CONTROL YOUR H-ENERGY WITHOUT THE DEVICE?
GUH...
IT'S NO USE!
GLANCE
WOULD HOSHINO EVEN...
Gulp

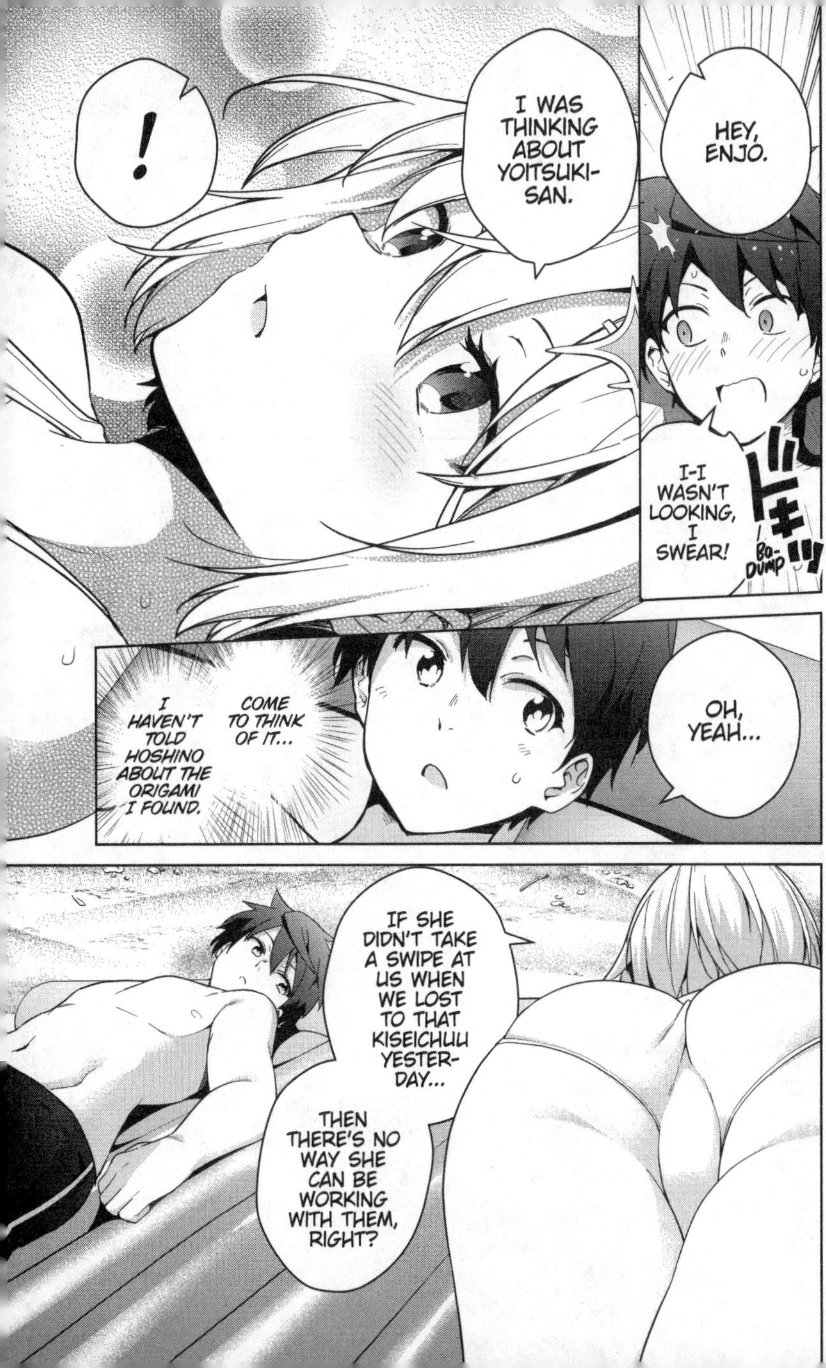
HEY, ENJO.
I-I WASN'T LOOKING, I SWEAR!
BA-DUMP
I WAS THINKING ABOUT YOITSUKI-SAN.
!
OH, YEAH...
COME TO THINK OF IT...
I HAVEN'T TOLD HOSHINO ABOUT THE ORIGAMI I FOUND.
IF SHE DIDN'T TAKE A SWIPE AT US WHEN WE LOST TO THAT KISEICHUU YESTER-DAY...
THEN THERE'S NO WAY SHE CAN BE WORKING WITH THEM, RIGHT?

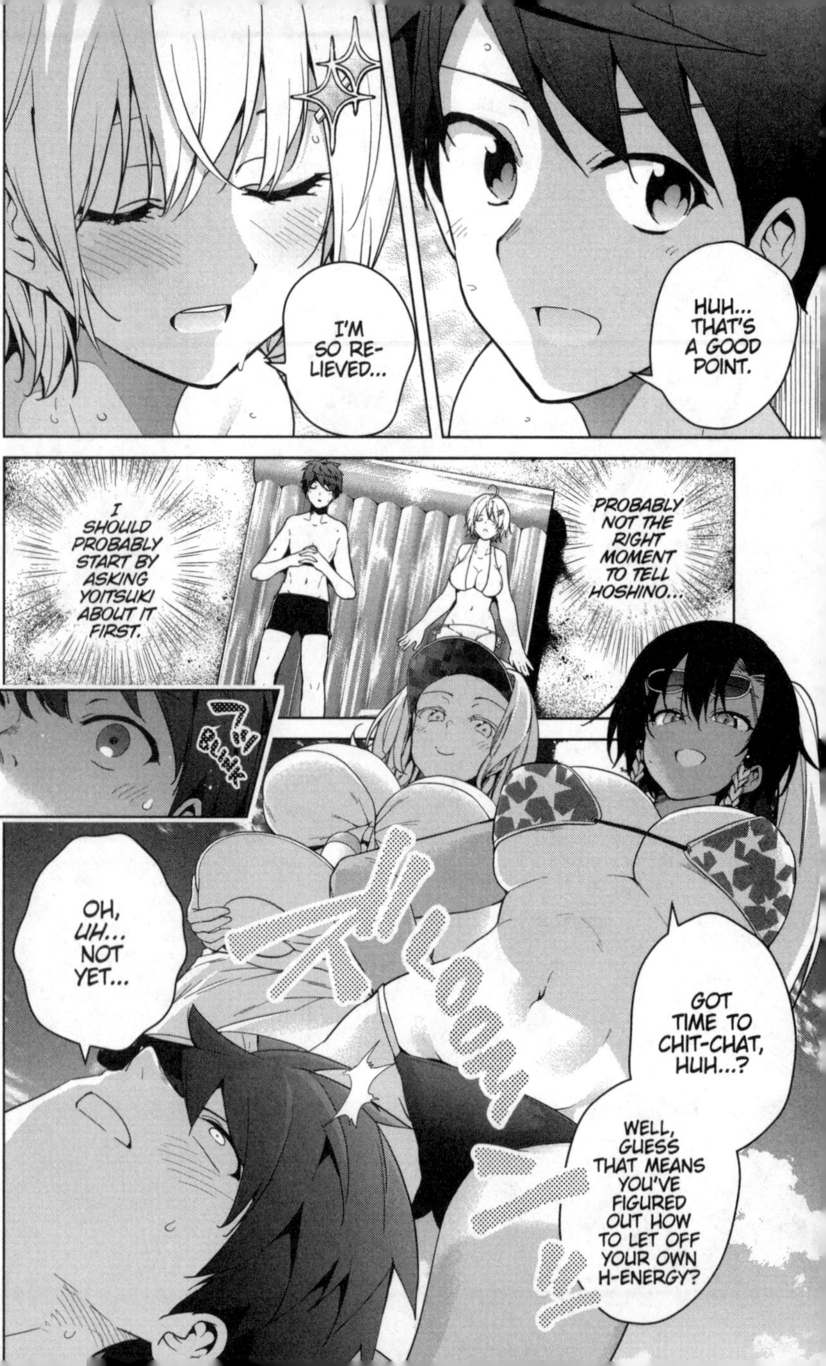
HUH... THAT'S A GOOD POINT.
I'M SO RE-LIEVED...
PROBABLY NOT THE RIGHT MOMENT TO TELL HOSHINO...
I SHOULD PROBABLY START BY ASKING YOITSUKI ABOUT IT FIRST.
BLINK
GOT TIME TO CHIT-CHAT, HUH...?
WELL, GUESS THAT MEANS YOU'VE FIGURED OUT HOW TO LET OFF YOUR OWN H-ENERGY?
LOOM
OH, UH... NOT YET...

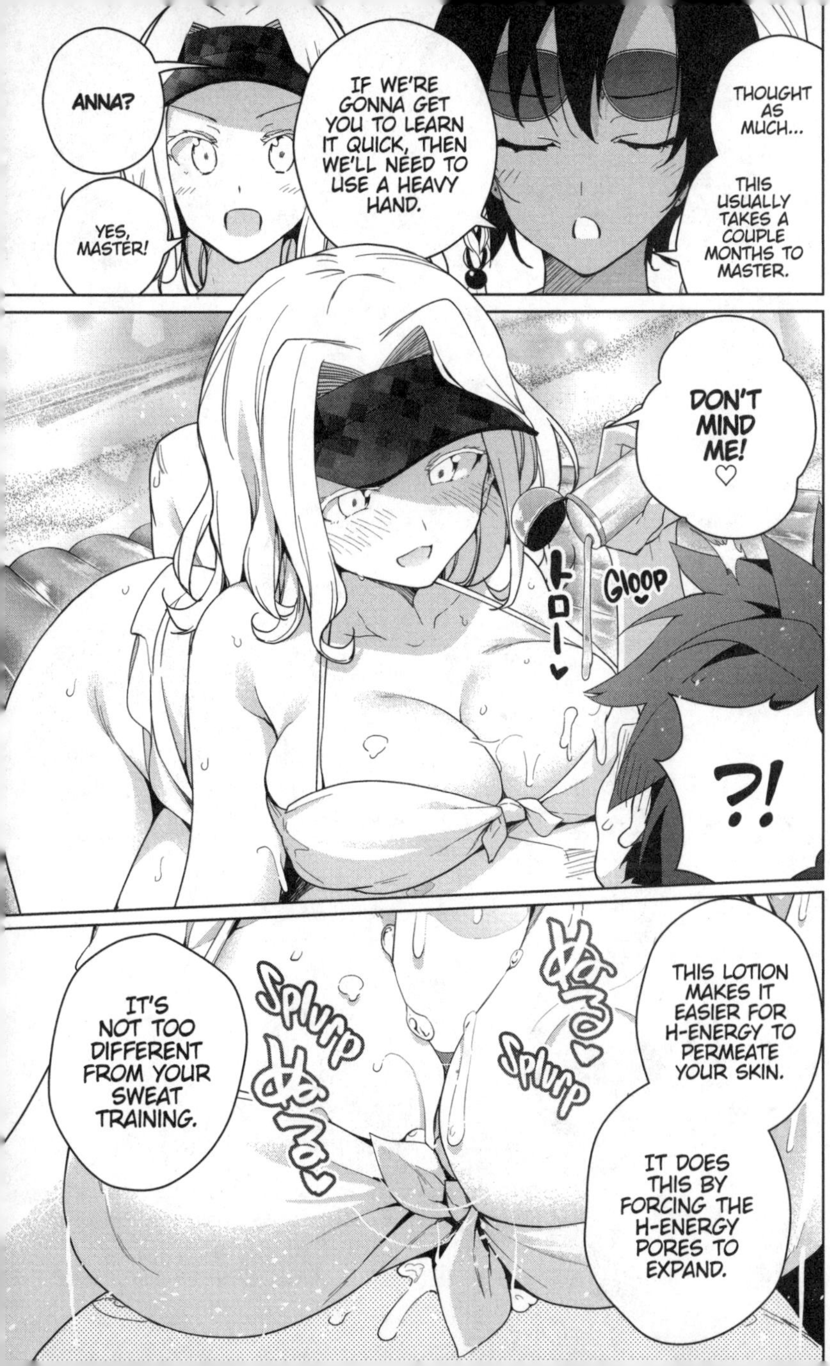
THOUGHT AS MUCH...
THIS USUALLY TAKES A COUPLE MONTHS TO MASTER.
IF WE'RE GONNA GET YOU TO LEARN IT QUICK, THEN WE'LL NEED TO USE A HEAVY HAND.
ANNA?
YES, MASTER!
DON'T MIND ME! ♡
GLOOP
トロー
?!
THIS LOTION MAKES IT EASIER FOR H-ENERGY TO PERMEATE YOUR SKIN.
IT DOES THIS BY FORCING THE H-ENERGY PORES TO EXPAND.
ぬる
Splurp
Splurp
ぬる
IT'S NOT TOO DIFFERENT FROM YOUR SWEAT TRAINING.

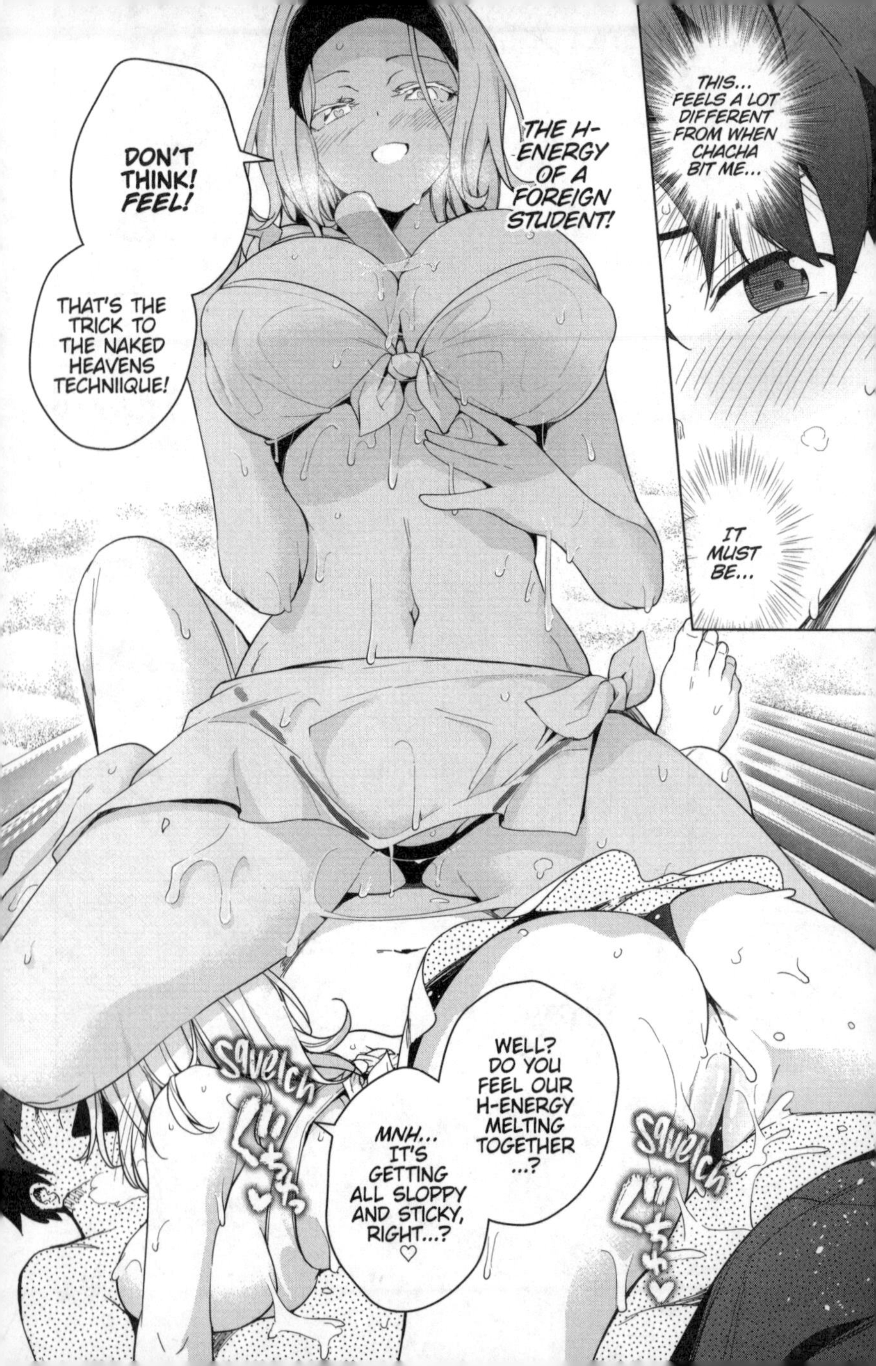
THIS... FEELS A LOT DIFFERENT FROM WHEN CHACHA BIT ME...
IT MUST BE...
THE H-ENERGY OF A FOREIGN STUDENT!
DON'T THINK! FEEL!
THAT'S THE TRICK TO THE NAKED HEAVENS TECHNIIQUE!
squelch
WELL? DO YOU FEEL OUR H-ENERGY MELTING TOGETHER ...?
MNH... IT'S GETTING ALL SLOPPY AND STICKY, RIGHT...? ♡
squelch

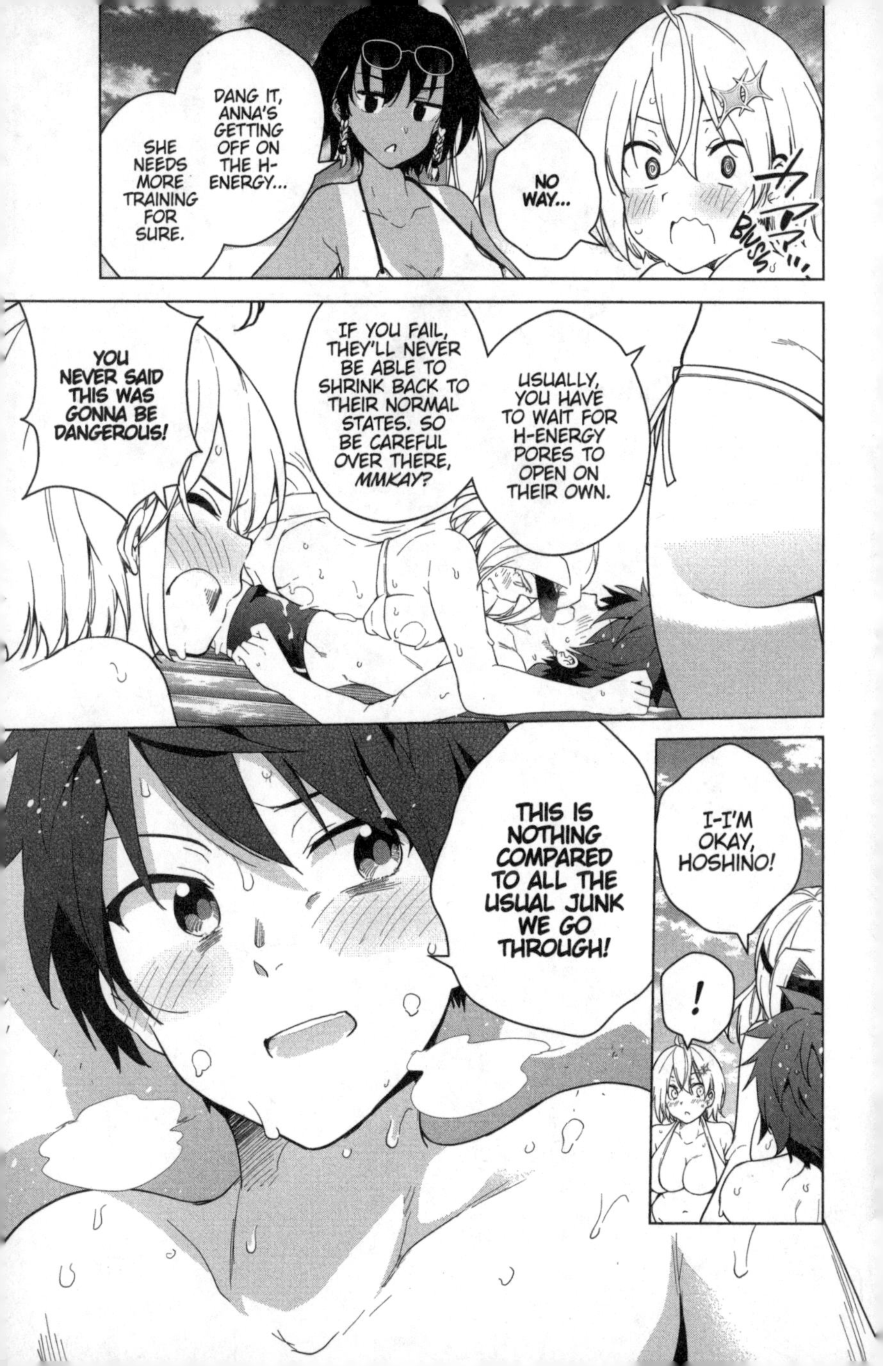
NO WAY...
BLUSH
DANG IT, ANNA'S GETTING OFF ON THE H-ENERGY...
SHE NEEDS MORE TRAINING FOR SURE.
USUALLY, YOU HAVE TO WAIT FOR H-ENERGY PORES TO OPEN ON THEIR OWN.
IF YOU FAIL, THEY'LL NEVER BE ABLE TO SHRINK BACK TO THEIR NORMAL STATES. SO BE CAREFUL OVER THERE, *MMKAY?*
YOU NEVER SAID THIS WAS GONNA BE DANGEROUS!
I-I'M OKAY, HOSHINO!
!
THIS IS NOTHING COMPARED TO ALL THE USUAL JUNK WE GO THROUGH!

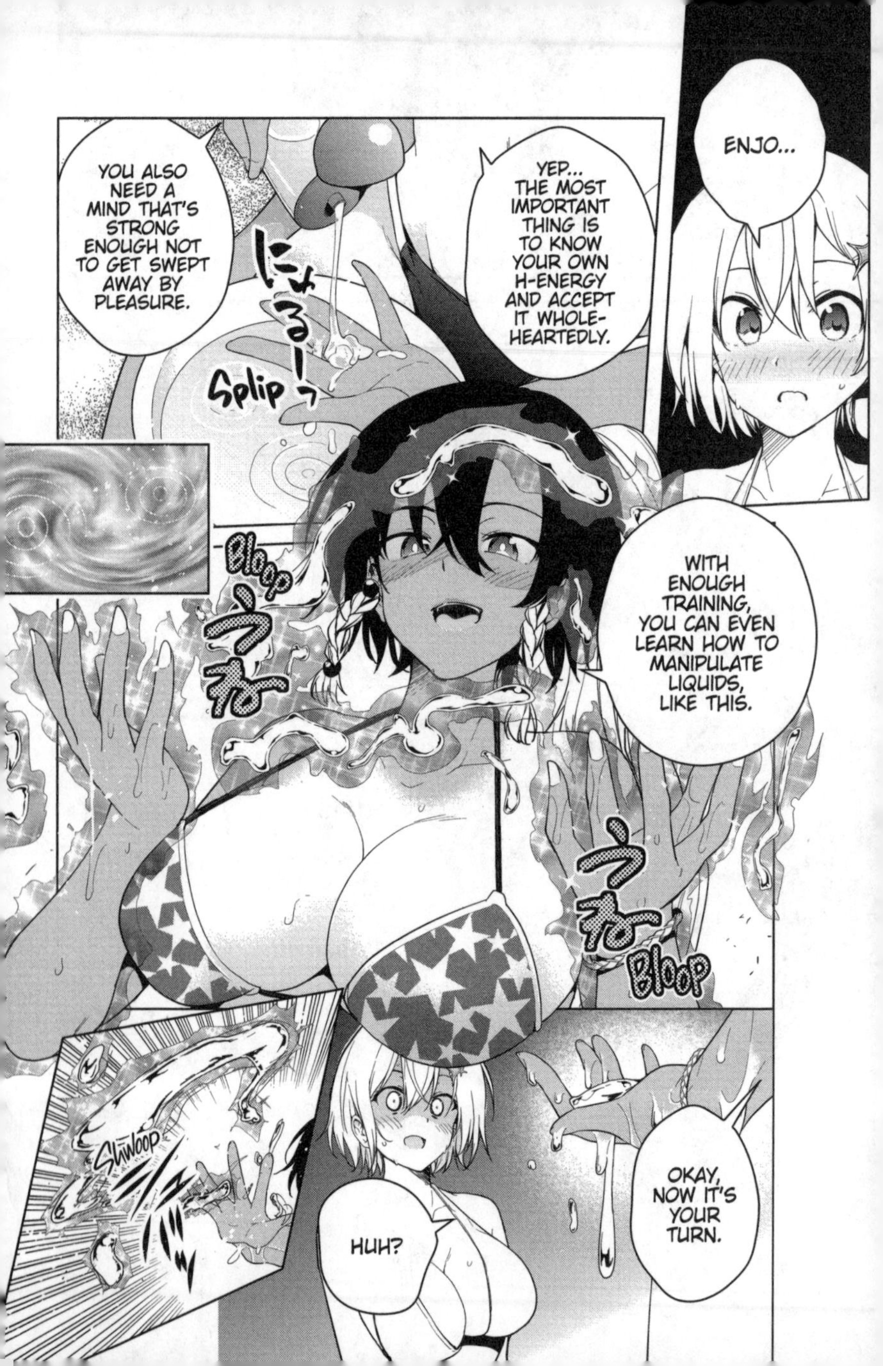

ENJO...
YEP... THE MOST IMPORTANT THING IS TO KNOW YOUR OWN H-ENERGY AND ACCEPT IT WHOLE-HEARTEDLY.
YOU ALSO NEED A MIND THAT'S STRONG ENOUGH NOT TO GET SWEPT AWAY BY PLEASURE.
にゅるーっ
Splip
WITH ENOUGH TRAINING, YOU CAN EVEN LEARN HOW TO MANIPULATE LIQUIDS, LIKE THIS.
うね
Bloop
うね
Bloop
OKAY, NOW IT'S YOUR TURN.
HUH?
Shwoop

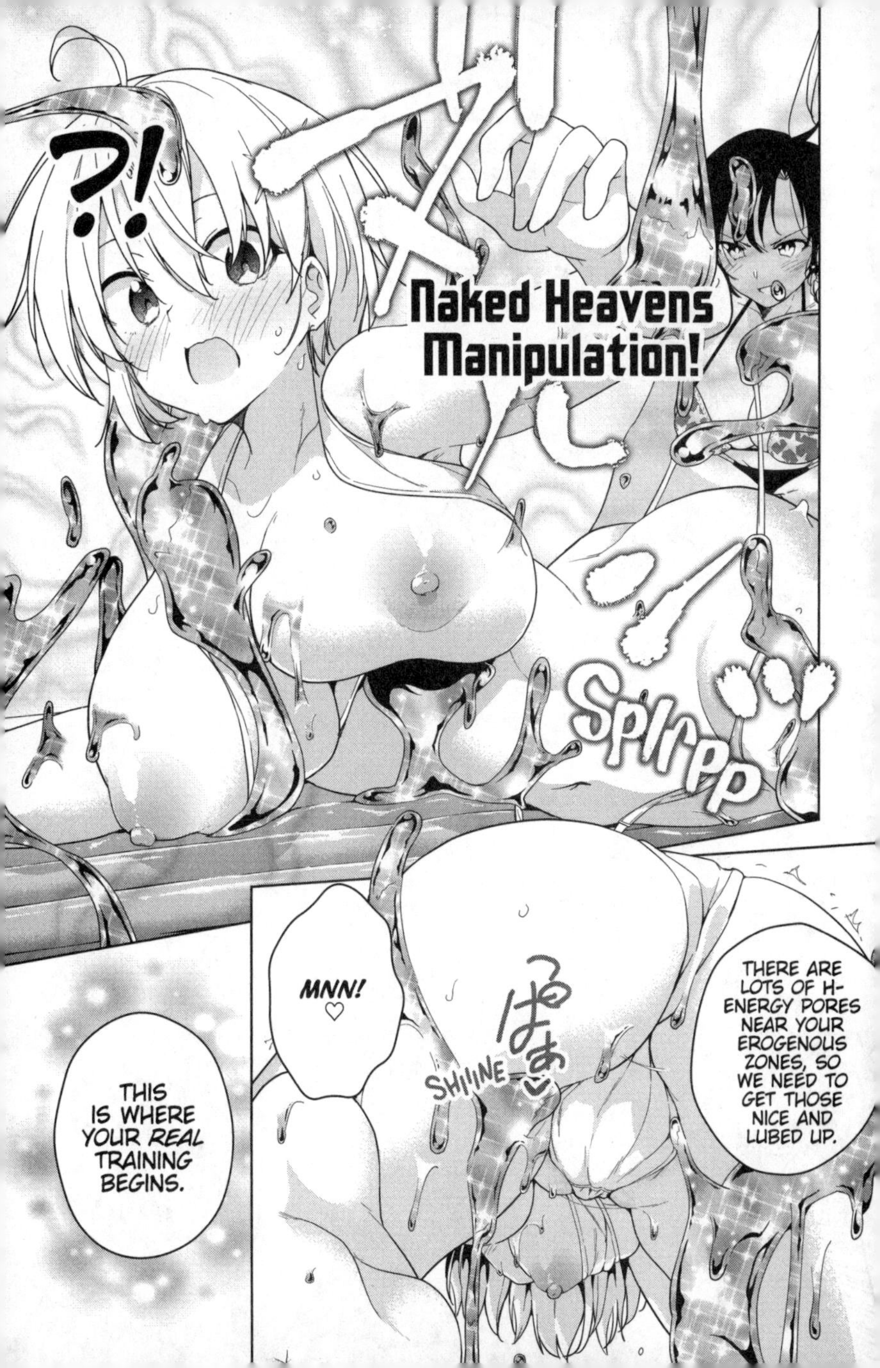
Naked Heavens Manipulation!
?!
Splrpp
THERE ARE LOTS OF H-ENERGY PORES NEAR YOUR EROGENOUS ZONES, SO WE NEED TO GET THOSE NICE AND LUBED UP.
SHIIINE
MNN! ♡
THIS IS WHERE YOUR REAL TRAINING BEGINS.

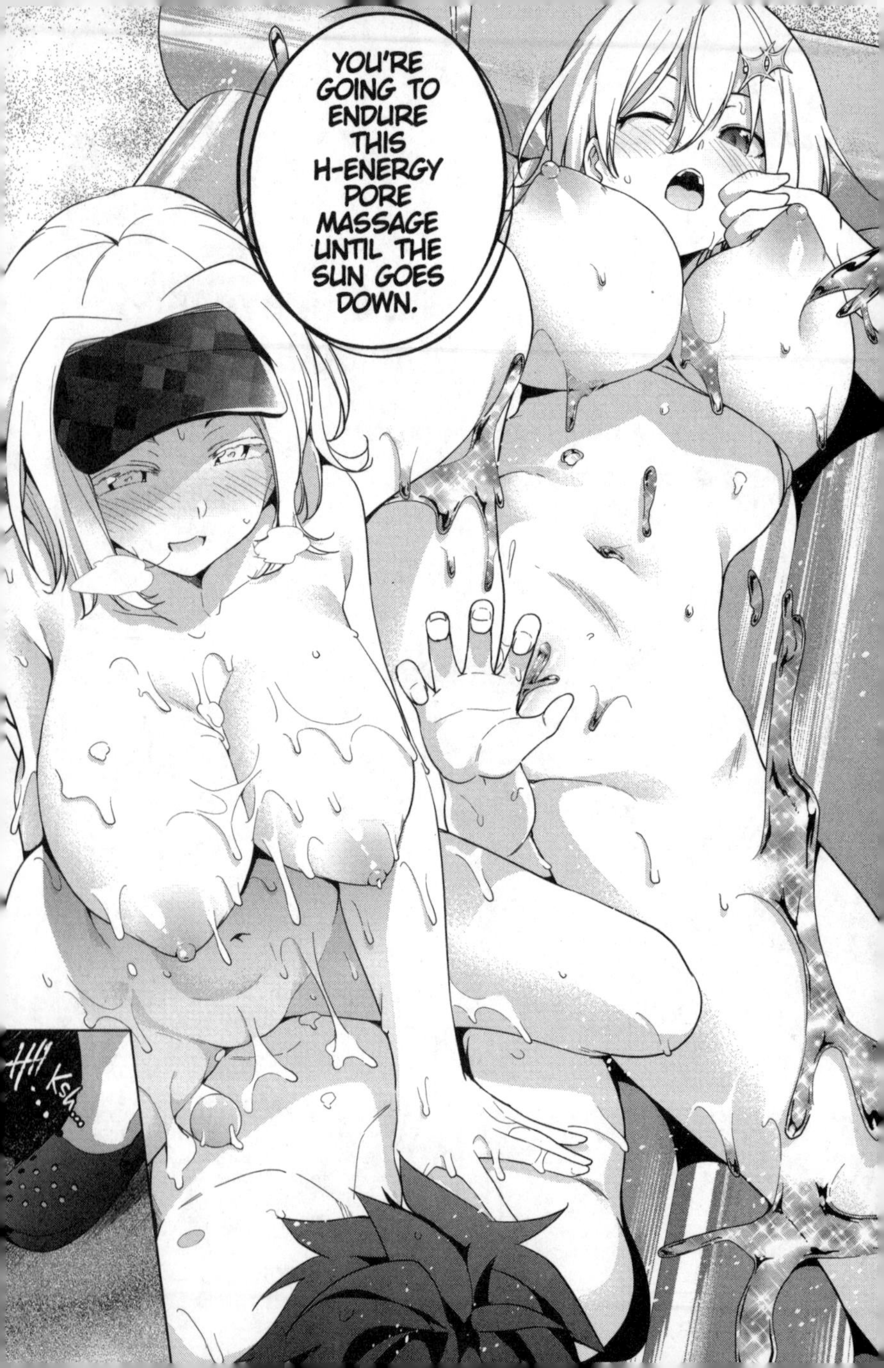
YOU'RE GOING TO ENDURE THIS H-ENERGY PORE MASSAGE UNTIL THE SUN GOES DOWN.
Ksh...

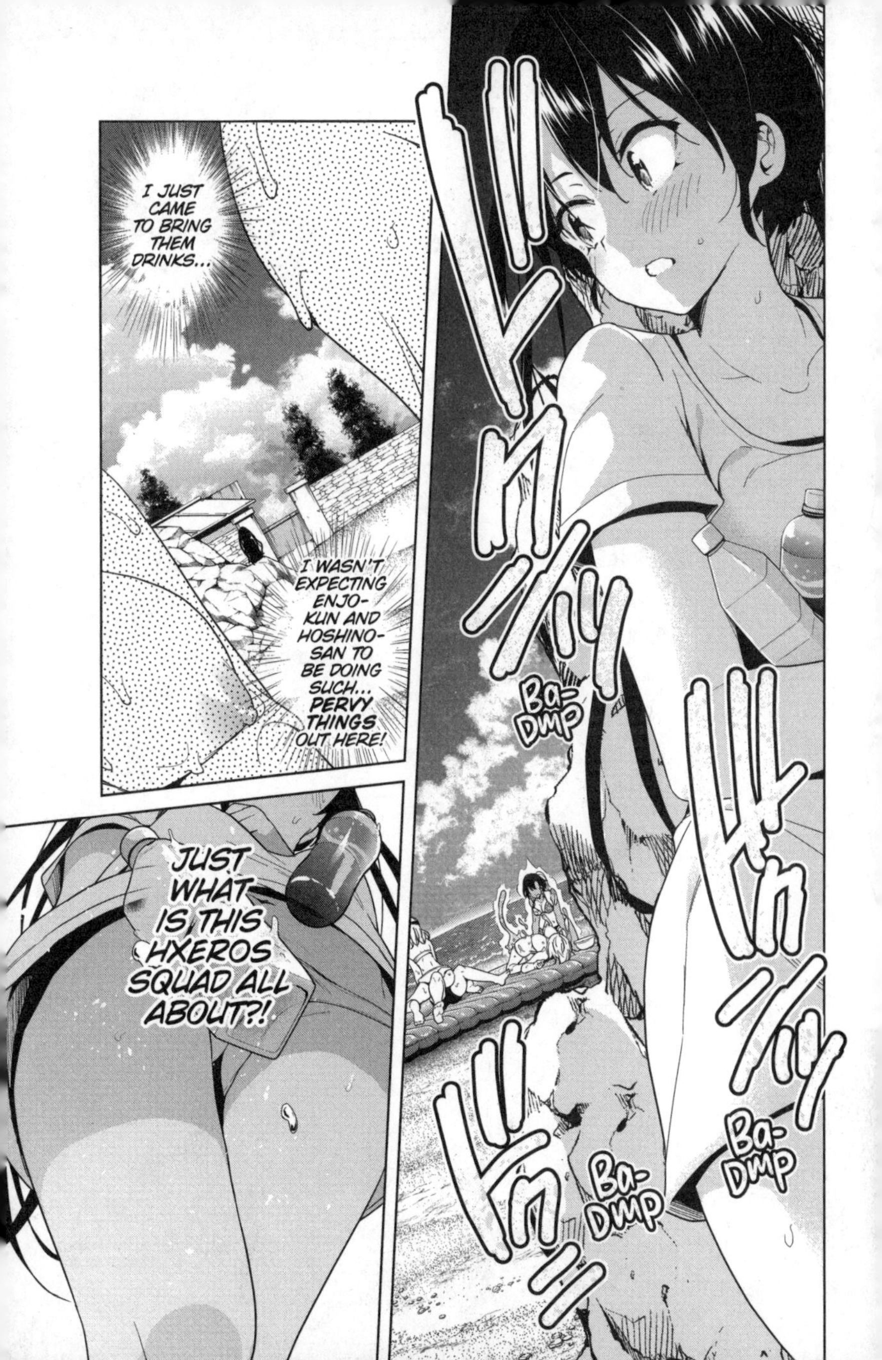
Ba-Dmp
Ba-Dmp
Ba-Dmp
I JUST CAME TO BRING THEM DRINKS...
I WASN'T EXPECTING ENJO-KUN AND HOSHINO-SAN TO BE DOING SUCH... PERVY THINGS OUT HERE!
JUST WHAT IS THIS HXEROS SQUAD ALL ABOUT?!

Extra Gallery

SUPER HxEROS

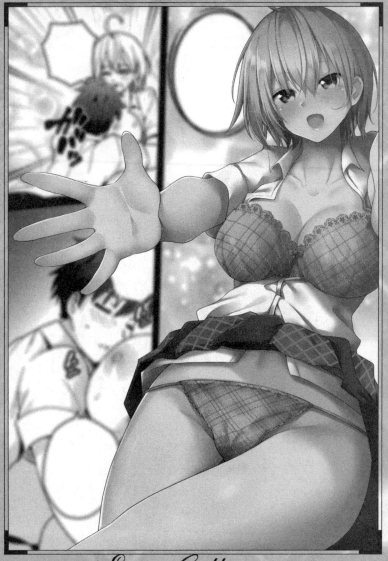

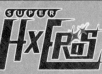

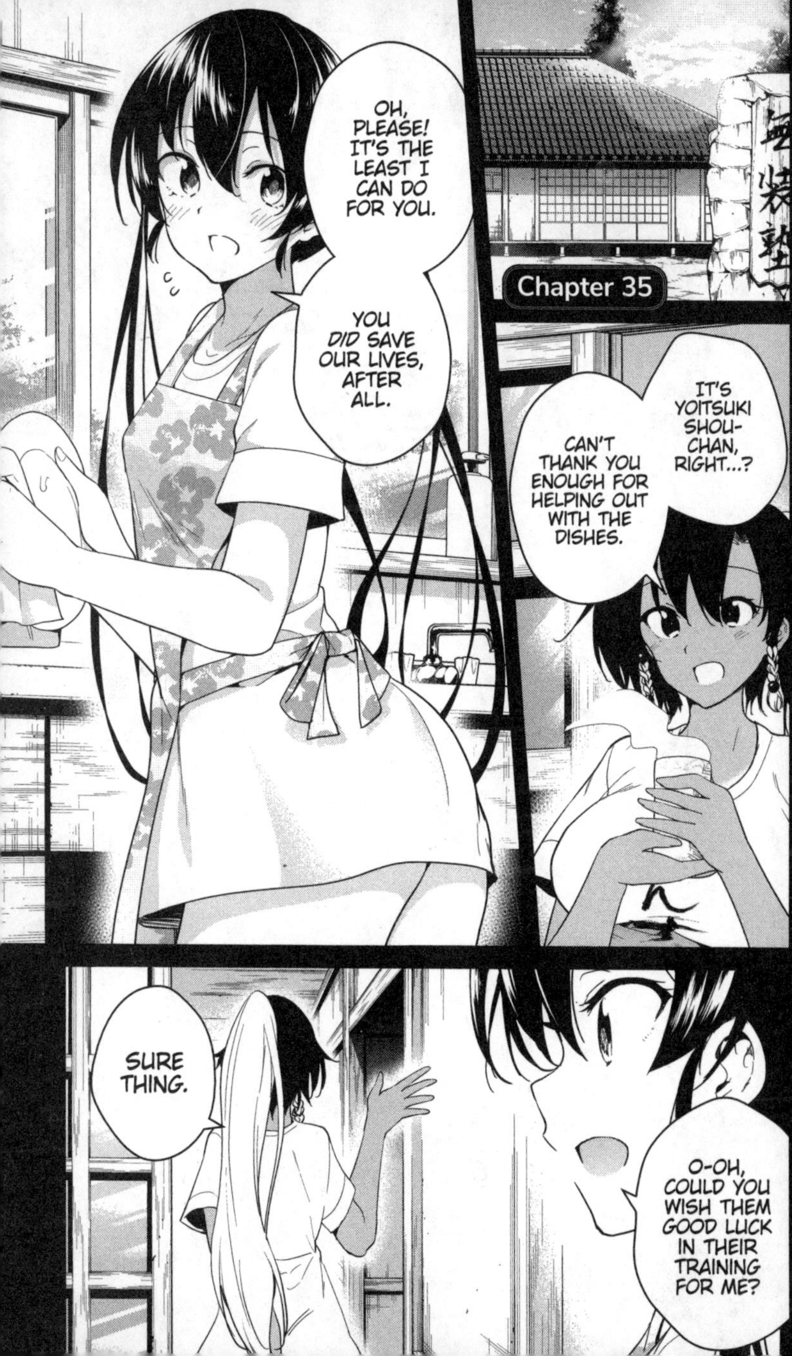
Chapter 35
IT'S YOITSUKI SHOU-CHAN, RIGHT...?
CAN'T THANK YOU ENOUGH FOR HELPING OUT WITH THE DISHES.
OH, PLEASE! IT'S THE LEAST I CAN DO FOR YOU.
YOU DID SAVE OUR LIVES, AFTER ALL.
O-OH, COULD YOU WISH THEM GOOD LUCK IN THEIR TRAINING FOR ME?
SURE THING.

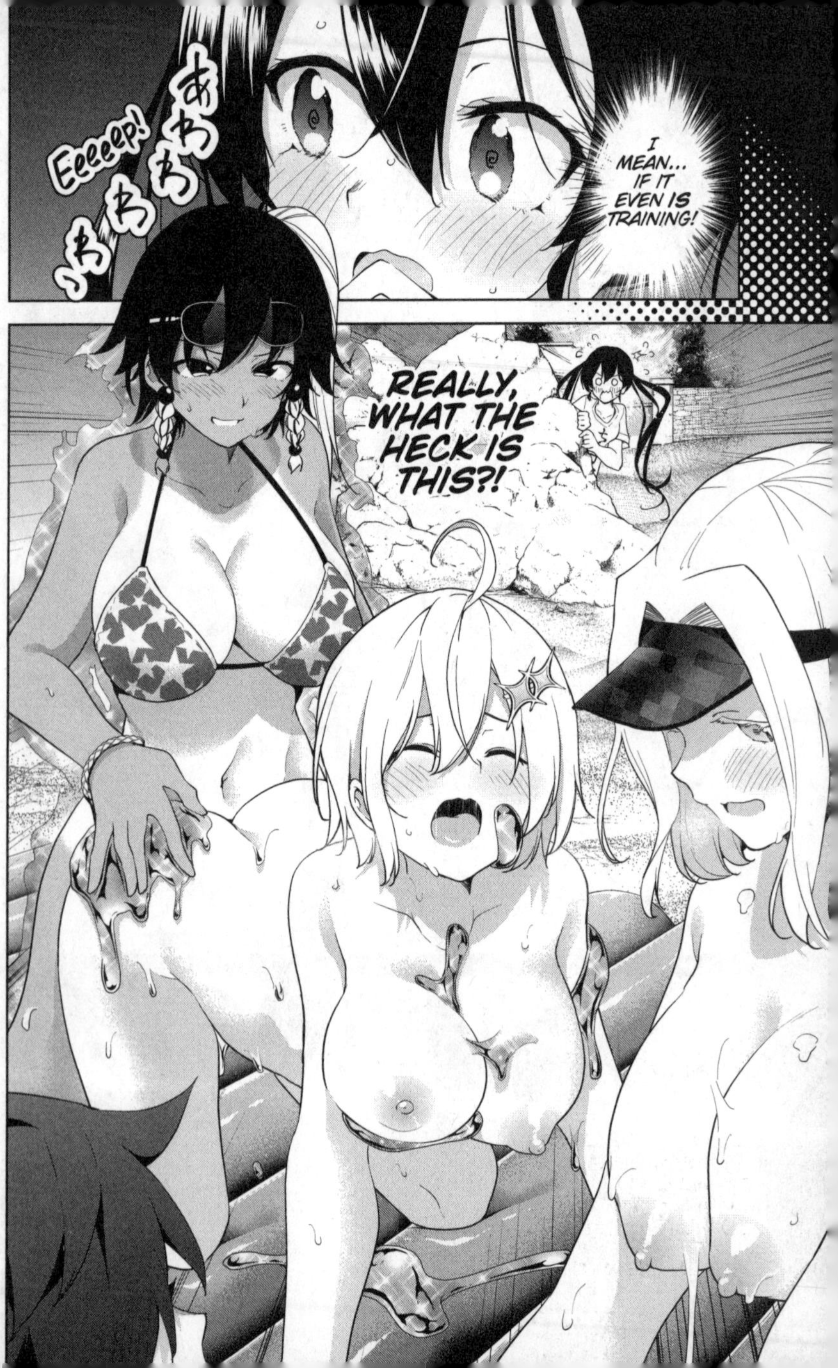
I MEAN... IF IT EVEN IS TRAINING!
Eeeeep!
あわわわわ
REALLY, WHAT THE HECK IS THIS?!

Chapter 35 Training Bears Fruit

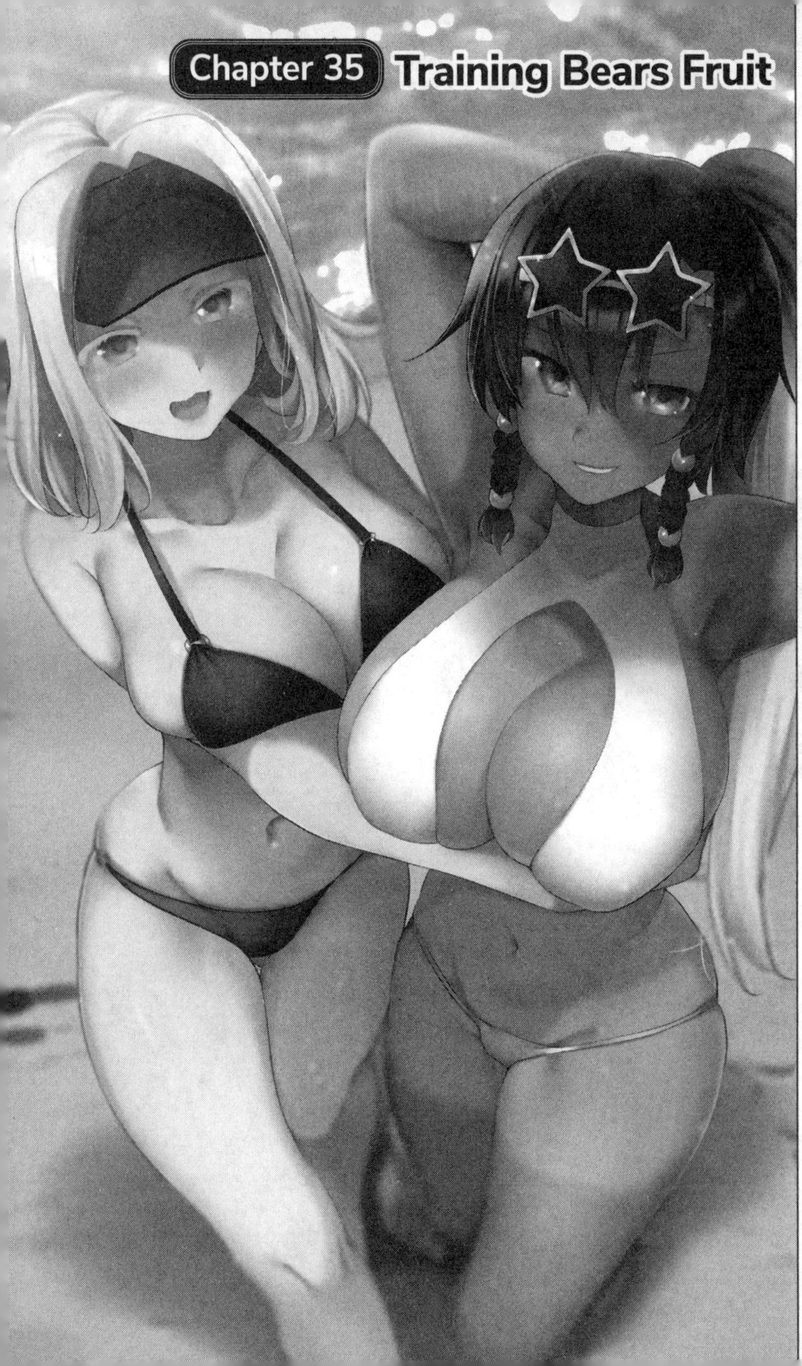

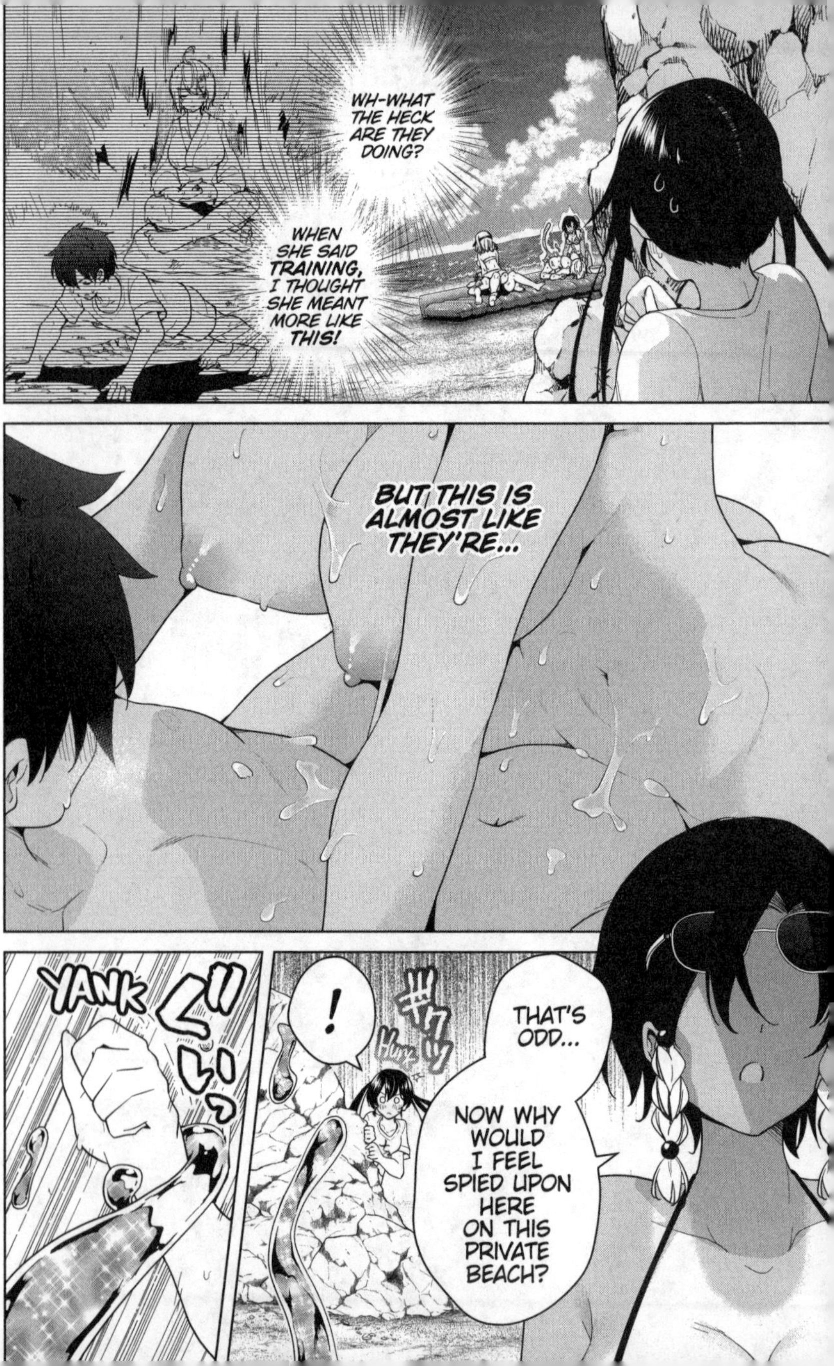
WH-WHAT THE HECK ARE THEY DOING?
WHEN SHE SAID TRAINING, I THOUGHT SHE MEANT MORE LIKE THIS!
BUT THIS IS ALMOST LIKE THEY'RE...
THAT'S ODD...
NOW WHY WOULD I FEEL SPIED UPON HERE ON THIS PRIVATE BEACH?
!
YANK

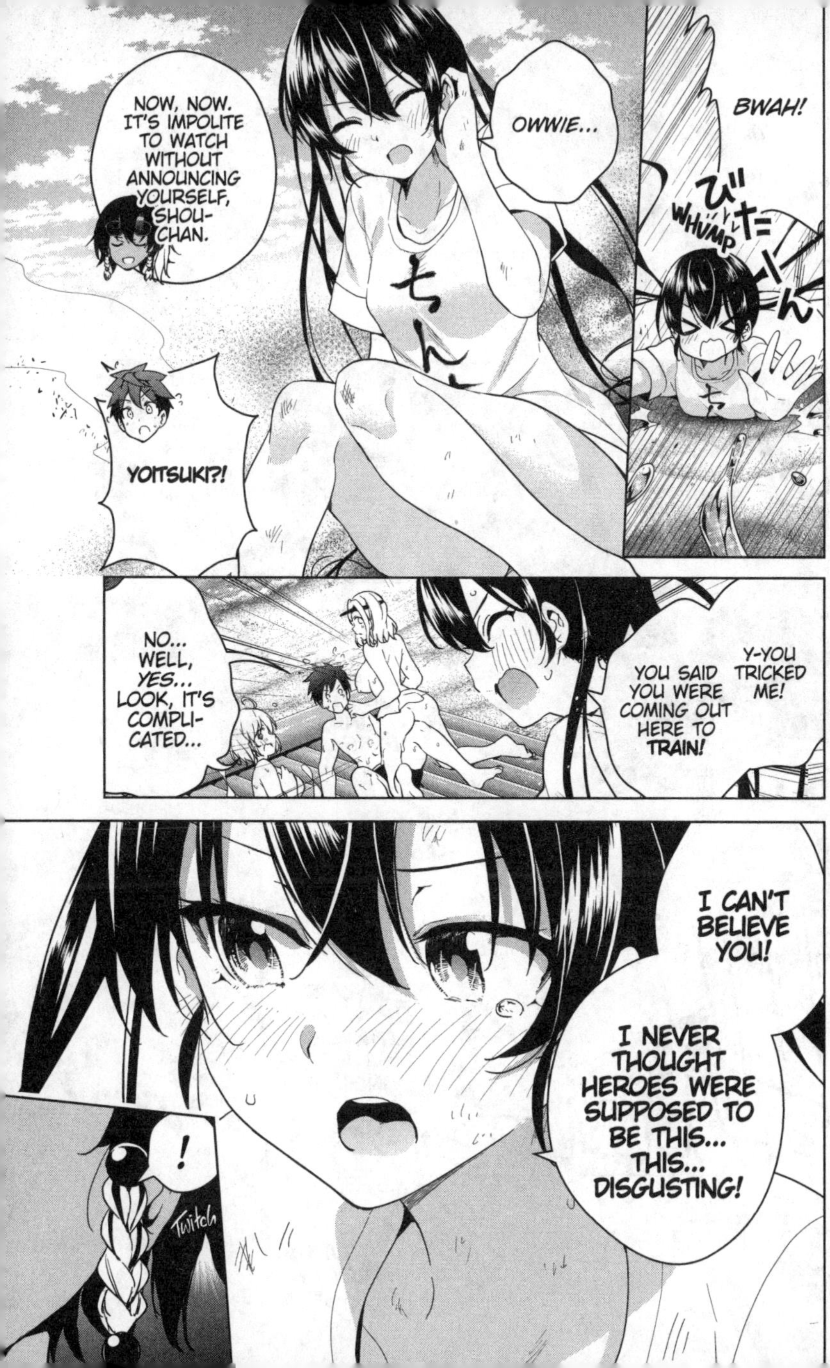

BWAH!
WHUMP
OWWIE...
NOW, NOW. IT'S IMPOLITE TO WATCH WITHOUT ANNOUNCING YOURSELF, SHOU-CHAN.
YOITSUKI?!
Y-YOU TRICKED ME!
YOU SAID YOU WERE COMING OUT HERE TO TRAIN!
NO... WELL, YES... LOOK, IT'S COMPLICATED...
I CAN'T BELIEVE YOU!
I NEVER THOUGHT HEROES WERE SUPPOSED TO BE THIS... THIS... DISGUSTING!
!
Twitch

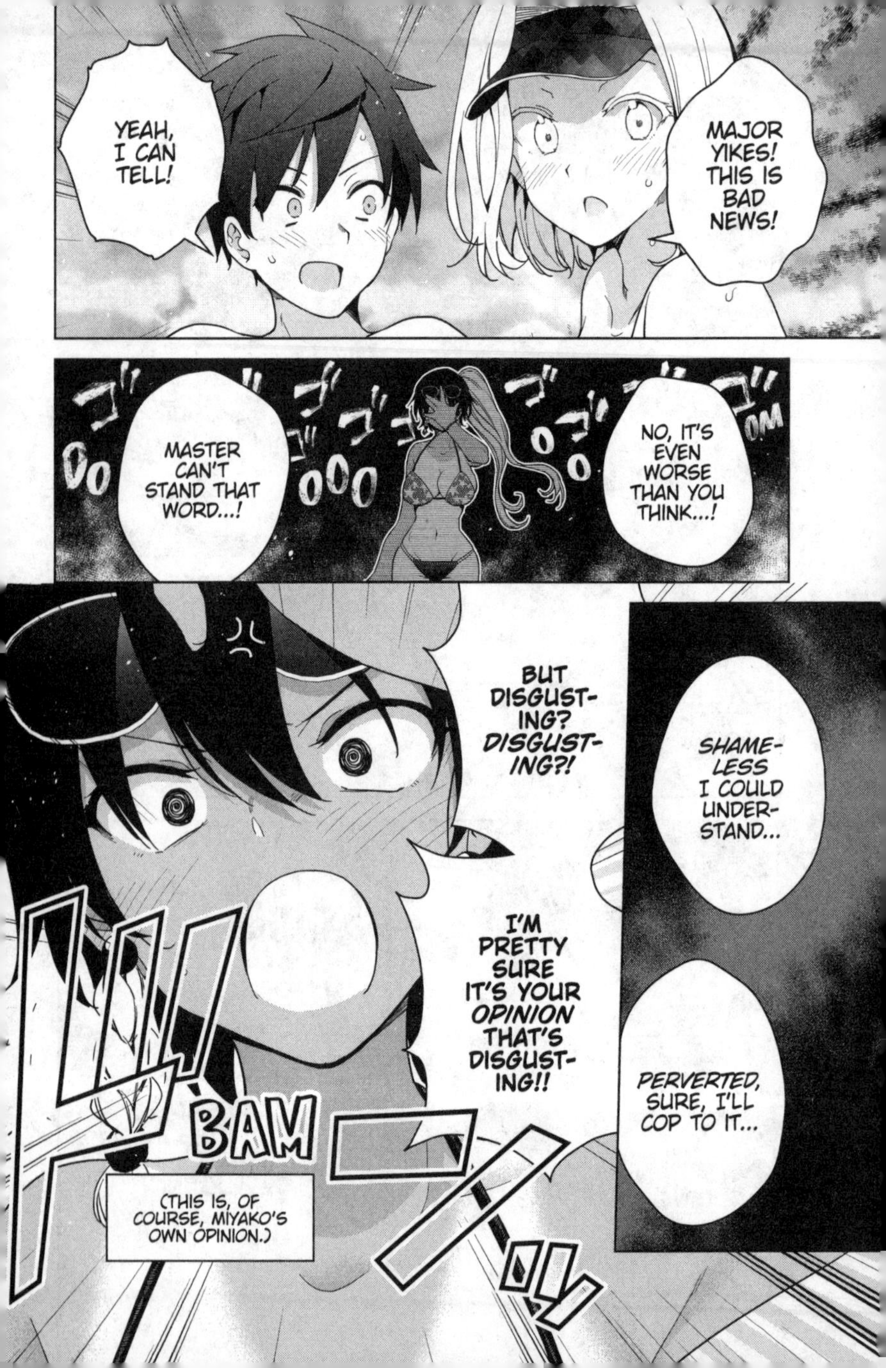
MAJOR YIKES! THIS IS BAD NEWS!
YEAH, I CAN TELL!
NO, IT'S EVEN WORSE THAN YOU THINK...!
MASTER CAN'T STAND THAT WORD...!
SHAME-LESS I COULD UNDER-STAND...
PERVERTED, SURE, I'LL COP TO IT...
BUT DISGUST-ING? DISGUST-ING?!
I'M PRETTY SURE IT'S YOUR OPINION THAT'S DISGUST-ING!!
BAM
(THIS IS, OF COURSE, MIYAKO'S OWN OPINION.)

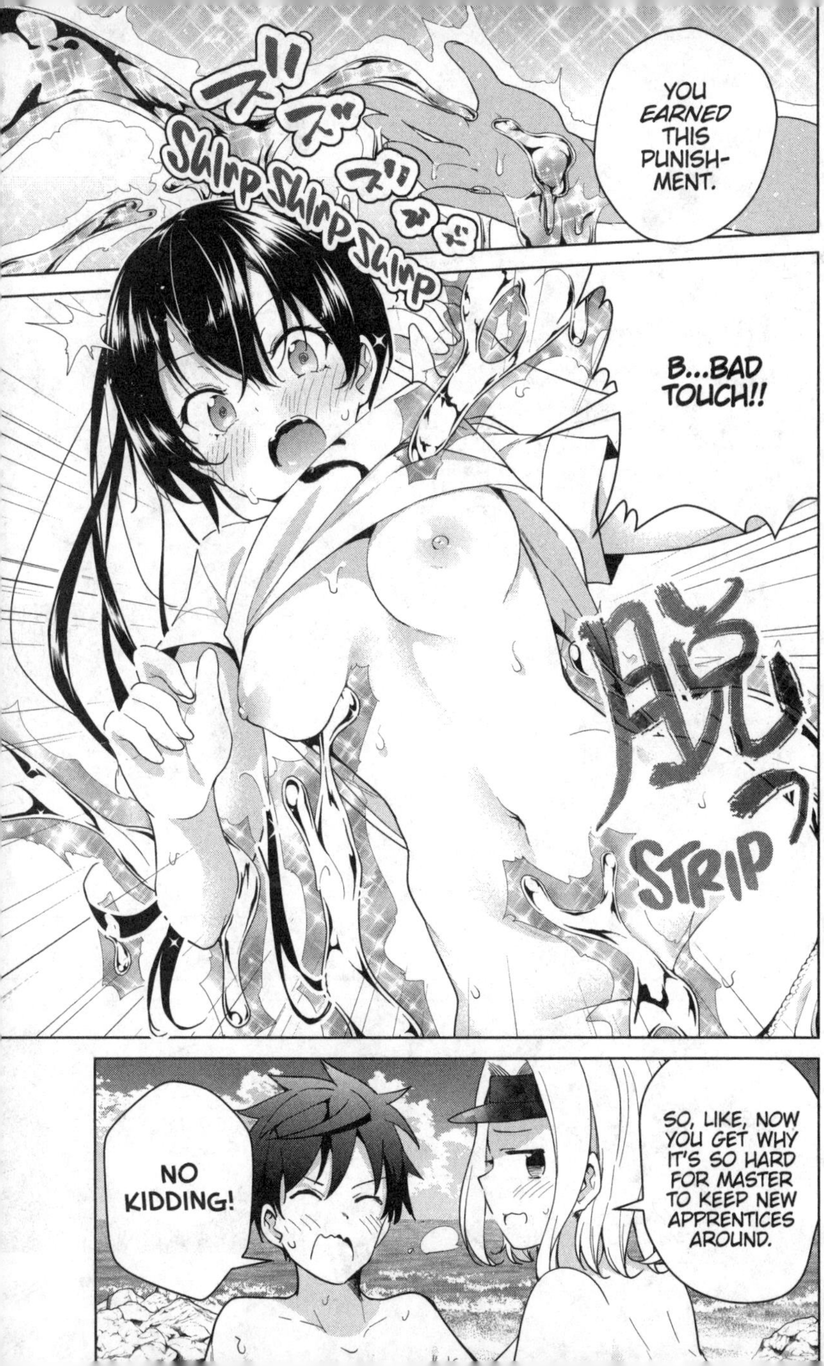
YOU EARNED THIS PUNISHMENT.
Shlrp Shlrp Shlrp Shlrp
B...BAD TOUCH!!
STRIP
SO, LIKE, NOW YOU GET WHY IT'S SO HARD FOR MASTER TO KEEP NEW APPRENTICES AROUND.
NO KIDDING!

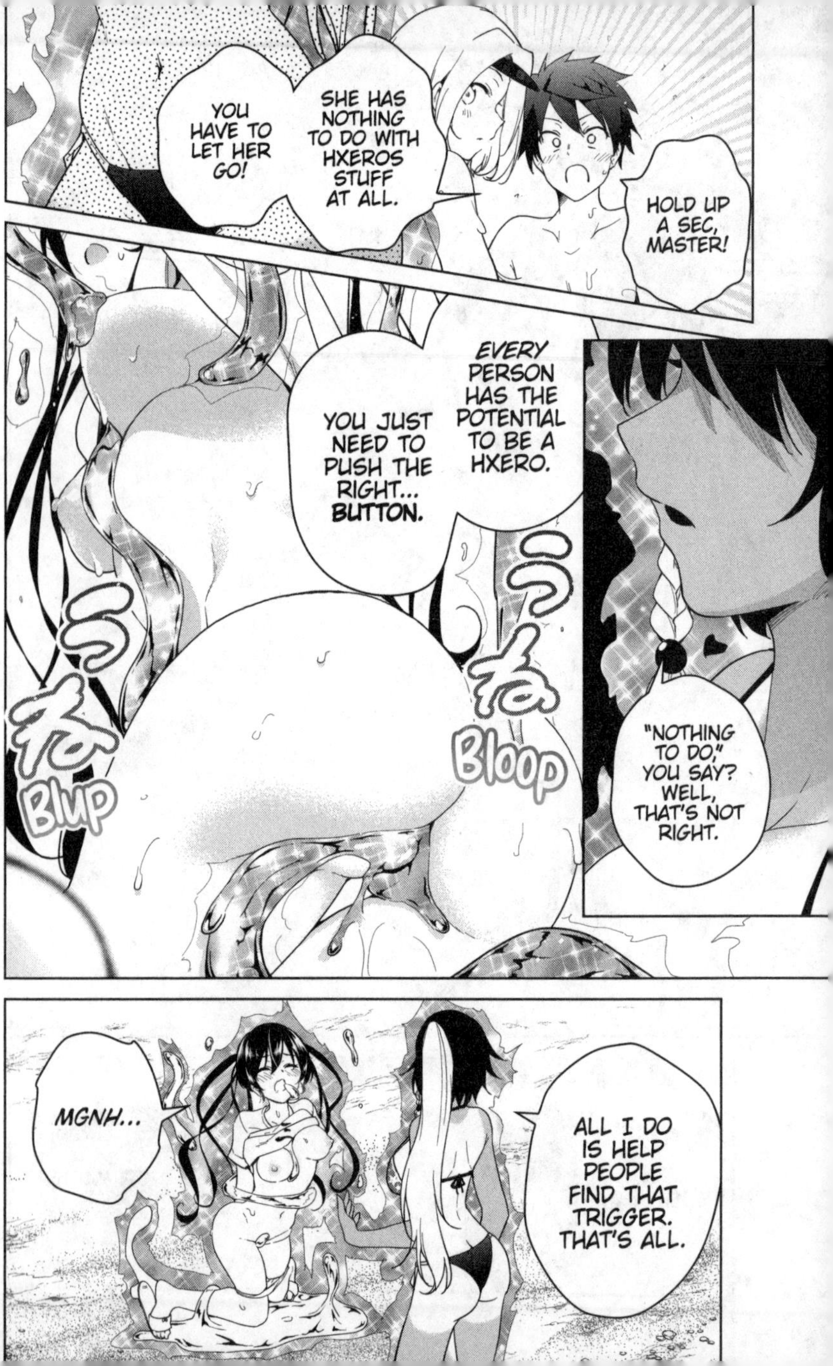
HOLD UP A SEC, MASTER!
SHE HAS NOTHING TO DO WITH HXEROS STUFF AT ALL.
YOU HAVE TO LET HER GO!
"NOTHING TO DO," YOU SAY? WELL, THAT'S NOT RIGHT.
EVERY PERSON HAS THE POTENTIAL TO BE A HXERO.
YOU JUST NEED TO PUSH THE RIGHT... BUTTON.
Bloop
Blup
ALL I DO IS HELP PEOPLE FIND THAT TRIGGER. THAT'S ALL.
MGNH...

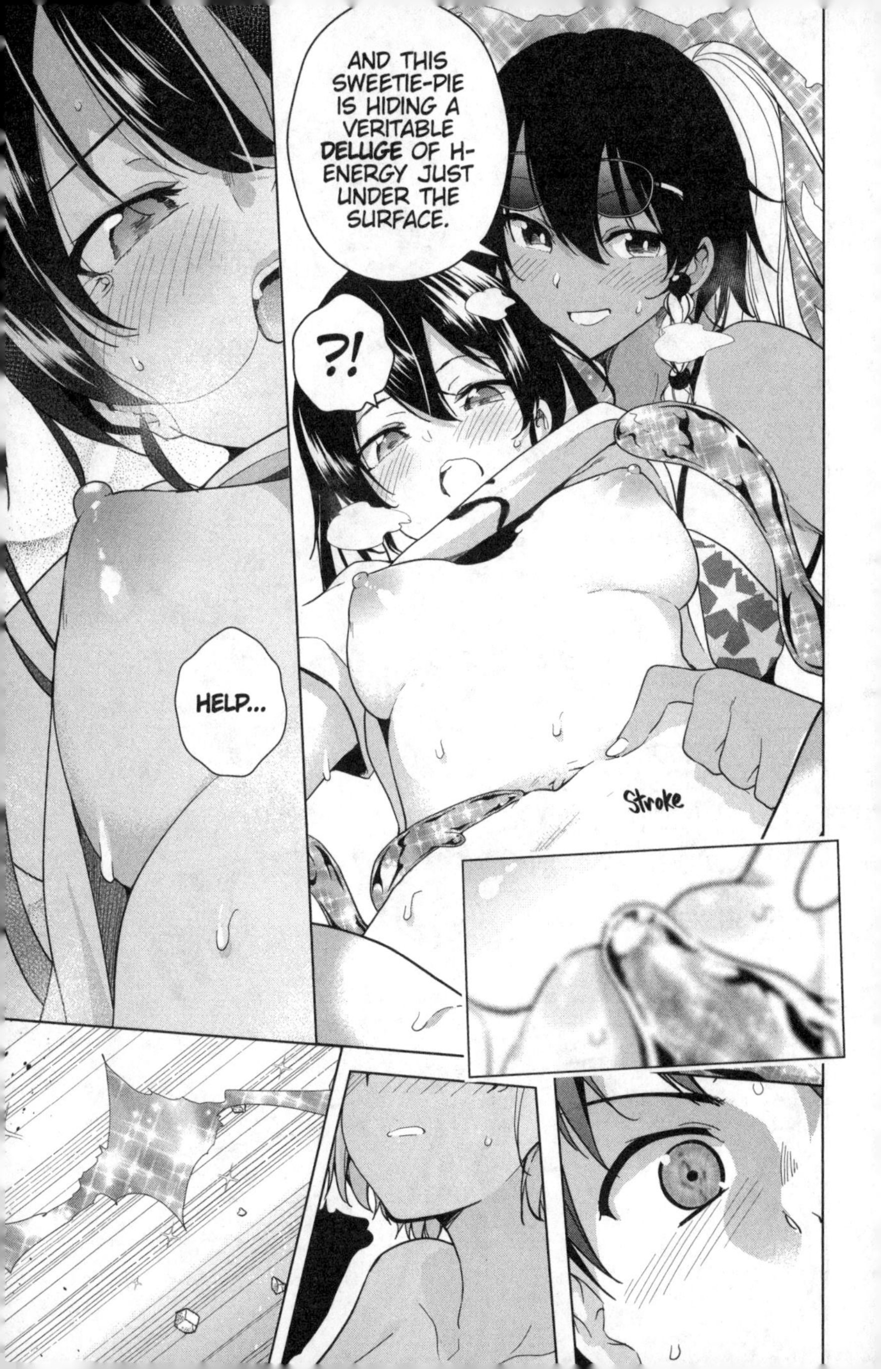
AND THIS SWEETIE-PIE IS HIDING A VERITABLE DELUGE OF H-ENERGY JUST UNDER THE SURFACE.
?!
Stroke
HELP...

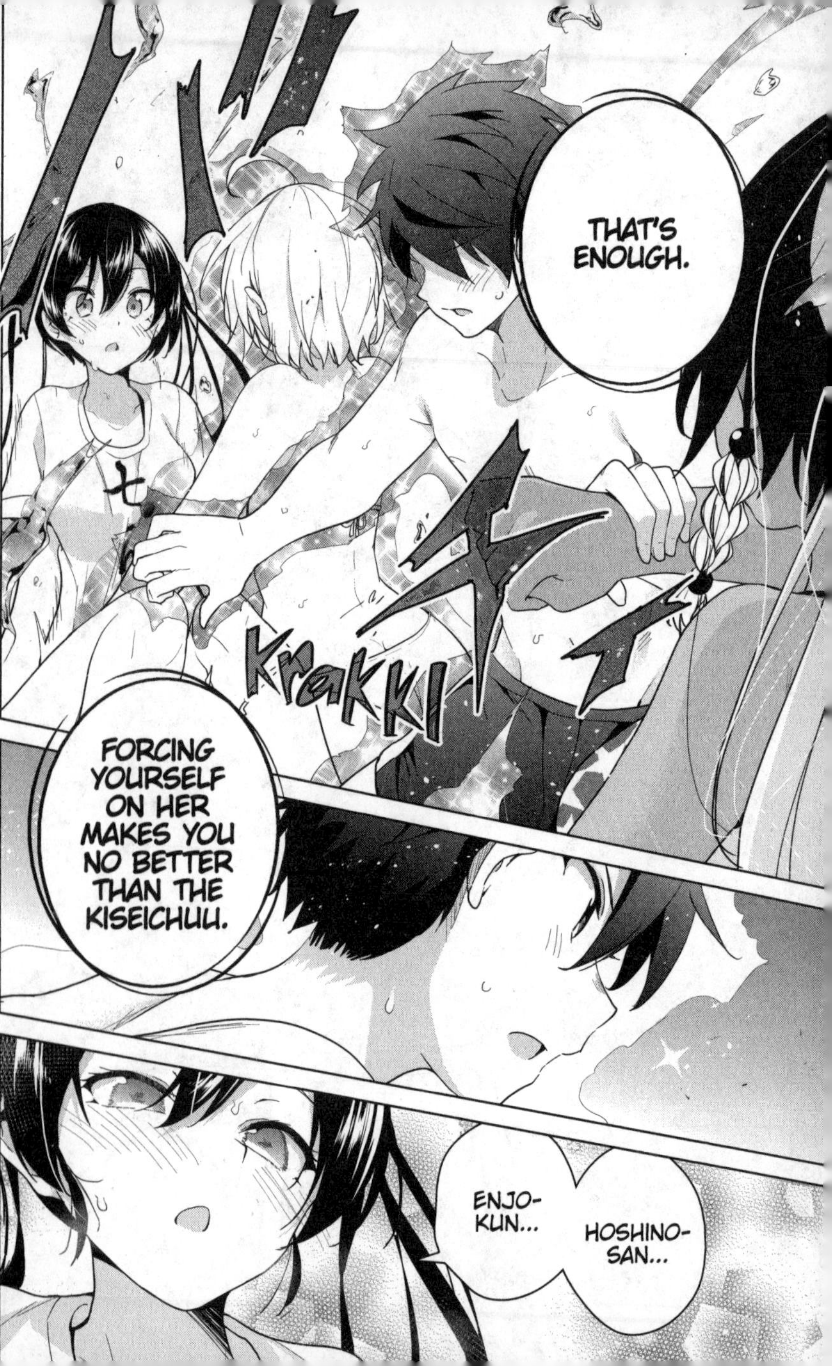
THAT'S ENOUGH.
KRAKKI
FORCING YOURSELF ON HER MAKES YOU NO BETTER THAN THE KISEICHUU.
HOSHINO-SAN...
ENJO-KUN...

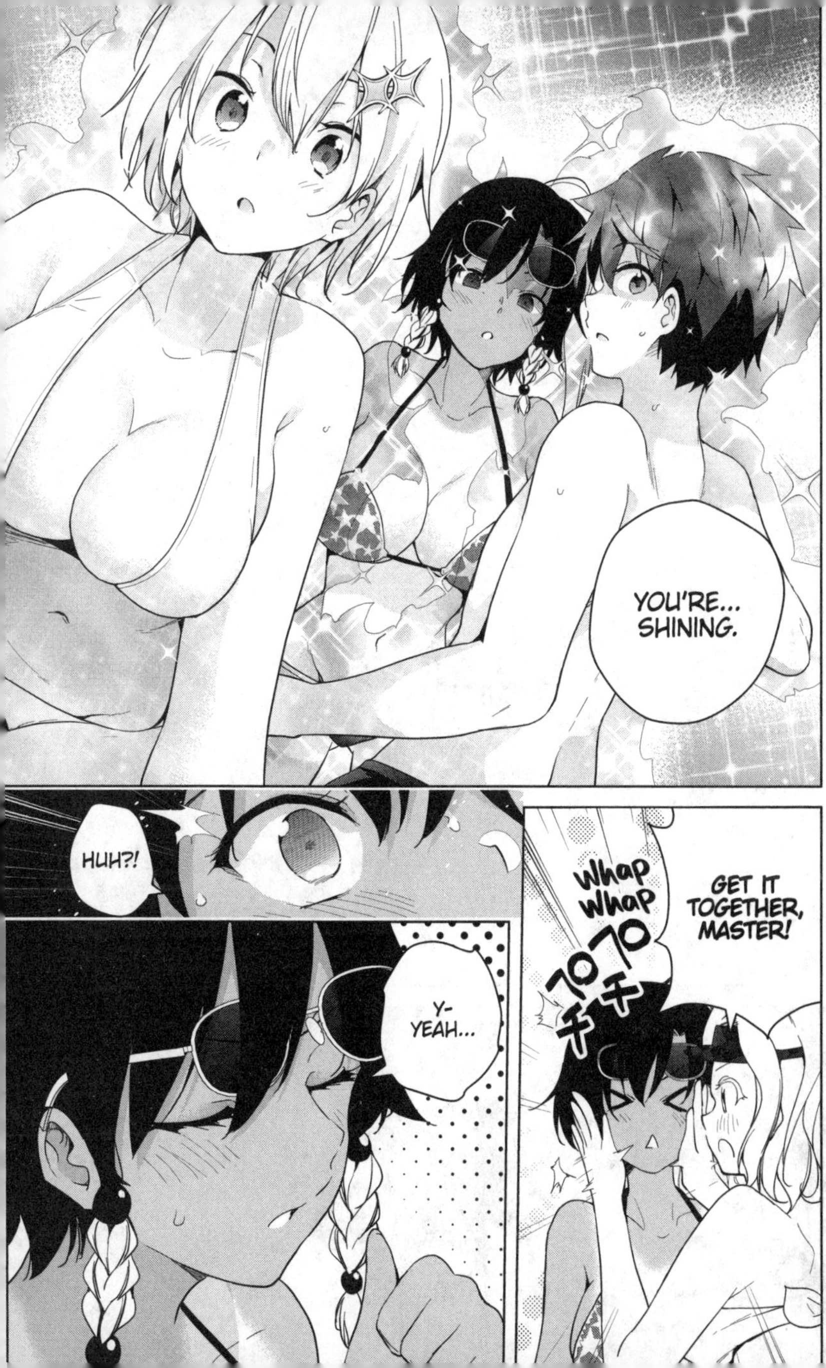
YOU'RE... SHINING.
GET IT TOGETHER, MASTER!
whap whap
ペチペチ
HUH?!
Y- YEAH...

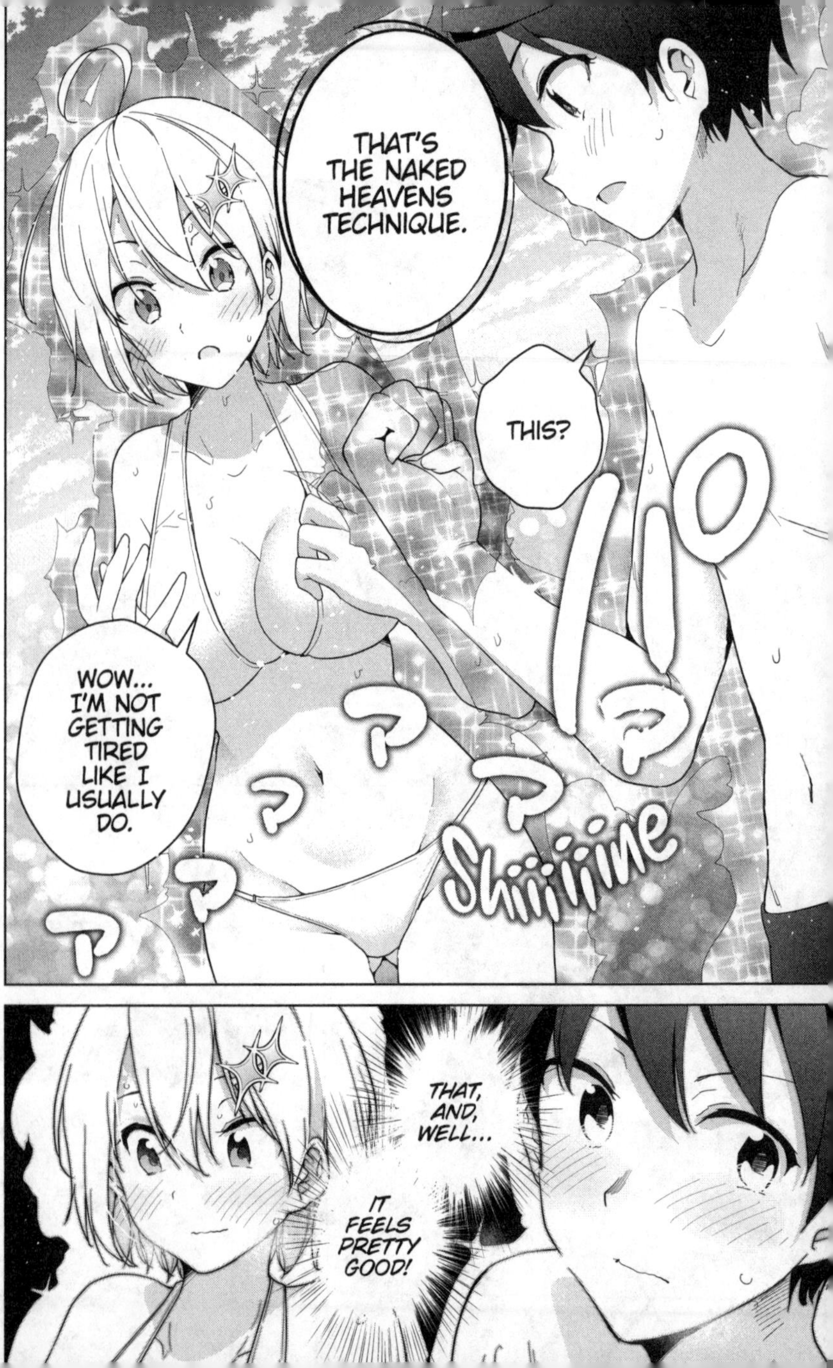
THAT'S THE NAKED HEAVENS TECHNIQUE.
THIS?
Shiiiiiine
WOW... I'M NOT GETTING TIRED LIKE I USUALLY DO.
THAT, AND, WELL...
IT FEELS PRETTY GOOD!

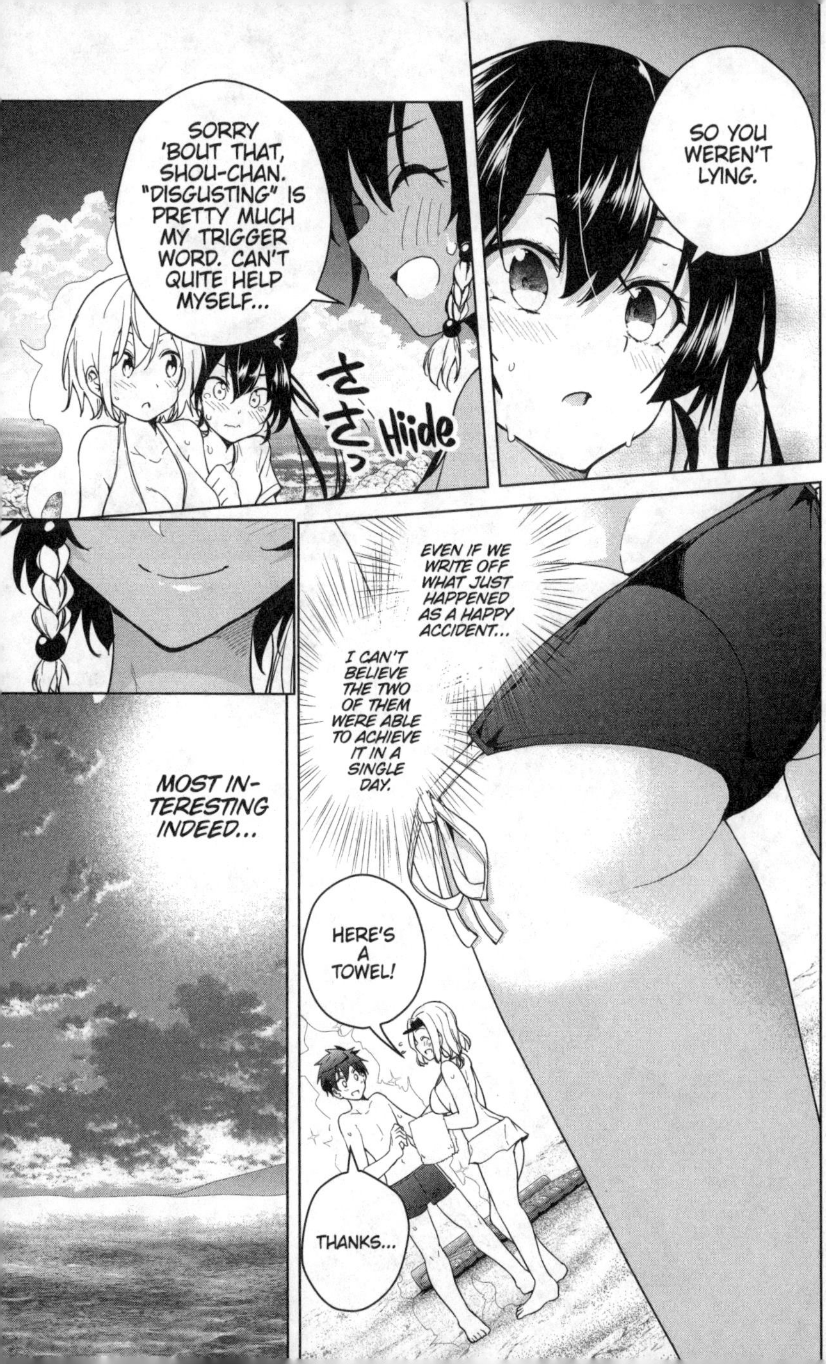
SO YOU WEREN'T LYING.
SORRY 'BOUT THAT, SHOU-CHAN. "DISGUSTING" IS PRETTY MUCH MY TRIGGER WORD. CAN'T QUITE HELP MYSELF...
さっ
Hiide
EVEN IF WE WRITE OFF WHAT JUST HAPPENED AS A HAPPY ACCIDENT...
I CAN'T BELIEVE THE TWO OF THEM WERE ABLE TO ACHIEVE IT IN A SINGLE DAY.
HERE'S A TOWEL!
THANKS...
MOST IN-TERESTING INDEED...

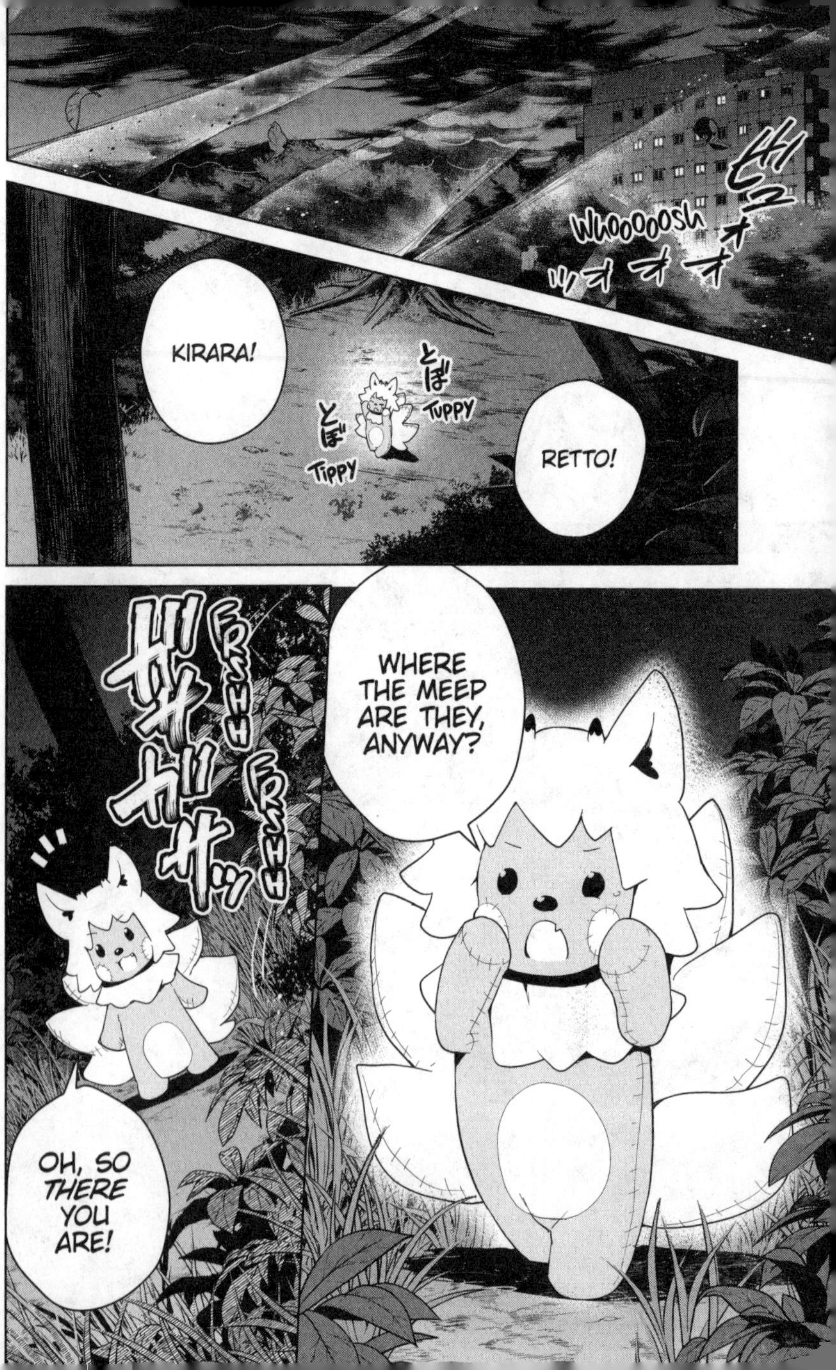
WHOOOOOSH
RETTO!
KIRARA!
とぼ
TUPPY
とぼ
TIPPY
WHERE THE MEEP ARE THEY, ANYWAY?
FRSHH FRSHH
OH, SO THERE YOU ARE!

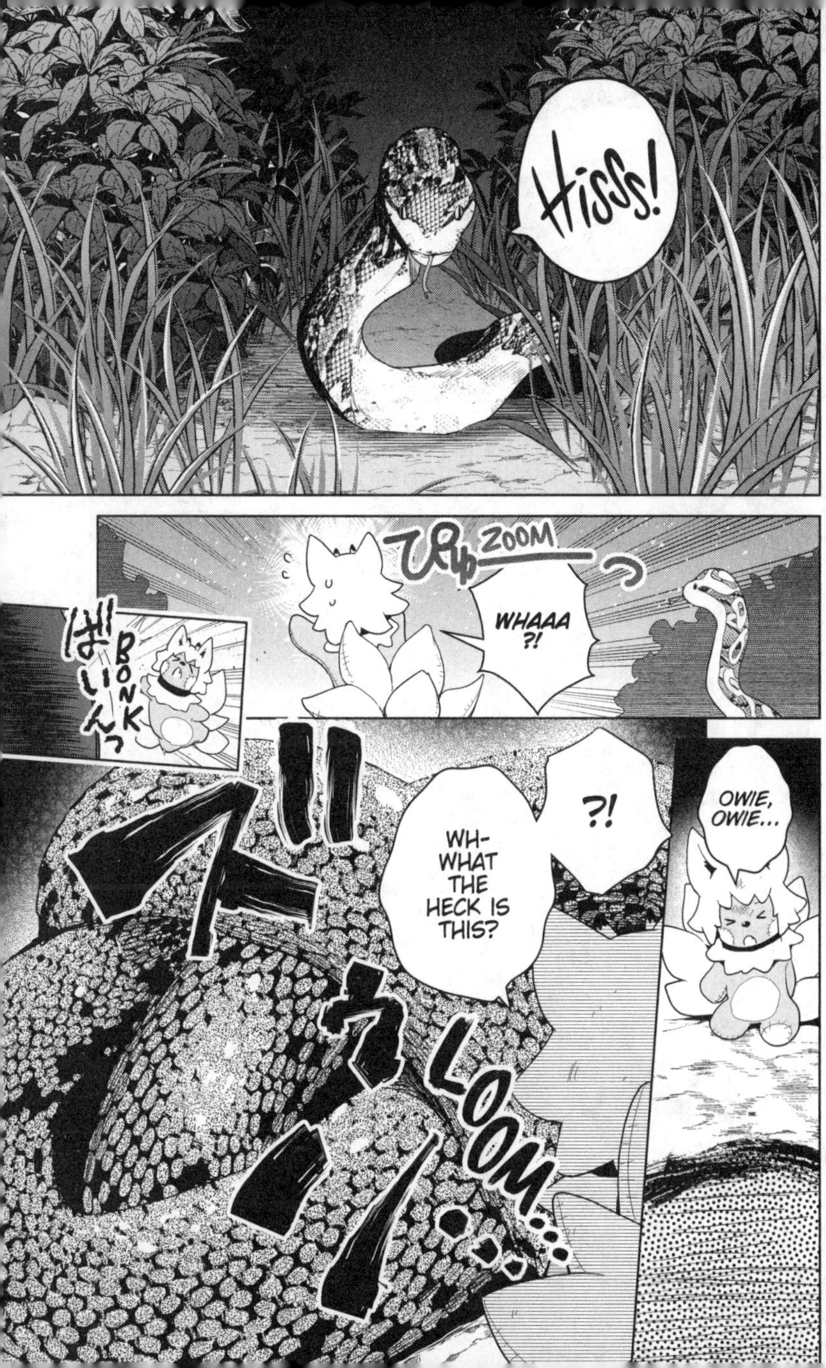

HISSS!
ZOOM
WHAAA?!
BONK
OWIE, OWIE...
?!
WH-WHAT THE HECK IS THIS?
LOOM...

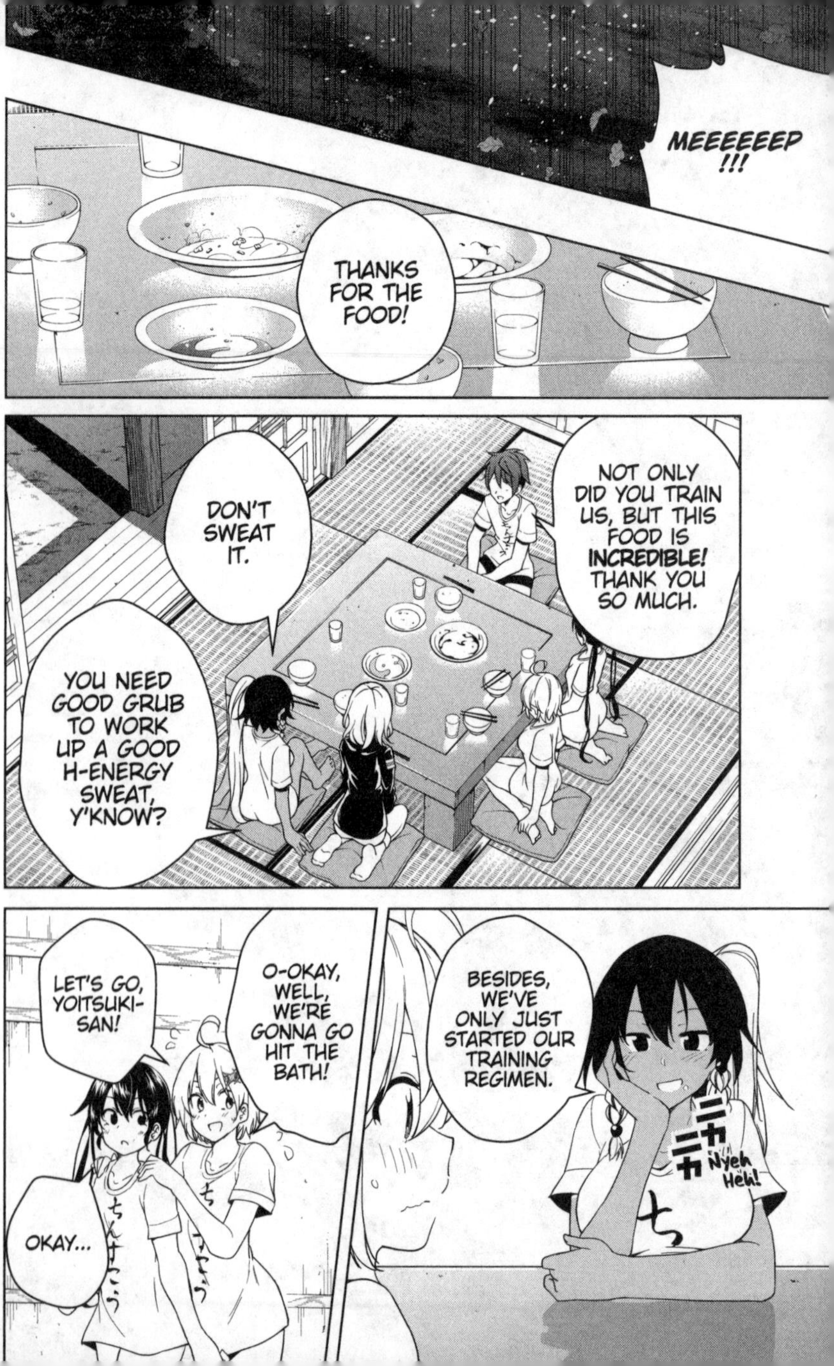
MEEEEEEP !!!
THANKS FOR THE FOOD!
NOT ONLY DID YOU TRAIN US, BUT THIS FOOD IS INCREDIBLE! THANK YOU SO MUCH.
DON'T SWEAT IT.
YOU NEED GOOD GRUB TO WORK UP A GOOD H-ENERGY SWEAT, Y'KNOW?
BESIDES, WE'VE ONLY JUST STARTED OUR TRAINING REGIMEN.
ニヤニヤ
Nyeh Heh!
O-OKAY, WELL, WE'RE GONNA GO HIT THE BATH!
LET'S GO, YOITSUKI-SAN!
OKAY...

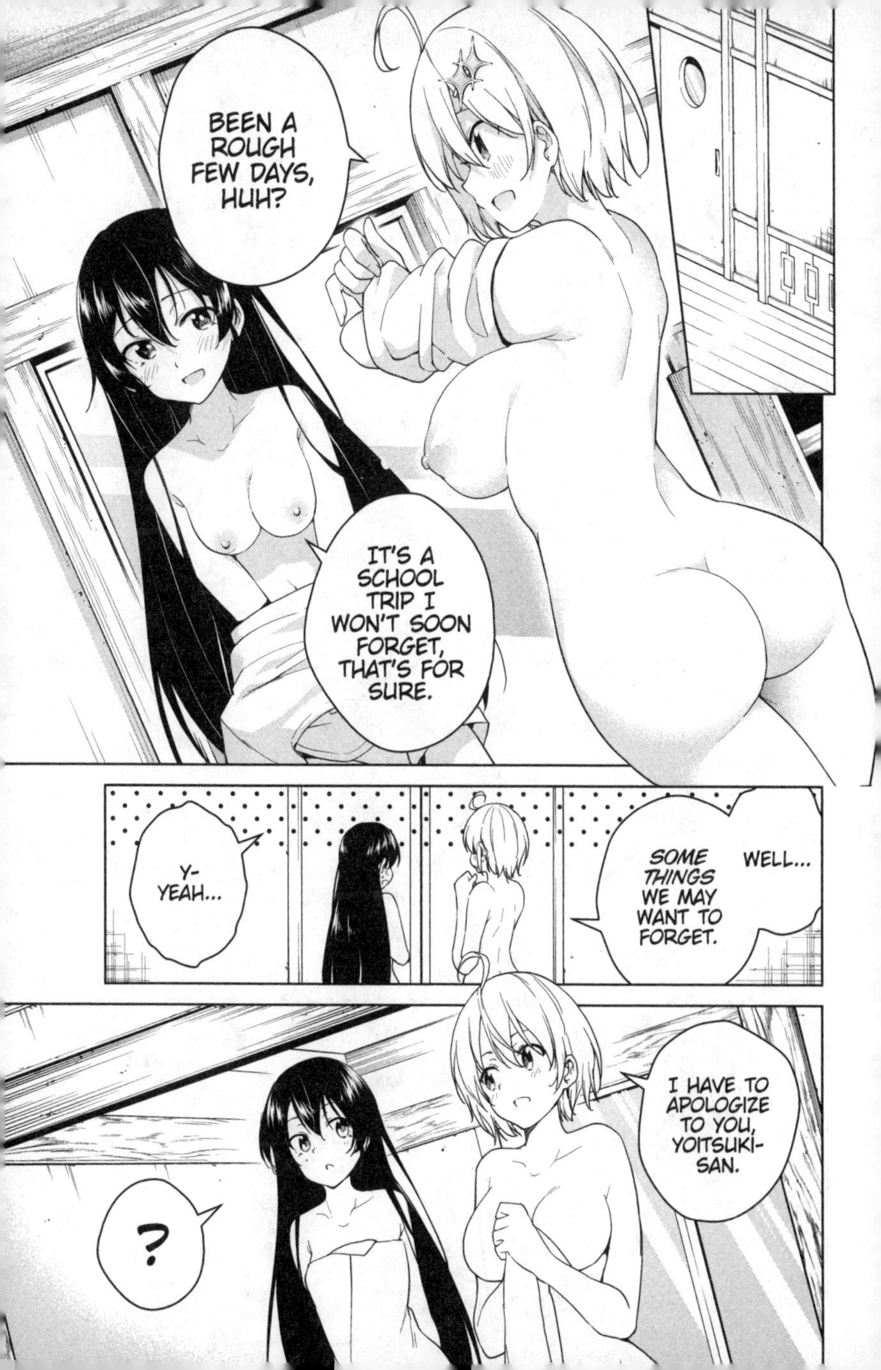
BEEN A ROUGH FEW DAYS, HUH?
IT'S A SCHOOL TRIP I WON'T SOON FORGET, THAT'S FOR SURE.
WELL...
SOME THINGS WE MAY WANT TO FORGET.
Y-YEAH...
I HAVE TO APOLOGIZE TO YOU, YOITSUKI-SAN.
?

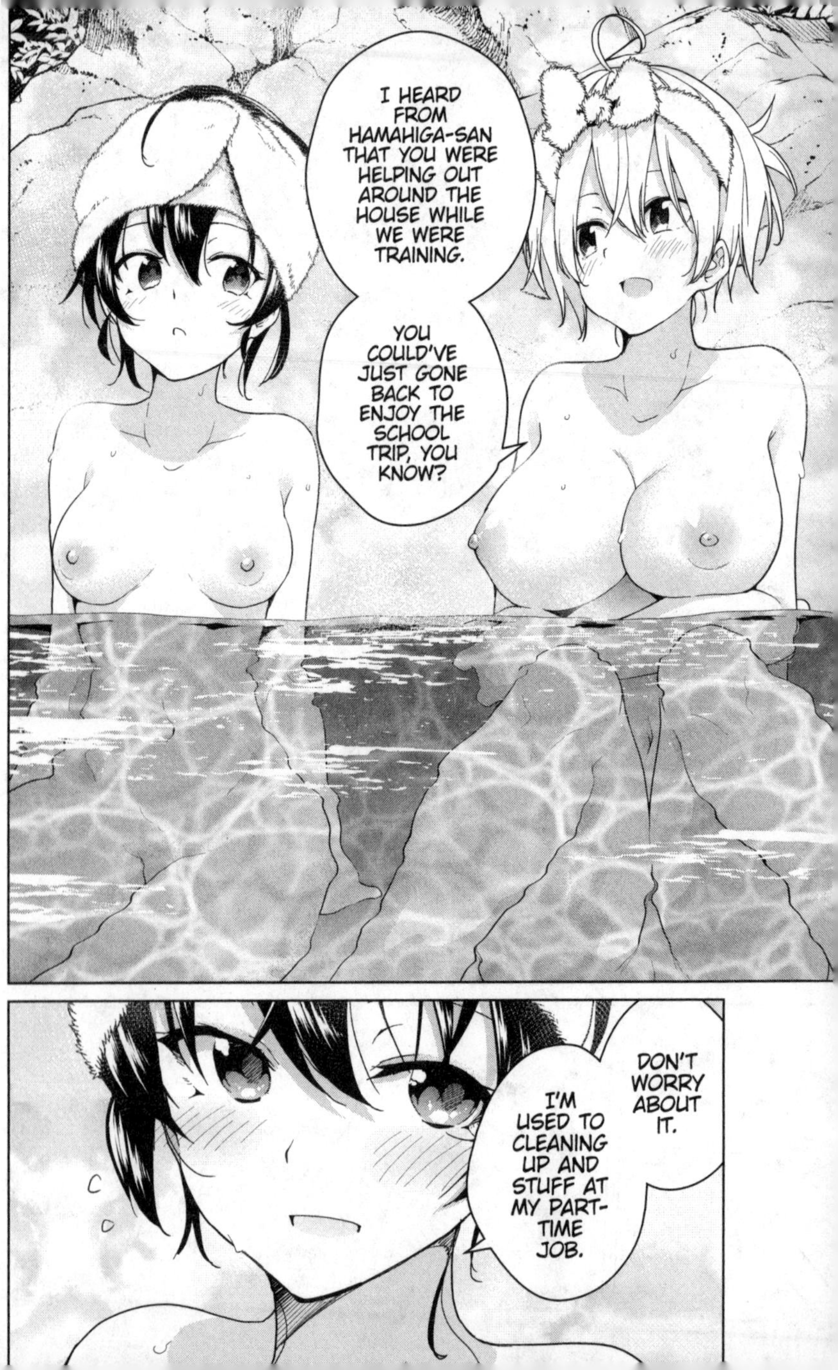
I HEARD FROM HAMAHIGA-SAN THAT YOU WERE HELPING OUT AROUND THE HOUSE WHILE WE WERE TRAINING.
YOU COULD'VE JUST GONE BACK TO ENJOY THE SCHOOL TRIP, YOU KNOW?
DON'T WORRY ABOUT IT.
I'M USED TO CLEANING UP AND STUFF AT MY PART-TIME JOB.

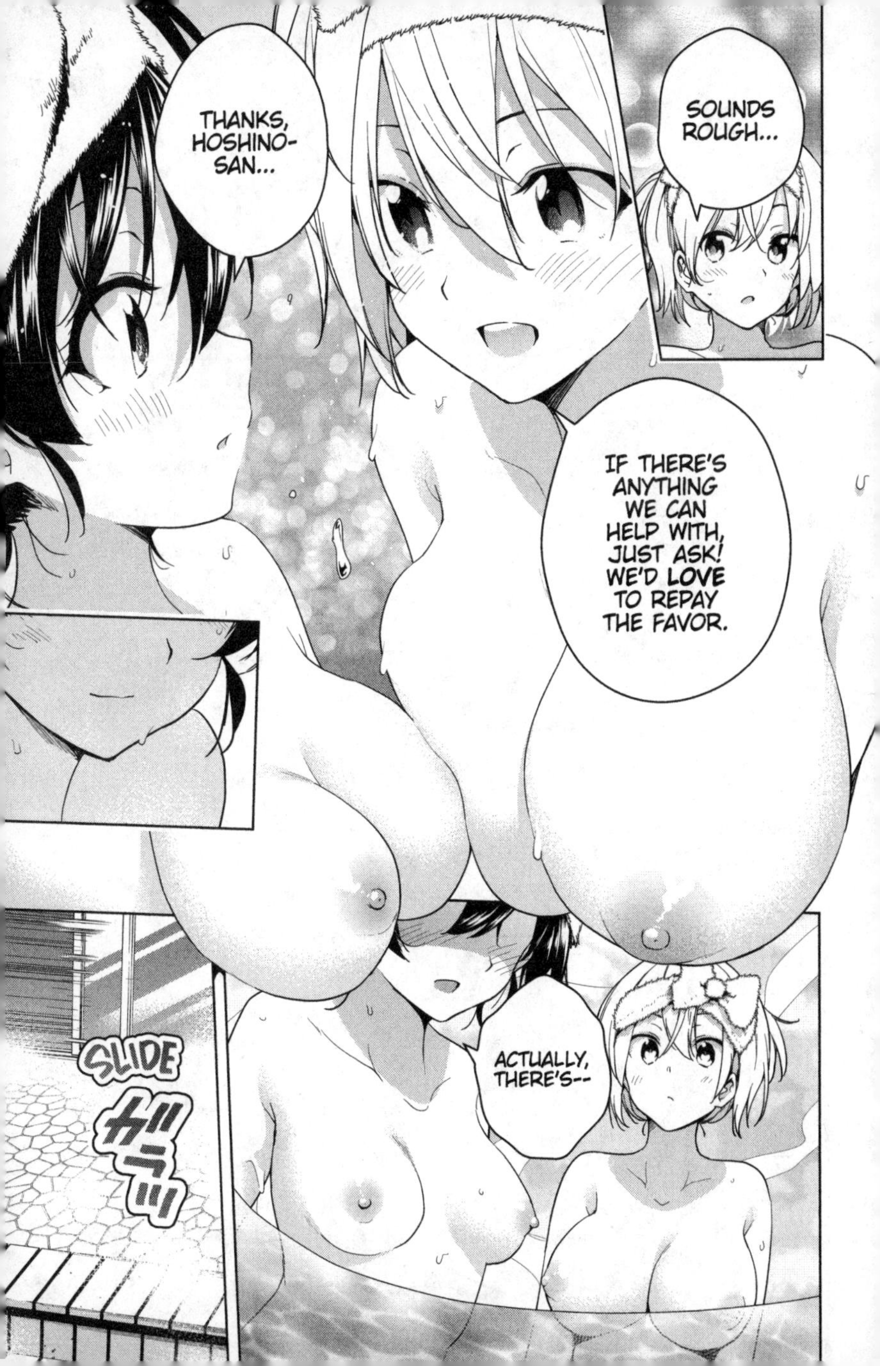
SOUNDS ROUGH...
THANKS, HOSHINO-SAN...
IF THERE'S ANYTHING WE CAN HELP WITH, JUST ASK! WE'D **LOVE** TO REPAY THE FAVOR.
ACTUALLY, THERE'S--
SLIDE
ガラッ

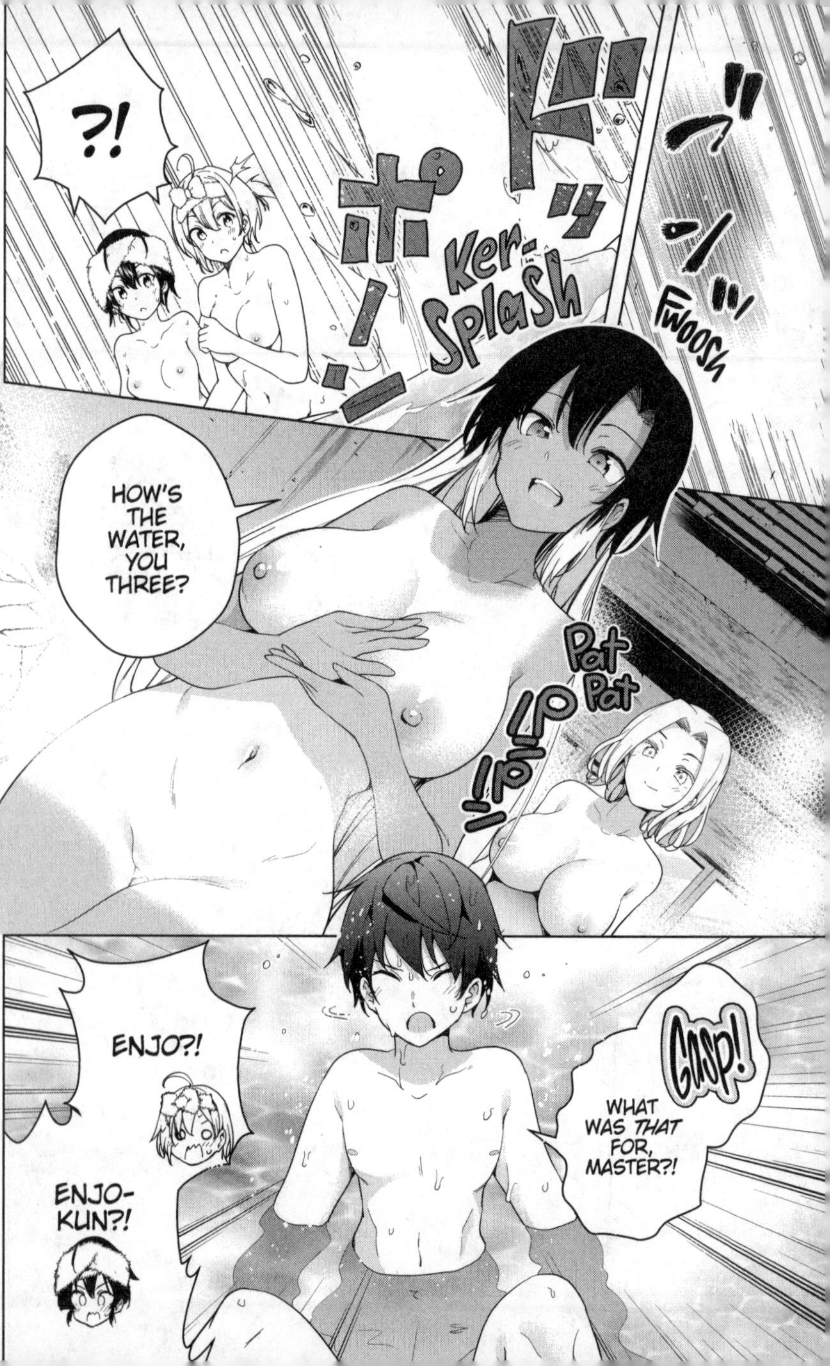
Fwoosh
Ker-Splash
?!
HOW'S THE WATER, YOU THREE?
Pat Pat
Gasp!
WHAT WAS THAT FOR, MASTER?!
ENJO?!
ENJO-KUN?!

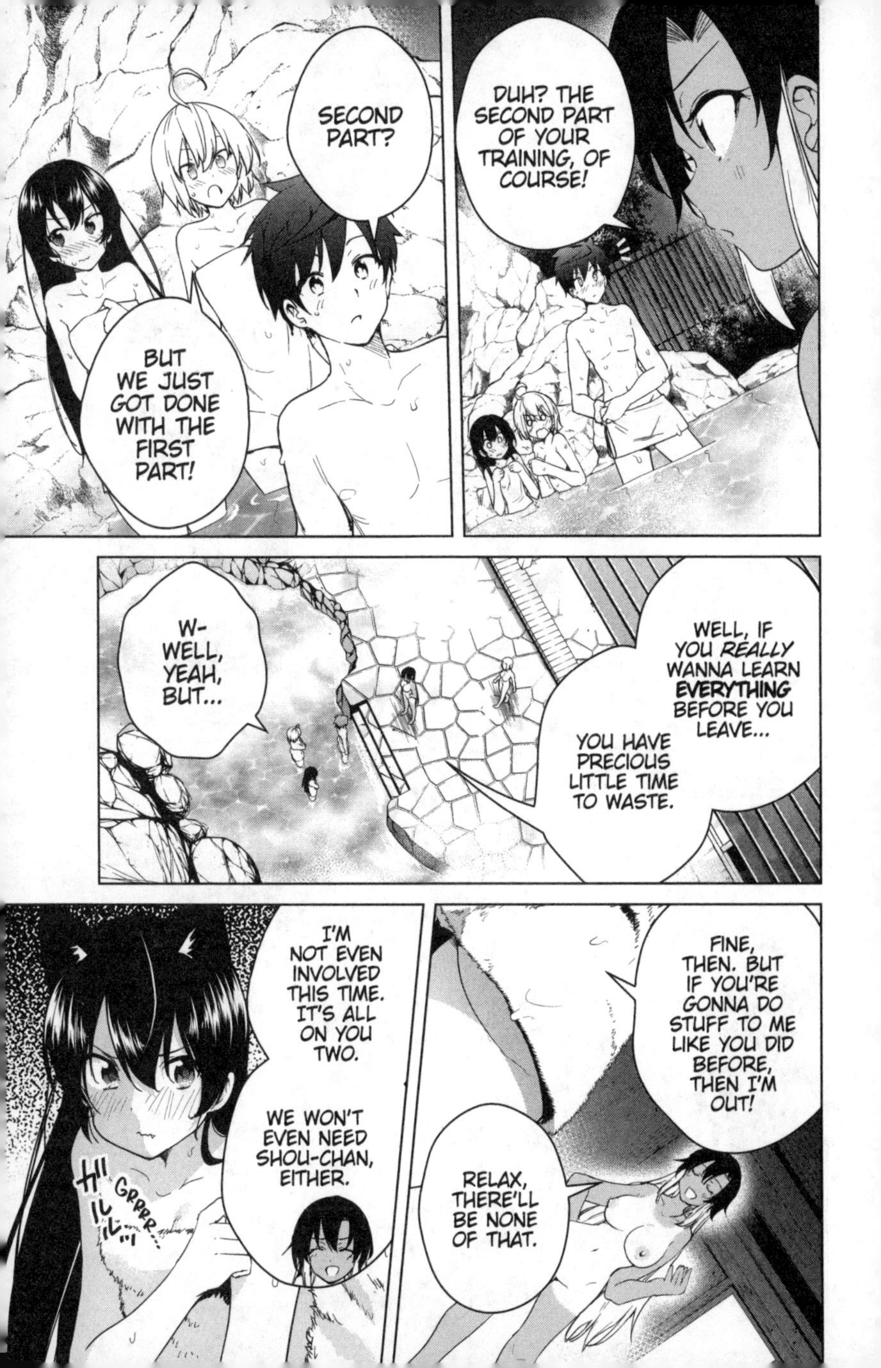
DUH? THE SECOND PART OF YOUR TRAINING, OF COURSE!
SECOND PART?
BUT WE JUST GOT DONE WITH THE FIRST PART!
WELL, IF YOU *REALLY* WANNA LEARN **EVERYTHING** BEFORE YOU LEAVE...
YOU HAVE PRECIOUS LITTLE TIME TO WASTE.
W- WELL, YEAH, BUT...
FINE, THEN. BUT IF YOU'RE GONNA DO STUFF TO ME LIKE YOU DID BEFORE, THEN I'M OUT!
RELAX, THERE'LL BE NONE OF THAT.
I'M NOT EVEN INVOLVED THIS TIME. IT'S ALL ON YOU TWO.
WE WON'T EVEN NEED SHOU-CHAN, EITHER.
GRRRR...

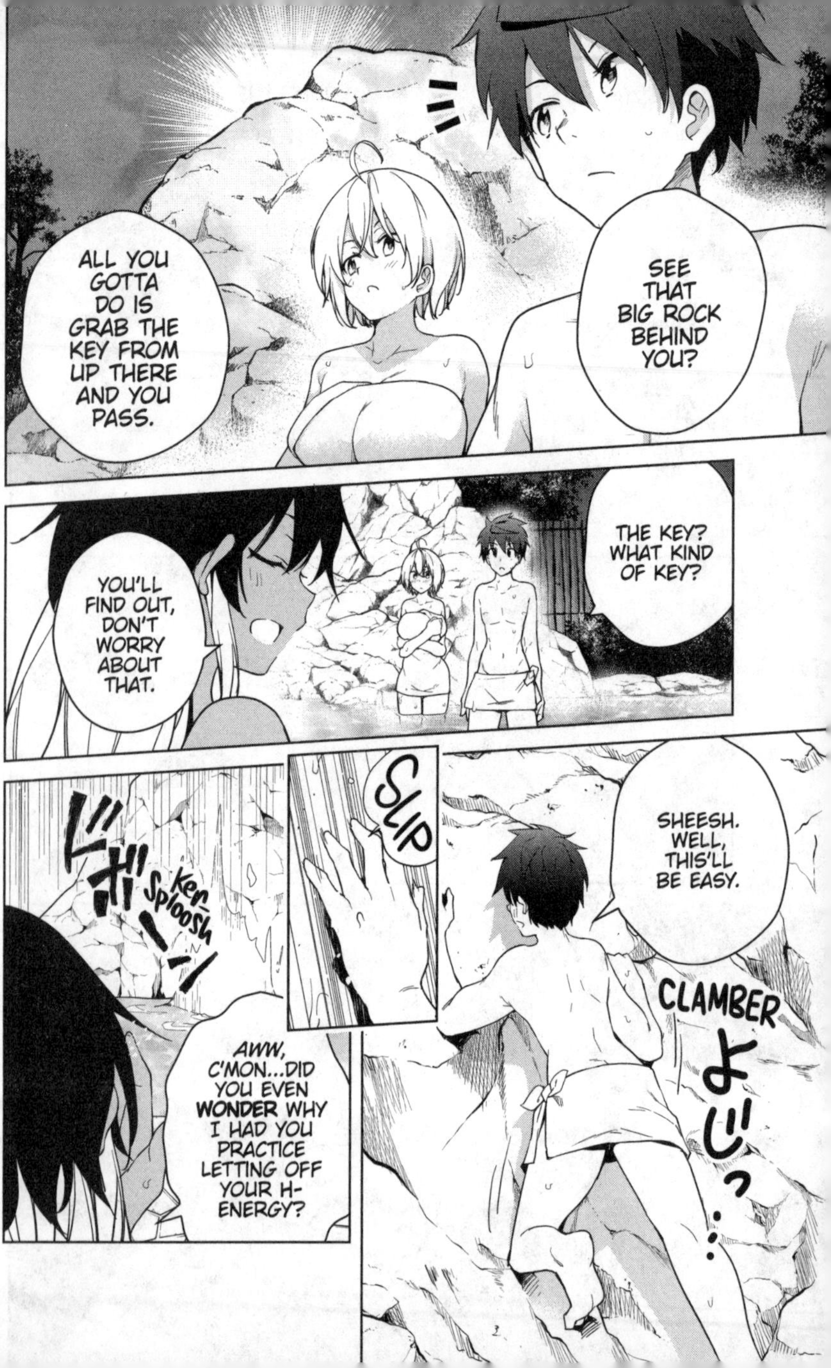
SEE THAT BIG ROCK BEHIND YOU?
ALL YOU GOTTA DO IS GRAB THE KEY FROM UP THERE AND YOU PASS.
THE KEY? WHAT KIND OF KEY?
YOU'LL FIND OUT, DON'T WORRY ABOUT THAT.
SHEESH. WELL, THIS'LL BE EASY.
CLAMBER
SLIP
KER-SPLOOSH
AWW, C'MON...DID YOU EVEN **WONDER** WHY I HAD YOU PRACTICE LETTING OFF YOUR H-ENERGY?

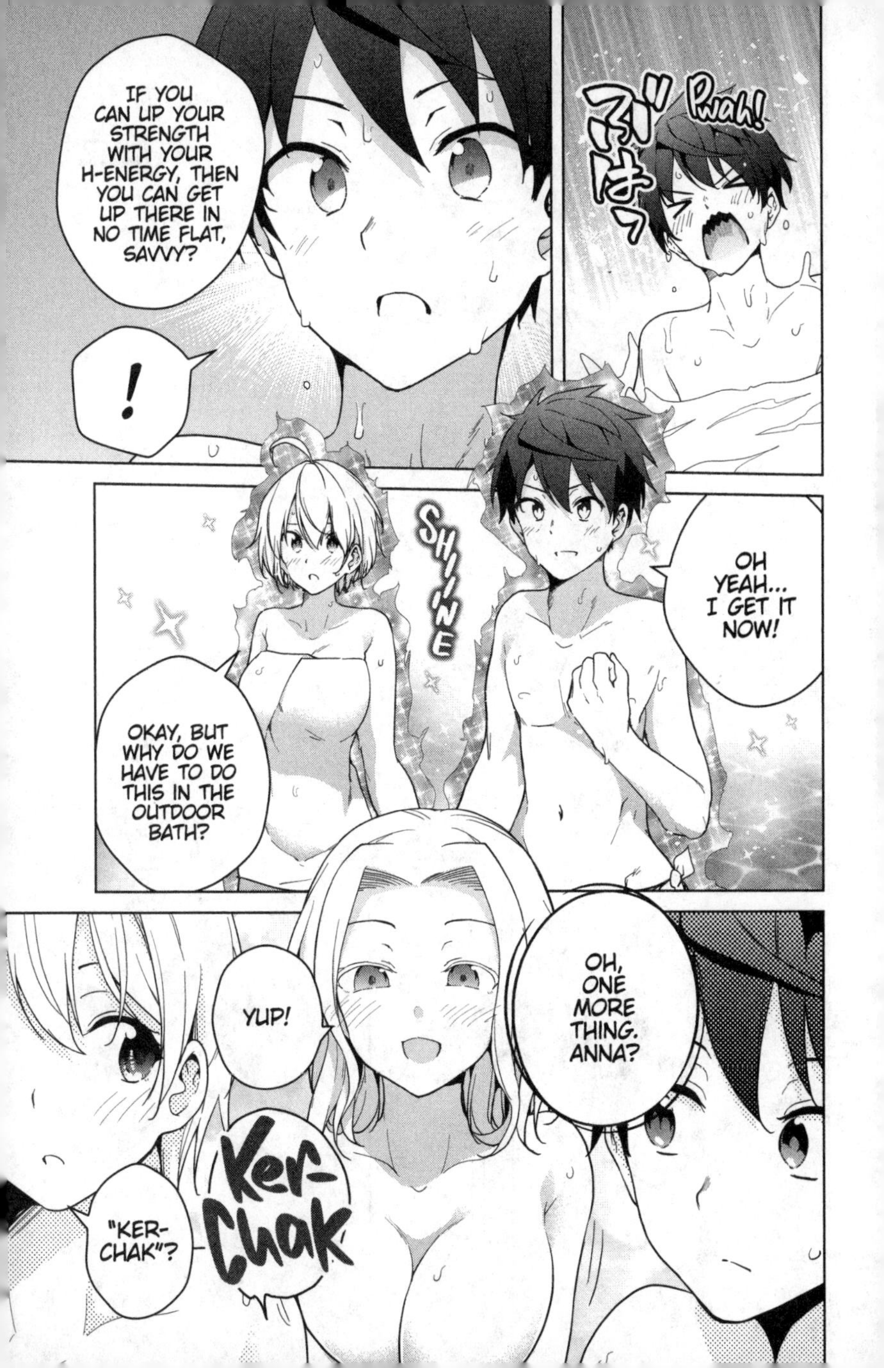
Pwah!
IF YOU CAN UP YOUR STRENGTH WITH YOUR H-ENERGY, THEN YOU CAN GET UP THERE IN NO TIME FLAT, SAVVY?
!
OH YEAH... I GET IT NOW!
SHIIINE
OKAY, BUT WHY DO WE HAVE TO DO THIS IN THE OUTDOOR BATH?
OH, ONE MORE THING. ANNA?
YUP!
Ker-Chak
"KER-CHAK"?

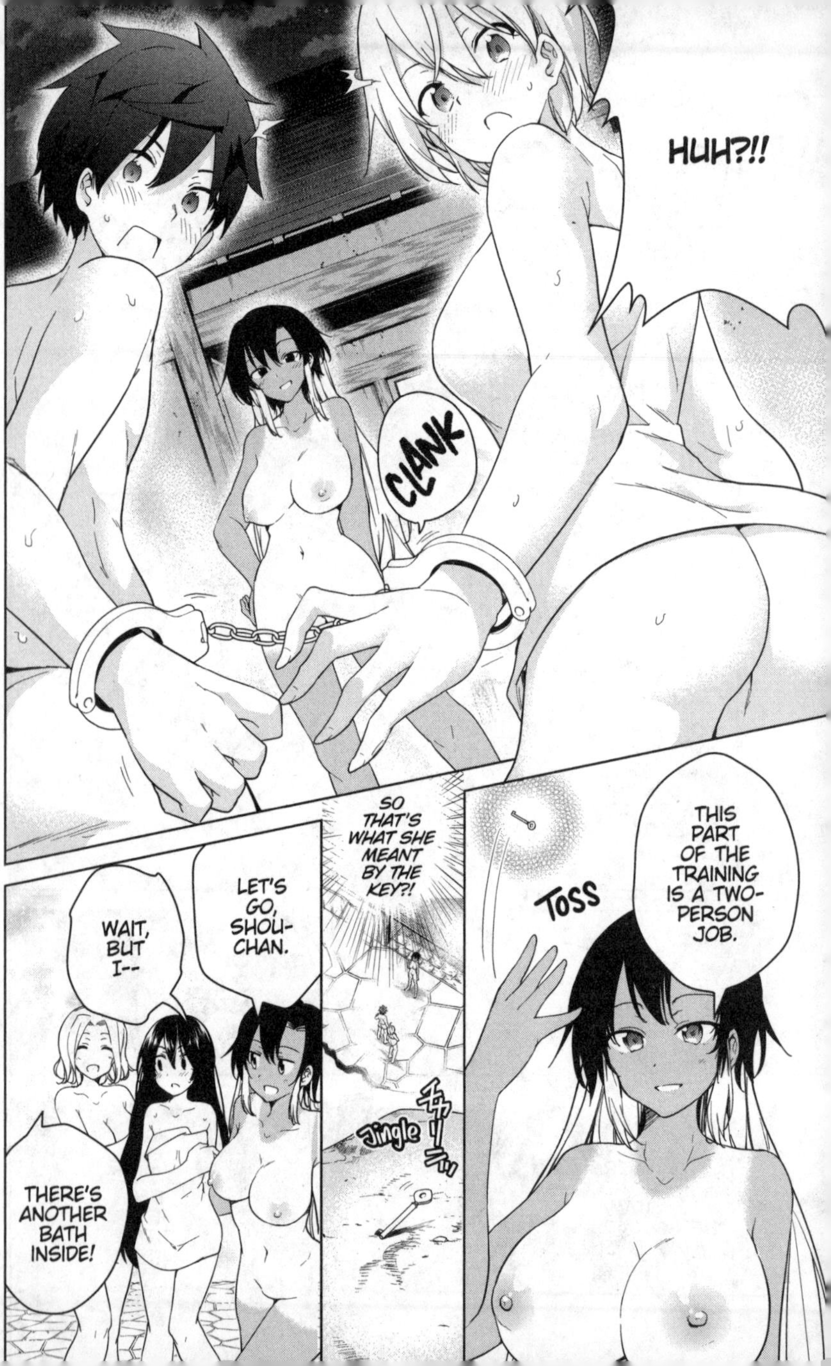
HUH?!!
CLANK
THIS PART OF THE TRAINING IS A TWO-PERSON JOB.
TOSS
SO THAT'S WHAT SHE MEANT BY THE KEY?!
Jingle
LET'S GO, SHOU-CHAN.
WAIT, BUT I--
THERE'S ANOTHER BATH INSIDE!

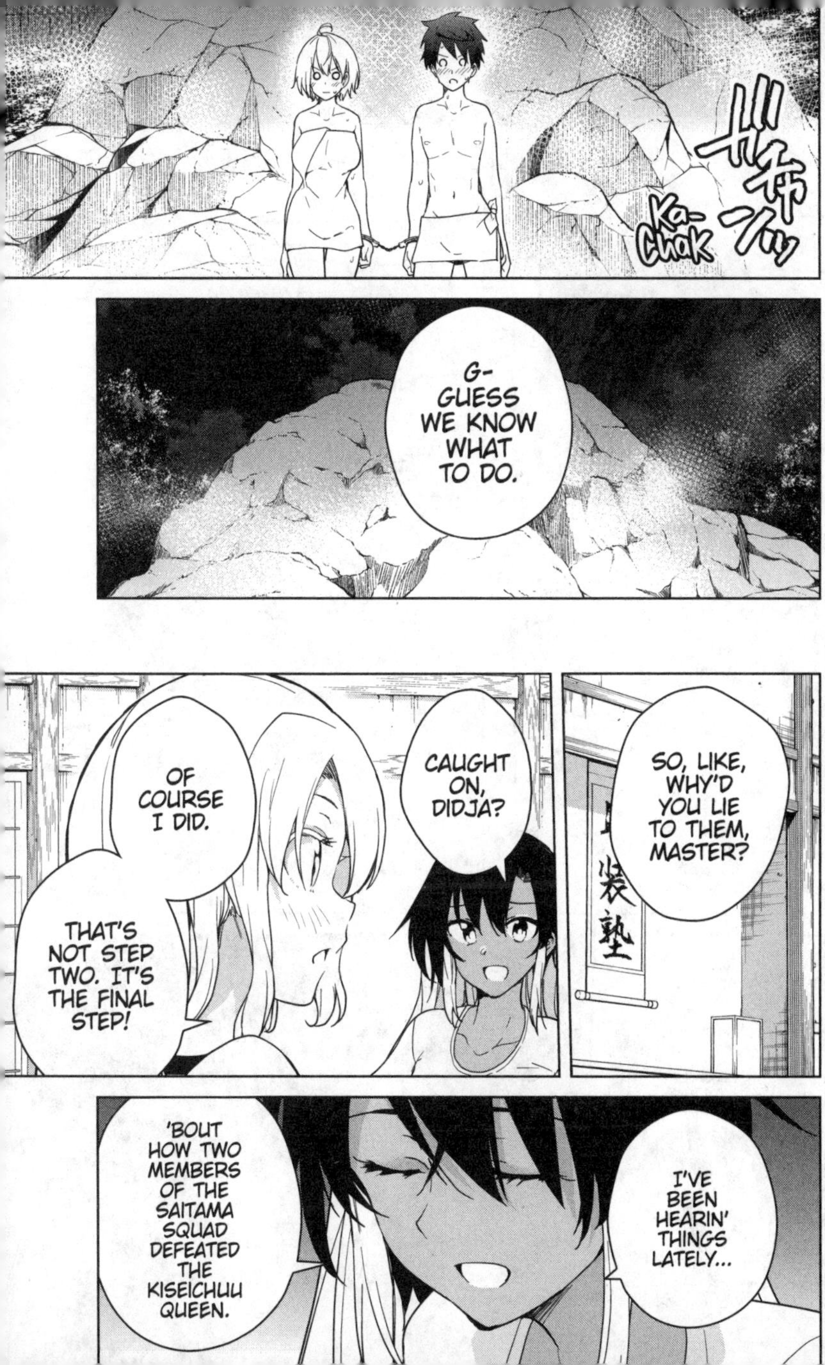
ガチャッ
Ka-Chak
G-GUESS WE KNOW WHAT TO DO.
SO, LIKE, WHY'D YOU LIE TO THEM, MASTER?
CAUGHT ON, DIDJA?
OF COURSE I DID.
THAT'S NOT STEP TWO. IT'S THE FINAL STEP!
I'VE BEEN HEARIN' THINGS LATELY...
'BOUT HOW TWO MEMBERS OF THE SAITAMA SQUAD DEFEATED THE KISEICHUU QUEEN.

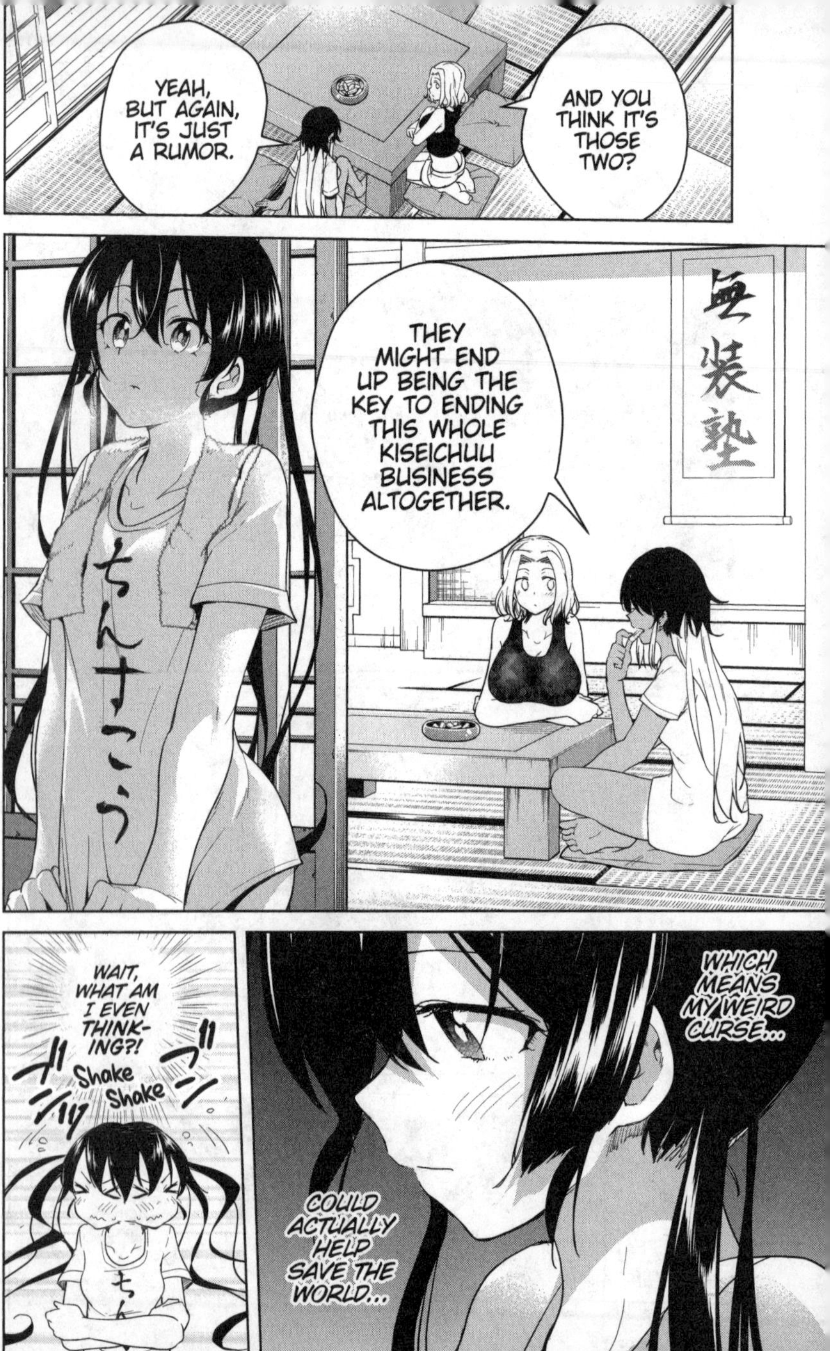
AND YOU THINK IT'S THOSE TWO?
YEAH, BUT AGAIN, IT'S JUST A RUMOR.
無装塾
THEY MIGHT END UP BEING THE KEY TO ENDING THIS WHOLE KISEICHUU BUSINESS ALTOGETHER.
ちんすこう
WHICH MEANS MY WEIRD CURSE...
COULD ACTUALLY HELP SAVE THE WORLD...
WAIT, WHAT AM I EVEN THINKING?!
Shake Shake

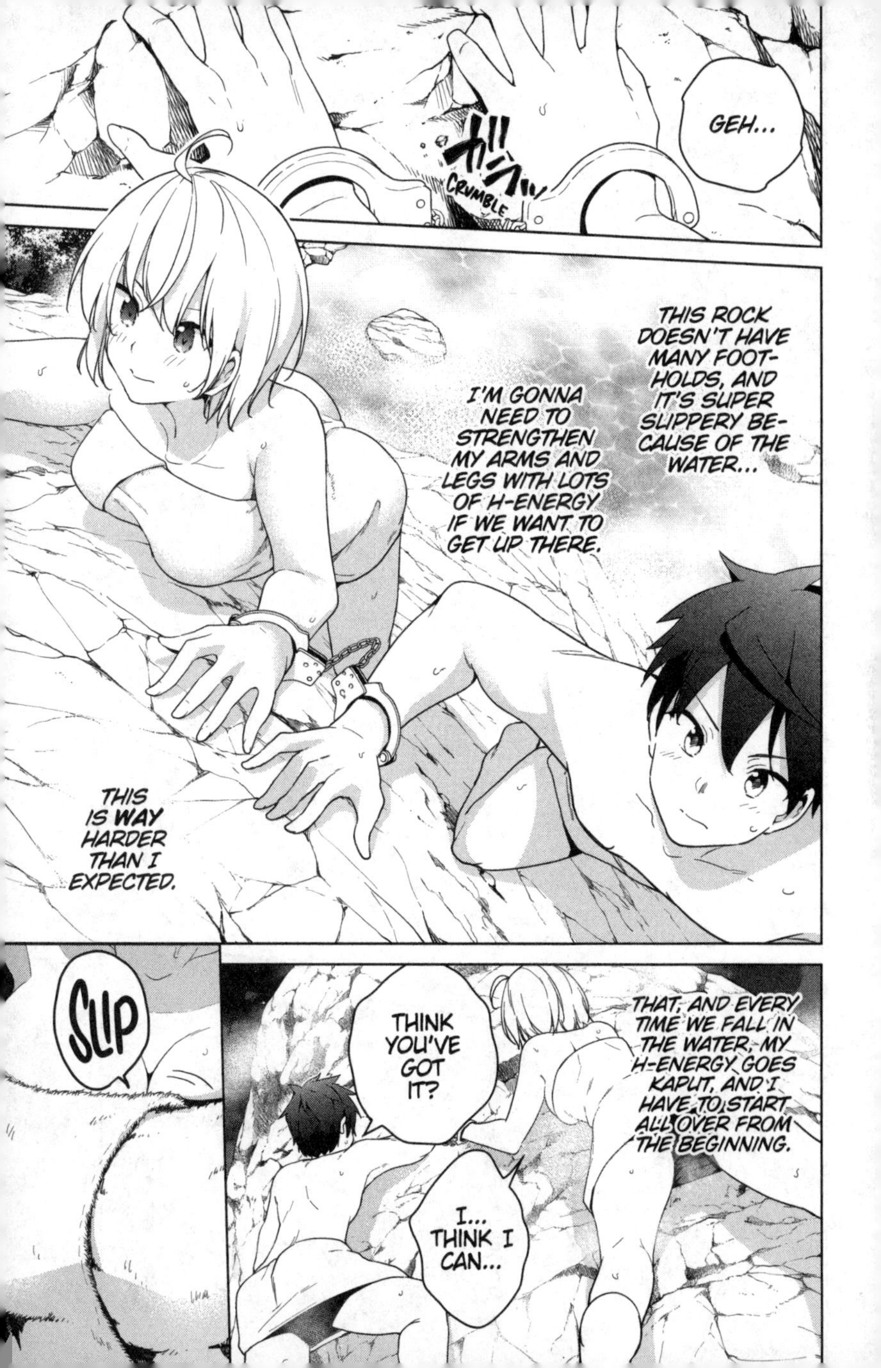
GEH...
CRUMBLE
THIS ROCK DOESN'T HAVE MANY FOOT-HOLDS, AND IT'S SUPER SLIPPERY BE-CAUSE OF THE WATER...
I'M GONNA NEED TO STRENGTHEN MY ARMS AND LEGS WITH LOTS OF H-ENERGY IF WE WANT TO GET UP THERE.
THIS IS WAY HARDER THAN I EXPECTED.
THAT, AND EVERY TIME WE FALL IN THE WATER, MY H-ENERGY GOES KAPUT, AND I HAVE TO START ALL OVER FROM THE BEGINNING.
THINK YOU'VE GOT IT?
I... THINK I CAN...
SLIP

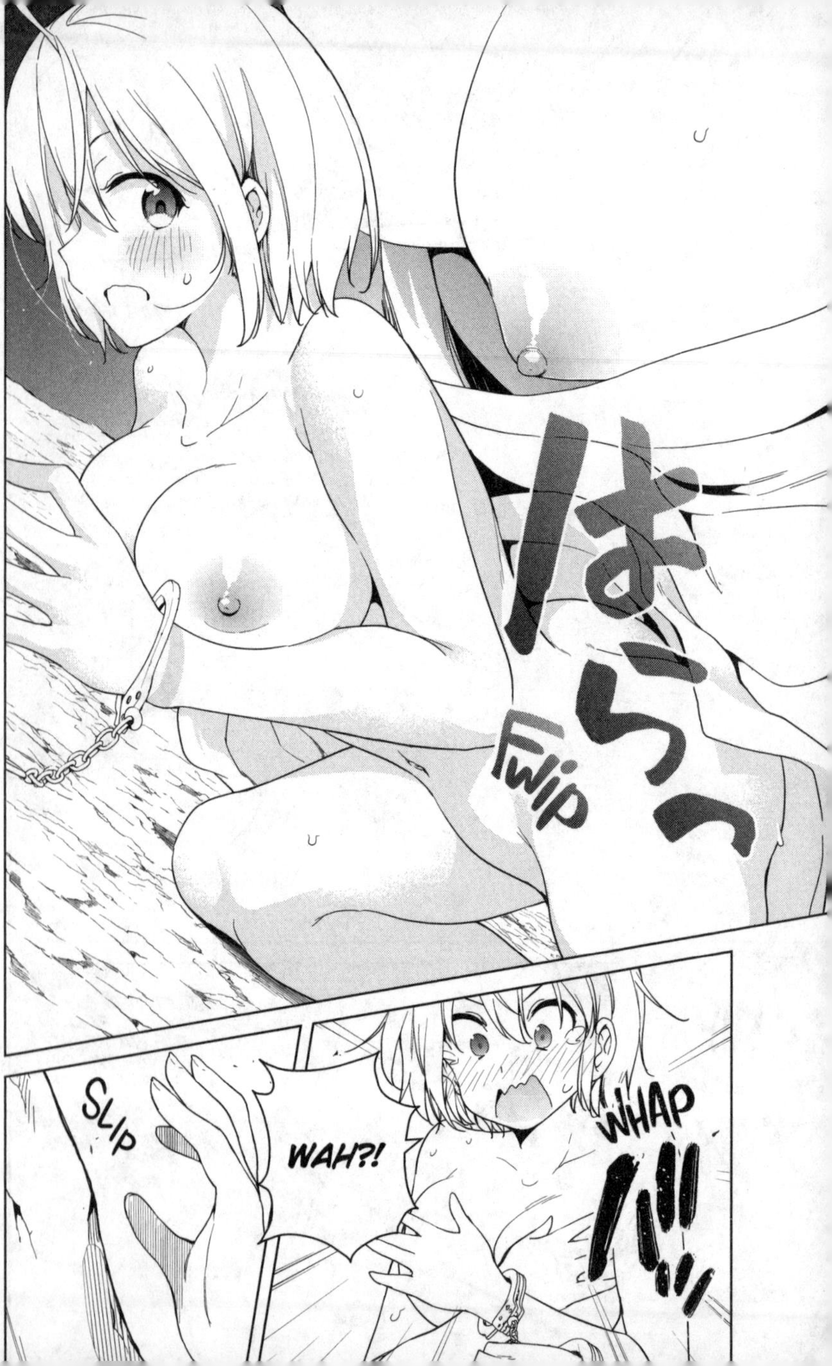
はらっ
Fwip
WHAP
バッ
WAH?!
SLip

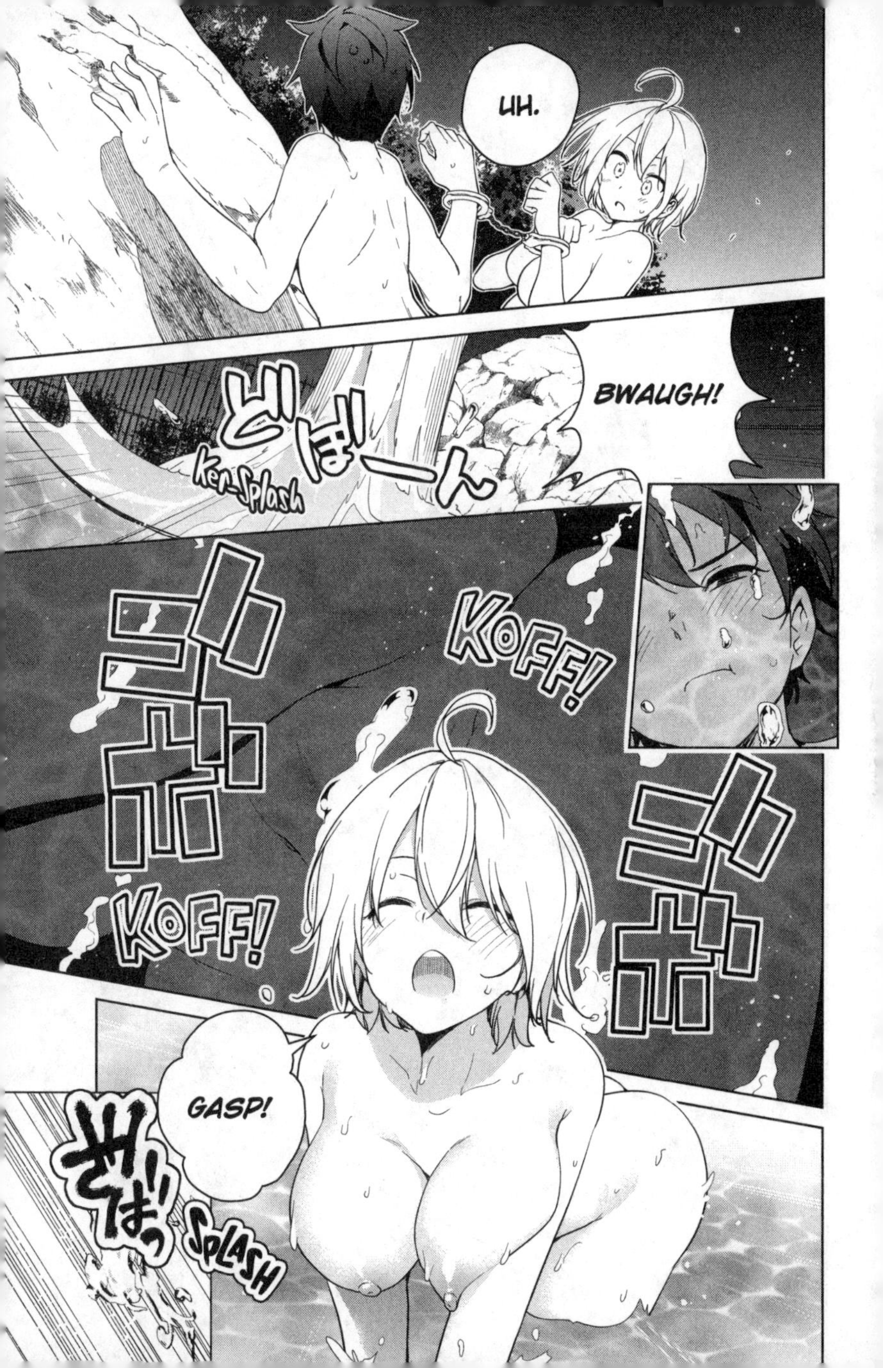

UH.
BWAUGH!
どぼーん
Ker-Splash
KOFF!
KOFF!
GASP!
ざばっ
SPLASH

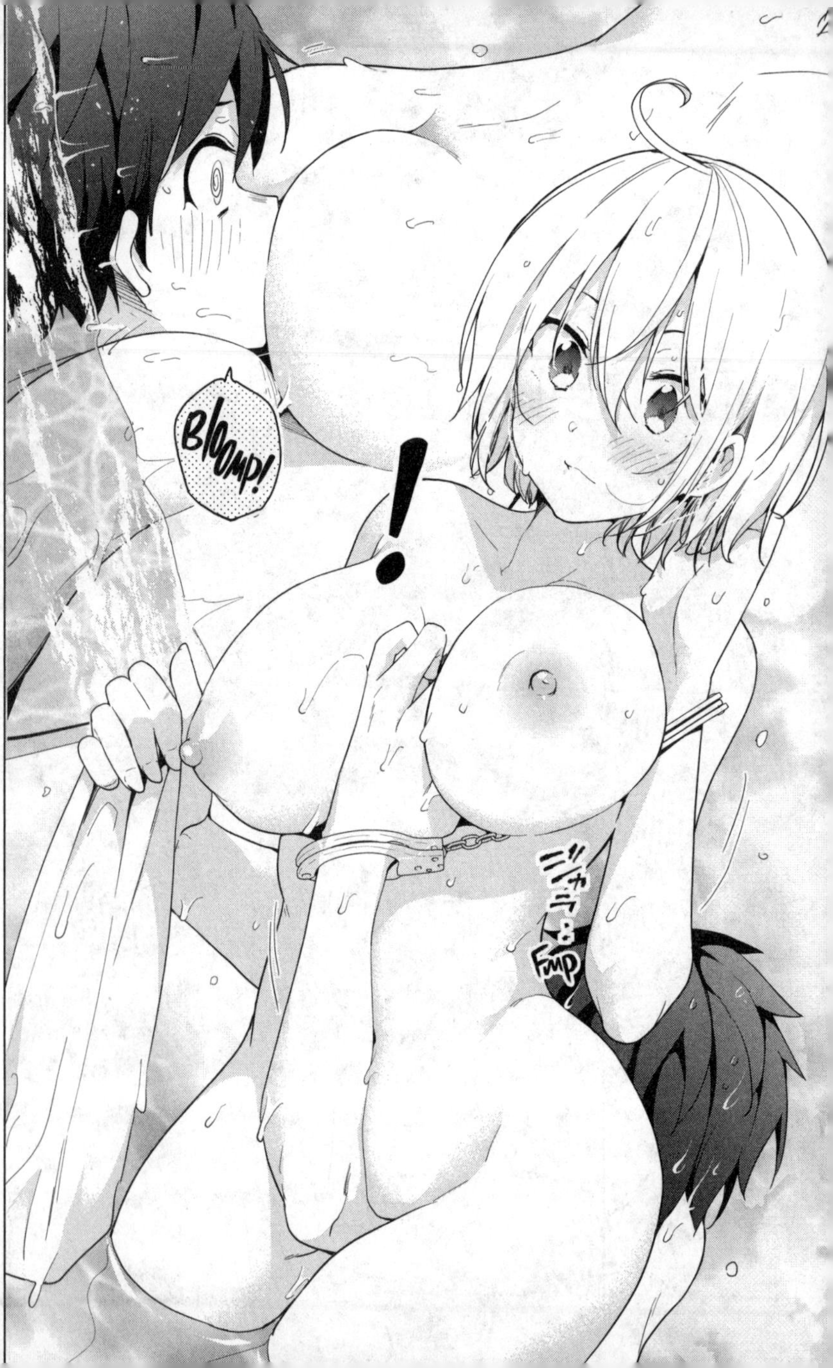
BLOOMP!
Fmp

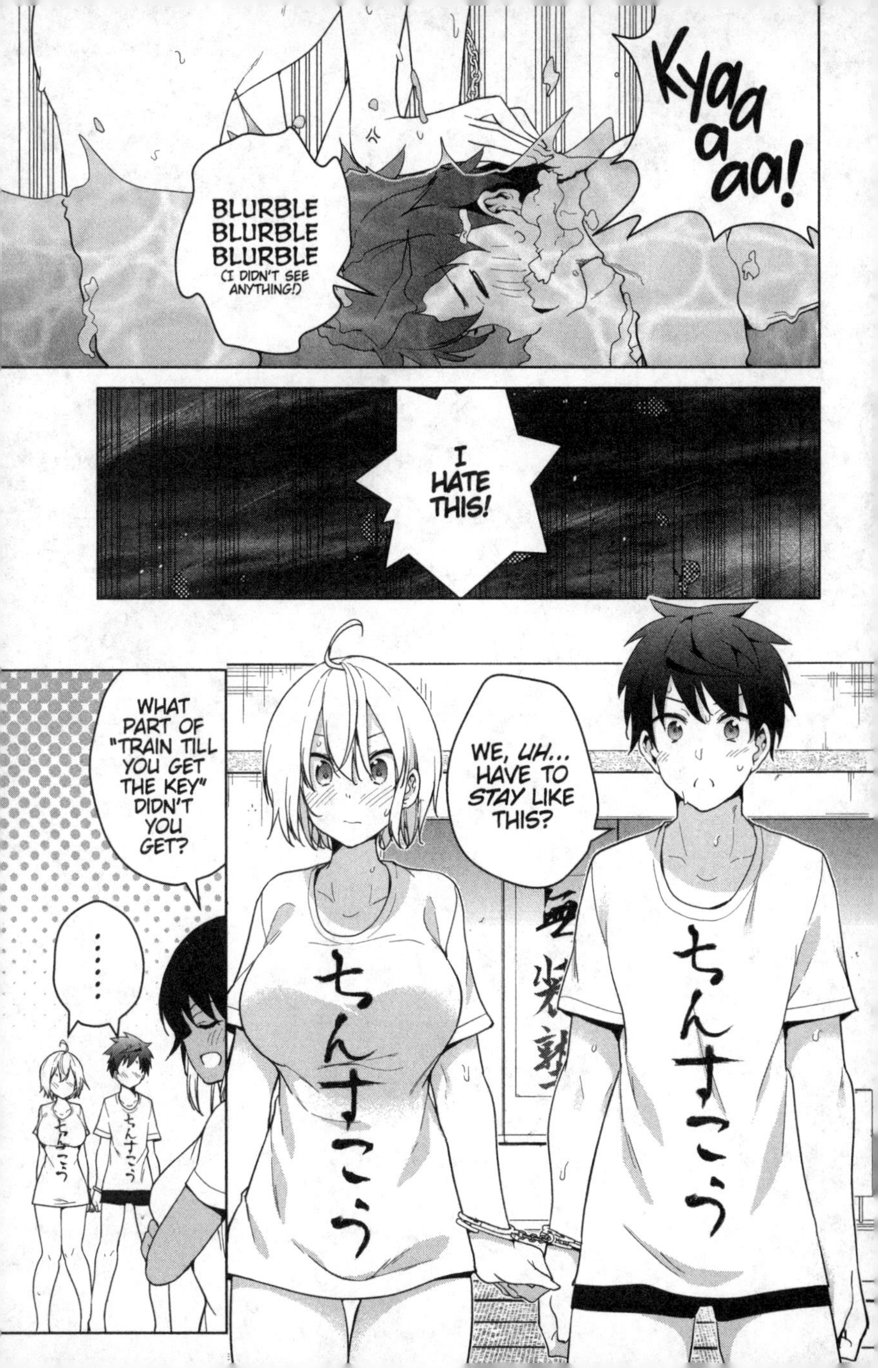
Kyaaaaa!
BLURBLE BLURBLE BLURBLE (I DIDN'T SEE ANYTHING!)
I HATE THIS!
WE, UH... HAVE TO STAY LIKE THIS?
WHAT PART OF "TRAIN TILL YOU GET THE KEY" DIDN'T YOU GET?
......
ちんすこう

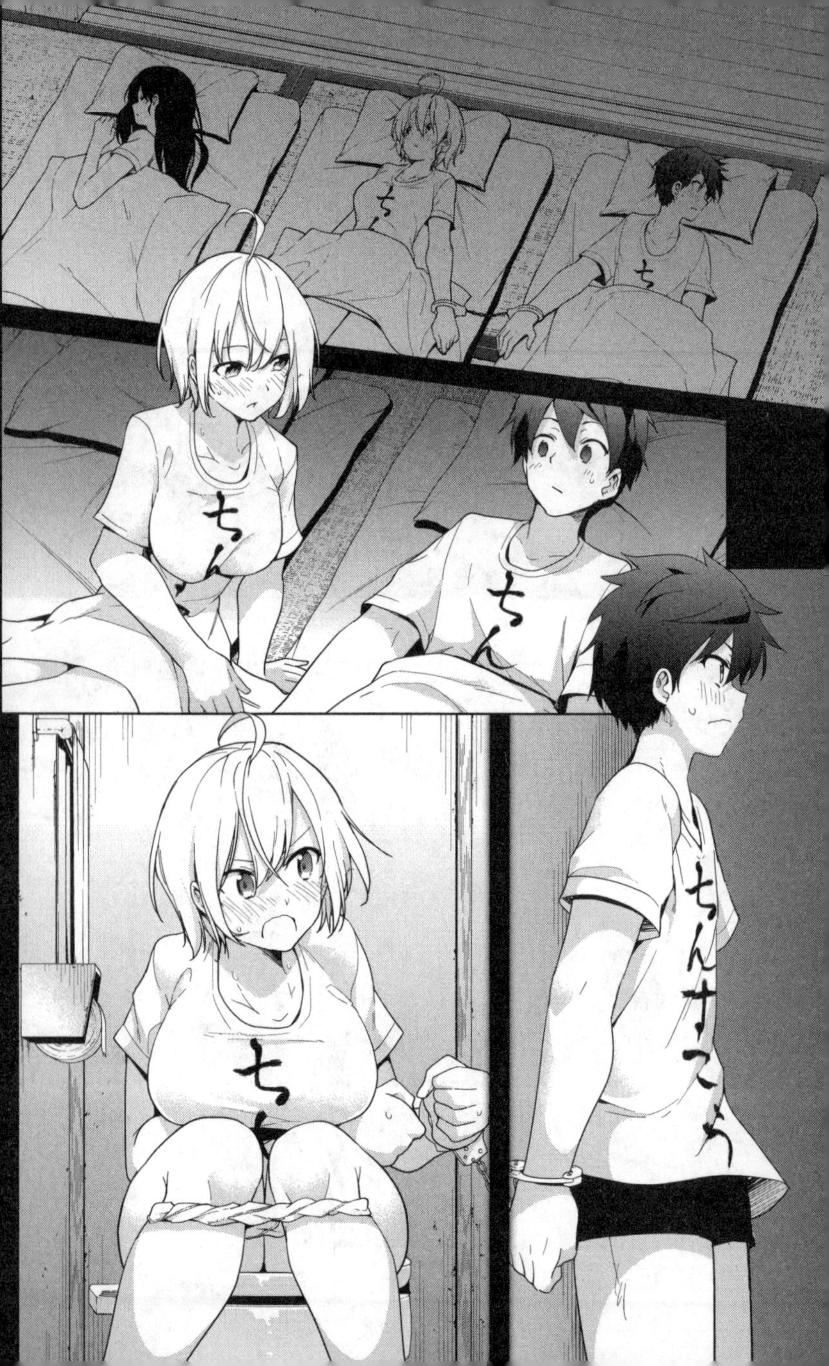

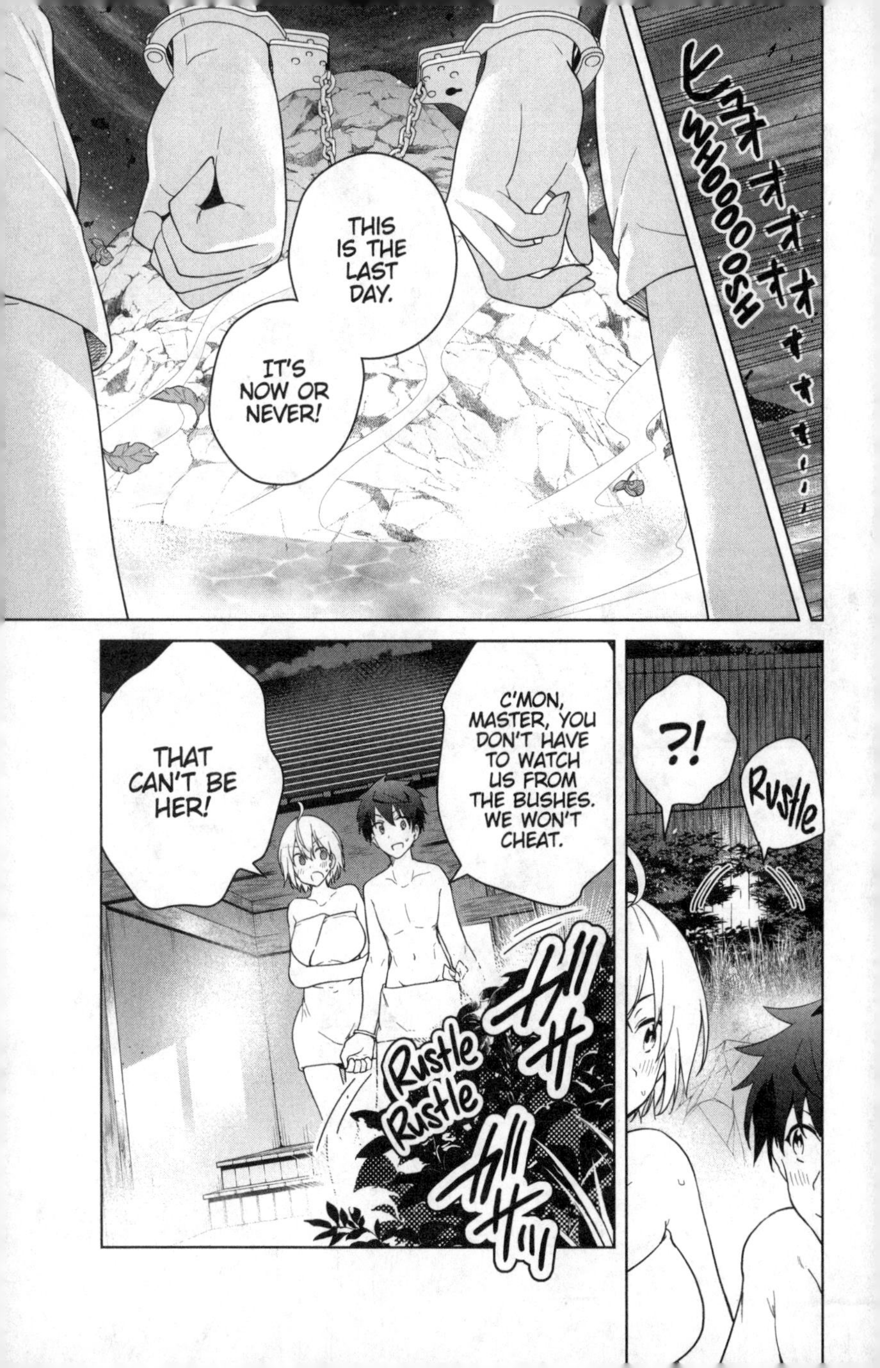
WHOOOOOSH
THIS IS THE LAST DAY.
IT'S NOW OR NEVER!
?!
Rustle
C'MON, MASTER, YOU DON'T HAVE TO WATCH US FROM THE BUSHES. WE WON'T CHEAT.
THAT CAN'T BE HER!
Rustle Rustle

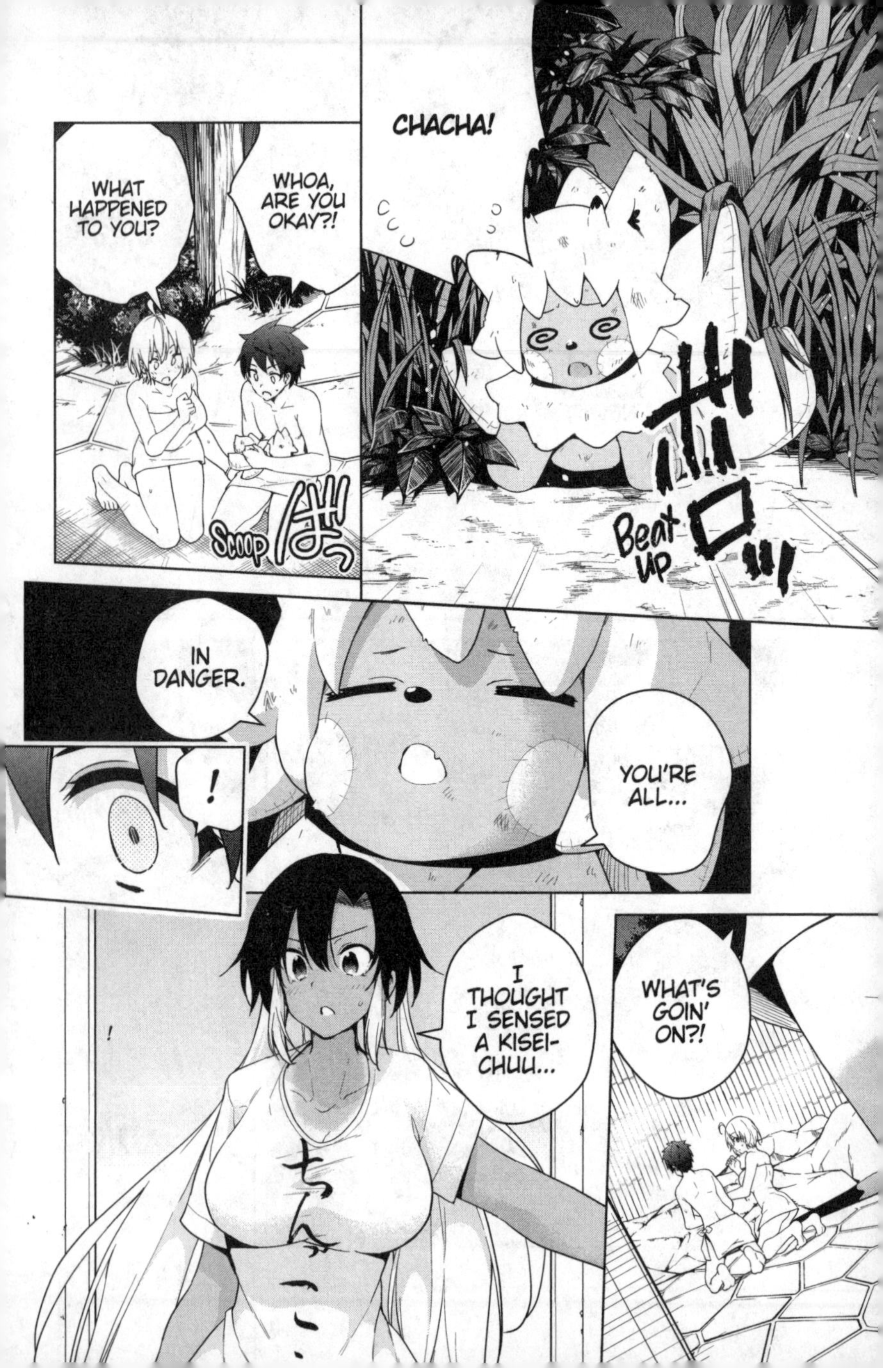
CHACHA!
Beat up
WHOA, ARE YOU OKAY?!
WHAT HAPPENED TO YOU?
Scoop ばっ
YOU'RE ALL...
IN DANGER.
!
WHAT'S GOIN' ON?!
I THOUGHT I SENSED A KISEI-CHUU...
!

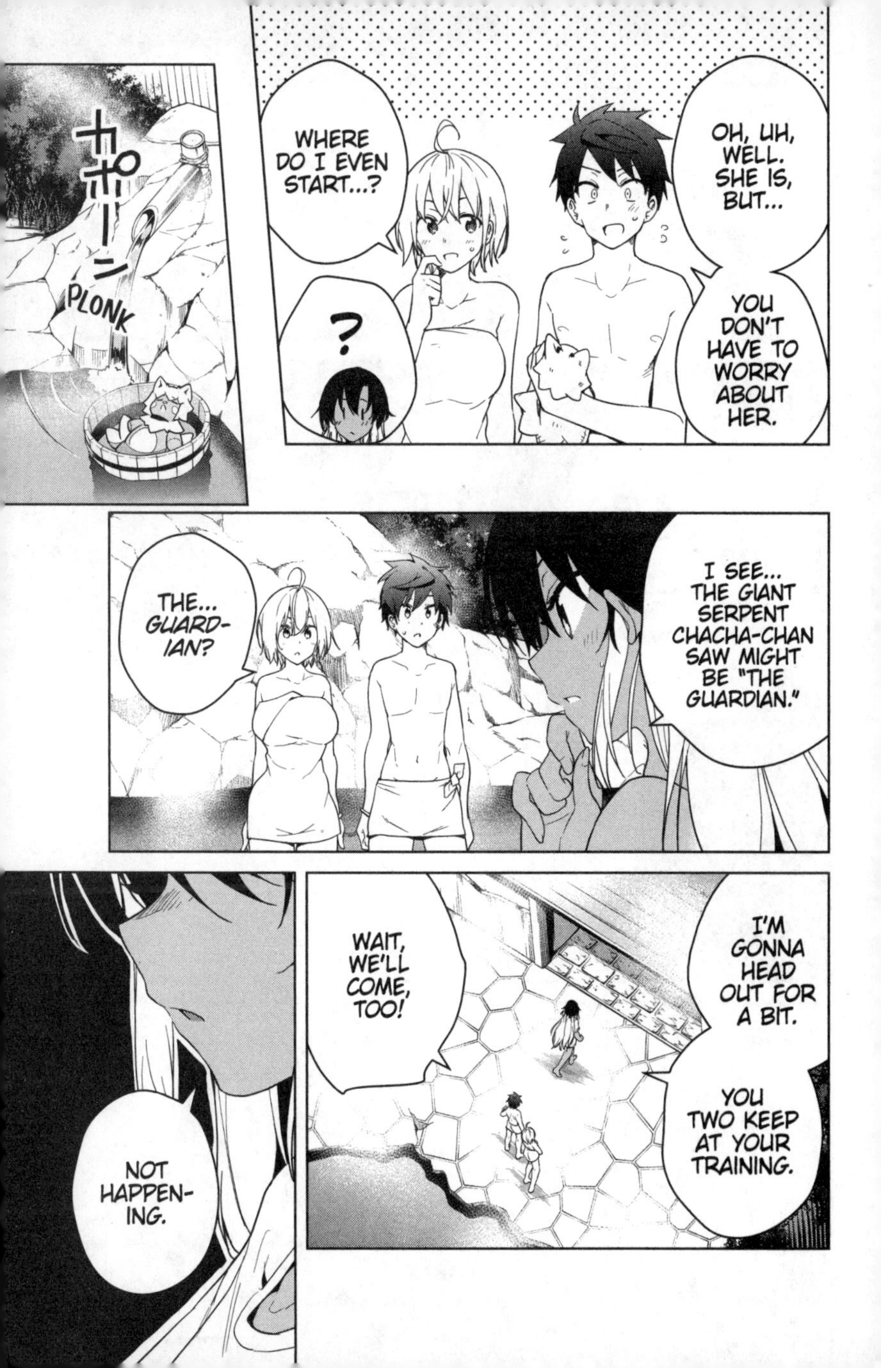
OH, UH, WELL. SHE IS, BUT...
WHERE DO I EVEN START...?
YOU DON'T HAVE TO WORRY ABOUT HER.
?
カポーン
PLONK
I SEE... THE GIANT SERPENT CHACHA-CHAN SAW MIGHT BE "THE GUARDIAN."
THE... GUARD-IAN?
I'M GONNA HEAD OUT FOR A BIT.
YOU TWO KEEP AT YOUR TRAINING.
WAIT, WE'LL COME, TOO!
NOT HAPPEN-ING.

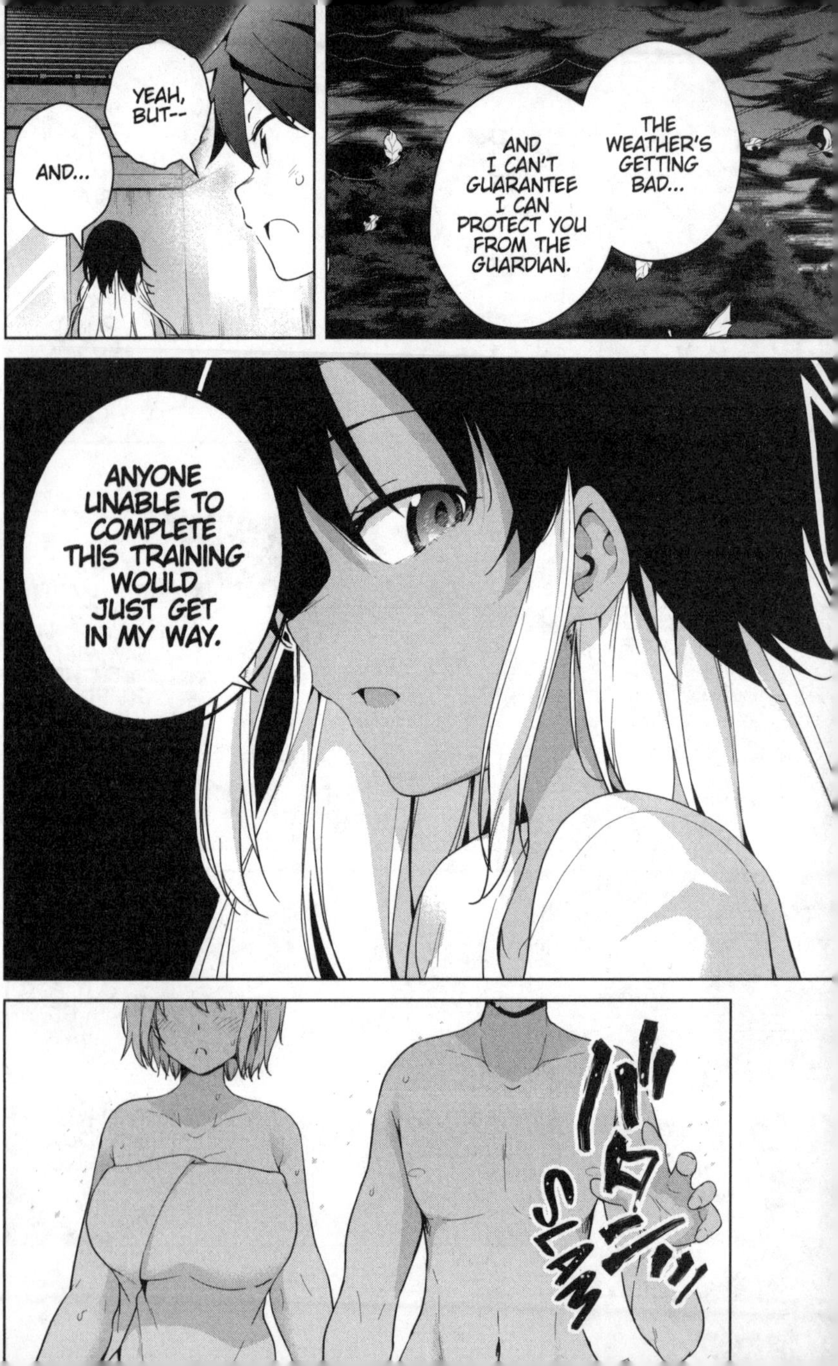
THE WEATHER'S GETTING BAD...
AND I CAN'T GUARANTEE I CAN PROTECT YOU FROM THE GUARDIAN.
YEAH, BUT--
AND...
ANYONE UNABLE TO COMPLETE THIS TRAINING WOULD JUST GET IN MY WAY.
SLAM

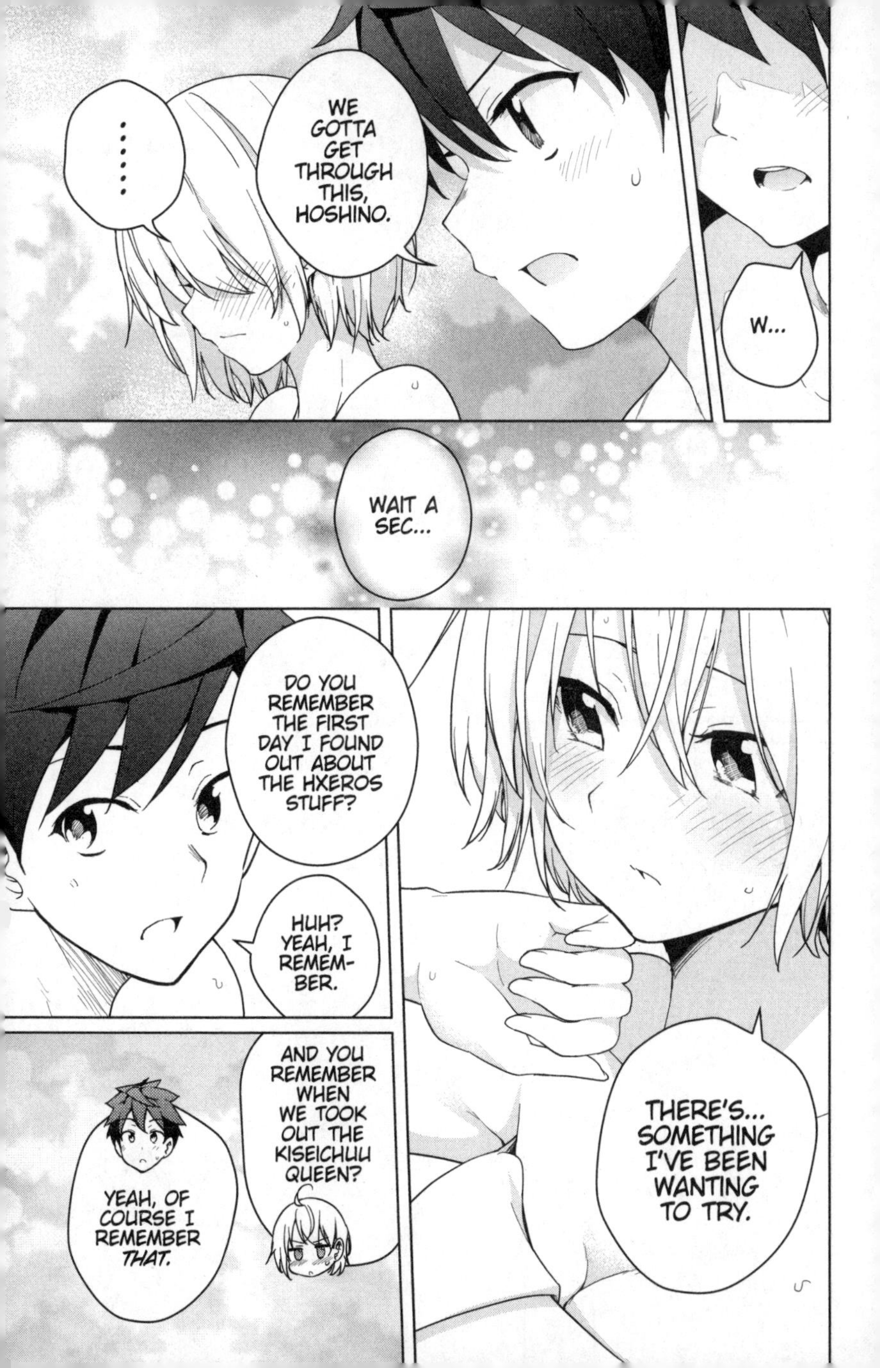
W...
WE GOTTA GET THROUGH THIS, HOSHINO.
......
WAIT A SEC...
THERE'S... SOMETHING I'VE BEEN WANTING TO TRY.
DO YOU REMEMBER THE FIRST DAY I FOUND OUT ABOUT THE HXEROS STUFF?
HUH? YEAH, I REMEMBER.
AND YOU REMEMBER WHEN WE TOOK OUT THE KISEICHUU QUEEN?
YEAH, OF COURSE I REMEMBER *THAT*.

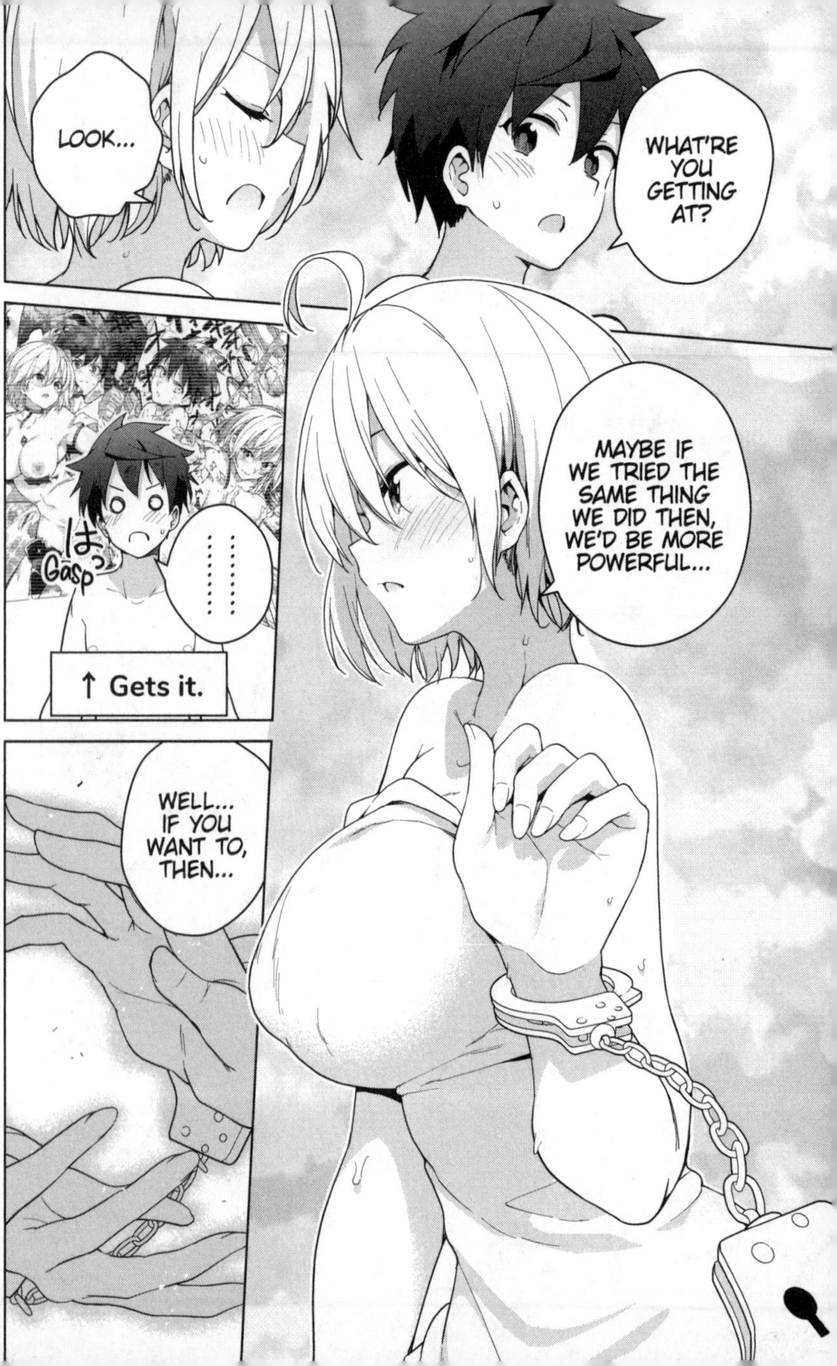
WHAT'RE YOU GETTING AT?
LOOK...
MAYBE IF WE TRIED THE SAME THING WE DID THEN, WE'D BE MORE POWERFUL...
はっ
Gasp
......
↑ Gets it.
WELL... IF YOU WANT TO, THEN...

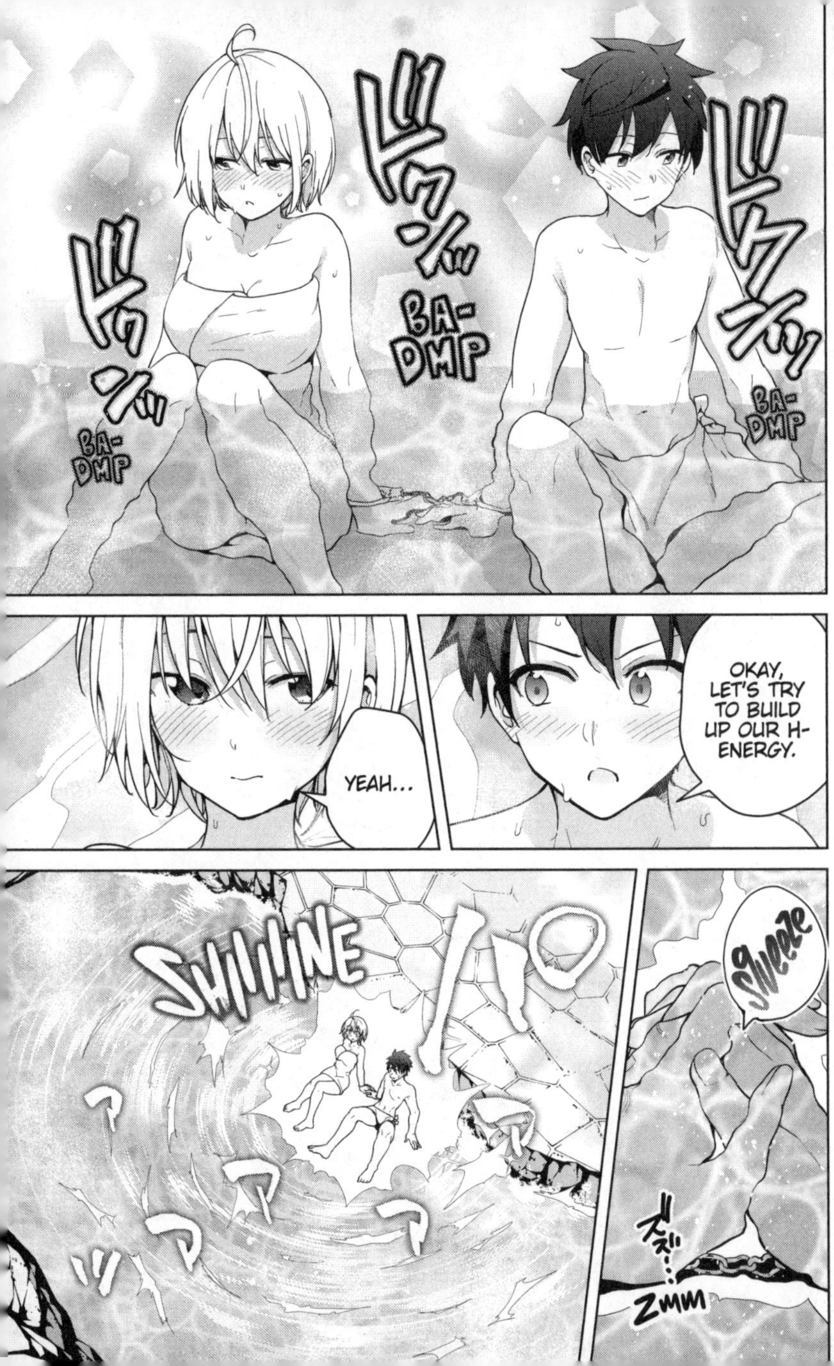
BA-DMP
BA-DMP
BA-DMP
OKAY, LET'S TRY TO BUILD UP OUR H-ENERGY.
YEAH...
squeeze
ZMM
SHIIIINE

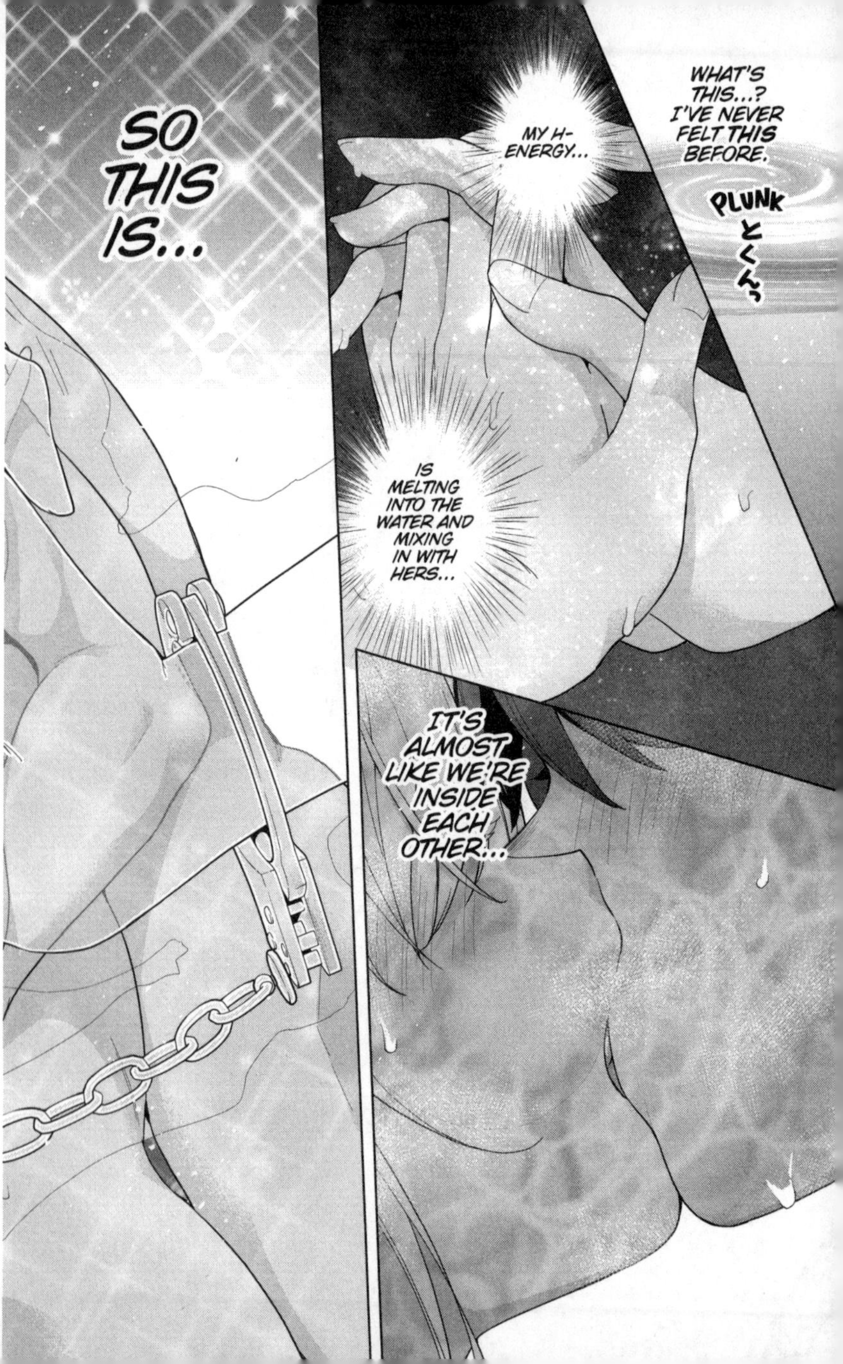
WHAT'S THIS...? I'VE NEVER FELT THIS BEFORE.
PLUNK
とくん
MY H-ENERGY...
IS MELTING INTO THE WATER AND MIXING IN WITH HERS...
IT'S ALMOST LIKE WE'RE INSIDE EACH OTHER...
SO THIS IS...

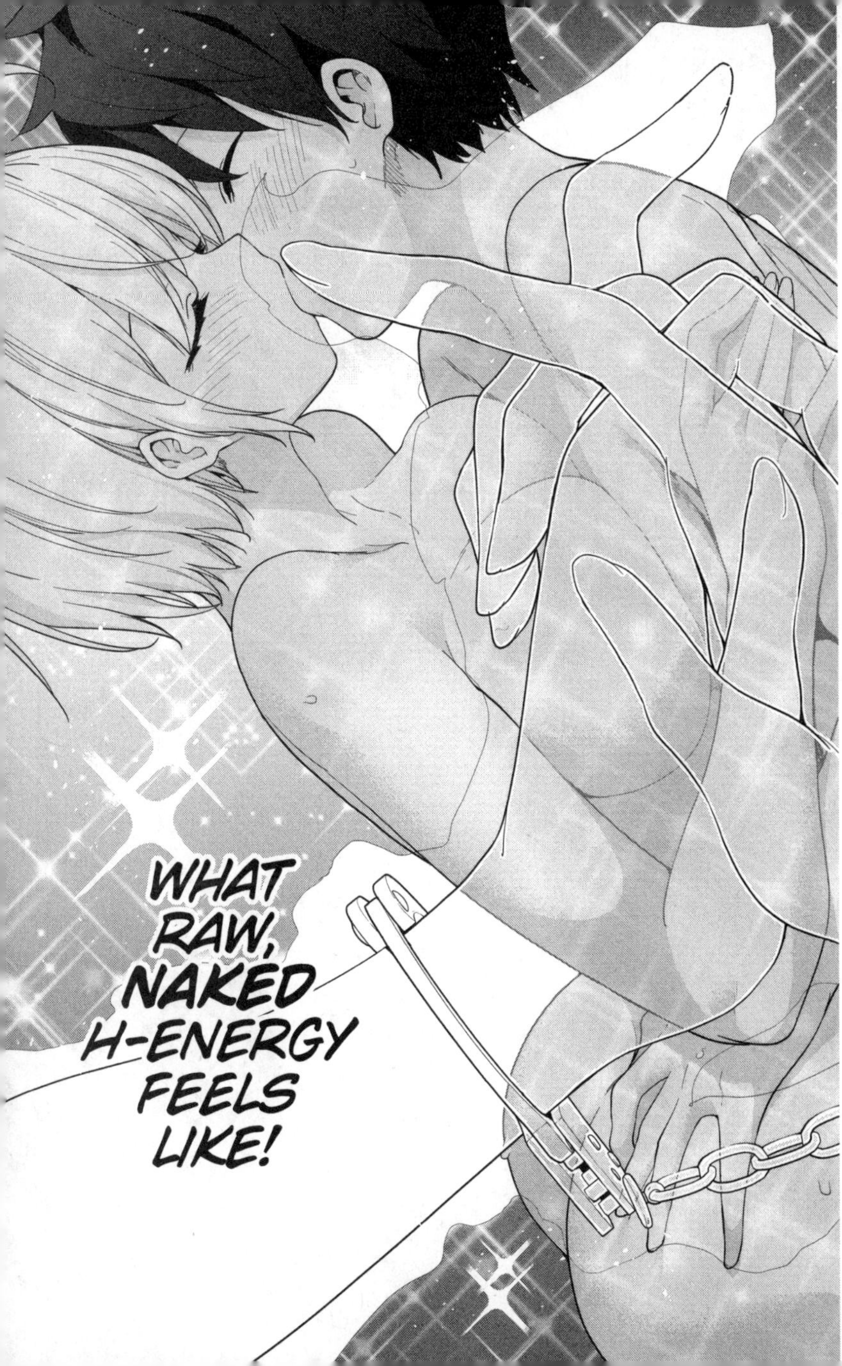
WHAT RAW, NAKED H-ENERGY FEELS LIKE!

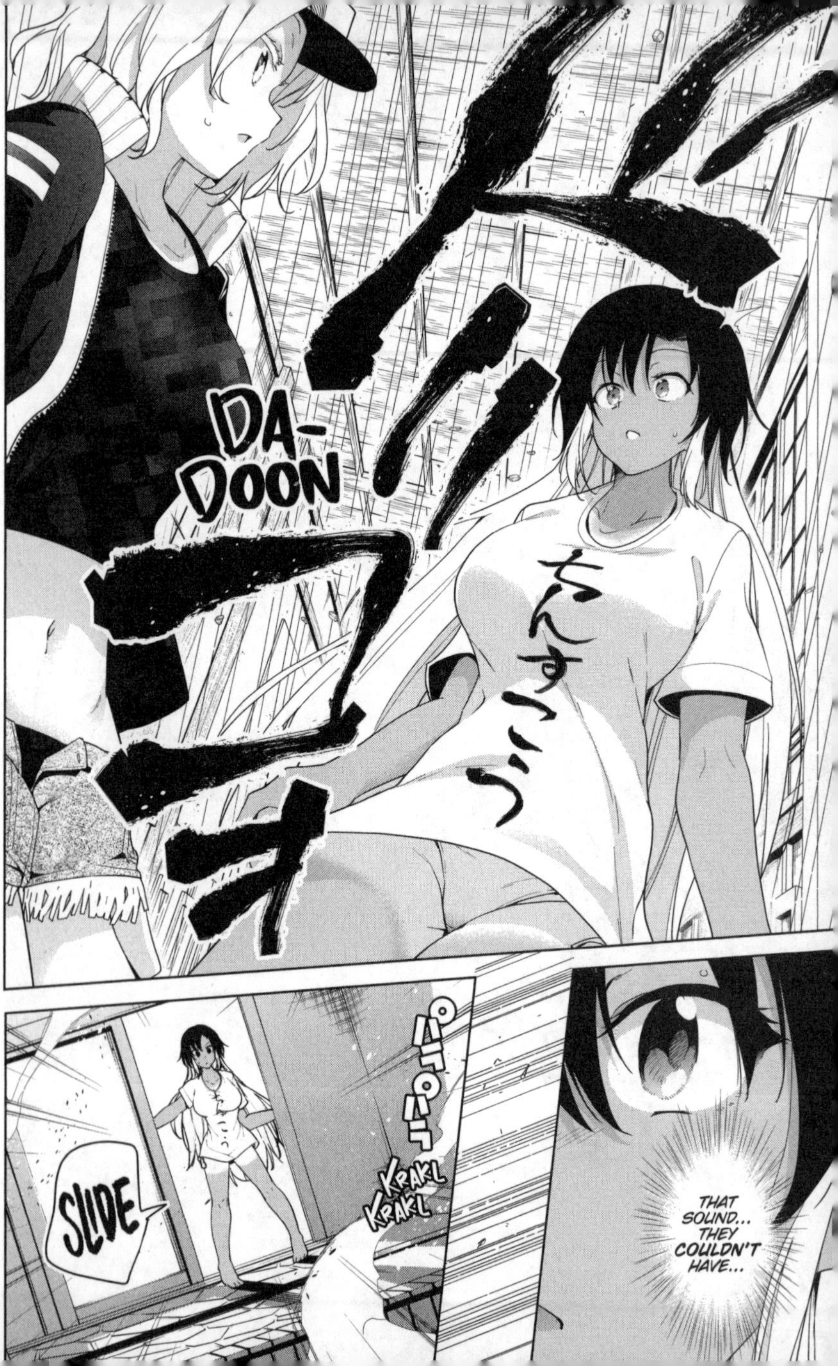
DA-DOON
ちんすこう
THAT SOUND... THEY COULDN'T HAVE...
KRAKL KRAKL
SLIDE

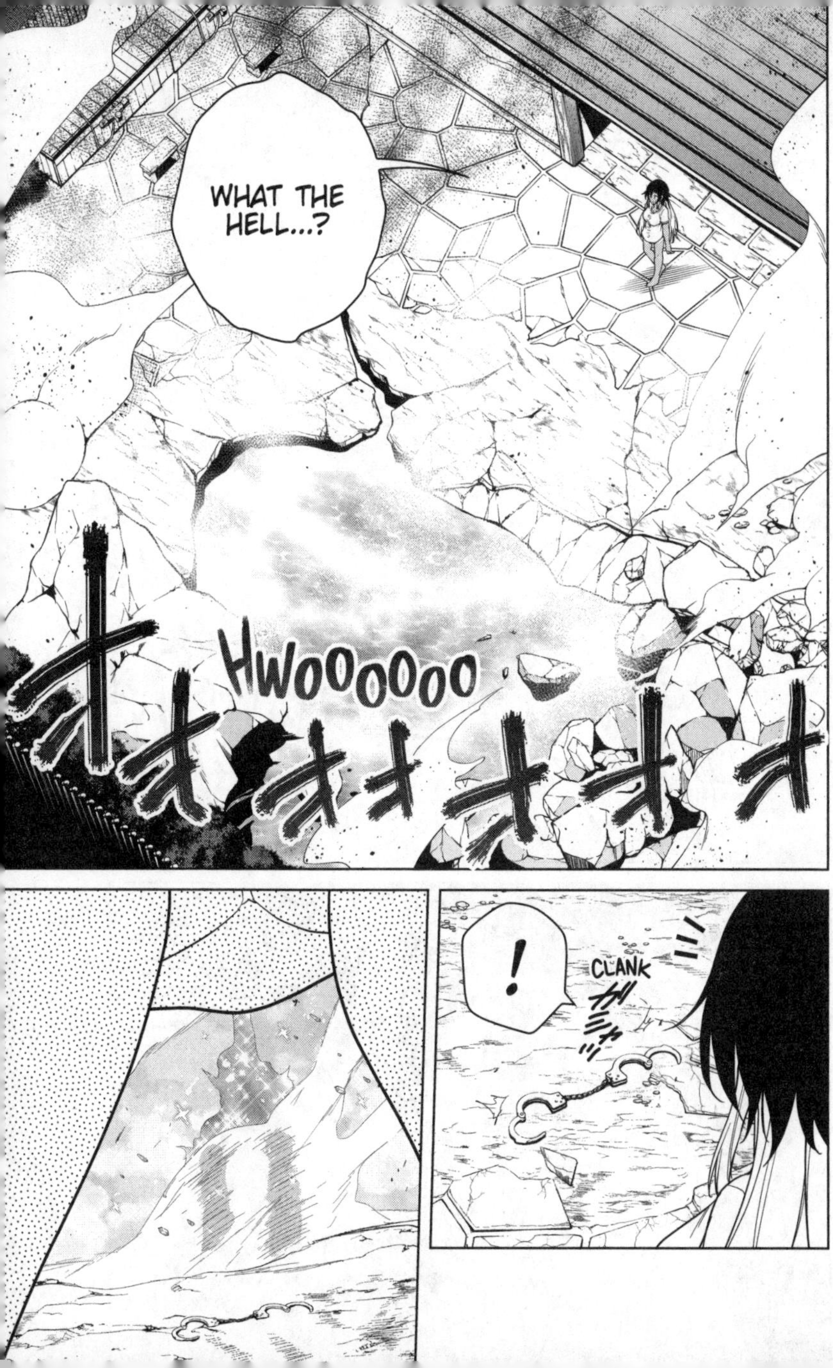
WHAT THE HELL...?
HWOOOOOO
!
CLANK

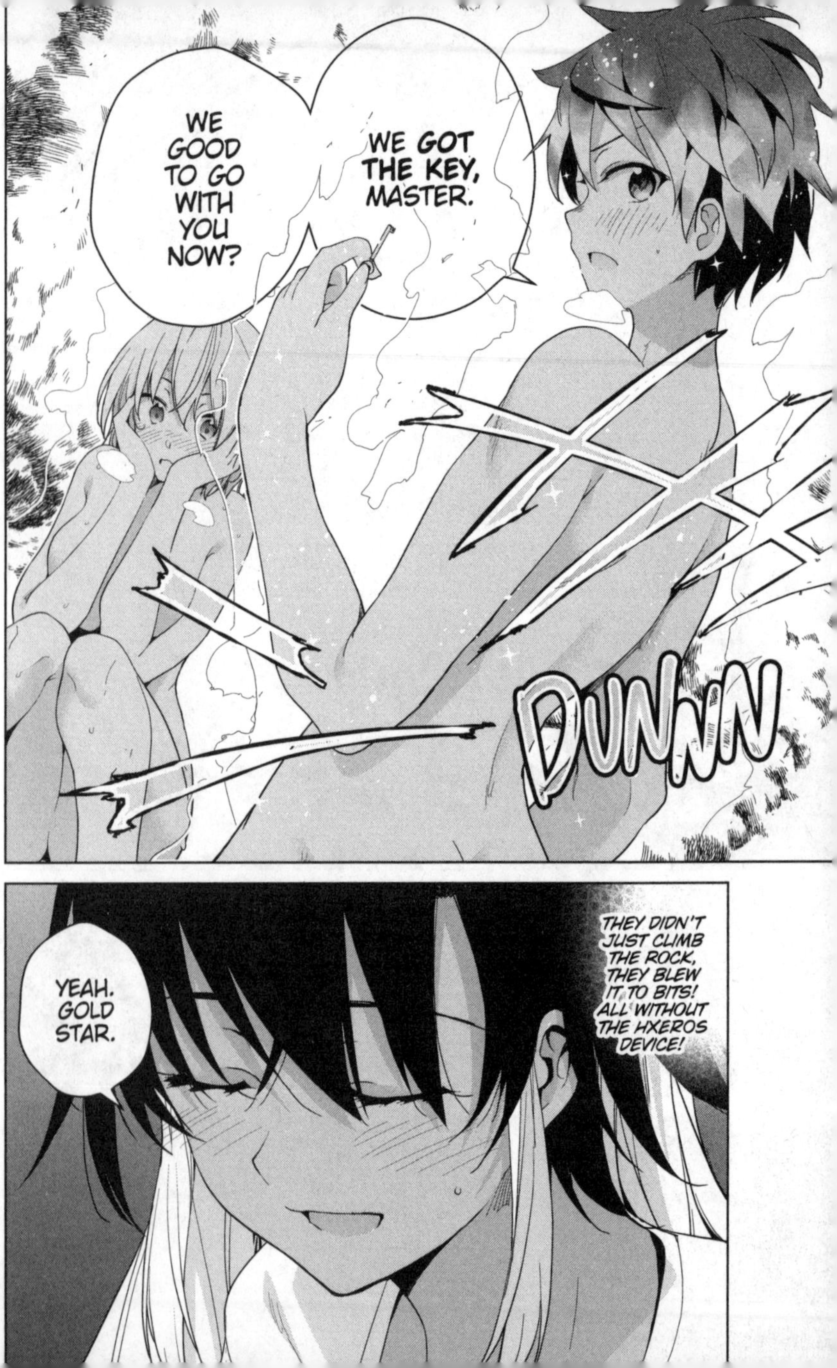
WE GOT THE KEY, MASTER.
WE GOOD TO GO WITH YOU NOW?
DUNNN
THEY DIDN'T JUST CLIMB THE ROCK, THEY BLEW IT TO BITS! ALL WITHOUT THE HXEROS DEVICE!
YEAH. GOLD STAR.

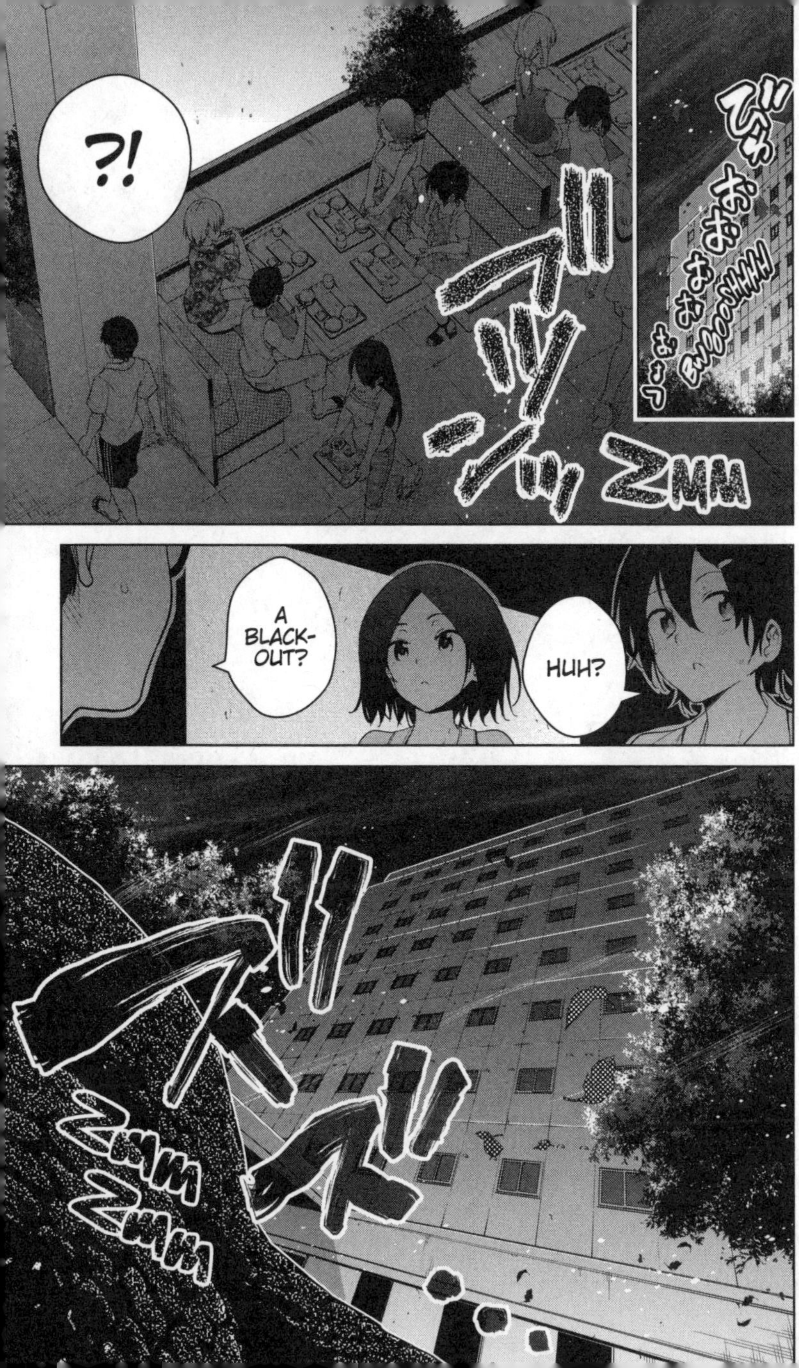
びゅおおおおおっ
BWOOOSHHHH
ブツッ
ZMM
?!
HUH?
A BLACK-OUT?
ズズ
ZMM ZMM

Extra Gallery

SUPER HxEROS

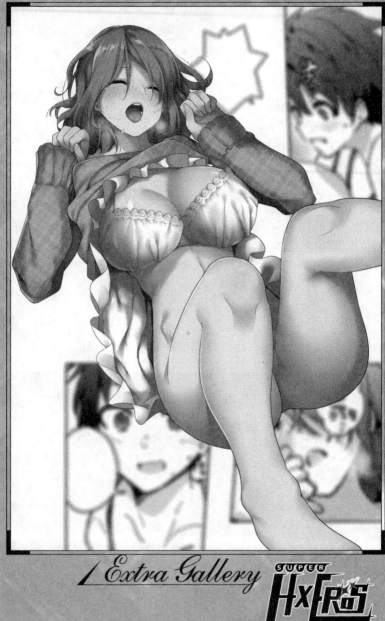

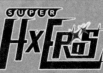

Chapter 36
HXEROS VS. Guardian

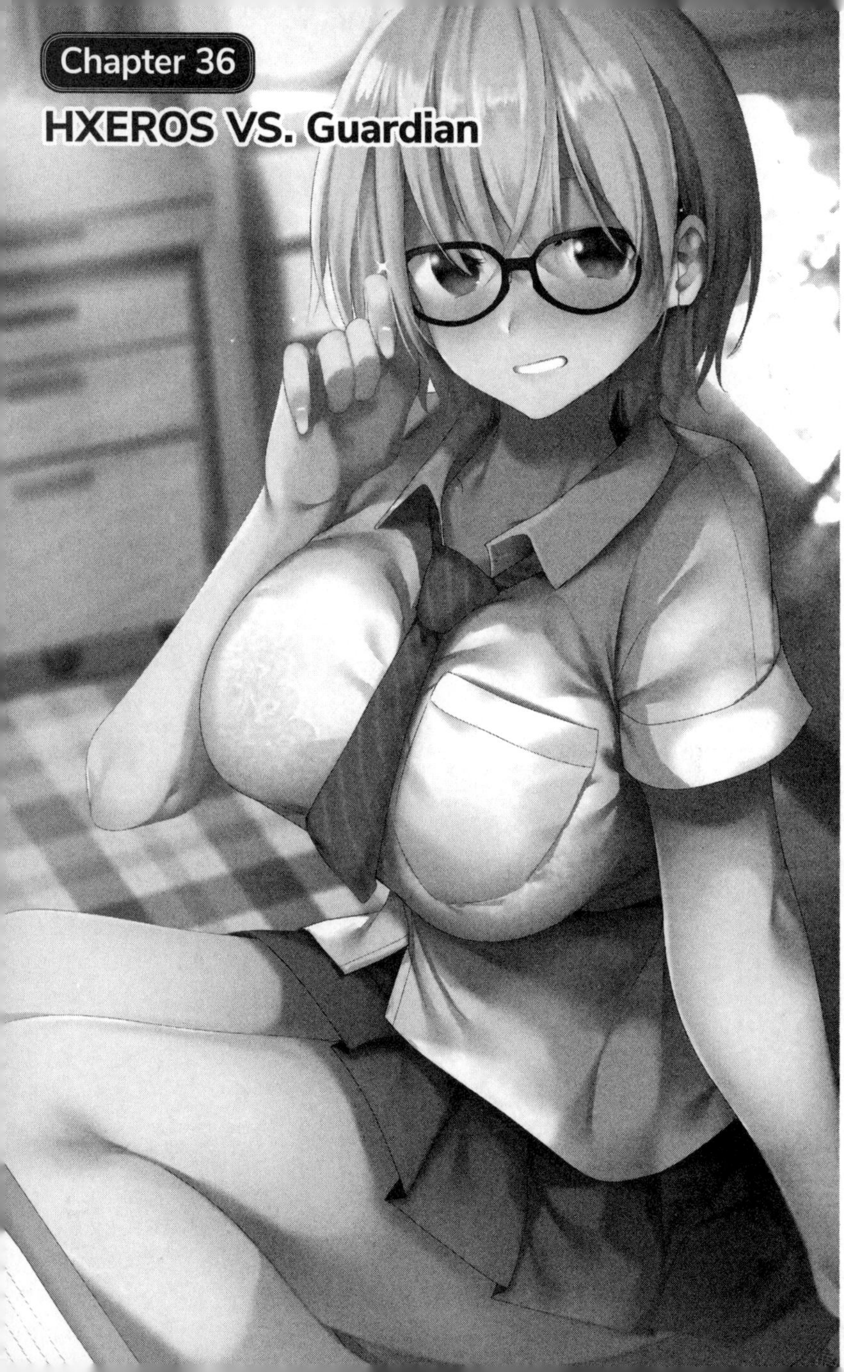

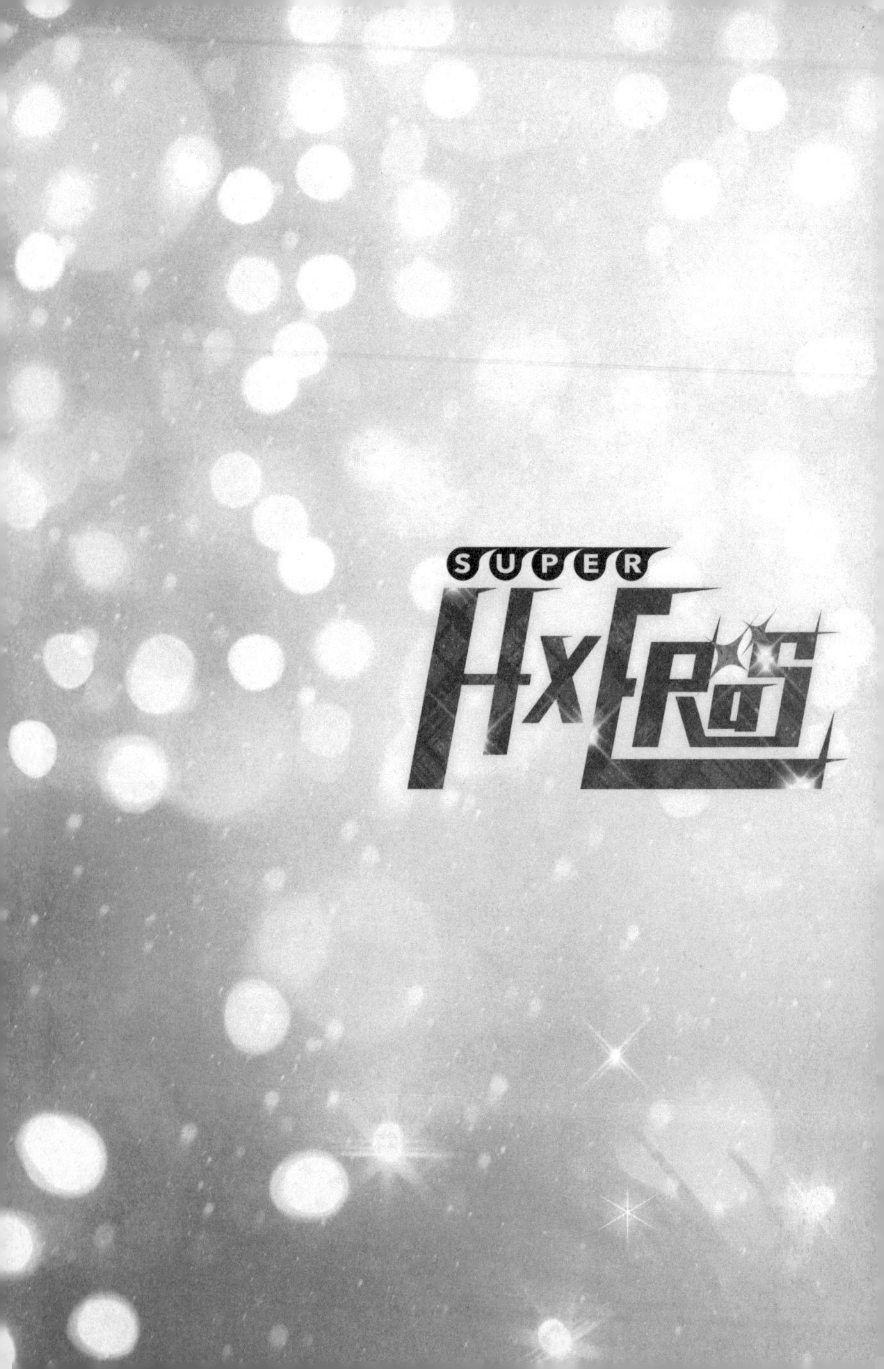
SUPER
HxEROS

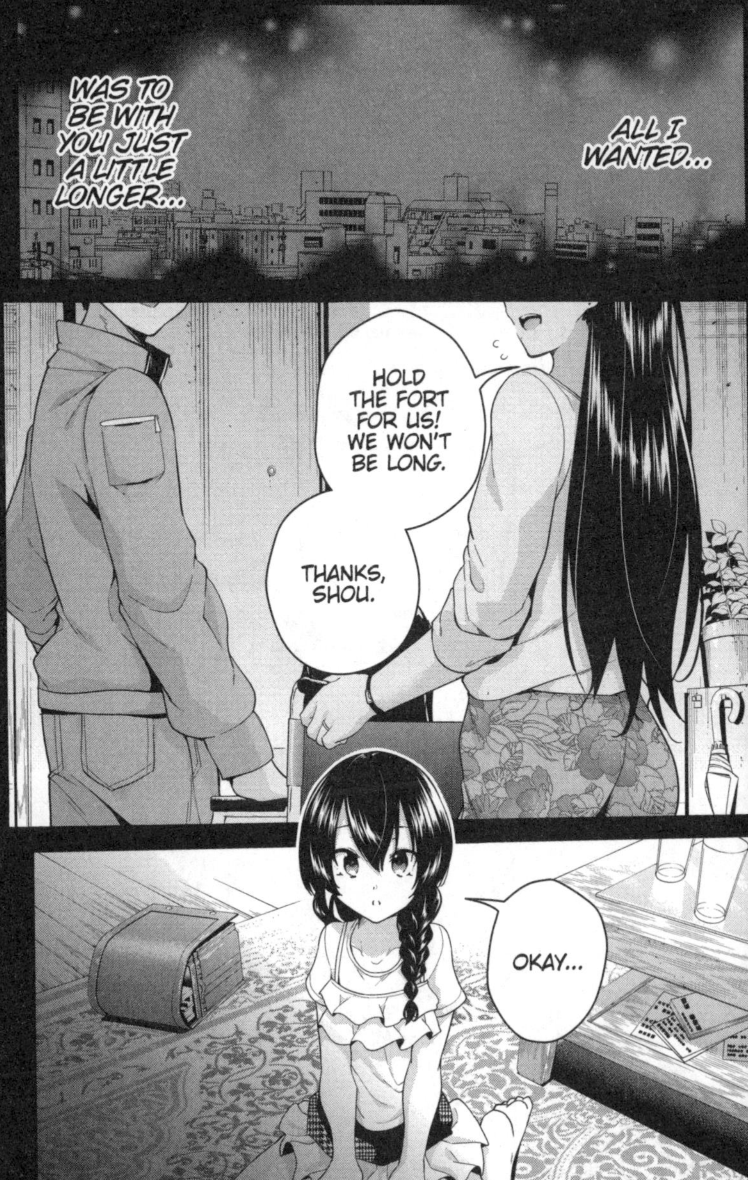
ALL I WANTED...
WAS TO BE WITH YOU JUST A LITTLE LONGER...
HOLD THE FORT FOR US! WE WON'T BE LONG.
THANKS, SHOU.
OKAY...

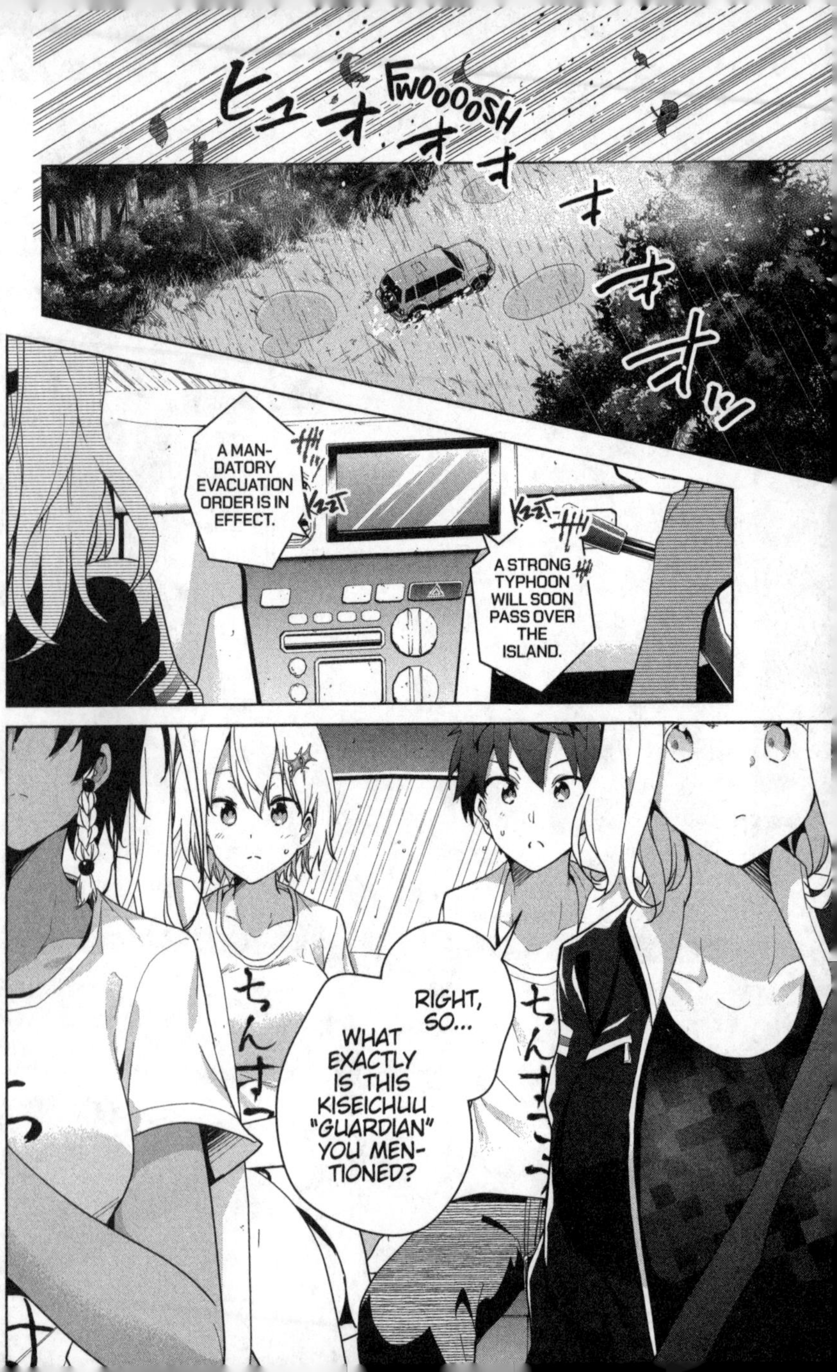
ヒュオォォォォオッ
FWOOOOSH
KZZT
A STRONG TYPHOON WILL SOON PASS OVER THE ISLAND.
KZZT
A MAN-DATORY EVACUATION ORDER IS IN EFFECT.
RIGHT, SO... WHAT EXACTLY IS THIS KISEICHUU "GUARDIAN" YOU MEN-TIONED?

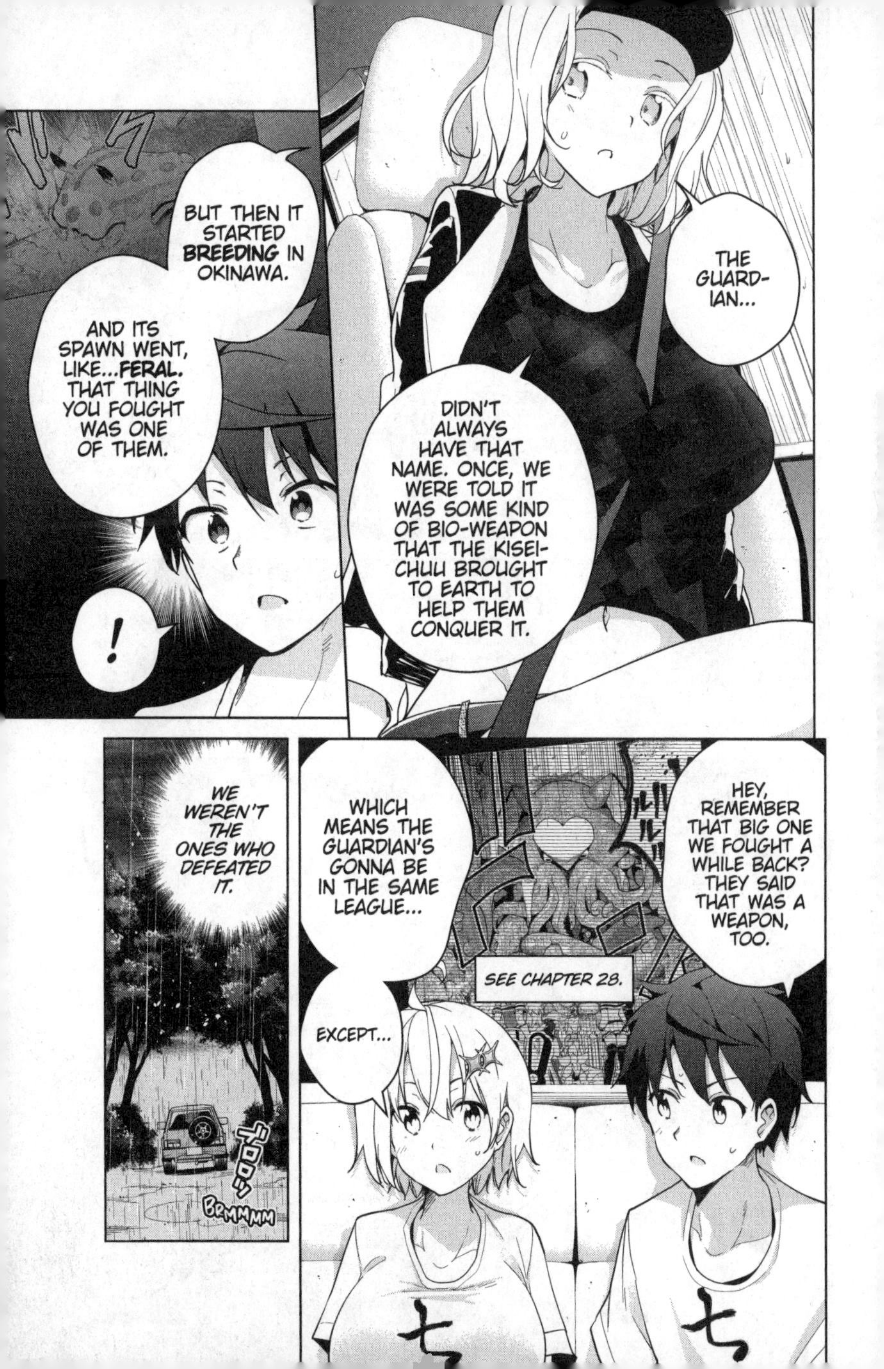
THE GUARDIAN...
DIDN'T ALWAYS HAVE THAT NAME. ONCE, WE WERE TOLD IT WAS SOME KIND OF BIO-WEAPON THAT THE KISEICHUU BROUGHT TO EARTH TO HELP THEM CONQUER IT.
BUT THEN IT STARTED **BREEDING** IN OKINAWA.
AND ITS SPAWN WENT, LIKE...**FERAL.** THAT THING YOU FOUGHT WAS ONE OF THEM.
!
HEY, REMEMBER THAT BIG ONE WE FOUGHT A WHILE BACK? THEY SAID THAT WAS A WEAPON, TOO.
SEE CHAPTER 28.
WHICH MEANS THE GUARDIAN'S GONNA BE IN THE SAME LEAGUE...
EXCEPT...
WE WEREN'T THE ONES WHO DEFEATED IT.
BRMMMM

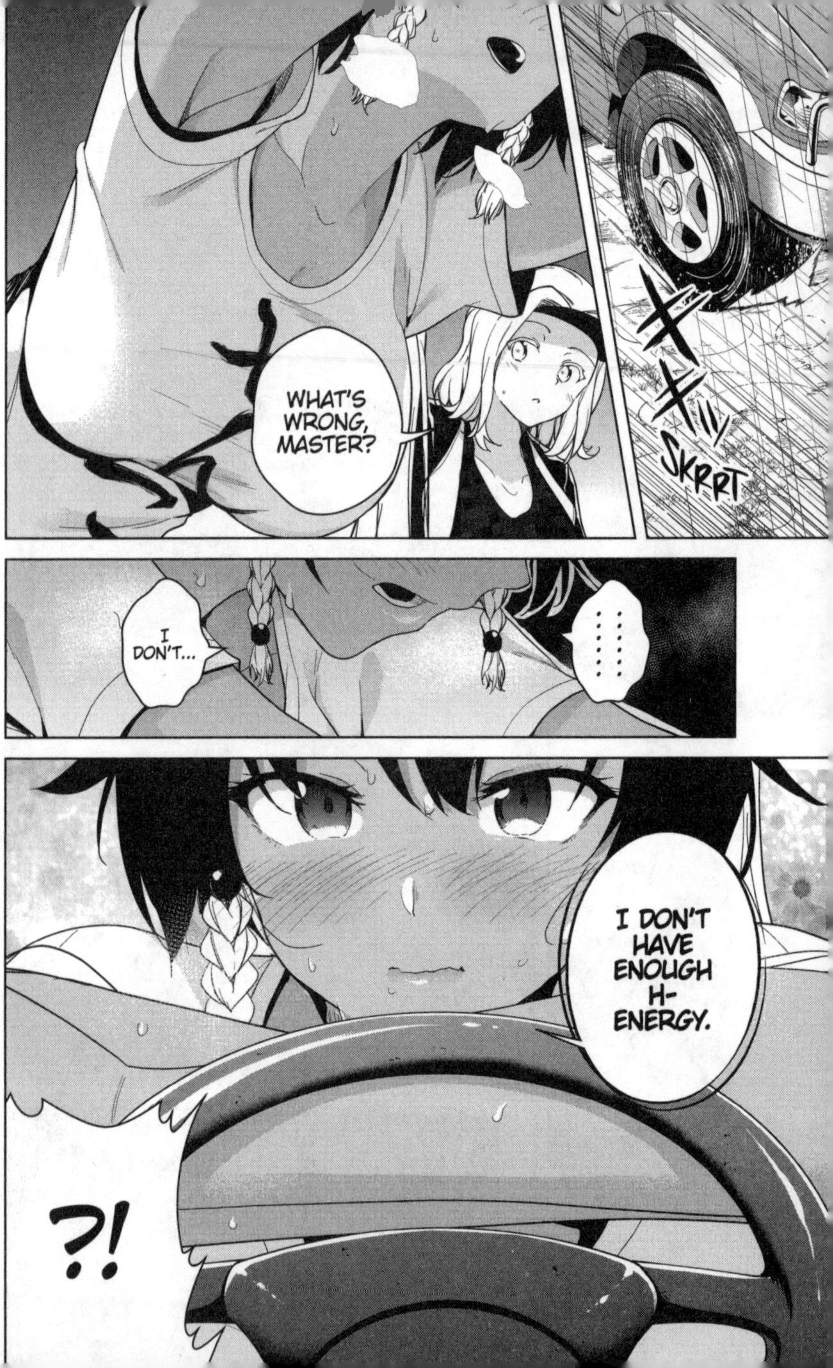
SKRRT
WHAT'S WRONG, MASTER?
......
I DON'T...
I DON'T HAVE ENOUGH H-ENERGY.
?!

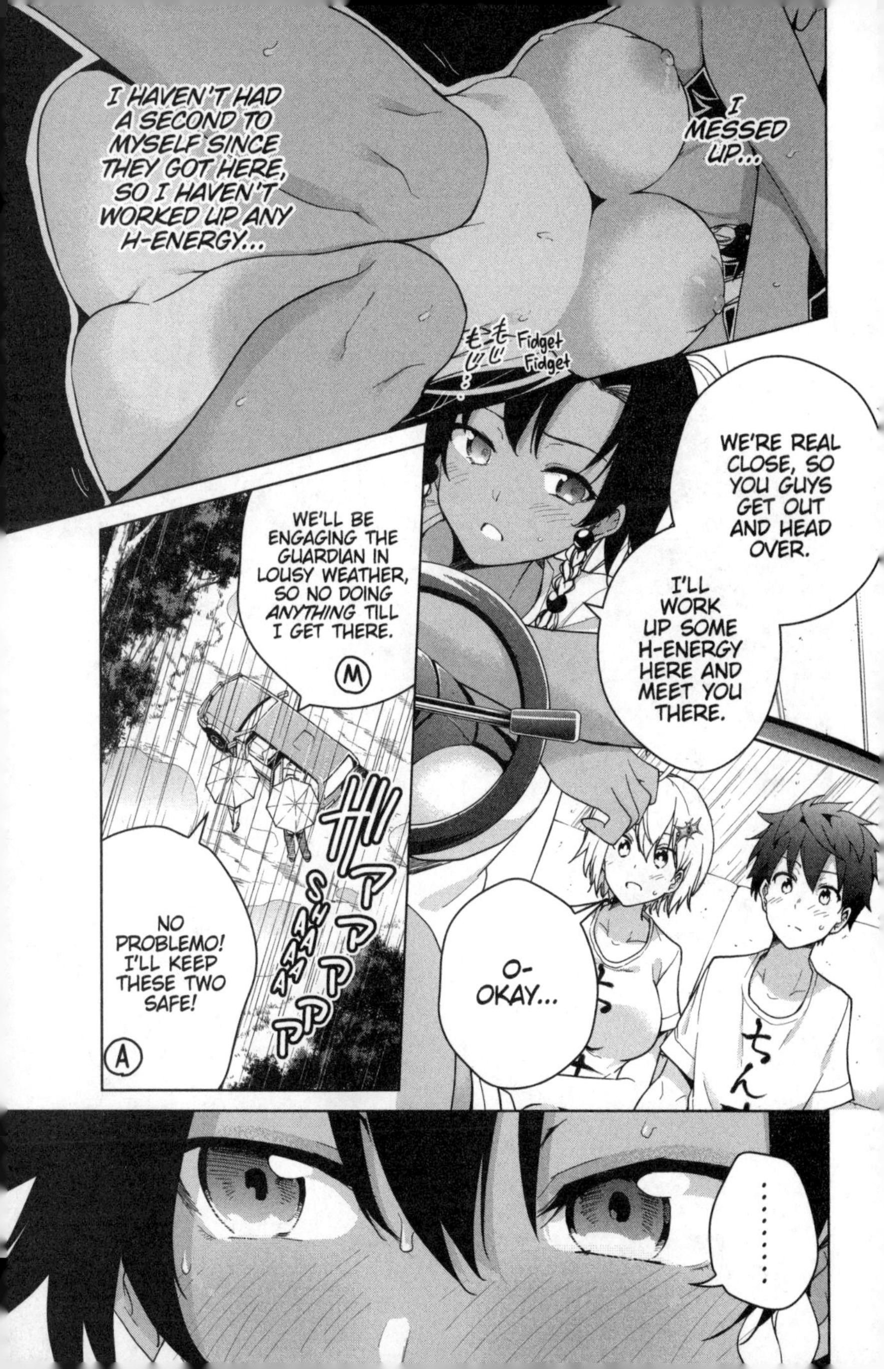

I MESSED UP...
I HAVEN'T HAD A SECOND TO MYSELF SINCE THEY GOT HERE, SO I HAVEN'T WORKED UP ANY H-ENERGY...
Fidget Fidget
WE'RE REAL CLOSE, SO YOU GUYS GET OUT AND HEAD OVER.
I'LL WORK UP SOME H-ENERGY HERE AND MEET YOU THERE.
O-OKAY...
WE'LL BE ENGAGING THE GUARDIAN IN LOUSY WEATHER, SO NO DOING *ANYTHING* TILL I GET THERE.
M
SHAAAAA
NO PROBLEMO! I'LL KEEP THESE TWO SAFE!
A
......

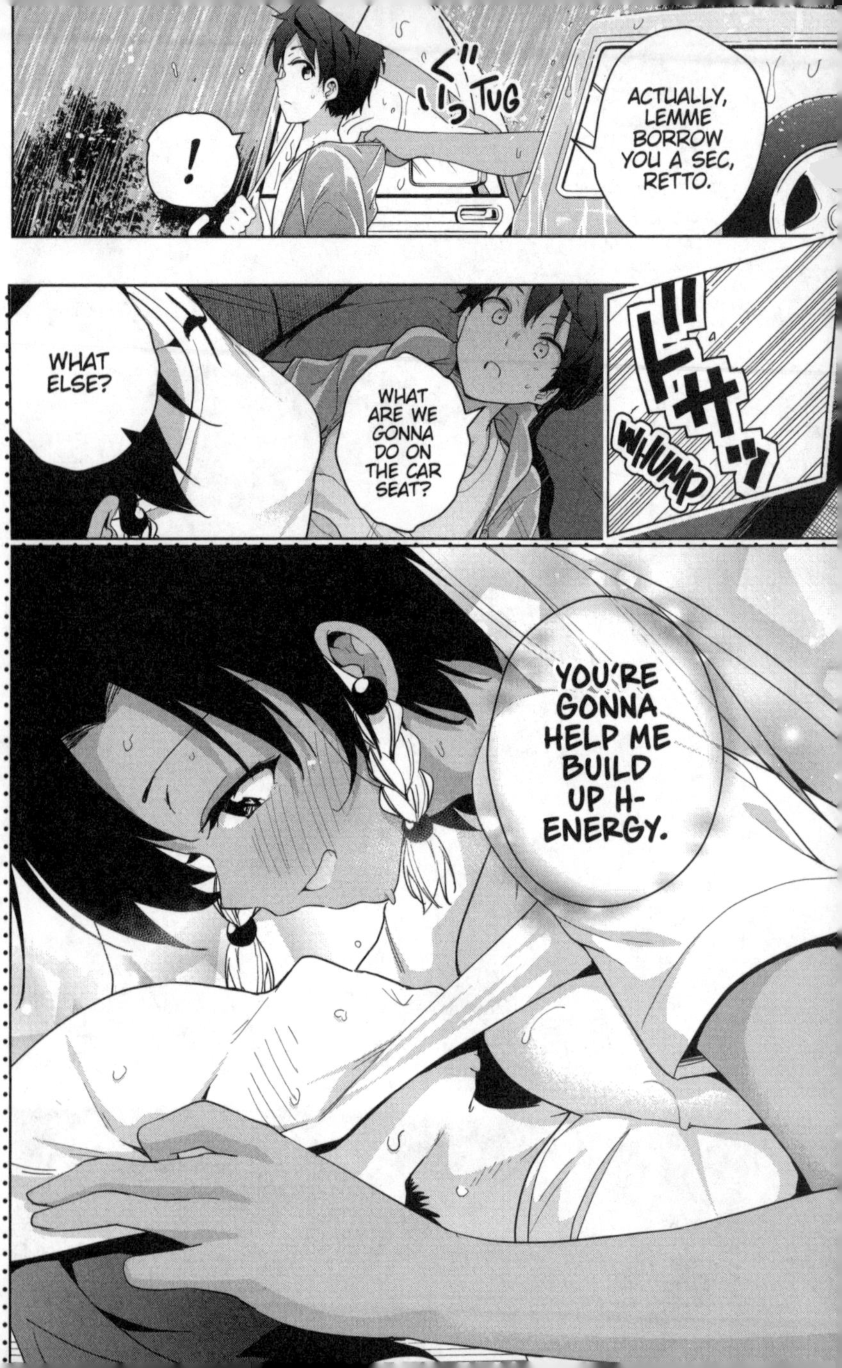
ACTUALLY, LEMME BORROW YOU A SEC, RETTO.
ぐいっ
TUG
!
ドサッ
WHUMP
WHAT ARE WE GONNA DO ON THE CAR SEAT?
WHAT ELSE?
YOU'RE GONNA HELP ME BUILD UP H-ENERGY.

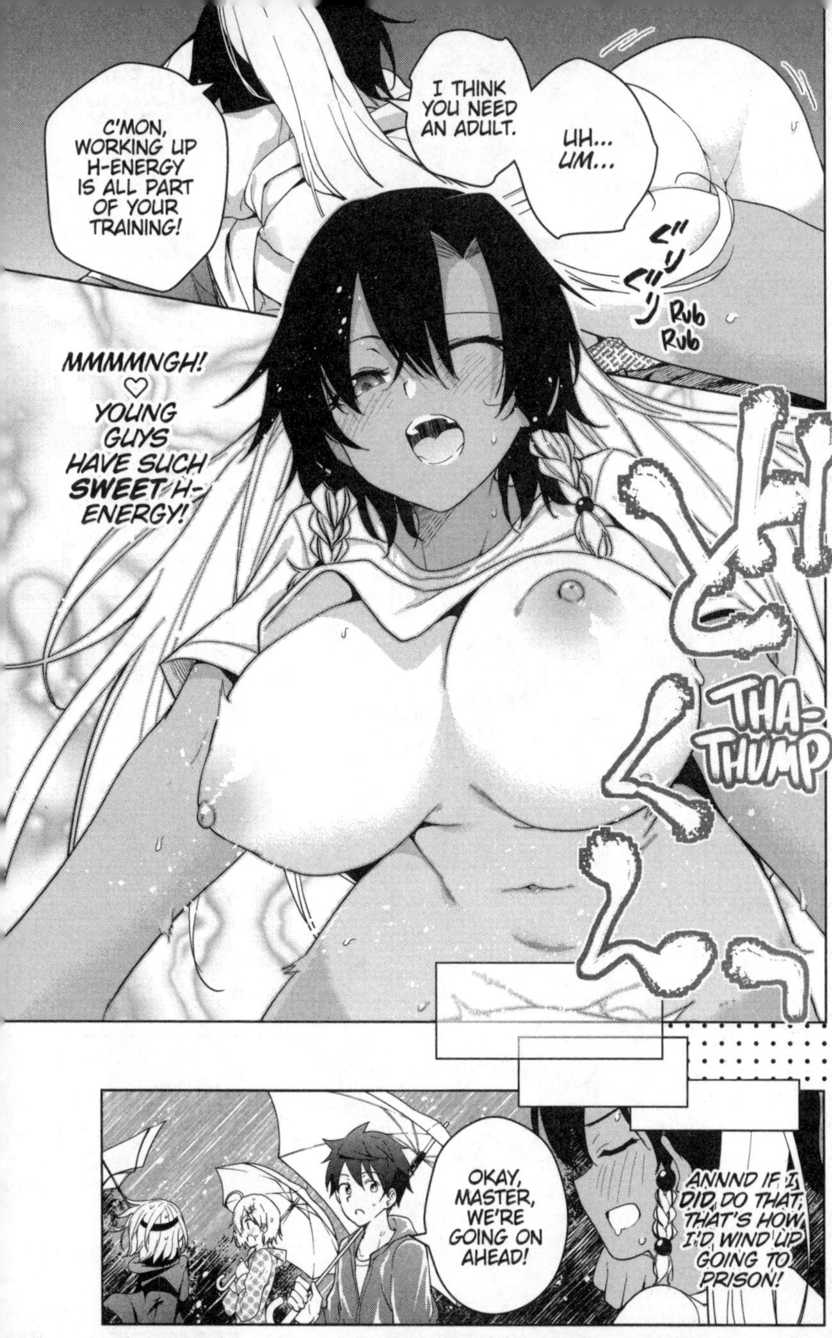
UH... UM...
I THINK YOU NEED AN ADULT.
C'MON, WORKING UP H-ENERGY IS ALL PART OF YOUR TRAINING!
ぐりぐり
Rub Rub
ドクン
THA-THUMP
MMMMNGH! ♡ YOUNG GUYS HAVE SUCH SWEET H-ENERGY!
ANNND IF I DID DO THAT, THAT'S HOW I'D WIND UP GOING TO PRISON!
OKAY, MASTER, WE'RE GOING ON AHEAD!

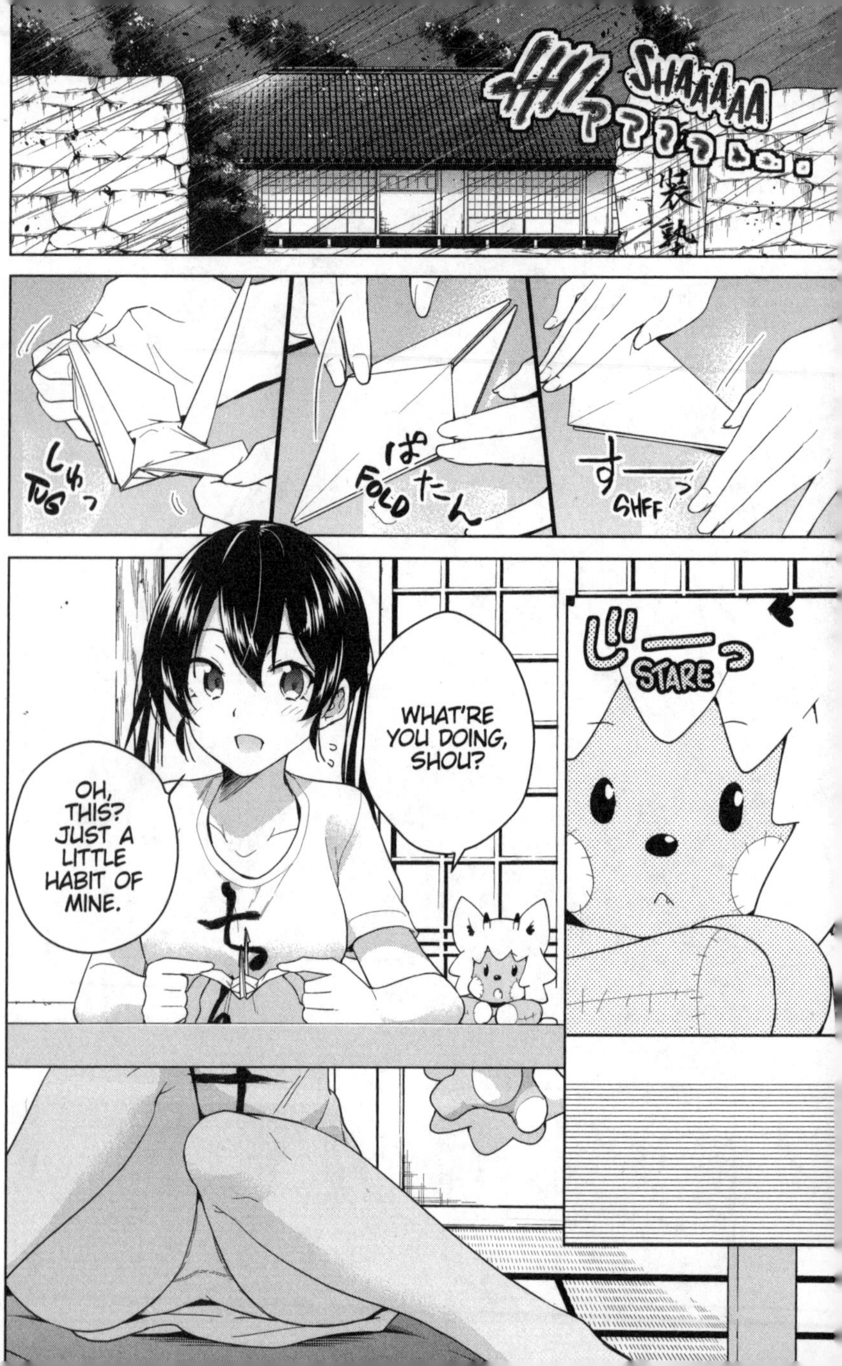
SHAAAAA
すー
SHFF
ぱたん
FOLD
しゅっ
TUG
じーっ
STARE
WHAT'RE YOU DOING, SHOU?
OH, THIS? JUST A LITTLE HABIT OF MINE.

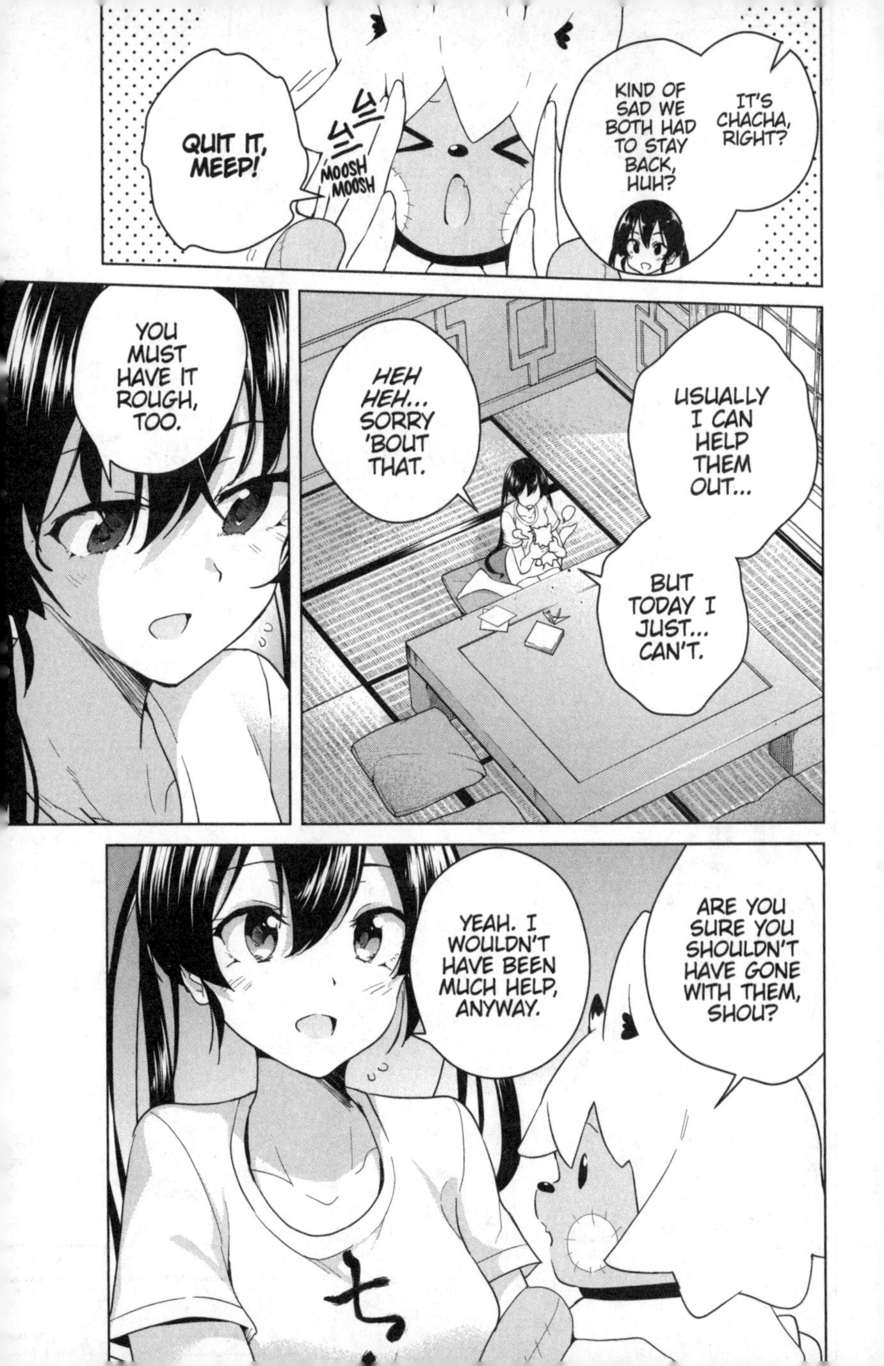
IT'S CHACHA, RIGHT?
KIND OF SAD WE BOTH HAD TO STAY BACK, HUH?
MOOSH MOOSH
QUIT IT, MEEP!
USUALLY I CAN HELP THEM OUT...
BUT TODAY I JUST... CAN'T.
HEH HEH... SORRY 'BOUT THAT.
YOU MUST HAVE IT ROUGH, TOO.
ARE YOU SURE YOU SHOULDN'T HAVE GONE WITH THEM, SHOU?
YEAH. I WOULDN'T HAVE BEEN MUCH HELP, ANYWAY.

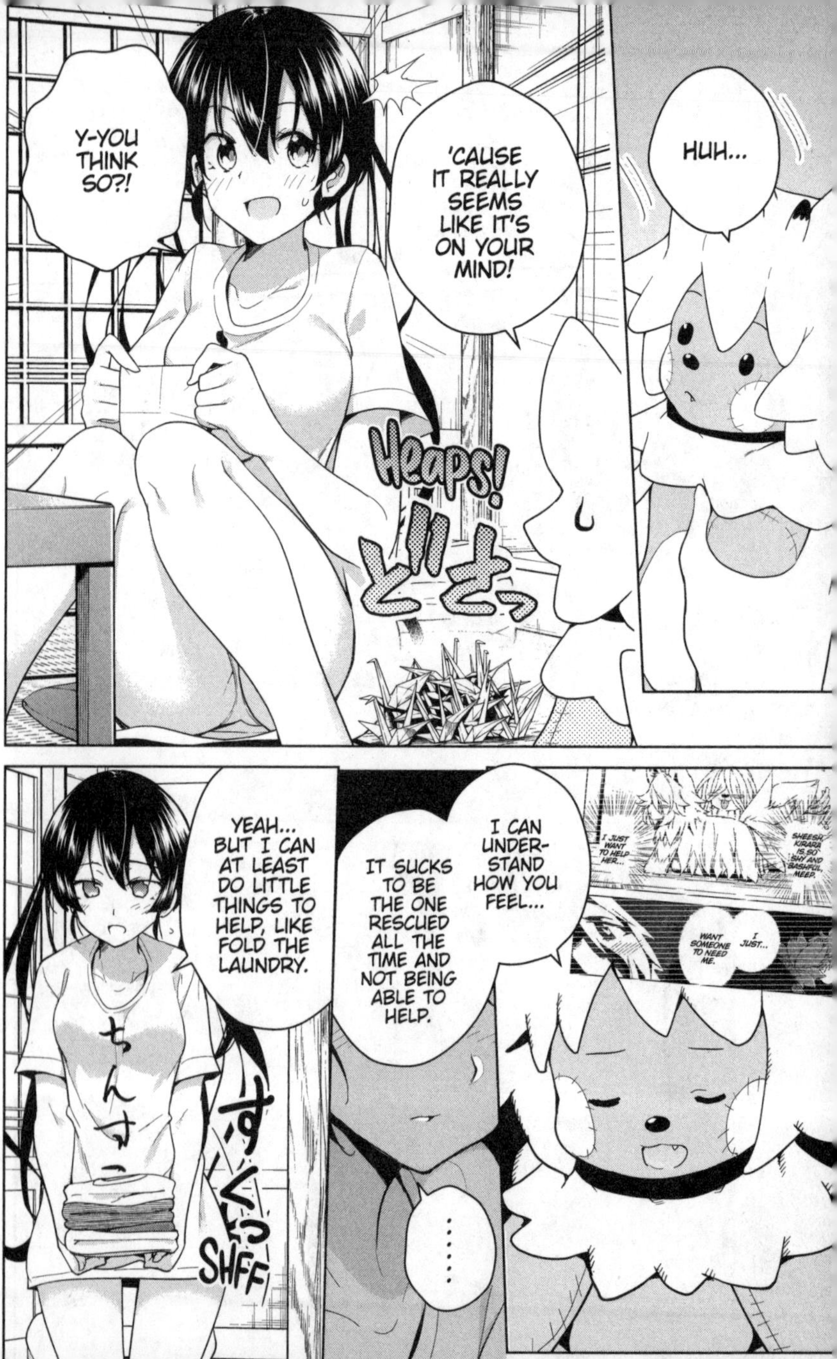
HUH...
'CAUSE IT REALLY SEEMS LIKE IT'S ON YOUR MIND!
Y-YOU THINK SO?!
Heaps!
どさっ
I CAN UNDERSTAND HOW YOU FEEL...
SHEESH, KIRARA IS SO SHY AND BASHFUL, MEEP.
I JUST WANT TO HELP HER...
I JUST...
WANT SOMEONE TO NEED ME.
IT SUCKS TO BE THE ONE RESCUED ALL THE TIME AND NOT BEING ABLE TO HELP.
......
YEAH... BUT I CAN AT LEAST DO LITTLE THINGS TO HELP, LIKE FOLD THE LAUNDRY.
すくっ
SHFF

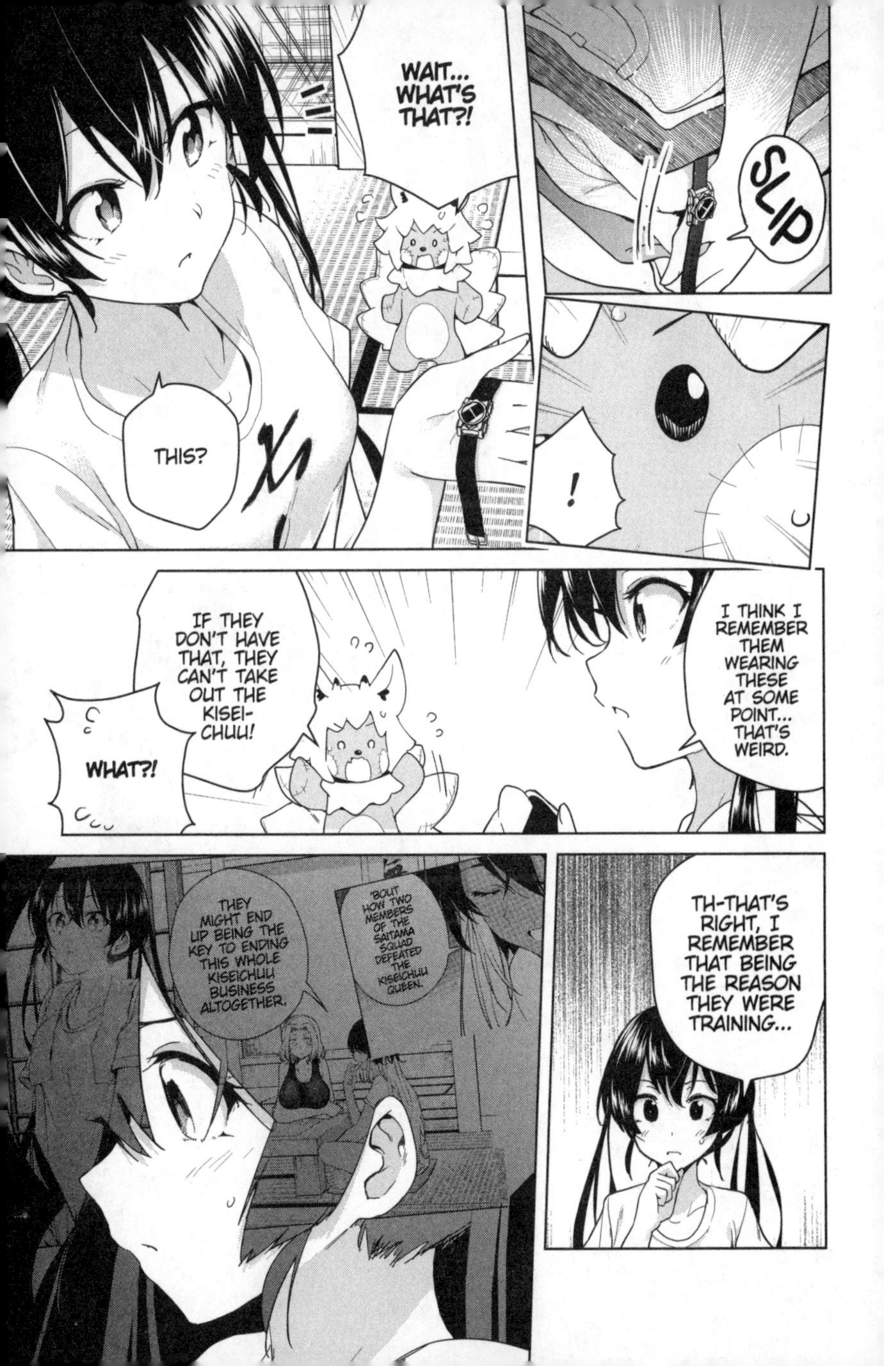
SLIP
!
WAIT... WHAT'S THAT?!
THIS?
I THINK I REMEMBER THEM WEARING THESE AT SOME POINT... THAT'S WEIRD.
IF THEY DON'T HAVE THAT, THEY CAN'T TAKE OUT THE KISEI-CHUU!
WHAT?!
TH-THAT'S RIGHT, I REMEMBER THAT BEING THE REASON THEY WERE TRAINING...
'BOUT HOW TWO MEMBERS OF THE SAITAMA SQUAD DEFEATED THE KISEICHUU QUEEN.
THEY MIGHT END UP BEING THE KEY TO ENDING THIS WHOLE KISEICHUU BUSINESS ALTOGETHER.

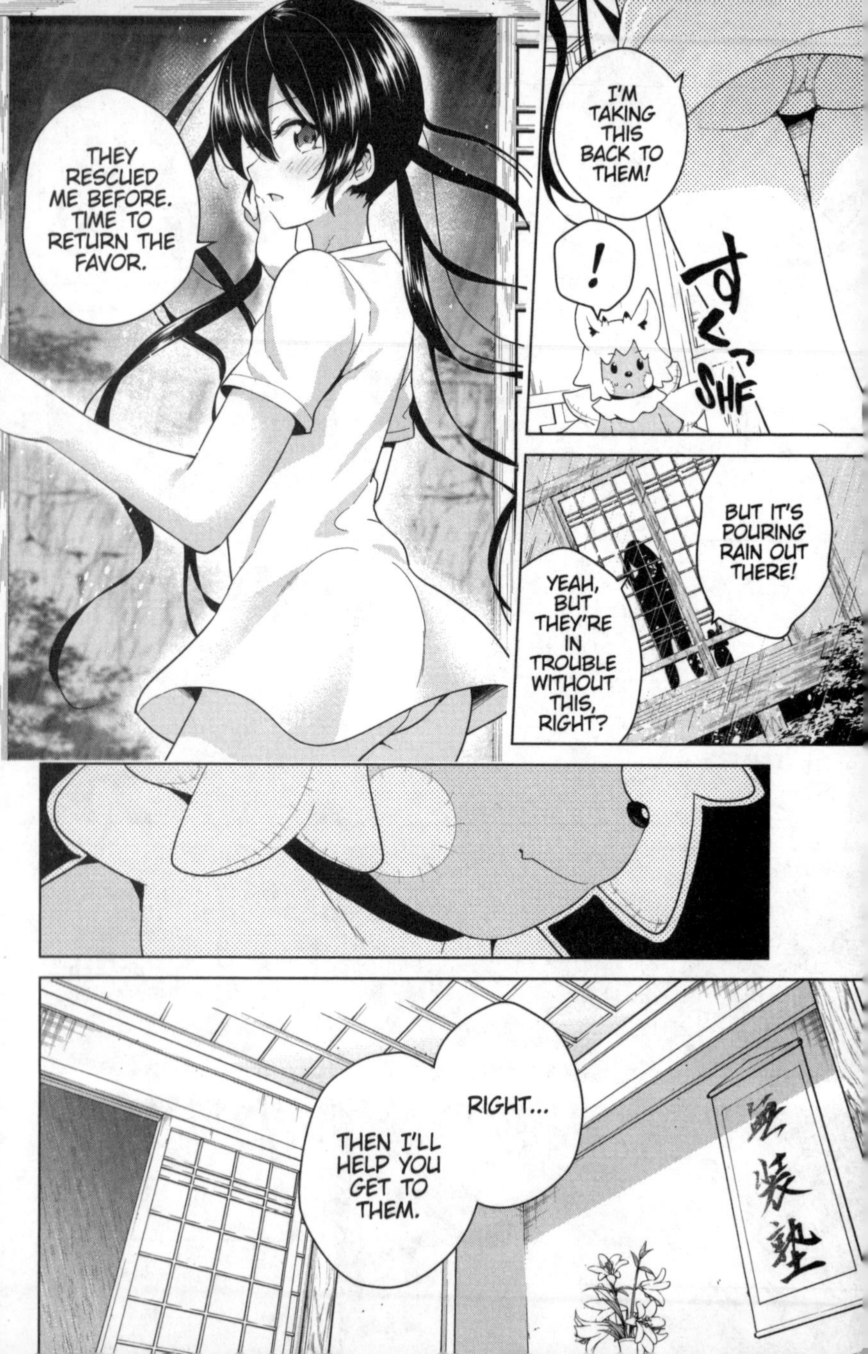
I'M TAKING THIS BACK TO THEM!
!
すくっ
SHF
BUT IT'S POURING RAIN OUT THERE!
YEAH, BUT THEY'RE IN TROUBLE WITHOUT THIS, RIGHT?
THEY RESCUED ME BEFORE. TIME TO RETURN THE FAVOR.
RIGHT...
THEN I'LL HELP YOU GET TO THEM.

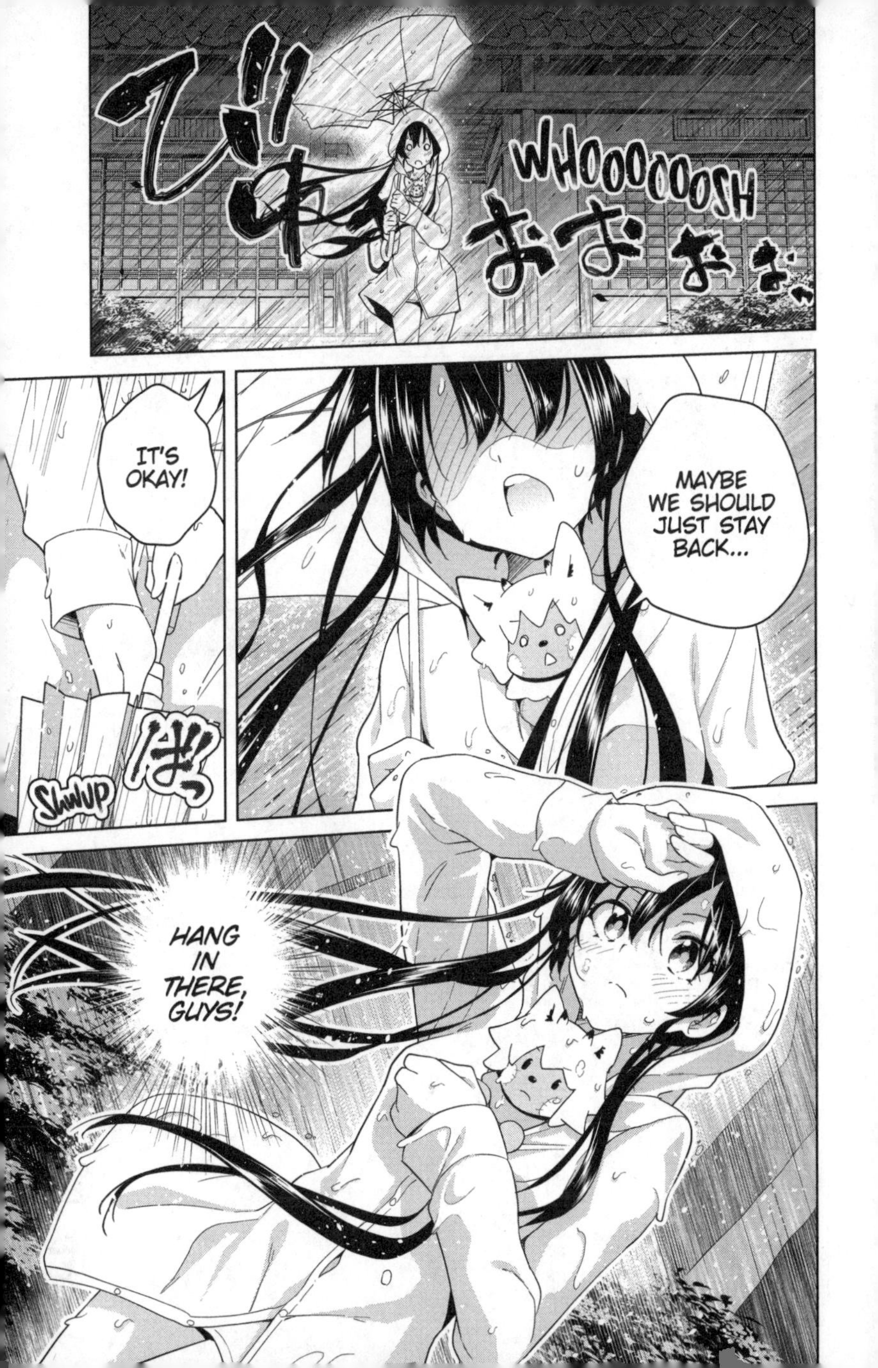
WHOOOOOOSH
MAYBE WE SHOULD JUST STAY BACK...
IT'S OKAY!
SHWUP
HANG IN THERE, GUYS!

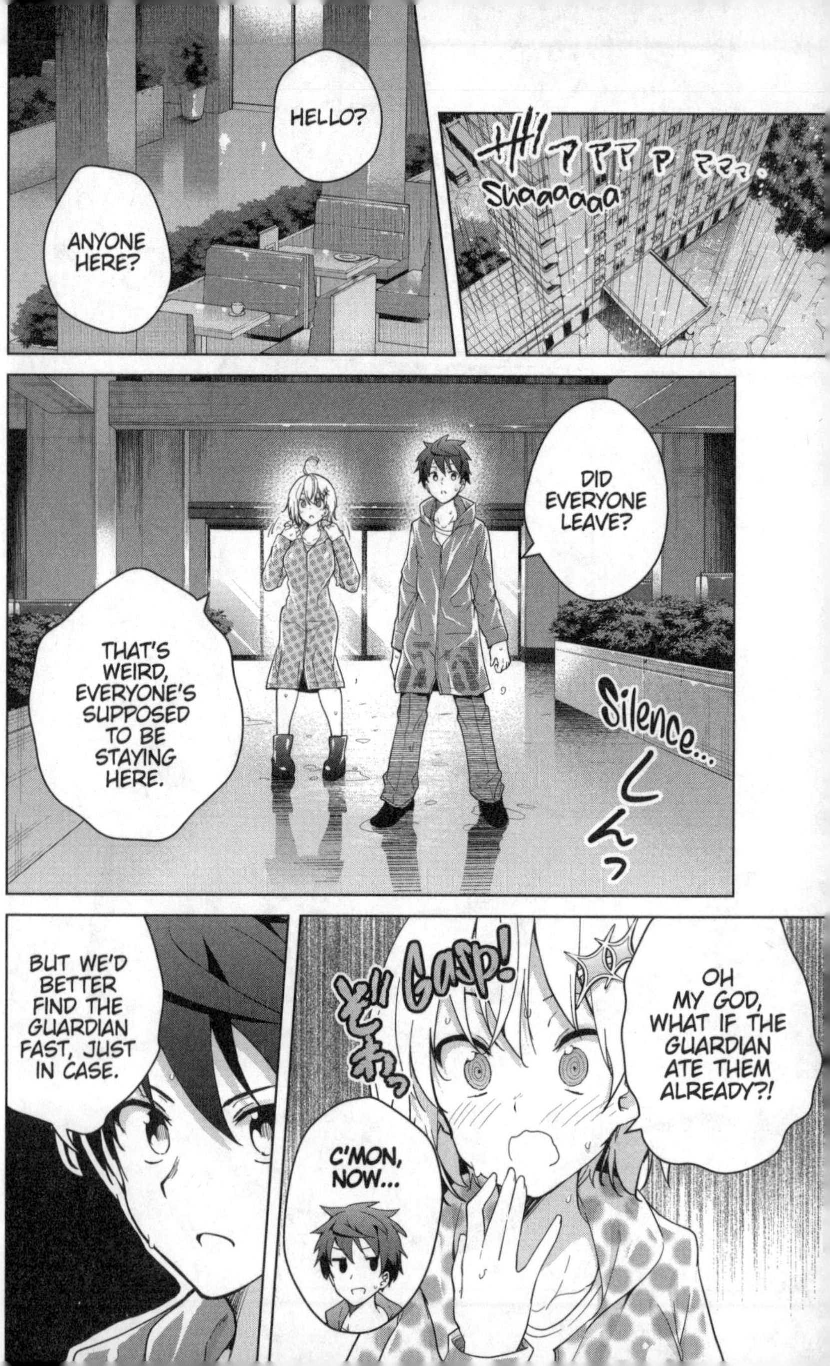
Shaaaaaa
HELLO?
ANYONE HERE?
DID EVERYONE LEAVE?
THAT'S WEIRD, EVERYONE'S SUPPOSED TO BE STAYING HERE.
Silence...
しんっ
OH MY GOD, WHAT IF THE GUARDIAN ATE THEM ALREADY?!
Gasp!
ぞわっ
C'MON, NOW...
BUT WE'D BETTER FIND THE GUARDIAN FAST, JUST IN CASE.

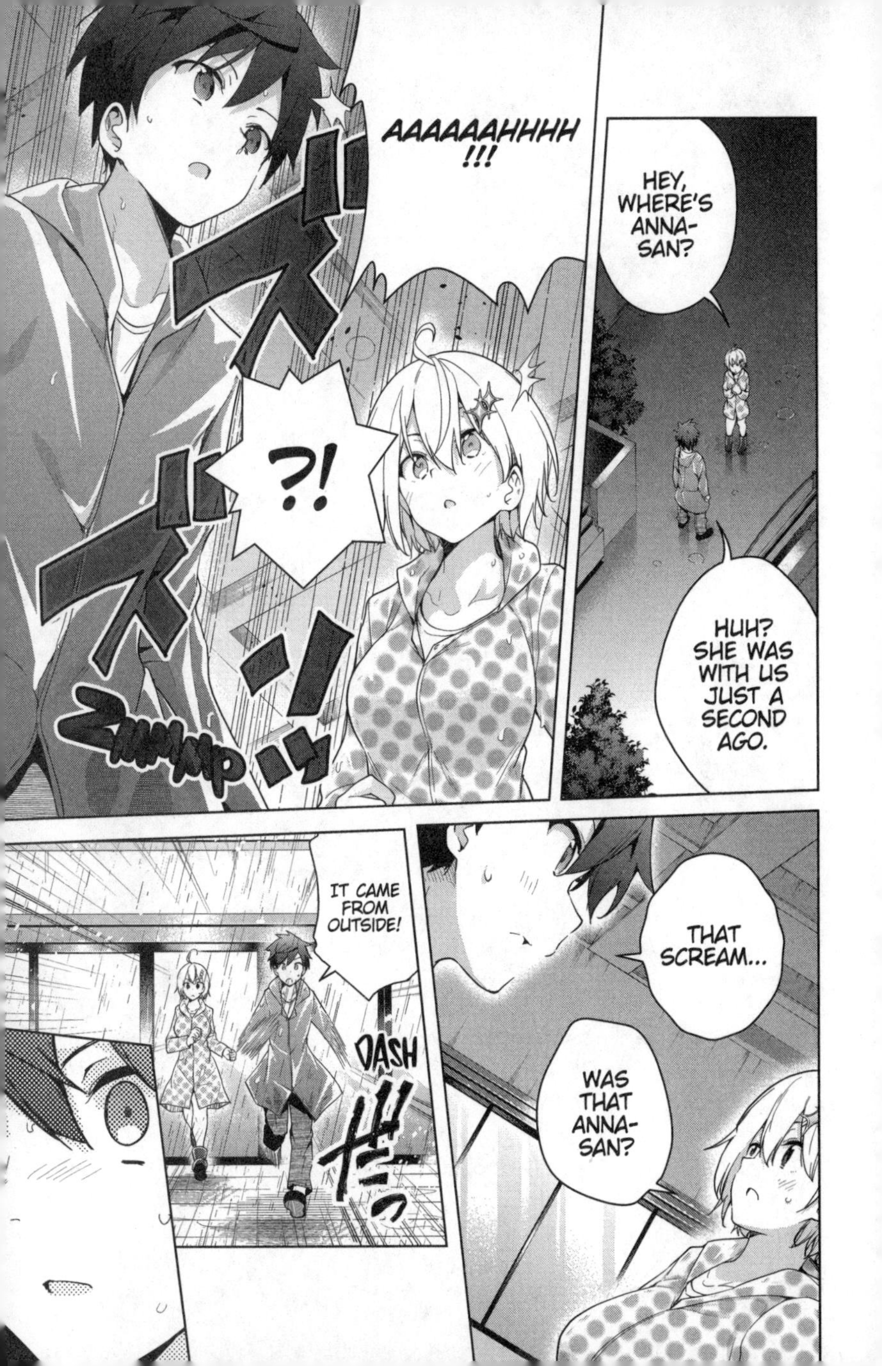
HEY, WHERE'S ANNA-SAN?
HUH? SHE WAS WITH US JUST A SECOND AGO.
AAAAAAHHHH!!!
?!
THAT SCREAM...
WAS THAT ANNA-SAN?
IT CAME FROM OUTSIDE!
DASH

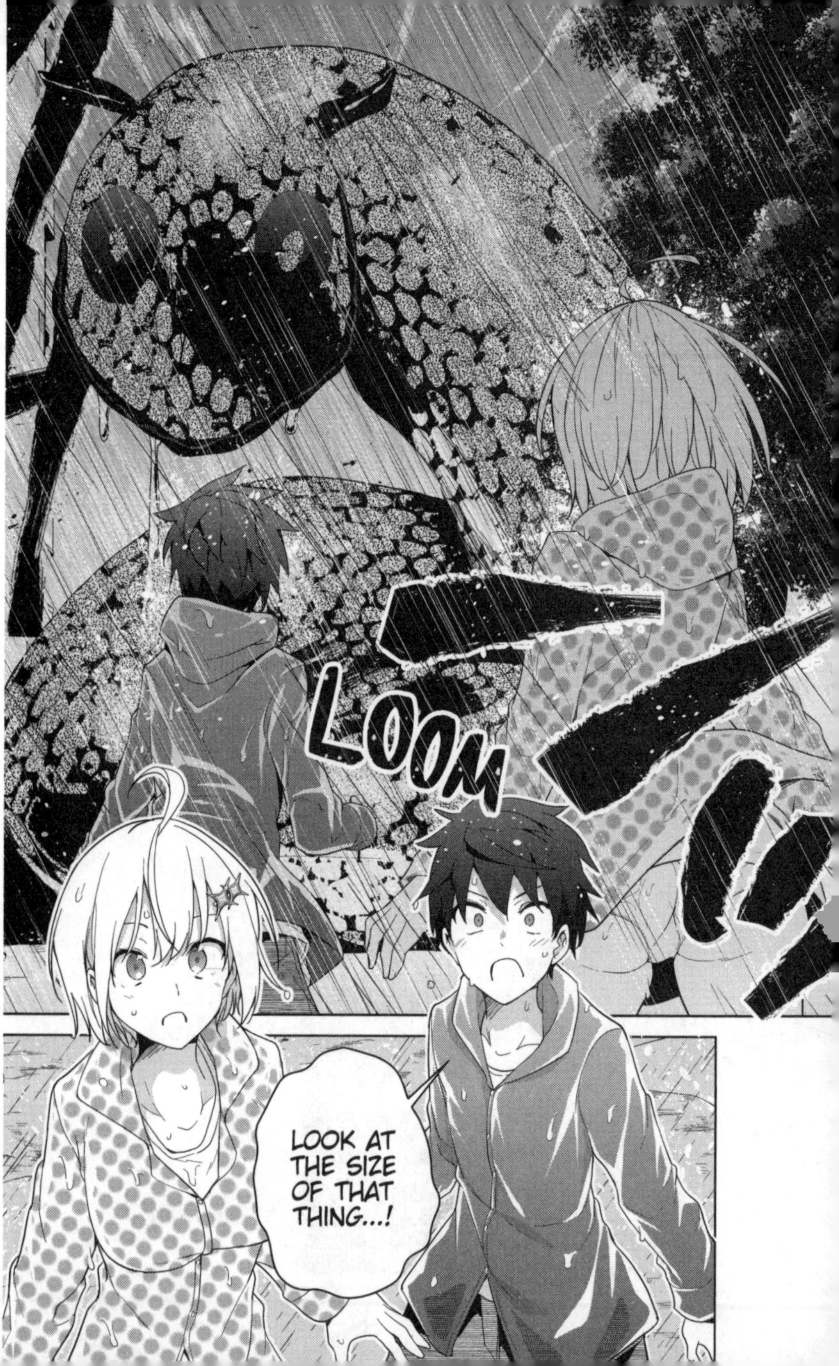
LOOM
LOOK AT THE SIZE OF THAT THING...!

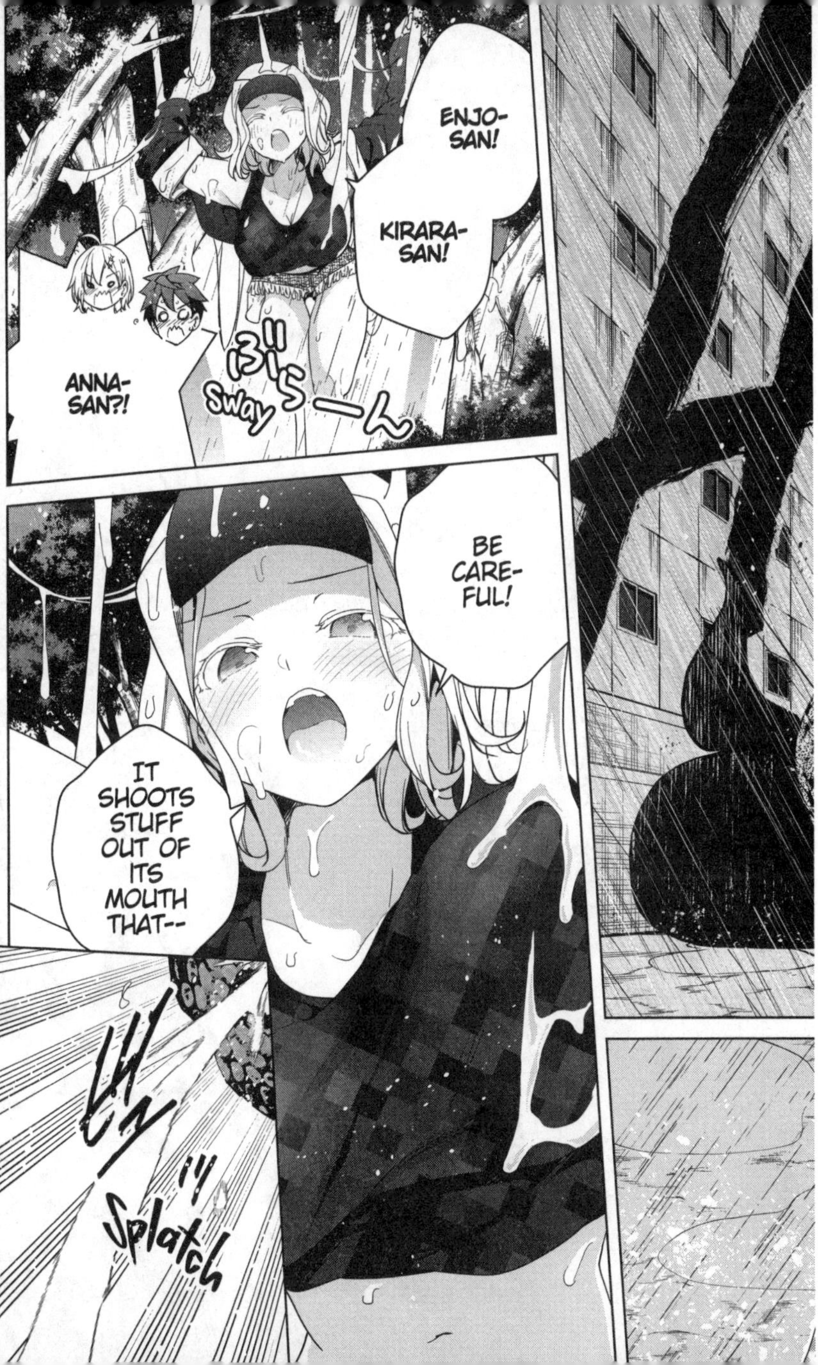
ENJO-SAN!
KIRARA-SAN!
ぶらーん
sway
ANNA-SAN?!
BE CARE-FUL!
IT SHOOTS STUFF OUT OF ITS MOUTH THAT--
Splatch

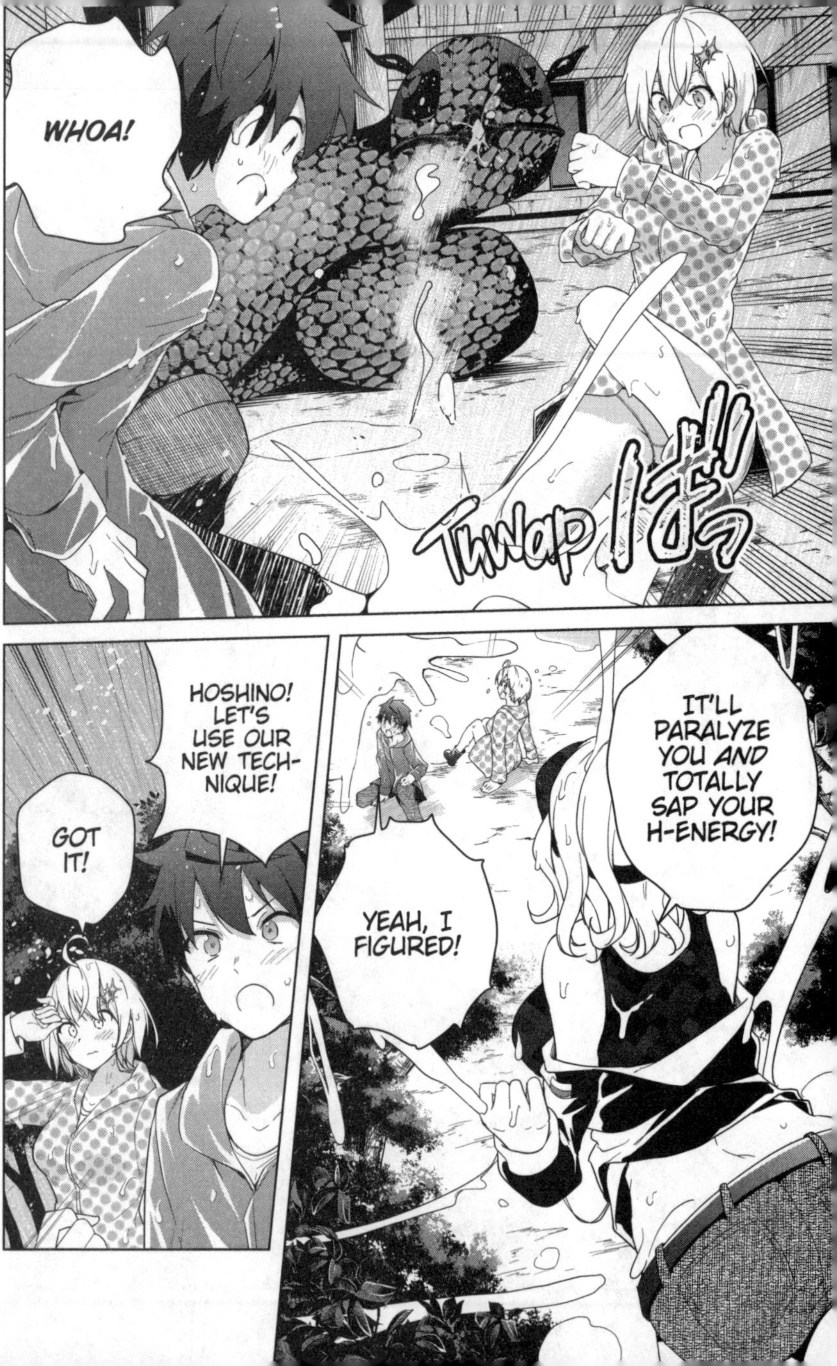
WHOA!
Thwap ばっ
IT'LL PARALYZE YOU AND TOTALLY SAP YOUR H-ENERGY!
YEAH, I FIGURED!
HOSHINO! LET'S USE OUR NEW TECH-NIQUE!
GOT IT!

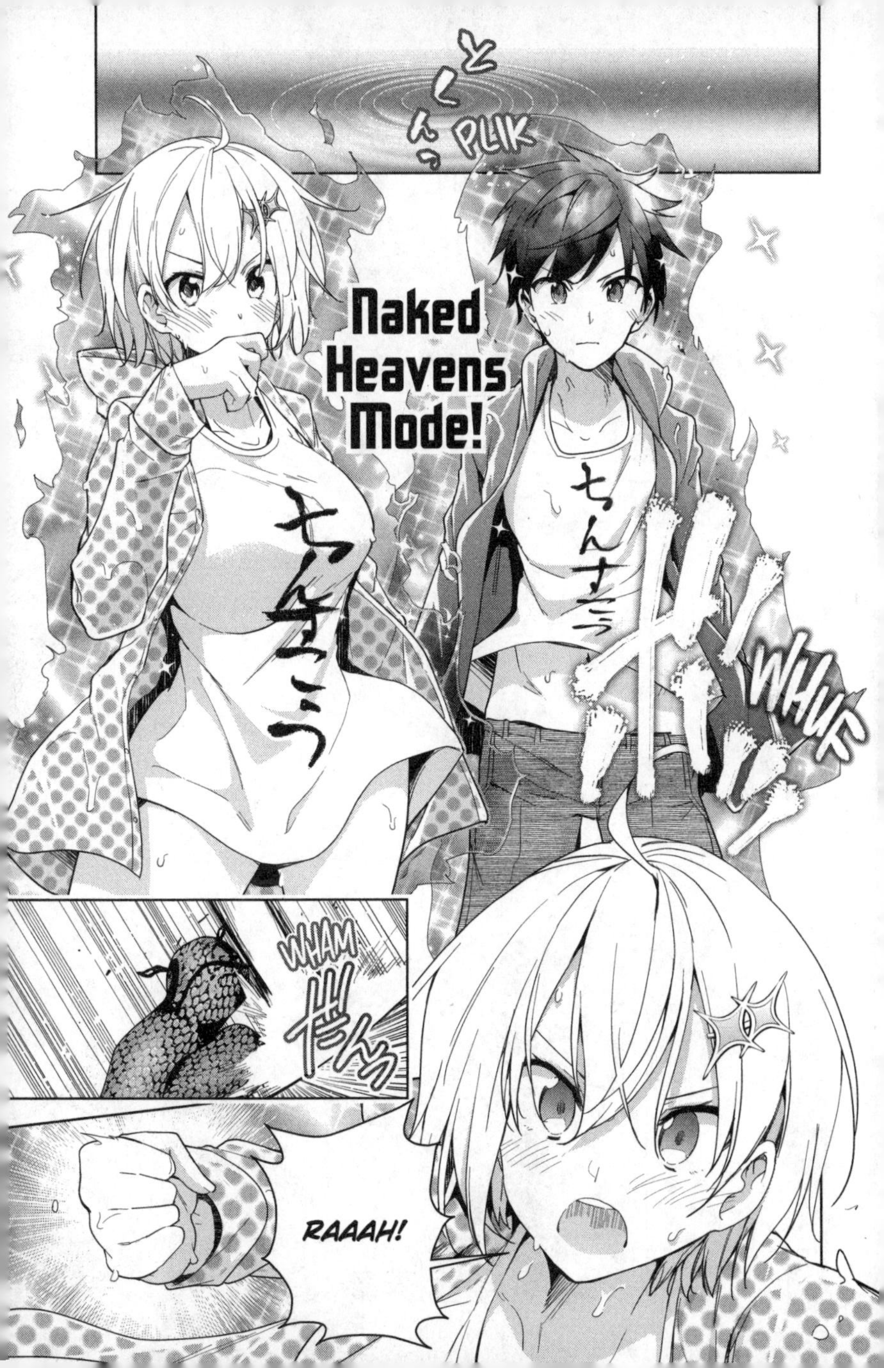
とくん
PLIK
Naked Heavens Mode!
WHUF
WHAM
RAAAH!

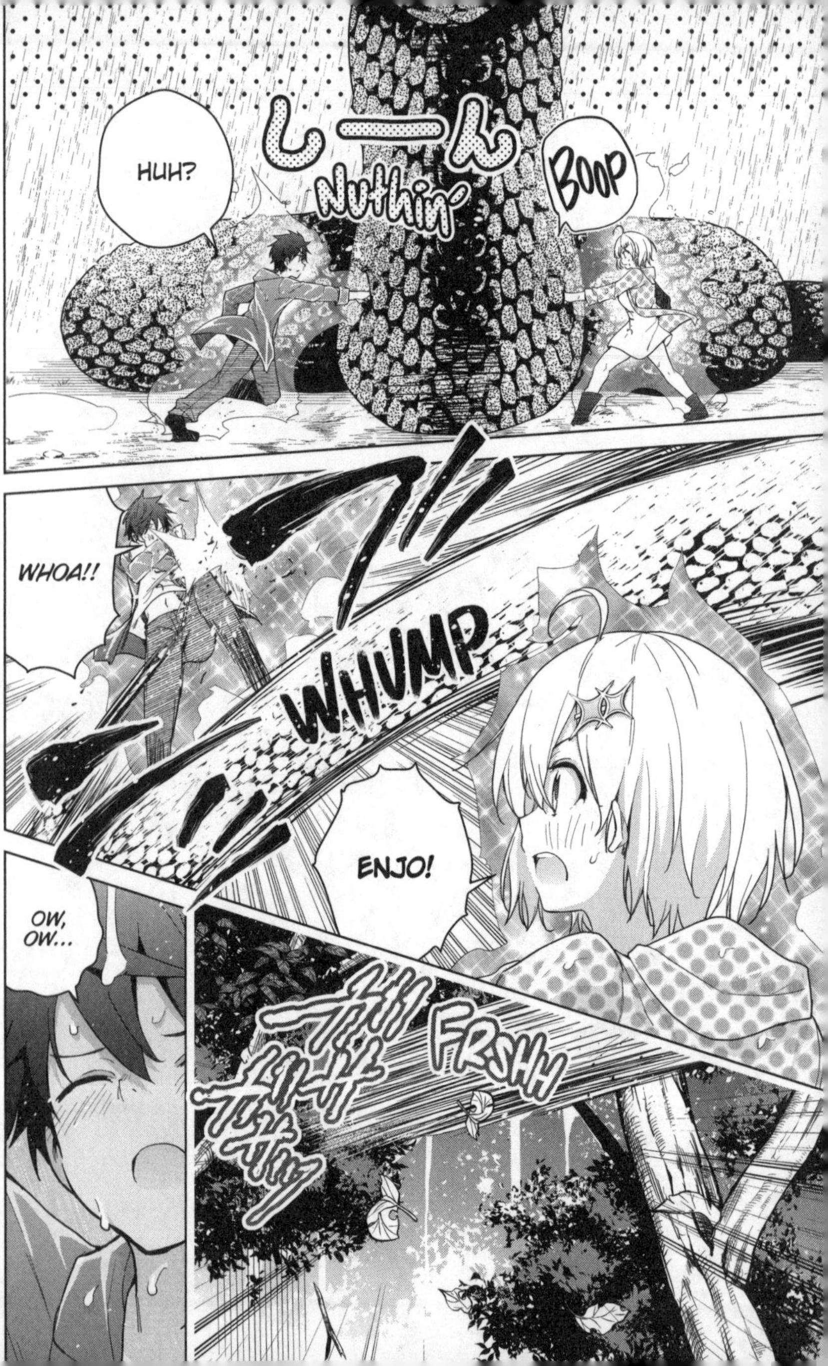

BOOP
しーん
Nuthin'
HUH?
WHUMP
WHOA!!
ENJO!
FRSHH
OW, OW...

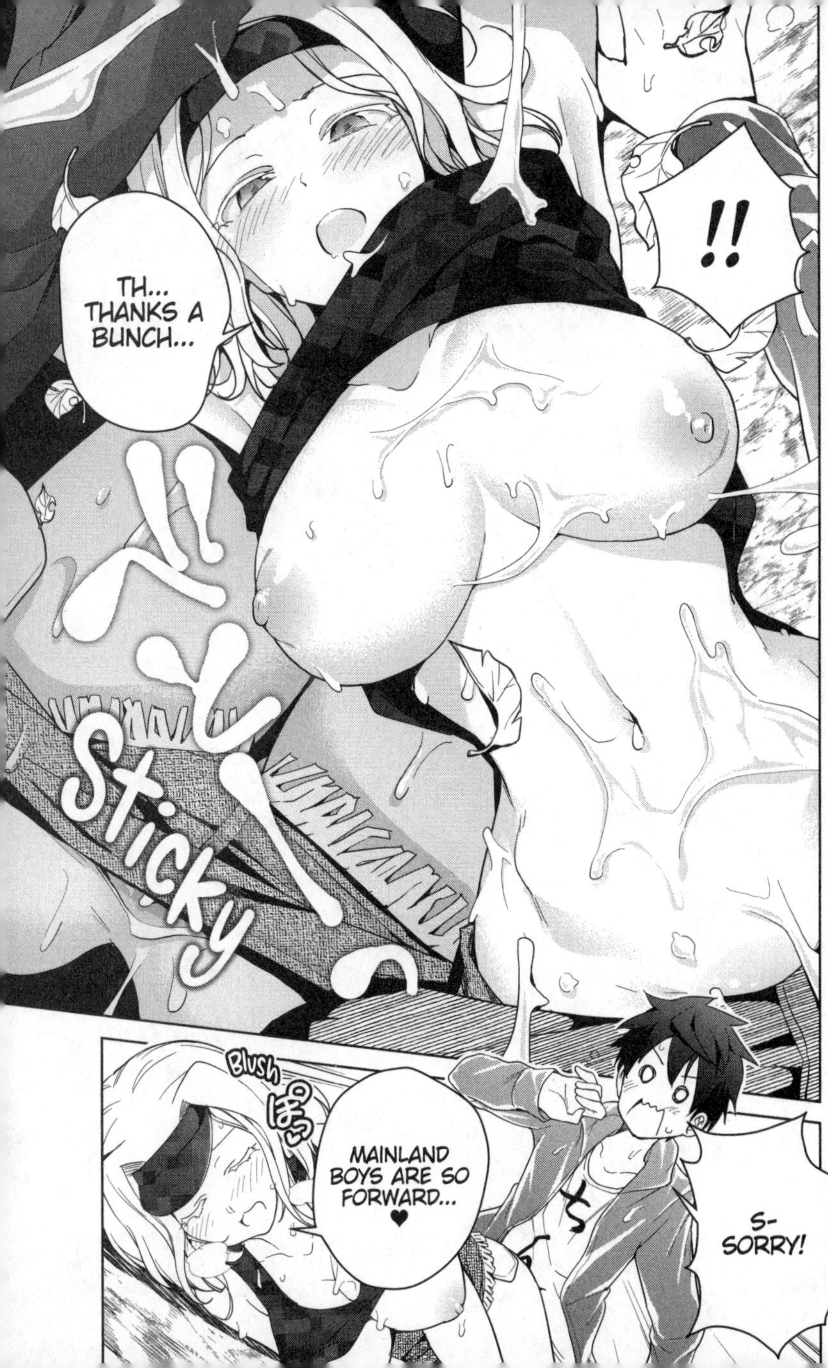
!!
TH... THANKS A BUNCH...
Sticky
S-SORRY!
Blush
ぽっ
MAINLAND BOYS ARE SO FORWARD... ♥

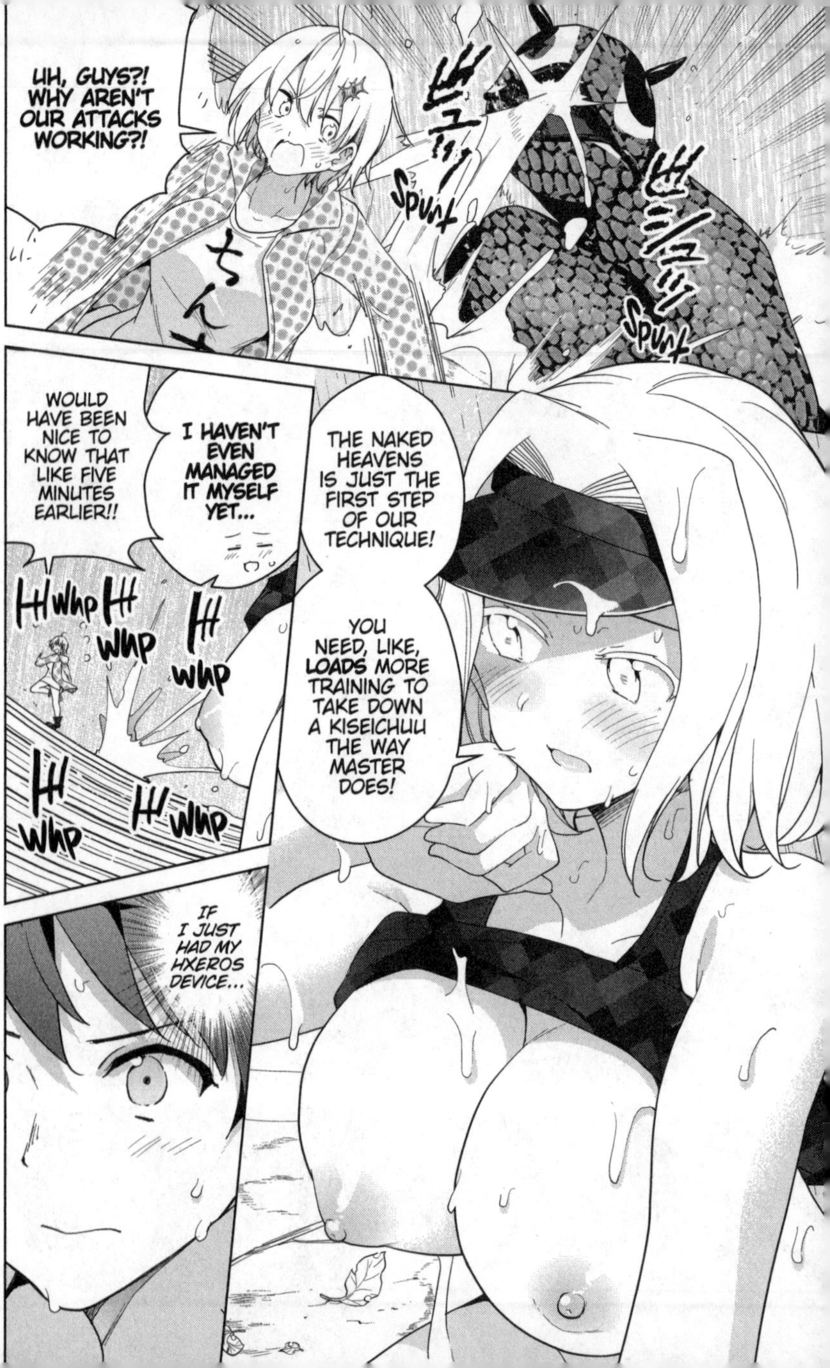
Spurt
Spurt
UH, GUYS?! WHY AREN'T OUR ATTACKS WORKING?!
THE NAKED HEAVENS IS JUST THE FIRST STEP OF OUR TECHNIQUE!
YOU NEED, LIKE, LOADS MORE TRAINING TO TAKE DOWN A KISEICHUU THE WAY MASTER DOES!
I HAVEN'T EVEN MANAGED IT MYSELF YET...
WOULD HAVE BEEN NICE TO KNOW THAT LIKE FIVE MINUTES EARLIER!!
whp
whp
whp
whp
whp
IF I JUST HAD MY HXEROS DEVICE...

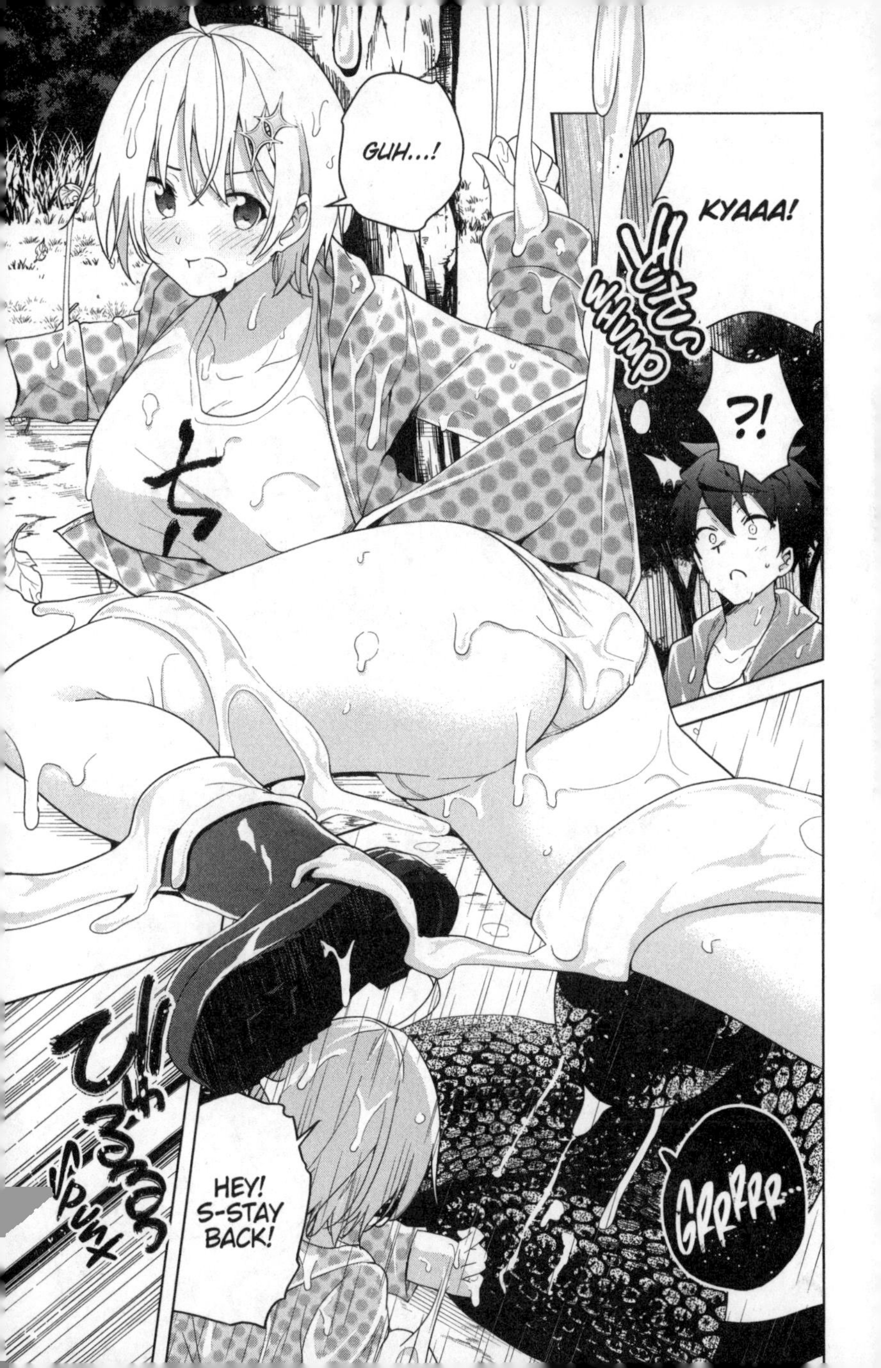
KYAAA!
WHUMP
?!
GUH...!
GRRRR...
HEY! S-STAY BACK!
SPUNT

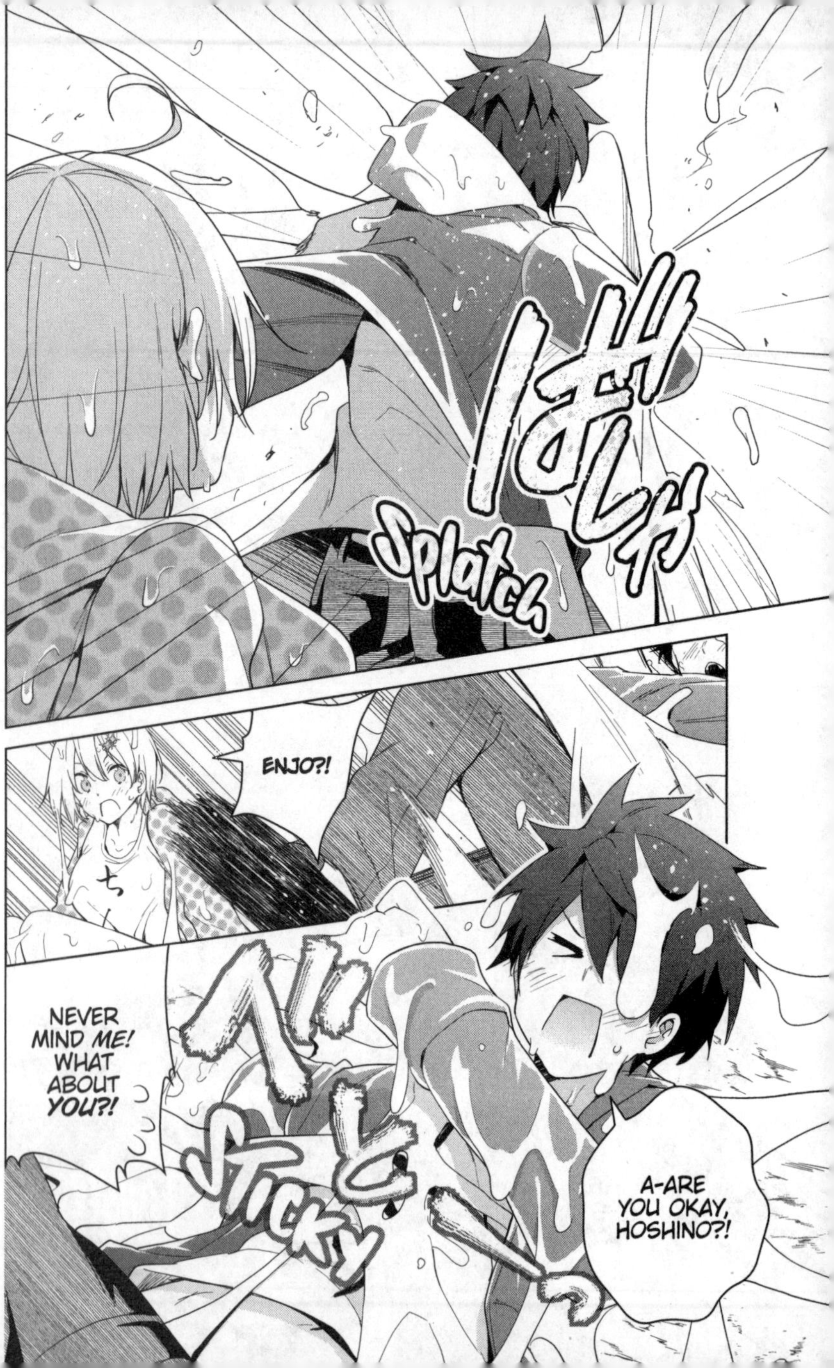
Splatch
ENJO?!
A-ARE YOU OKAY, HOSHINO?!
NEVER MIND ME! WHAT ABOUT YOU?!
Sticky

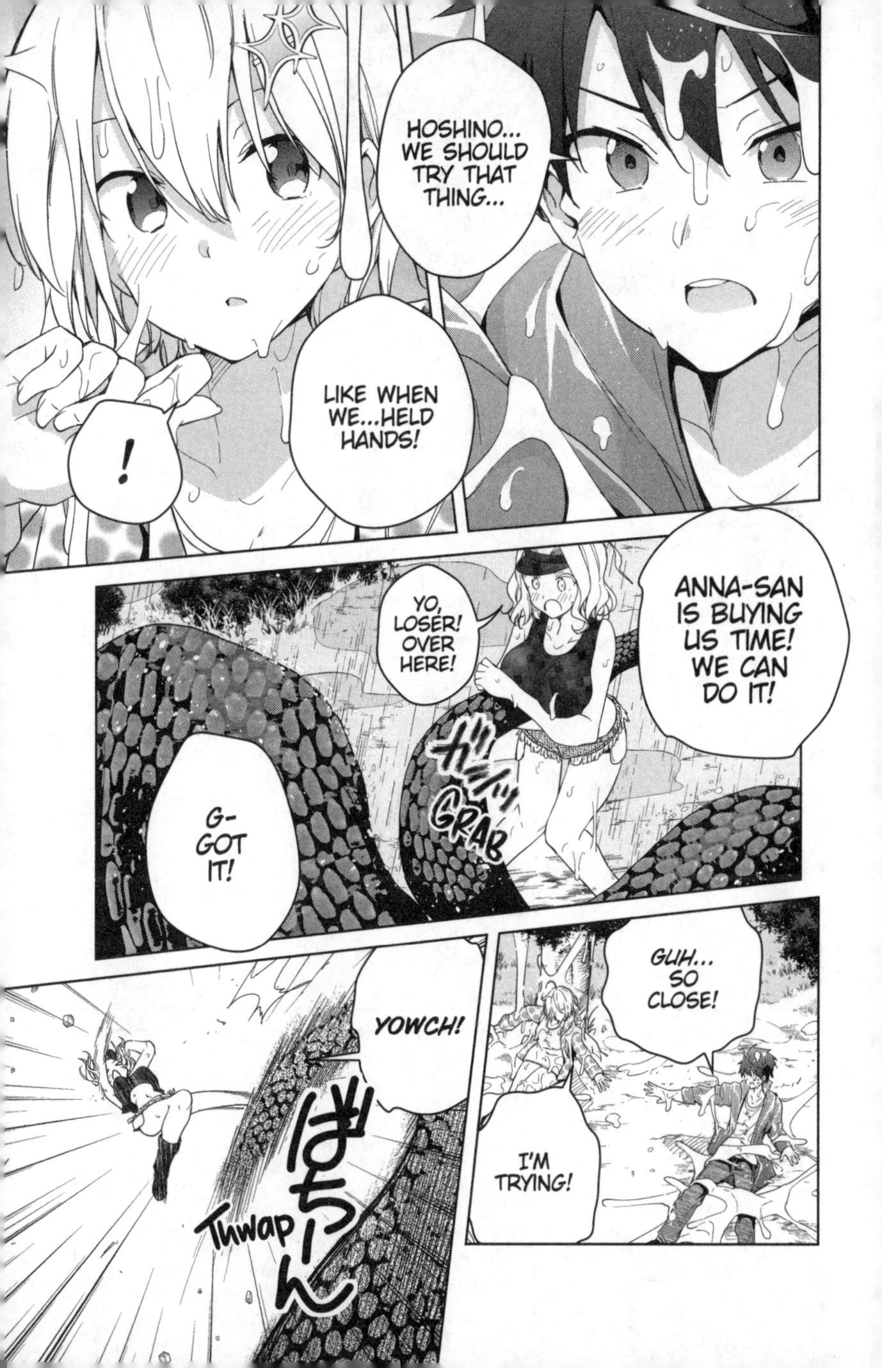
HOSHINO... WE SHOULD TRY THAT THING...
LIKE WHEN WE...HELD HANDS!
!
ANNA-SAN IS BUYING US TIME! WE CAN DO IT!
YO, LOSER! OVER HERE!
GRAB
G-GOT IT!
GUH... SO CLOSE!
I'M TRYING!
YOWCH!
Thwap

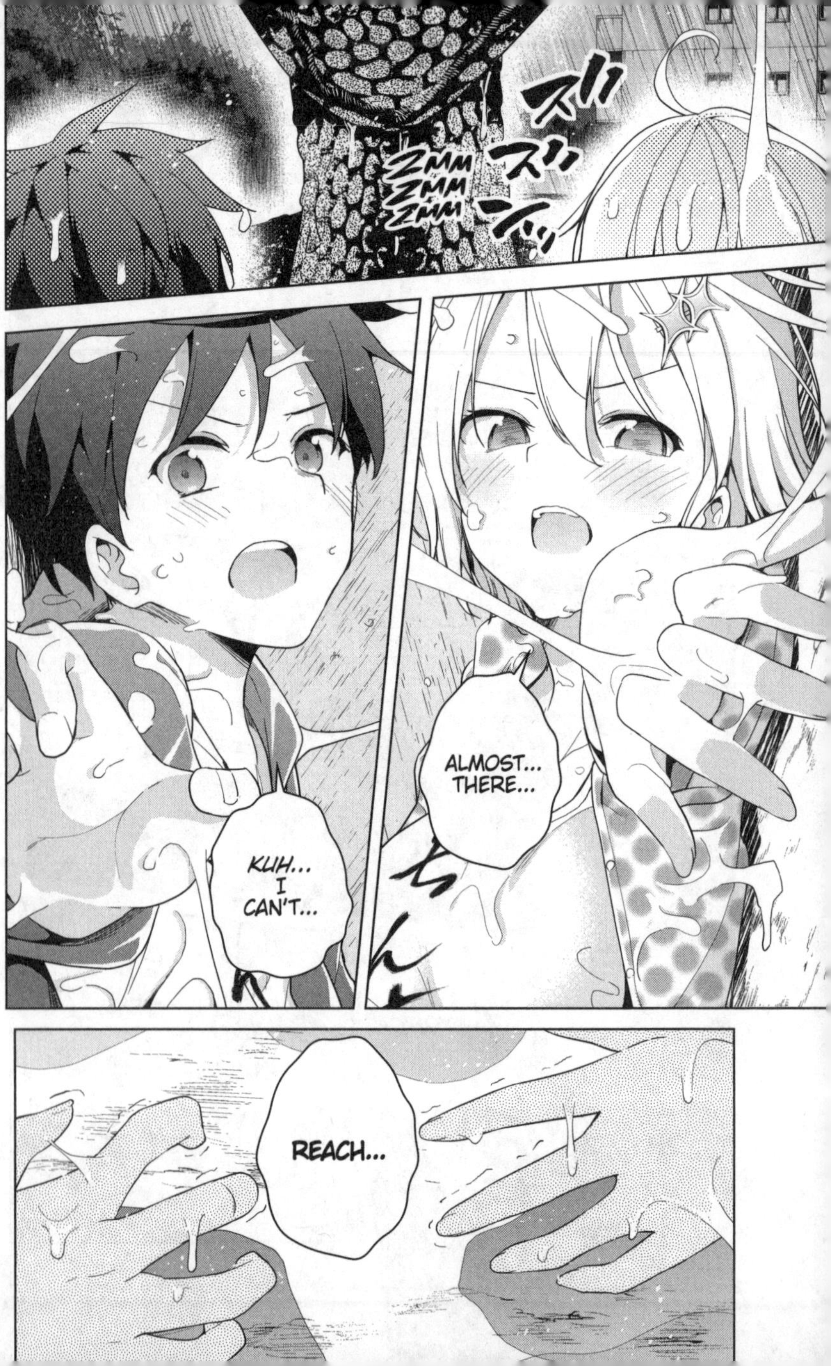
ZMMM
ZMMM
ZMMM
ALMOST... THERE...
KUH... I CAN'T...
REACH...

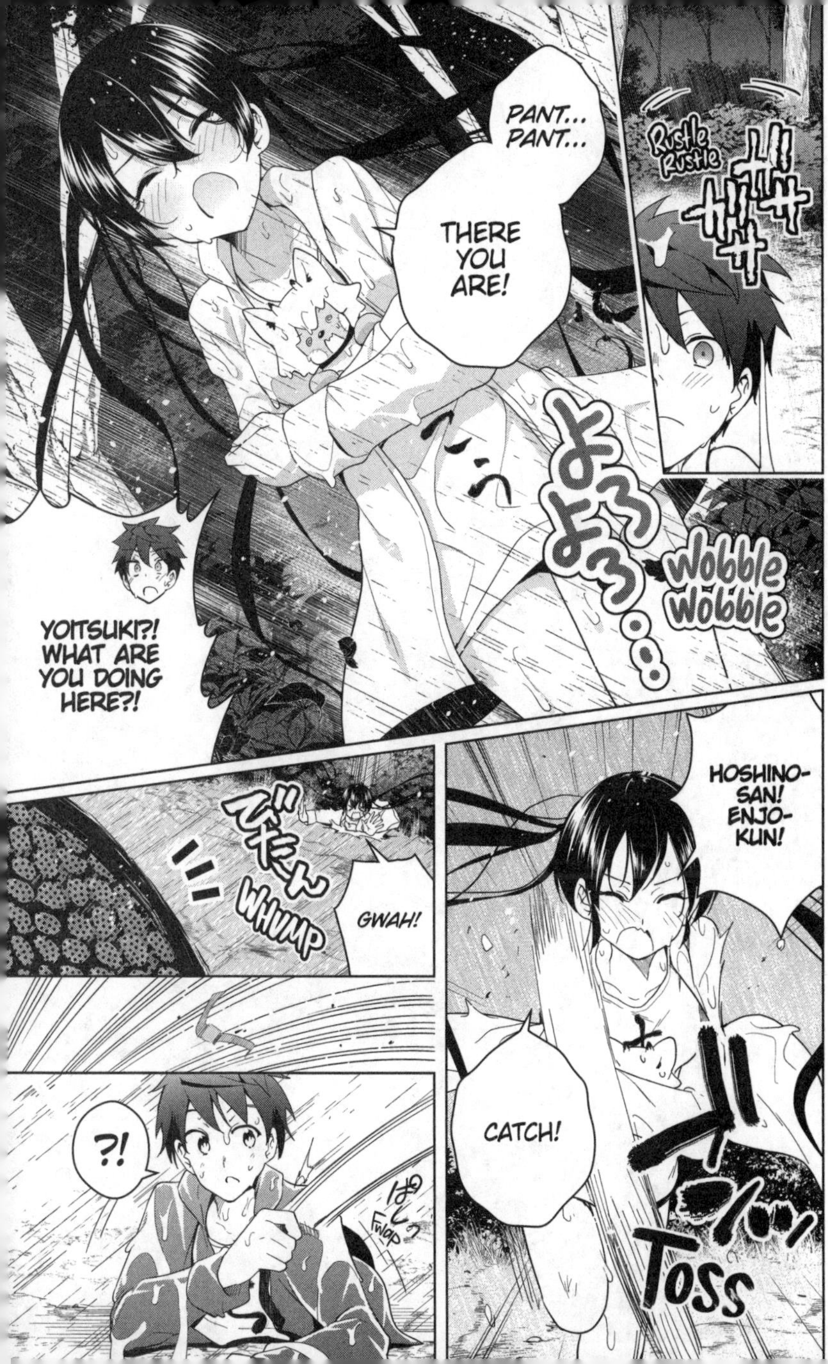

Rustle Rustle
PANT... PANT...
THERE YOU ARE!
よろよろ…
Wobble Wobble
YOITSUKI?! WHAT ARE YOU DOING HERE?!
HOSHINO-SAN! ENJO-KUN!
CATCH!
Toss
びたん
WHUMP
GWAH!
?!
ぱしっ
Fwap

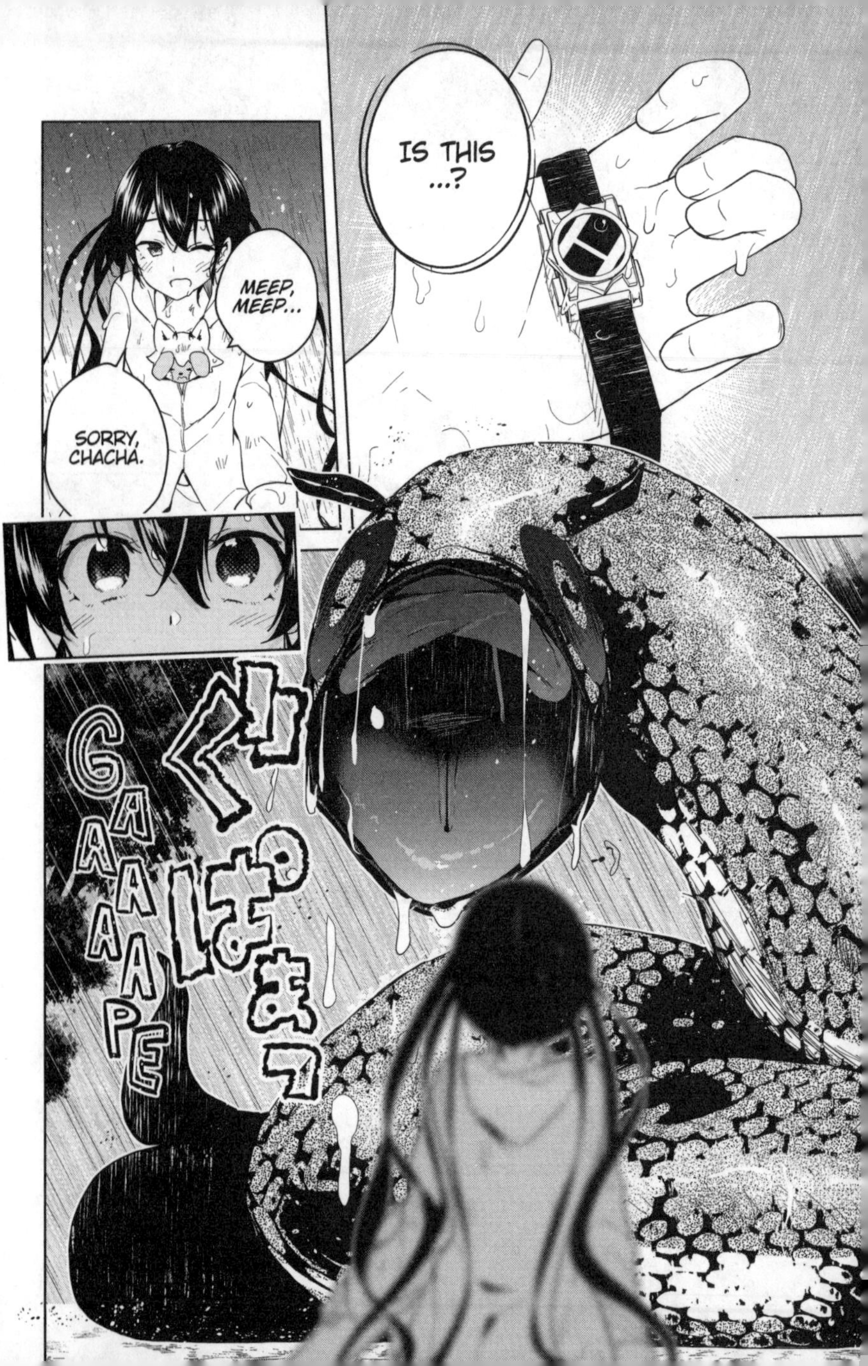
IS THIS ...?
MEEP, MEEP...
SORRY, CHACHA.
GAAAAAPE

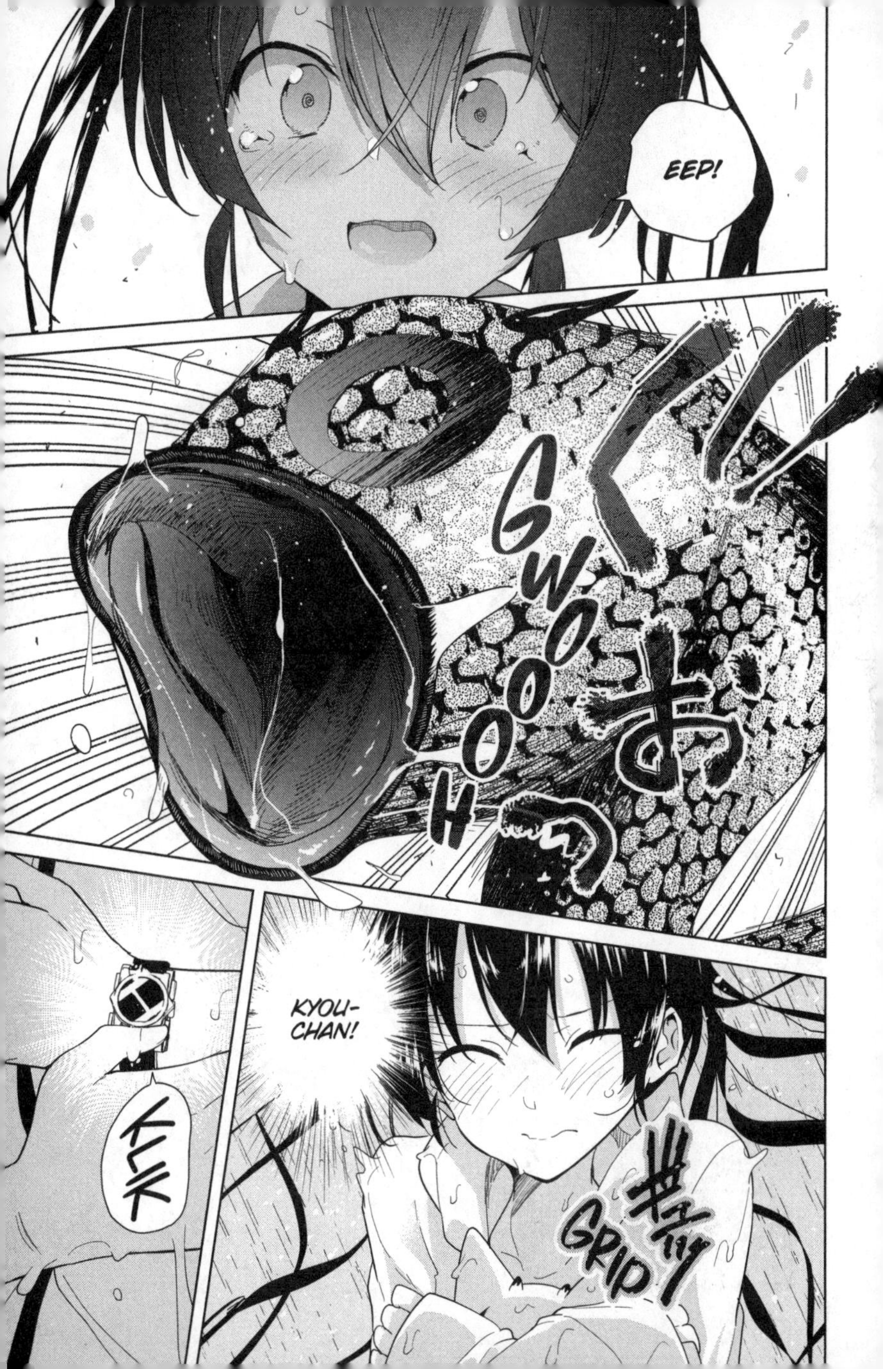
EEP!
GWOOOOH
KYOU-CHAN!
GRIP
KLIK

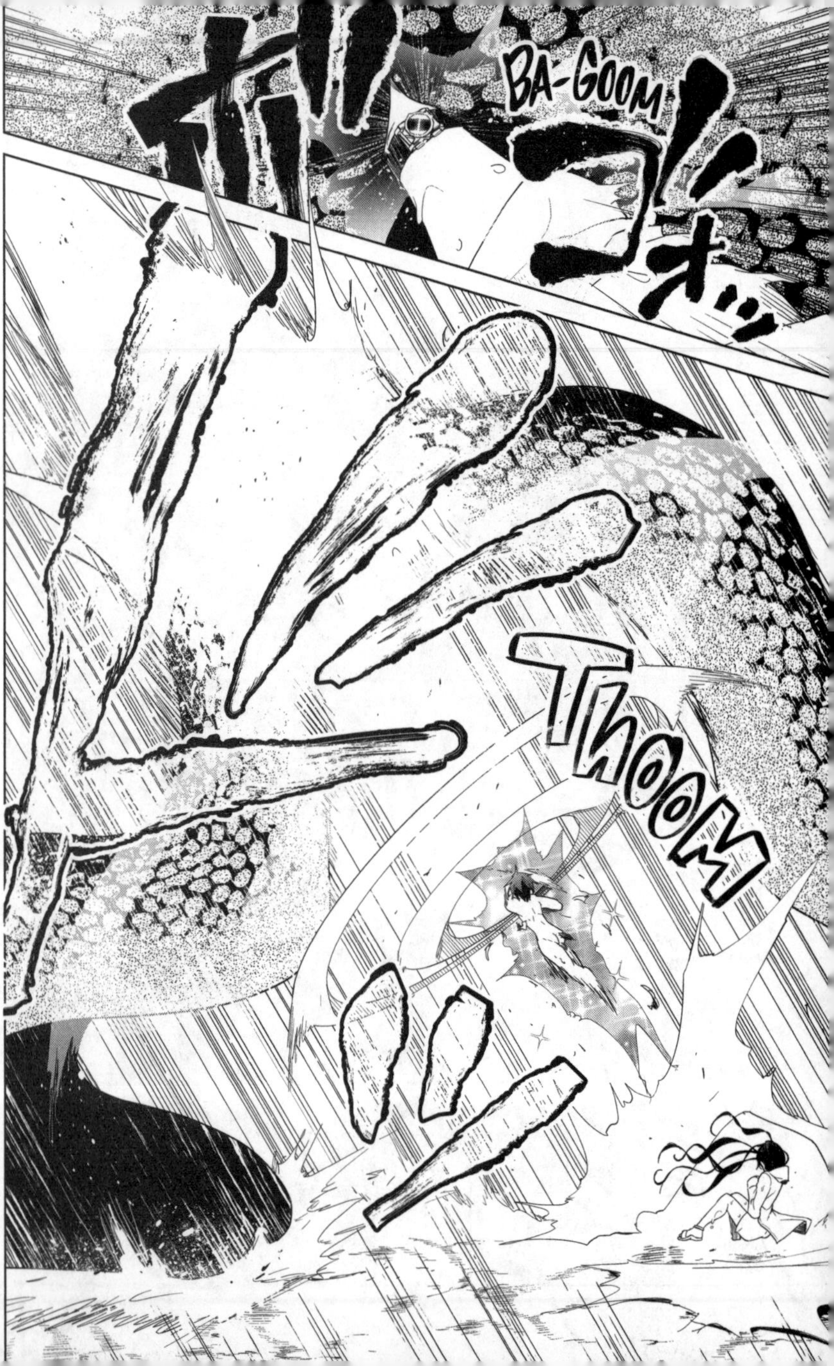
BA-GOOM
THOOM

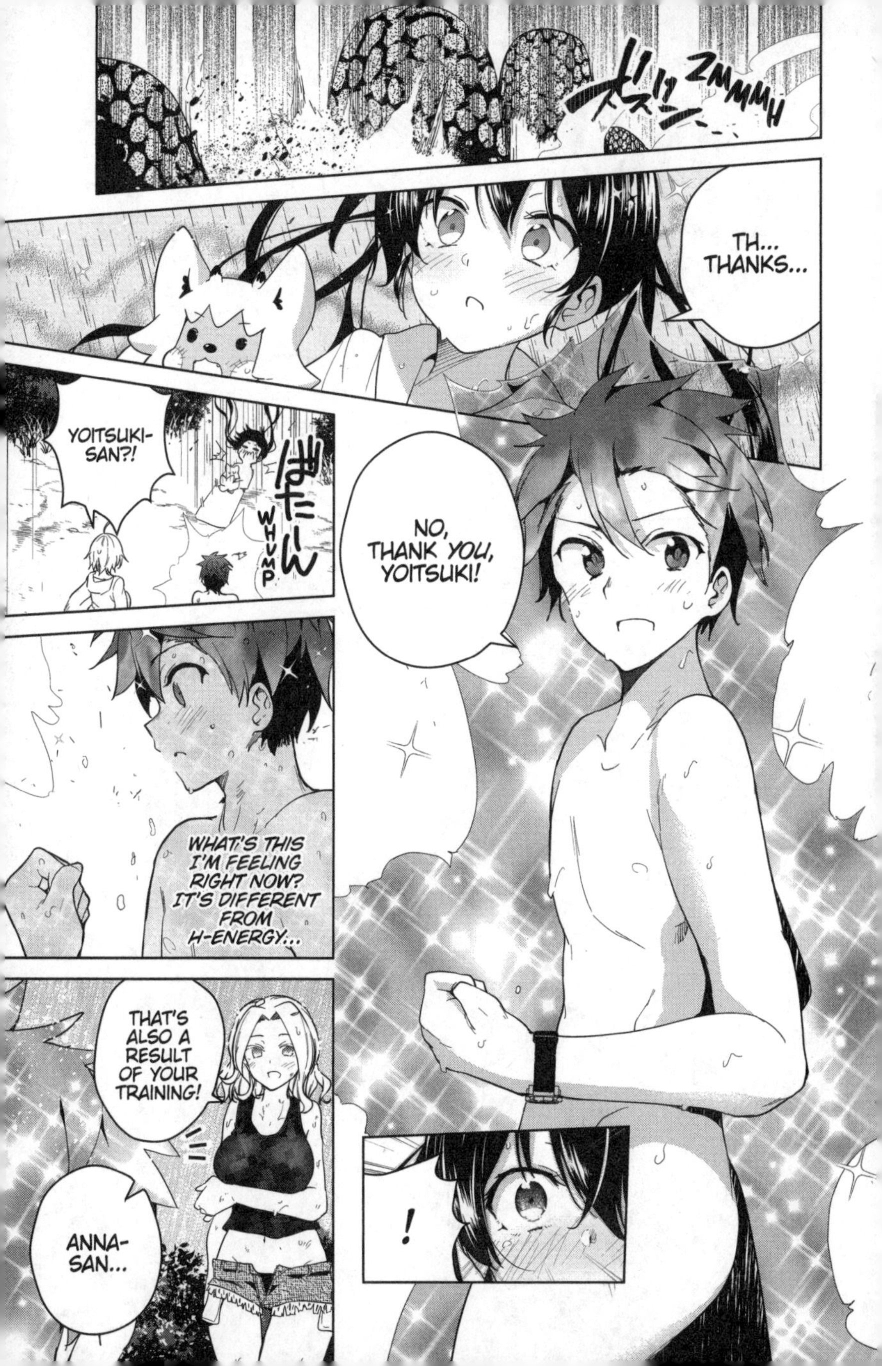
ZMMMMH
TH... THANKS...
NO, THANK YOU, YOITSUKI!
!
YOITSUKI-SAN?!
WHUMP
WHAT'S THIS I'M FEELING RIGHT NOW? IT'S DIFFERENT FROM H-ENERGY...
THAT'S ALSO A RESULT OF YOUR TRAINING!
ANNA-SAN...

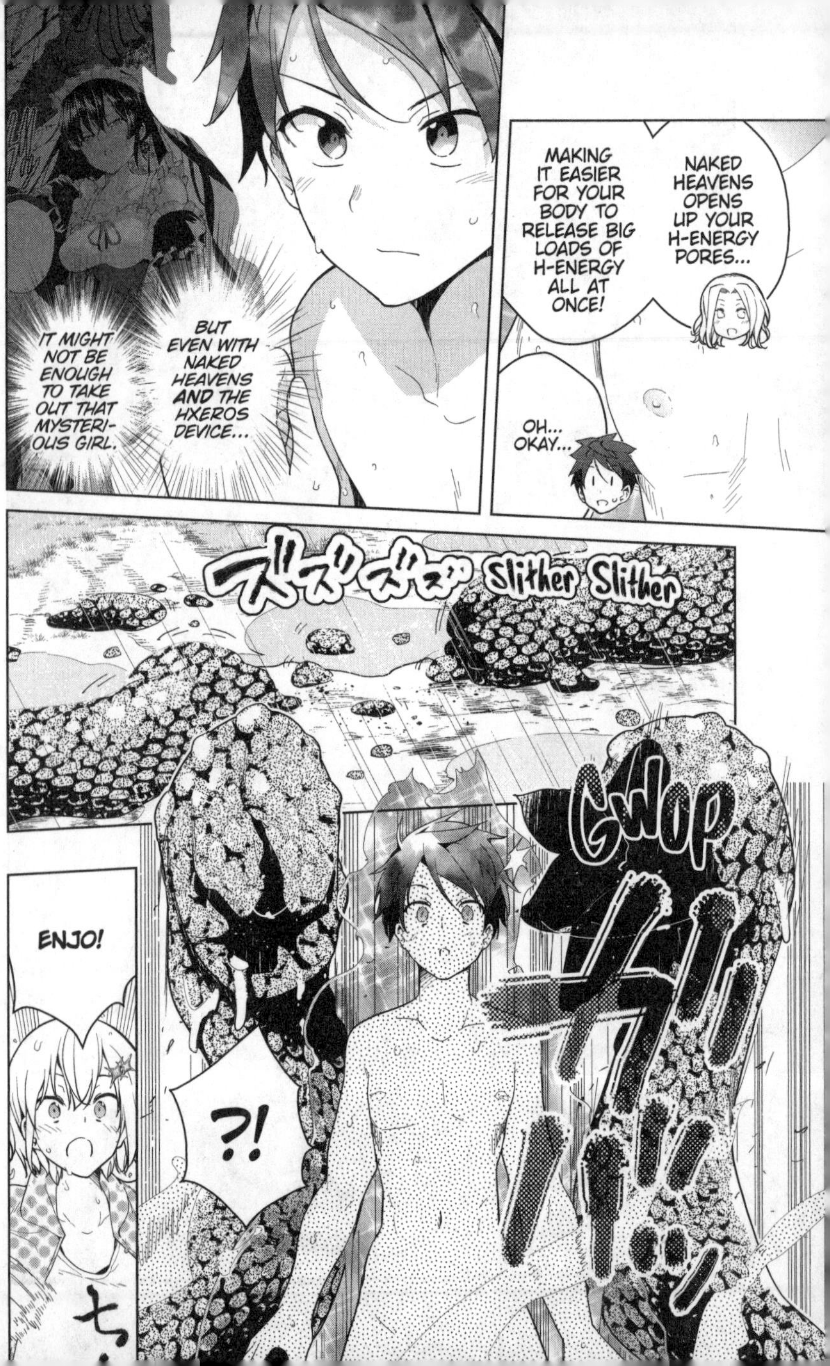
NAKED HEAVENS OPENS UP YOUR H-ENERGY PORES...
MAKING IT EASIER FOR YOUR BODY TO RELEASE BIG LOADS OF H-ENERGY ALL AT ONCE!
OH... OKAY...
BUT EVEN WITH NAKED HEAVENS AND THE HXEROS DEVICE...
IT MIGHT NOT BE ENOUGH TO TAKE OUT THAT MYSTERIOUS GIRL.
Slither Slither
GWOP
ENJO!
?!

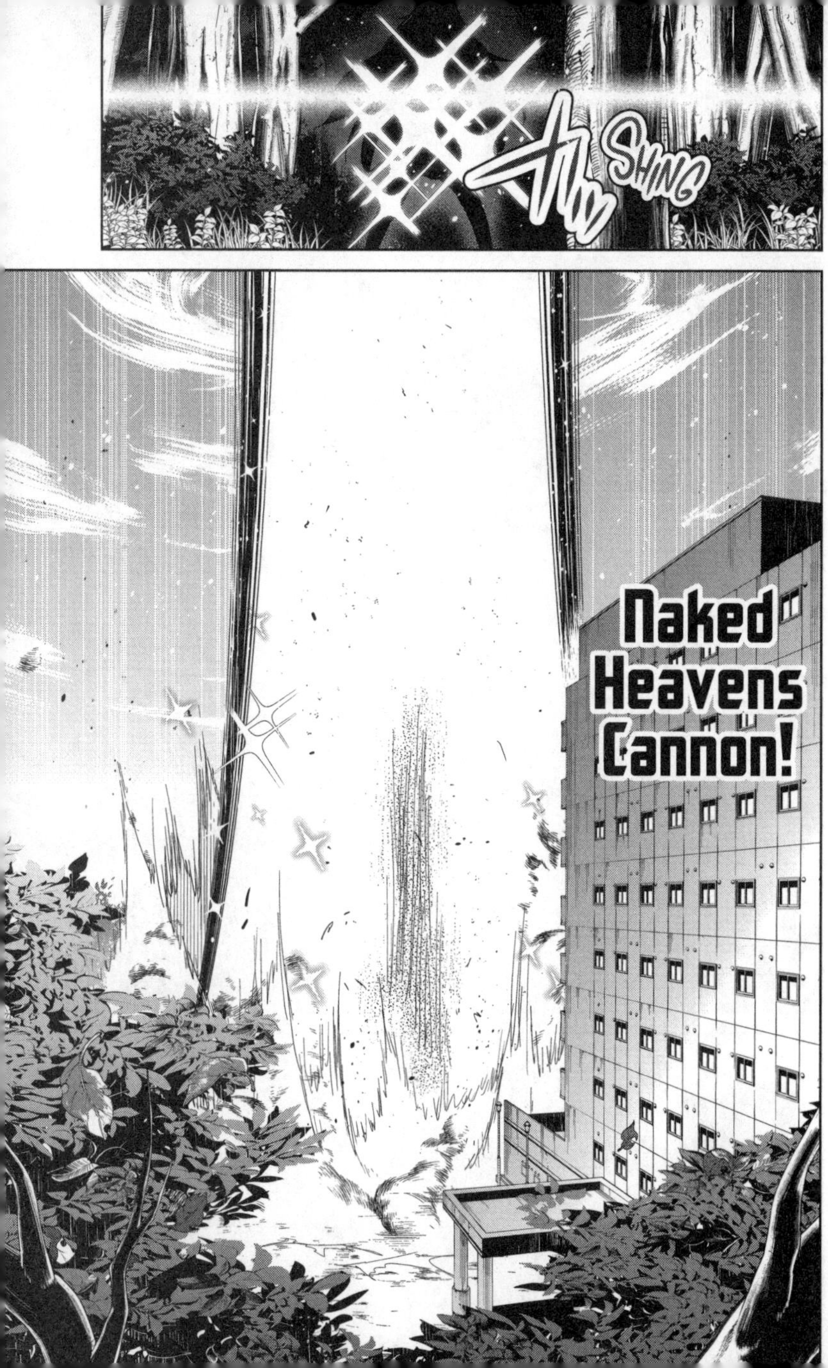
SHING
Naked Heavens Cannon!

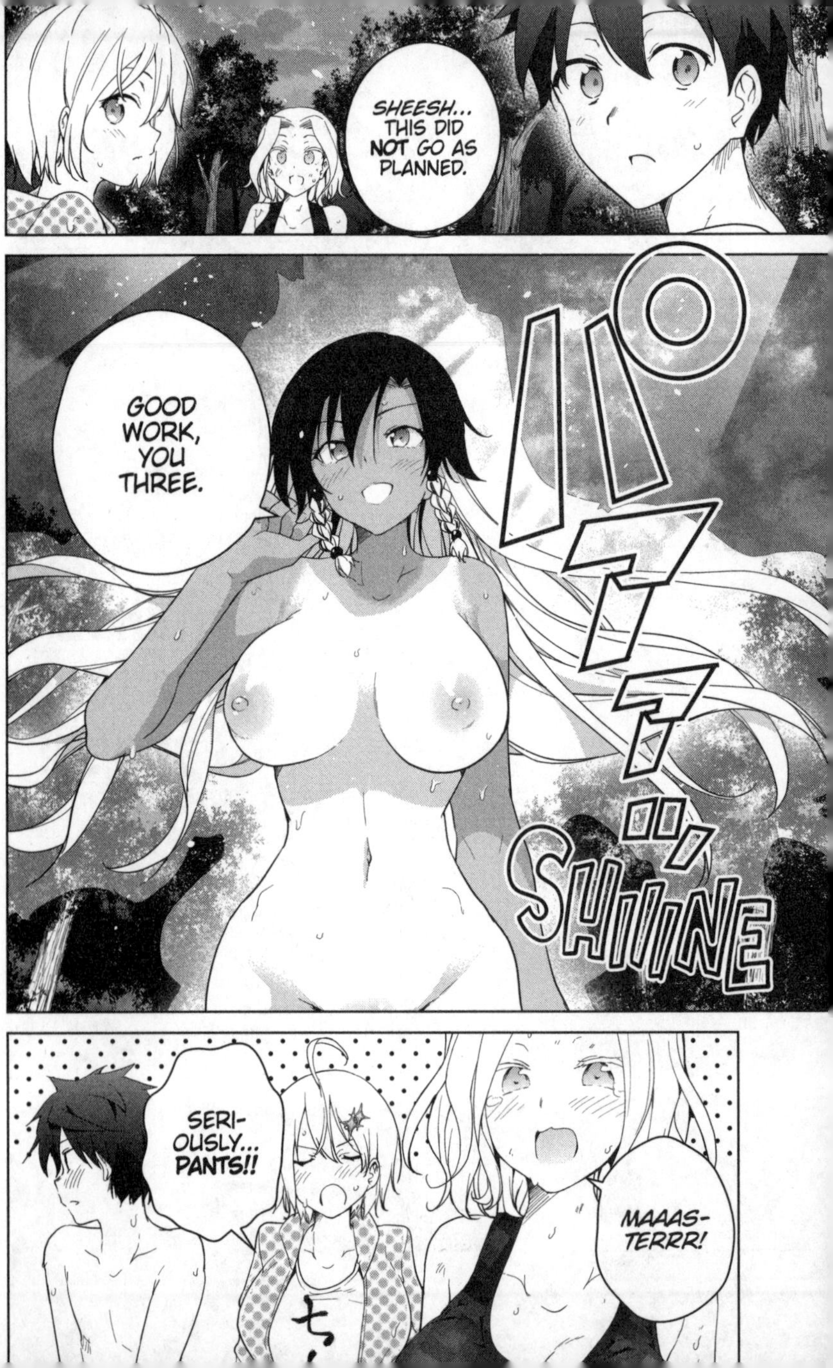
SHEESH... THIS DID NOT GO AS PLANNED.
GOOD WORK, YOU THREE.
SHIIINE
MAAAS-TERRR!
SERI-OUSLY... PANTS!!

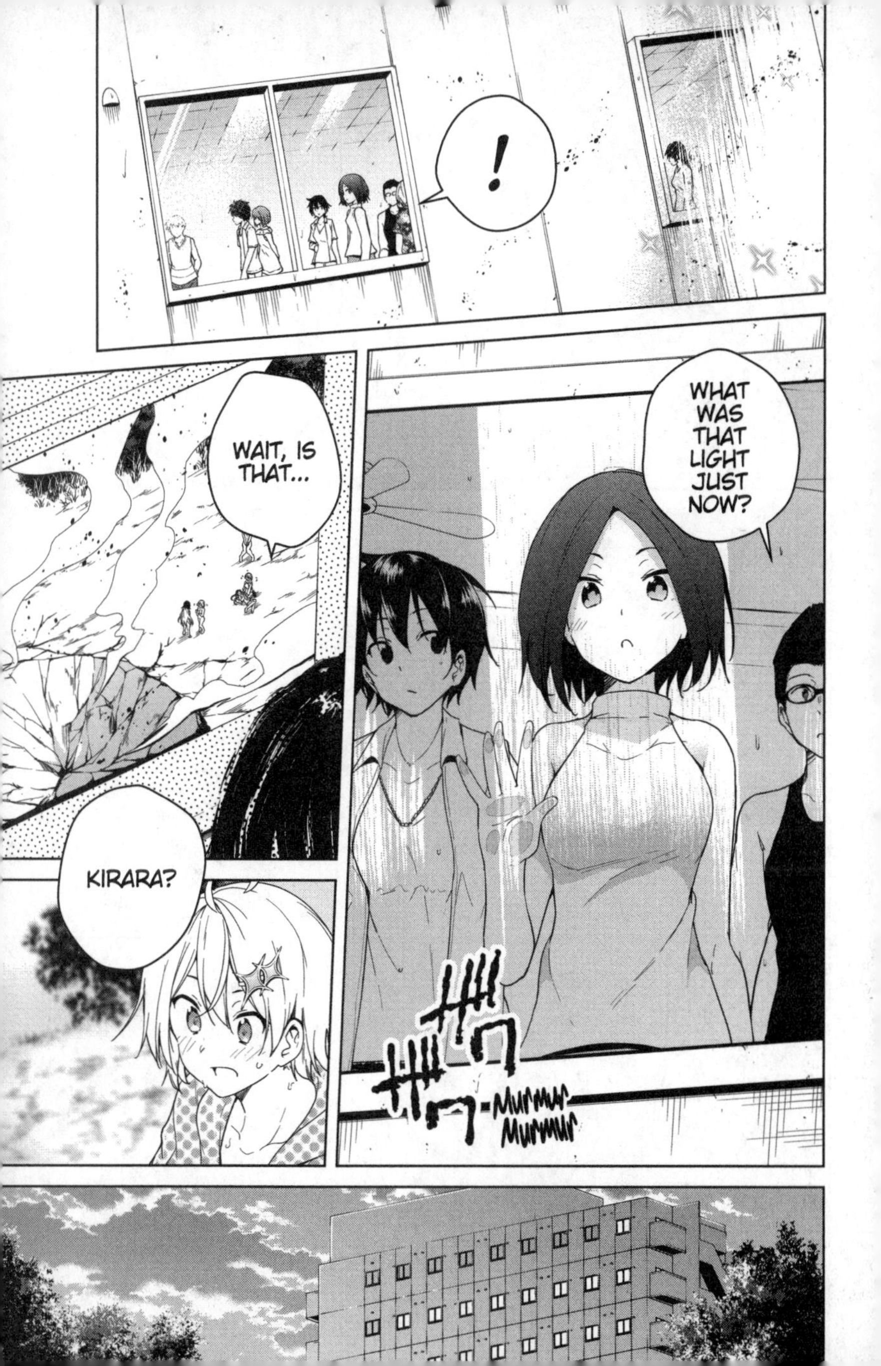
!
WHAT WAS THAT LIGHT JUST NOW?
Murmur Murmur
WAIT, IS THAT...
KIRARA?

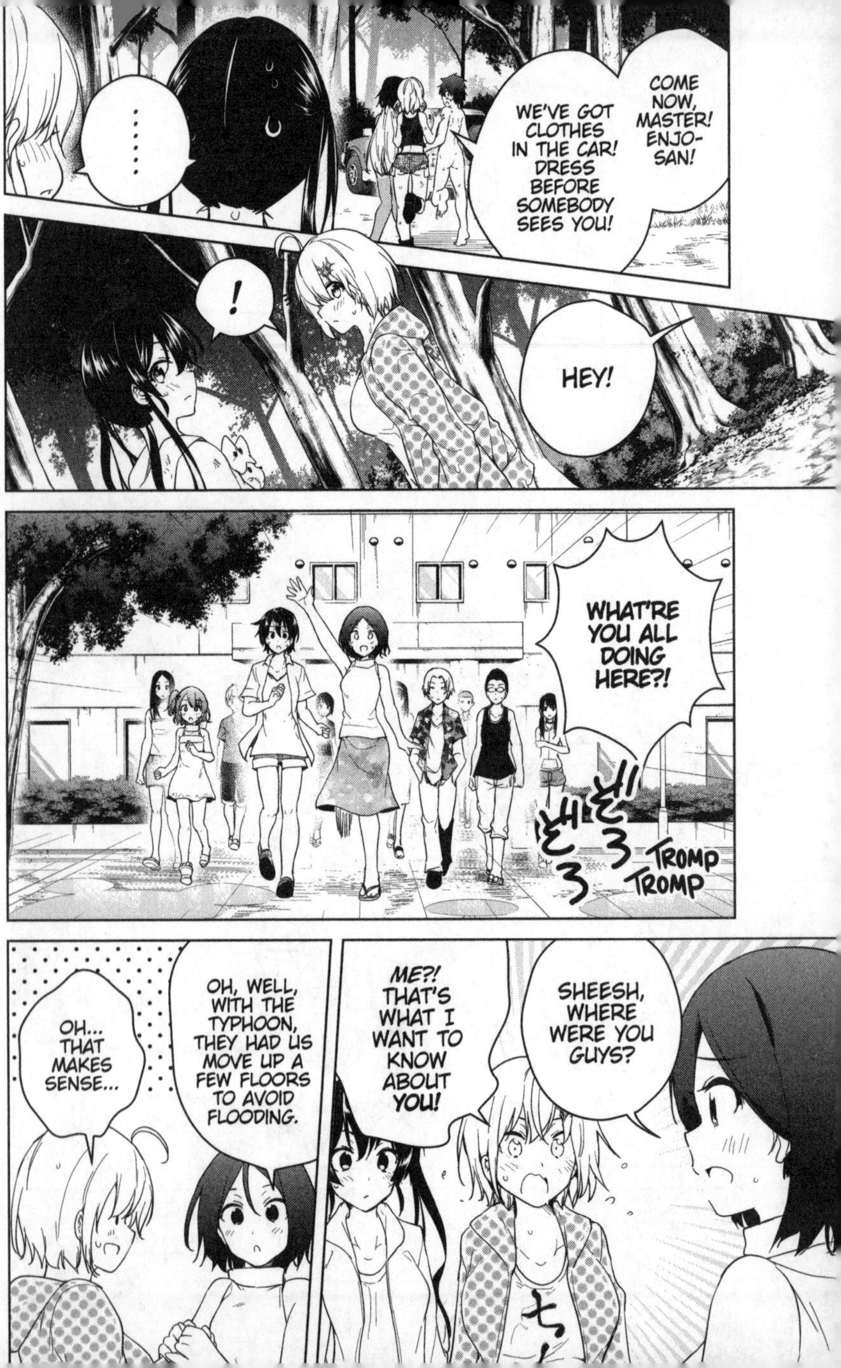
COME NOW, MASTER! ENJO-SAN!
WE'VE GOT CLOTHES IN THE CAR! DRESS BEFORE SOMEBODY SEES YOU!
......
HEY!
!
WHAT'RE YOU ALL DOING HERE?!
TROMP TROMP
SHEESH, WHERE WERE YOU GUYS?
ME?! THAT'S WHAT I WANT TO KNOW ABOUT YOU!
OH, WELL, WITH THE TYPHOON, THEY HAD US MOVE UP A FEW FLOORS TO AVOID FLOODING.
OH... THAT MAKES SENSE...

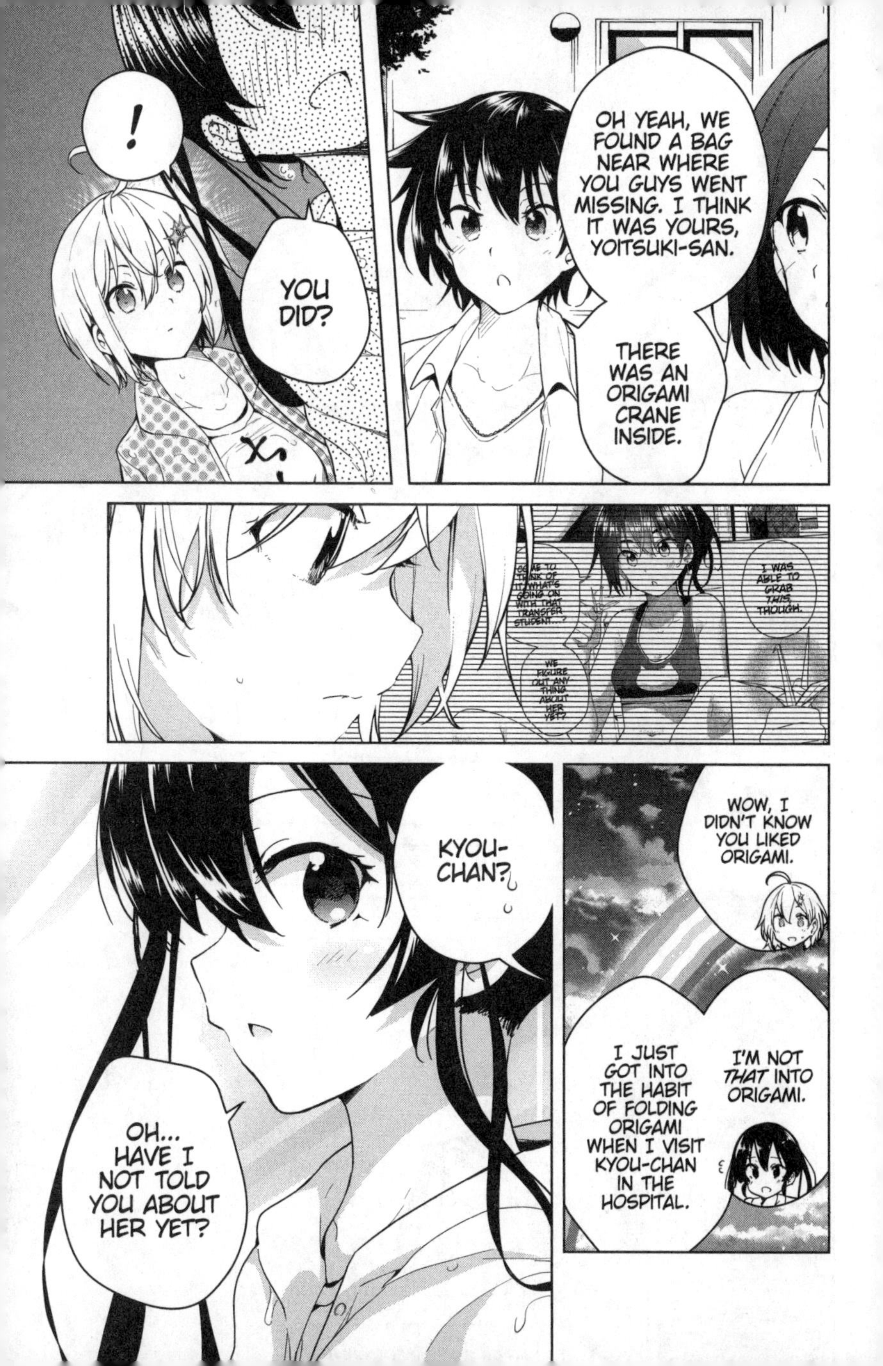
OH YEAH, WE FOUND A BAG NEAR WHERE YOU GUYS WENT MISSING. I THINK IT WAS YOURS, YOITSUKI-SAN.
THERE WAS AN ORIGAMI CRANE INSIDE.
!
YOU DID?
I WAS ABLE TO GRAB THIS, THOUGH.
COME TO THINK OF IT, WHAT'S GOING ON WITH THAT TRANSFER STUDENT...?
WE FIGURE OUT ANY-THING ABOUT HER YET?
WOW, I DIDN'T KNOW YOU LIKED ORIGAMI.
I'M NOT *THAT* INTO ORIGAMI.
I JUST GOT INTO THE HABIT OF FOLDING ORIGAMI WHEN I VISIT KYOU-CHAN IN THE HOSPITAL.
KYOU-CHAN?
OH... HAVE I NOT TOLD YOU ABOUT HER YET?

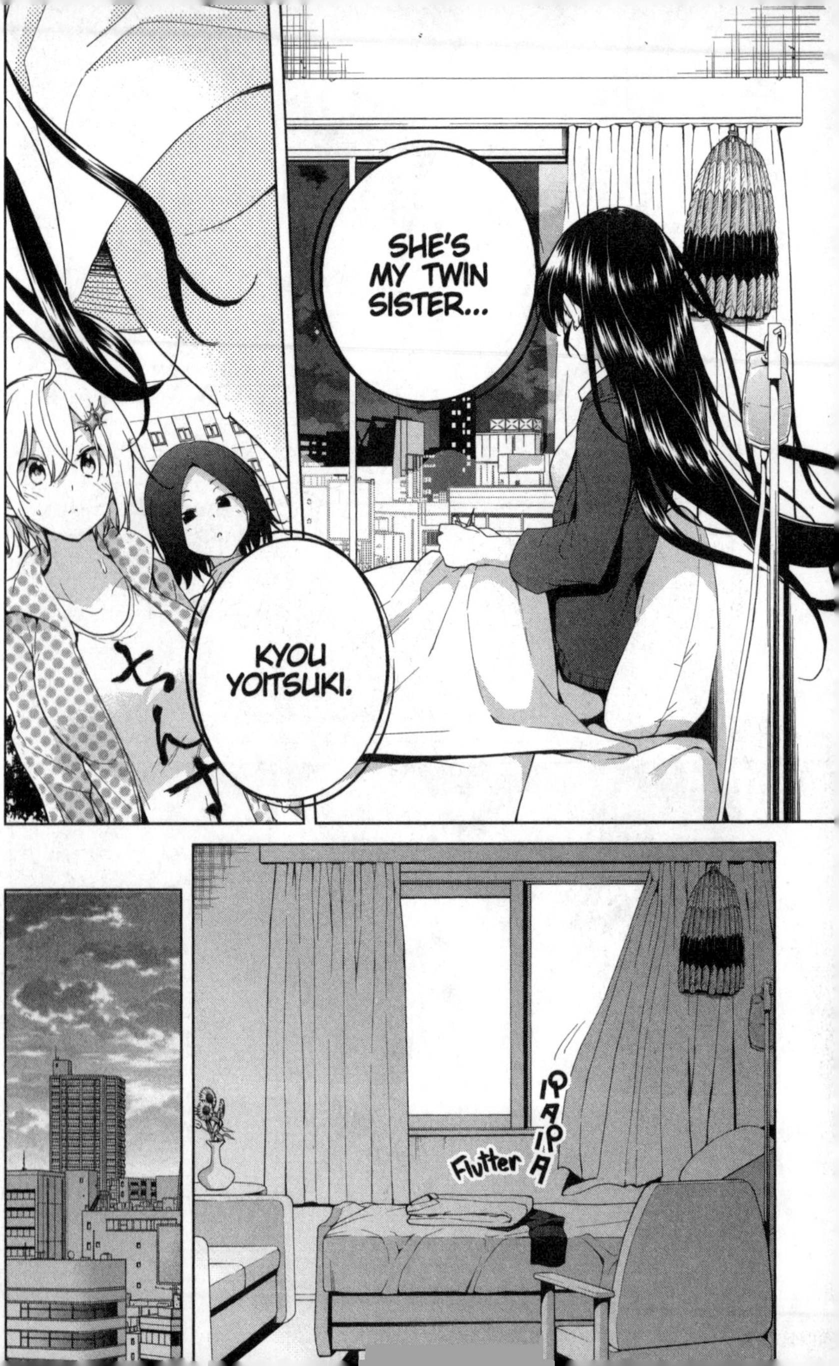
SHE'S MY TWIN SISTER...
KYOU YOITSUKI.
Flutter

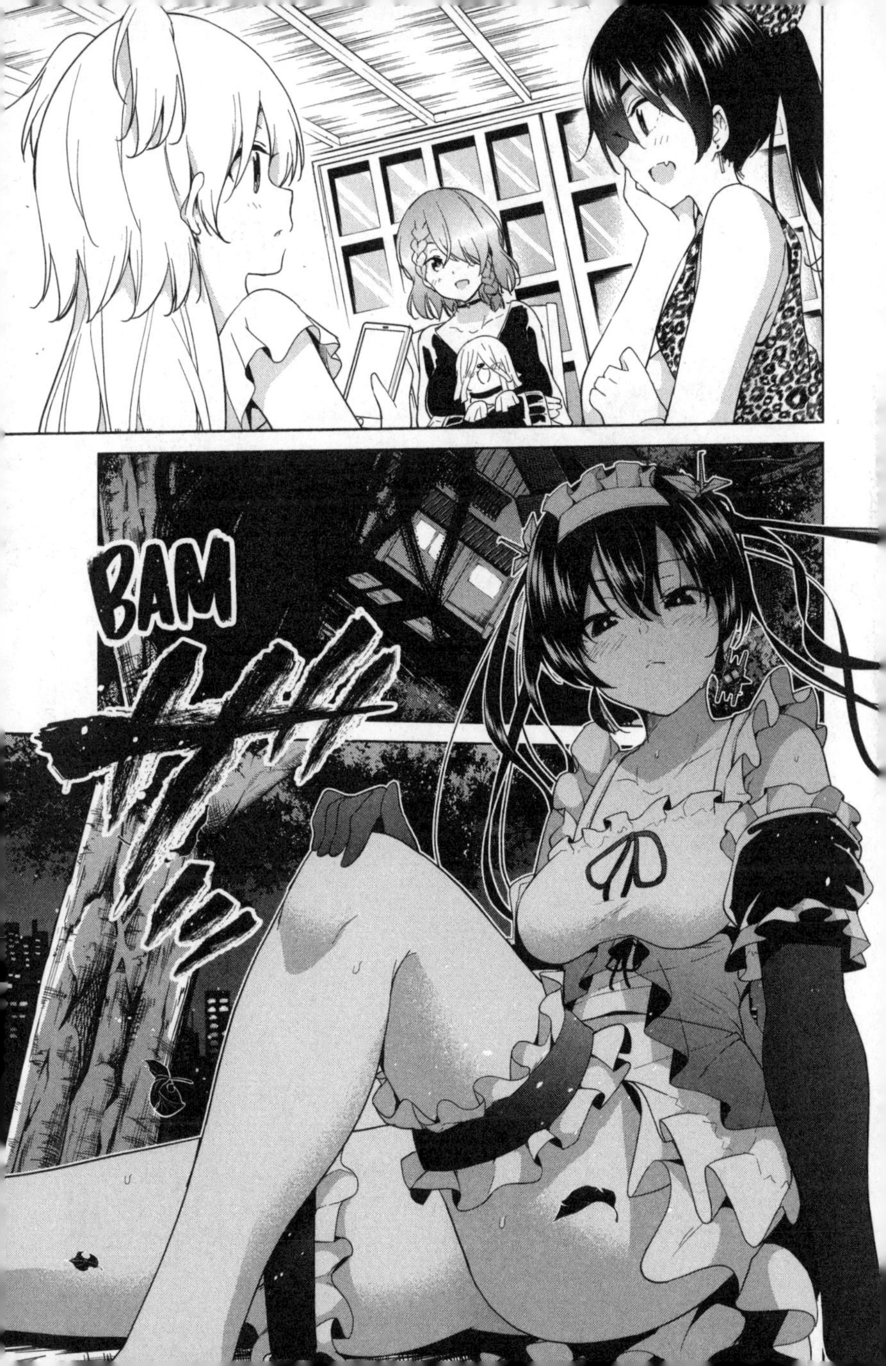
BAM

Extra Gallery

SUPER HxEROS

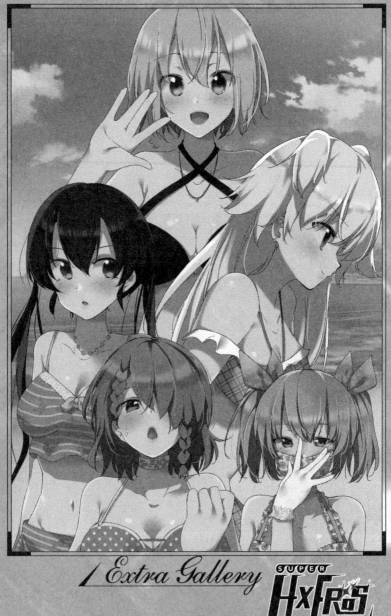

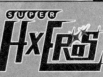

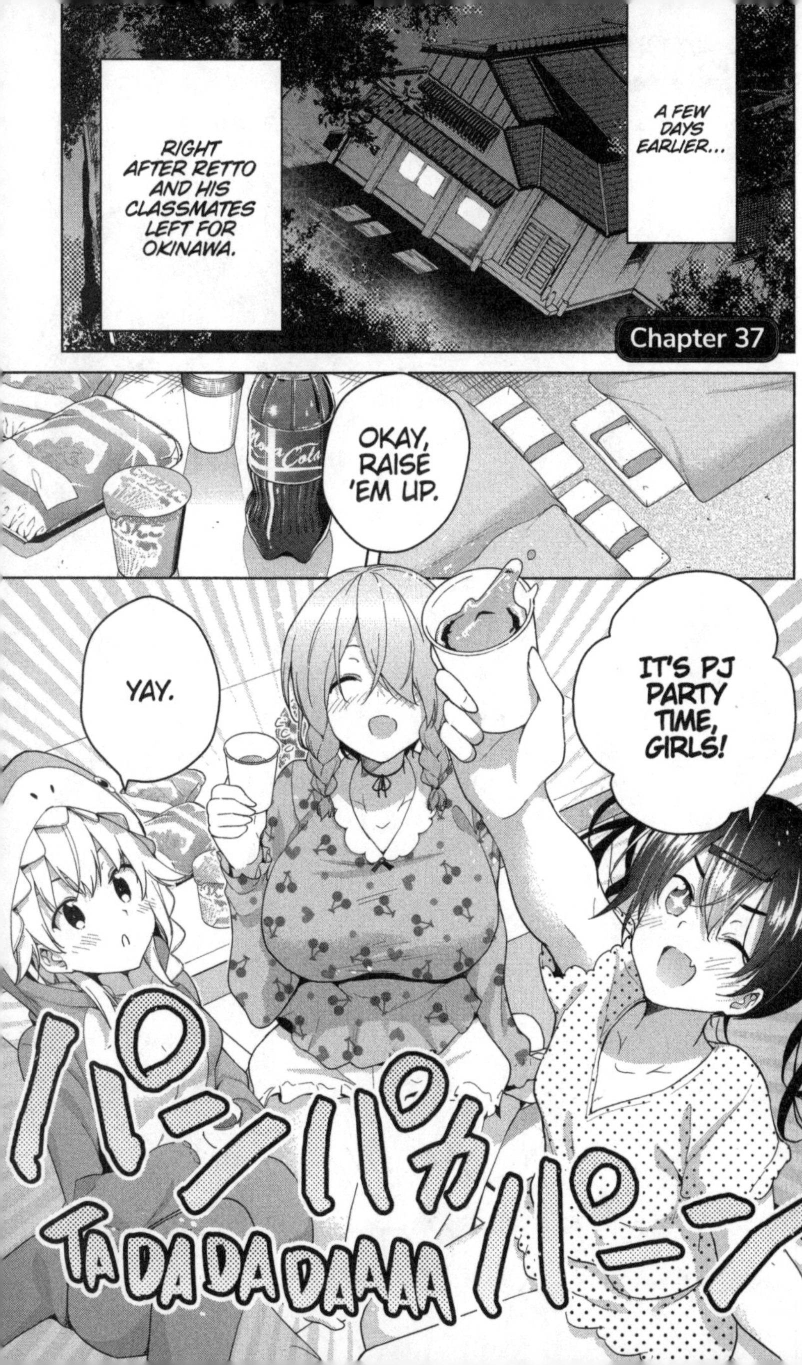
A FEW DAYS EARLIER...
RIGHT AFTER RETTO AND HIS CLASSMATES LEFT FOR OKINAWA.
Chapter 37
OKAY, RAISE 'EM UP.
IT'S PJ PARTY TIME, GIRLS!
YAY.
パンパカパーン
TA DA DA DAAAA

Chapter 37 Gossip Girls

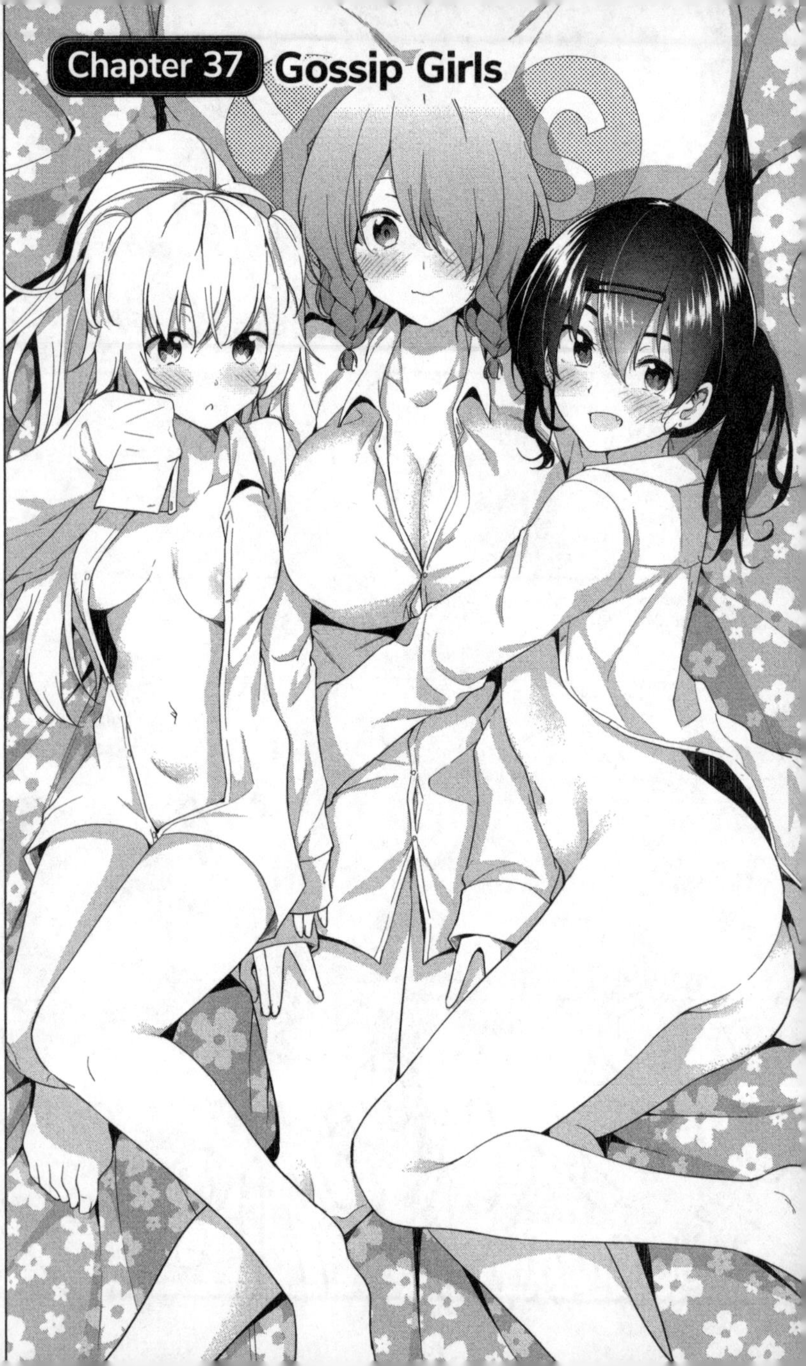

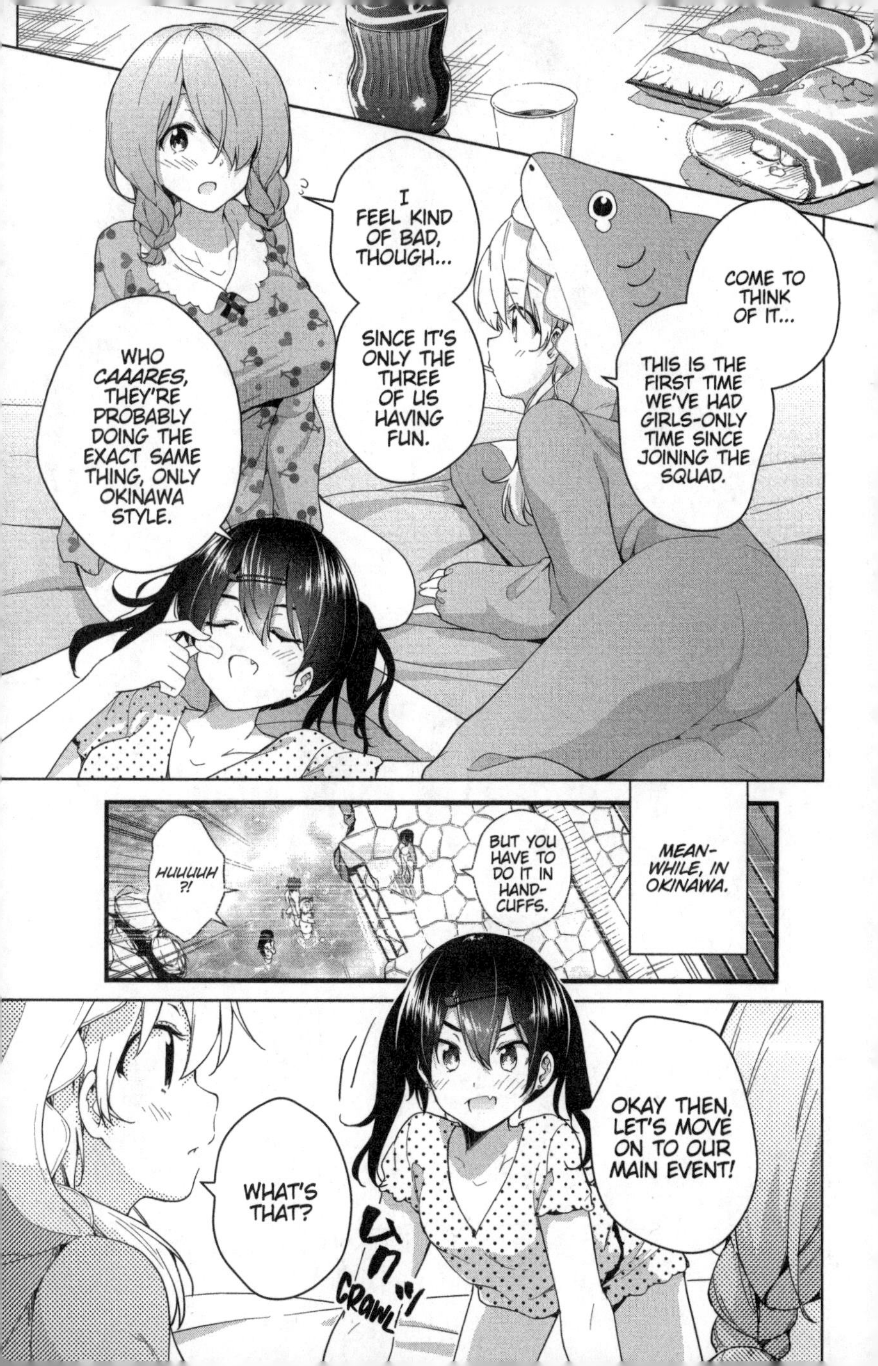
COME TO THINK OF IT...
THIS IS THE FIRST TIME WE'VE HAD GIRLS-ONLY TIME SINCE JOINING THE SQUAD.
I FEEL KIND OF BAD, THOUGH...
SINCE IT'S ONLY THE THREE OF US HAVING FUN.
WHO CAAARES, THEY'RE PROBABLY DOING THE EXACT SAME THING, ONLY OKINAWA STYLE.
MEAN-WHILE, IN OKINAWA.
BUT YOU HAVE TO DO IT IN HAND-CUFFS.
HUUUUH?!
OKAY THEN, LET'S MOVE ON TO OUR MAIN EVENT!
CRAWL
WHAT'S THAT?

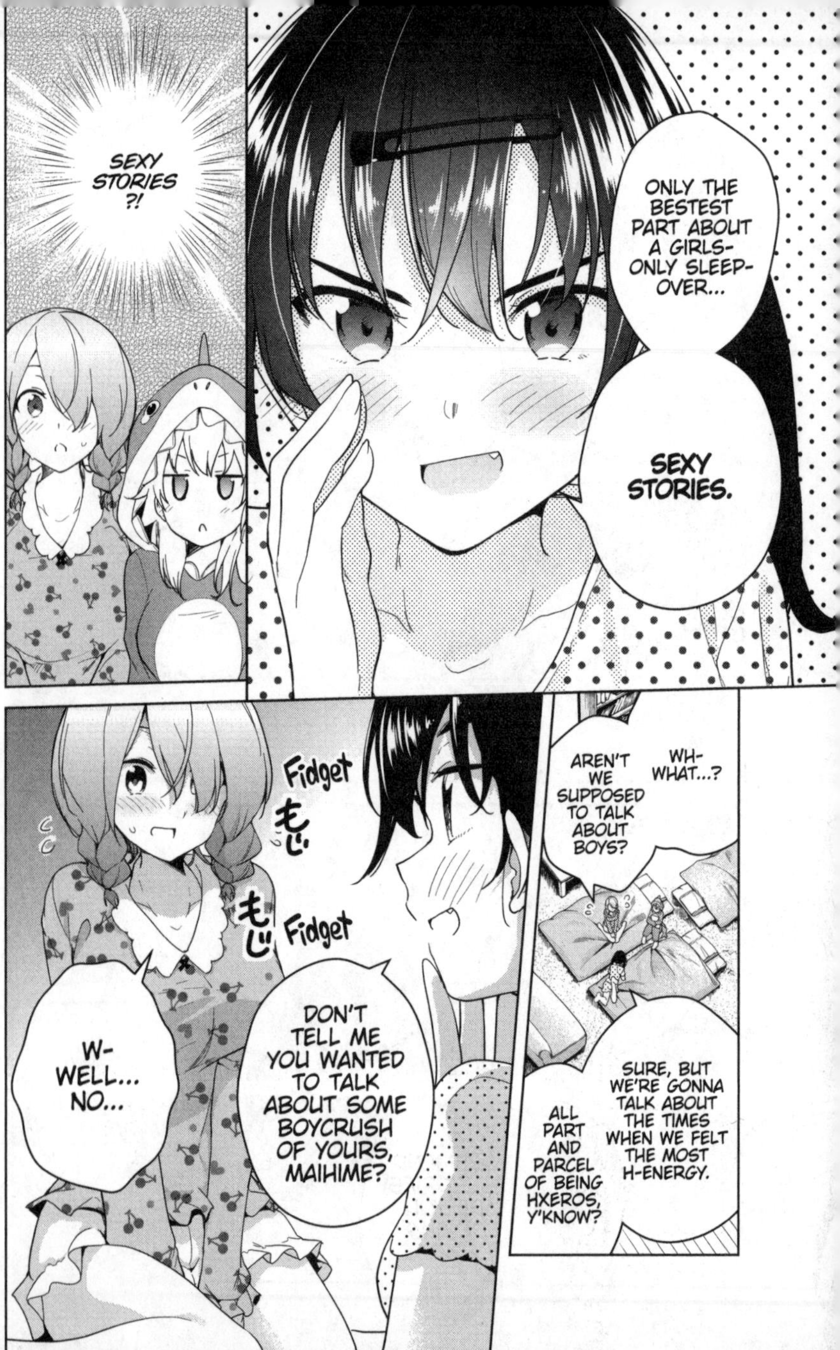
ONLY THE BESTEST PART ABOUT A GIRLS-ONLY SLEEP-OVER...
SEXY STORIES.
SEXY STORIES ?!
WH-WHAT...?
AREN'T WE SUPPOSED TO TALK ABOUT BOYS?
SURE, BUT WE'RE GONNA TALK ABOUT THE TIMES WHEN WE FELT THE MOST H-ENERGY.
ALL PART AND PARCEL OF BEING HXEROS, Y'KNOW?
Fidget もじ
もじ Fidget
DON'T TELL ME YOU WANTED TO TALK ABOUT SOME BOYCRUSH OF YOURS, MAIHIME?
W-WELL... NO...

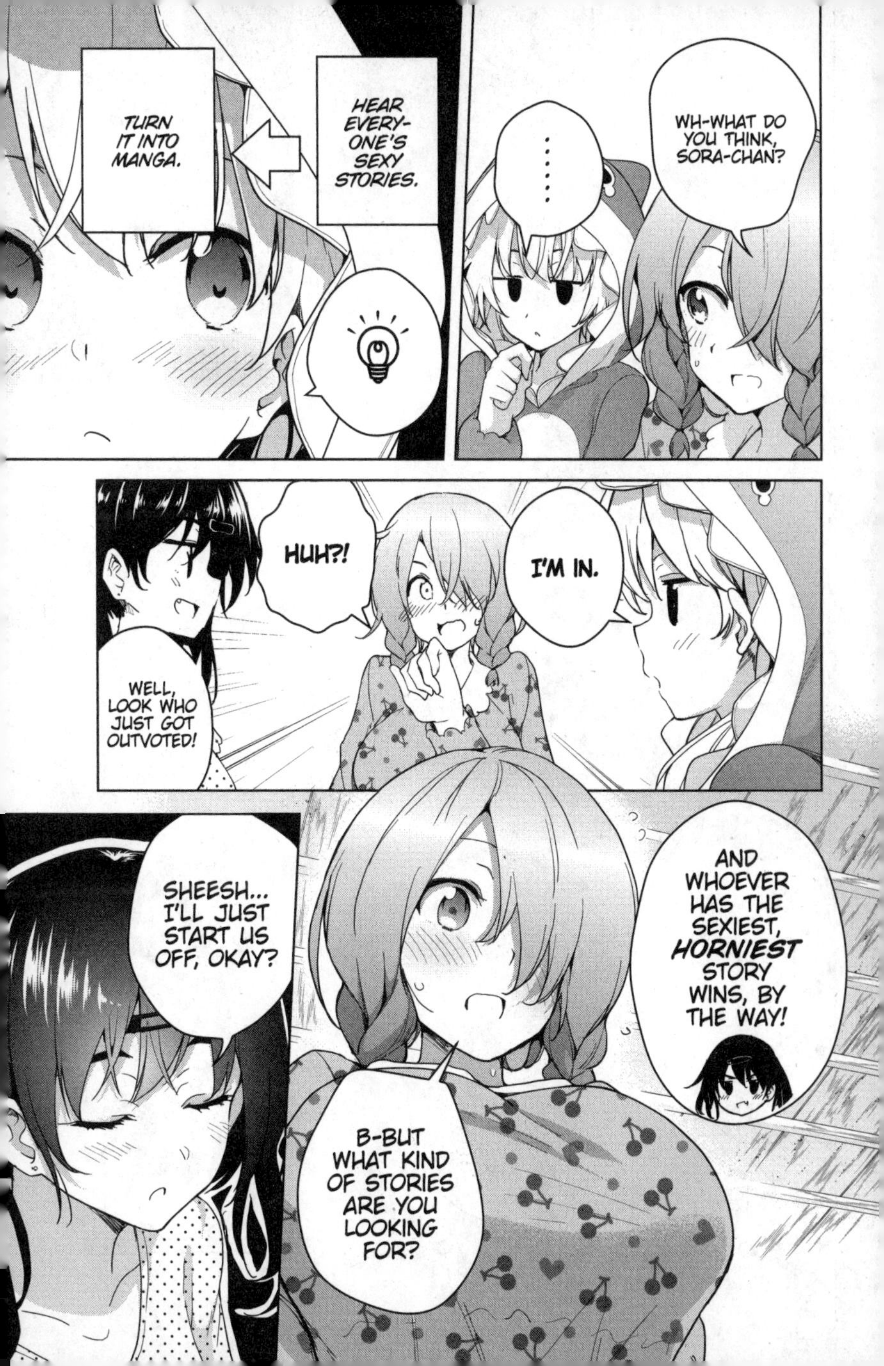
WH-WHAT DO YOU THINK, SORA-CHAN?
......
HEAR EVERY-ONE'S SEXY STORIES.
TURN IT INTO MANGA.
I'M IN.
HUH?!
WELL, LOOK WHO JUST GOT OUTVOTED!
AND WHOEVER HAS THE SEXIEST, HORNIEST STORY WINS, BY THE WAY!
B-BUT WHAT KIND OF STORIES ARE YOU LOOKING FOR?
SHEESH... I'LL JUST START US OFF, OKAY?

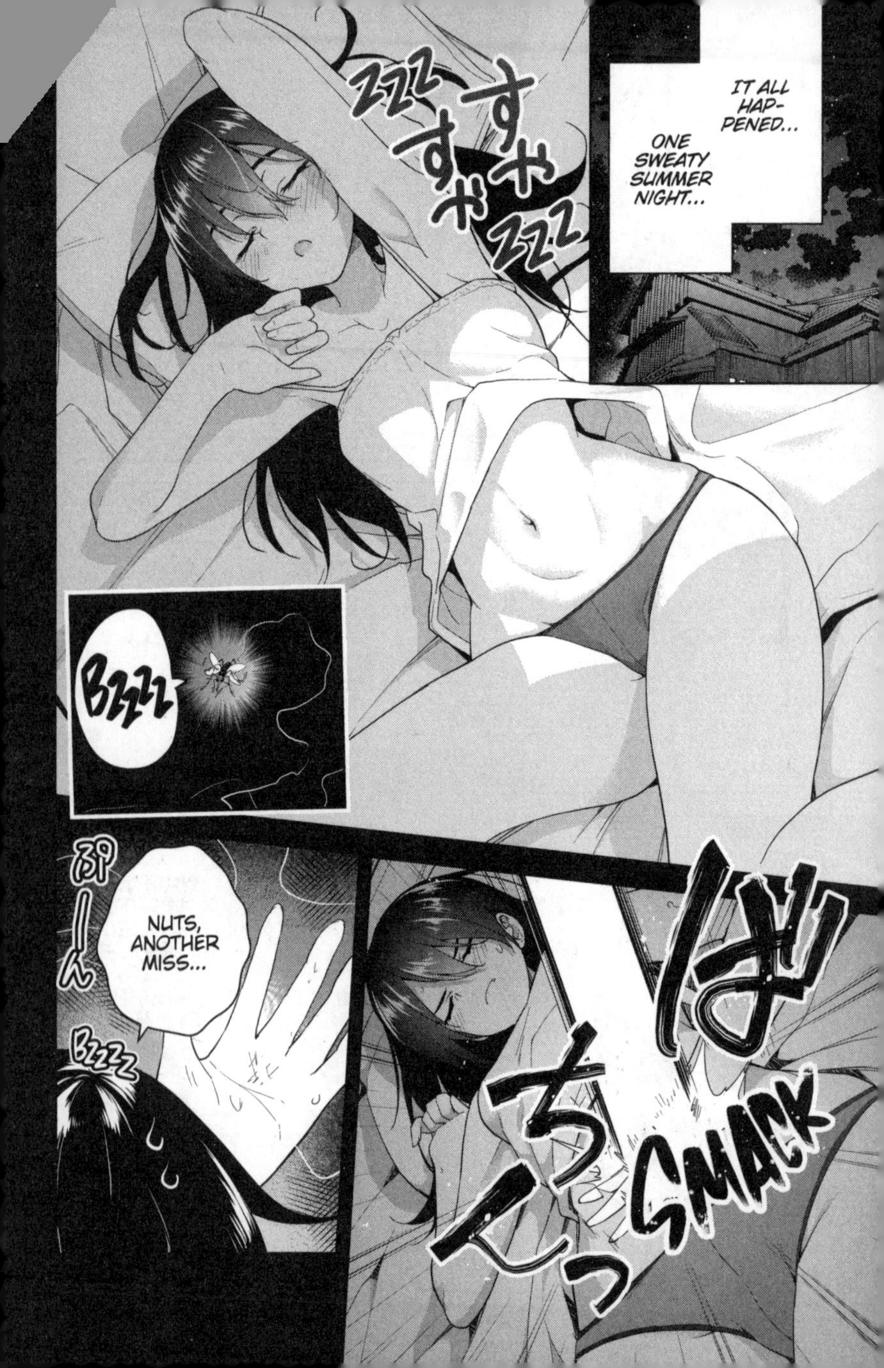
IT ALL HAP-PENED...
ONE SWEATY SUMMER NIGHT...
すやすや
ZZZ
ZZZ
BZZZZ
ぱちっ
SMACK
NUTS, ANOTHER MISS...
ぷーん
BZZZZ

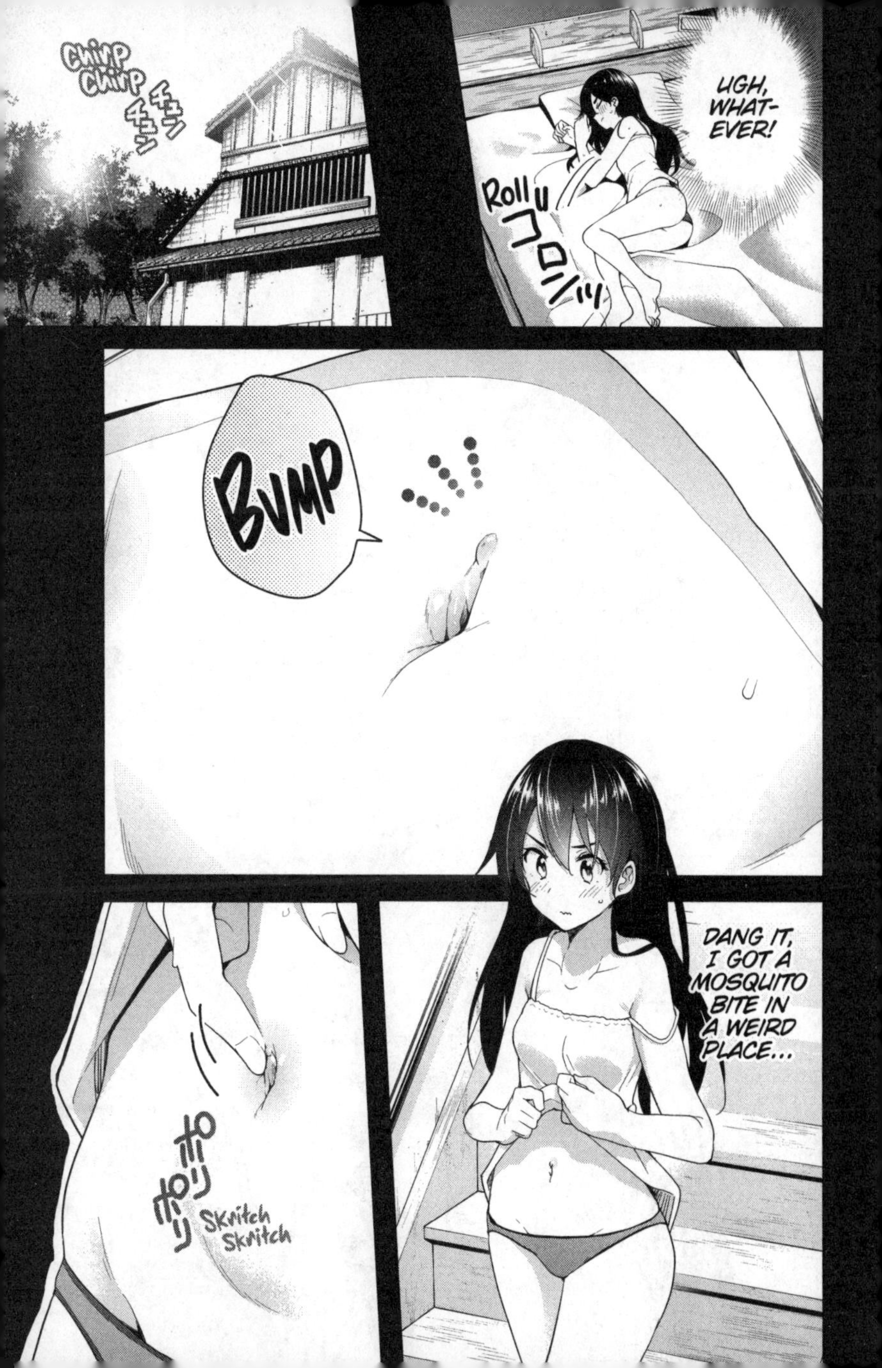
UGH, WHAT-EVER!
Roll コロンッ
Chirp Chirp チュンチュン
BUMP
DANG IT, I GOT A MOSQUITO BITE IN A WEIRD PLACE...
Skritch Skritch ポリポリ

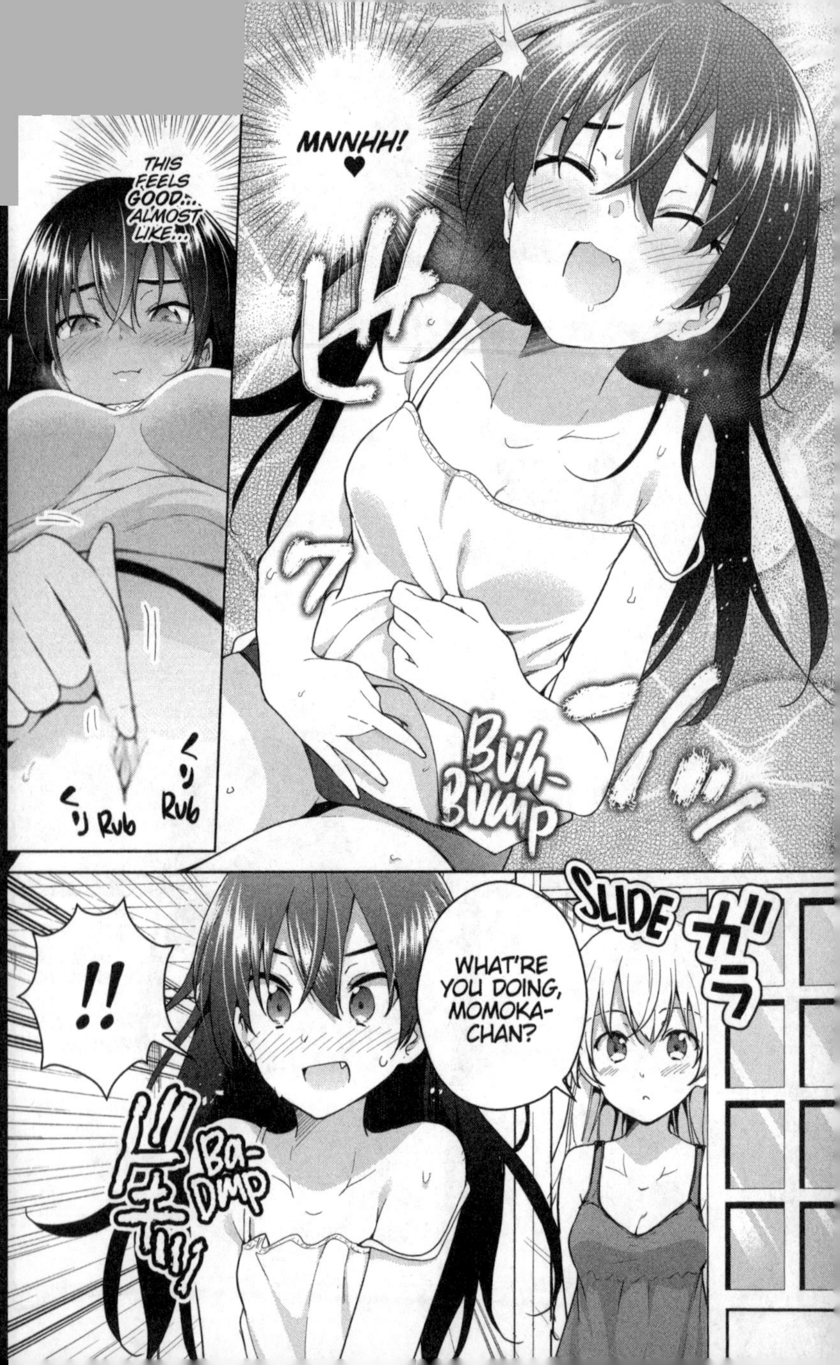
MNNHH! ♥
Buh-Bump
THIS FEELS GOOD... ALMOST LIKE...
くり Rub
くり Rub
SLIDE ガラ
WHAT'RE YOU DOING, MOMOKA-CHAN?
!!
Ba-Dmp

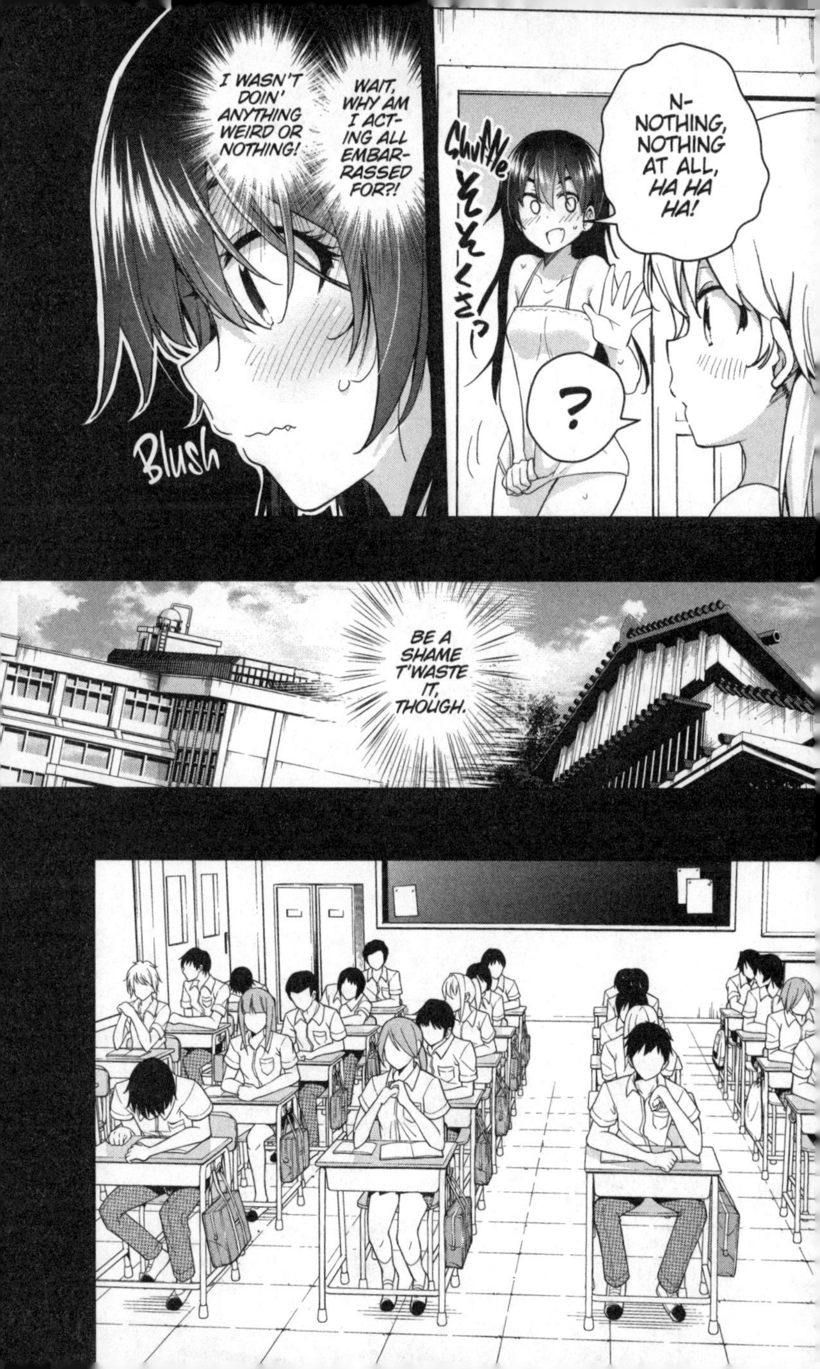
N-NOTHING, NOTHING AT ALL, HA HA HA!
Shuffle
そそくさっ
?
WAIT, WHY AM I ACTING ALL EMBARRASSED FOR?!
I WASN'T DOIN' ANYTHING WEIRD OR NOTHING!
Blush
BE A SHAME T'WASTE IT, THOUGH.

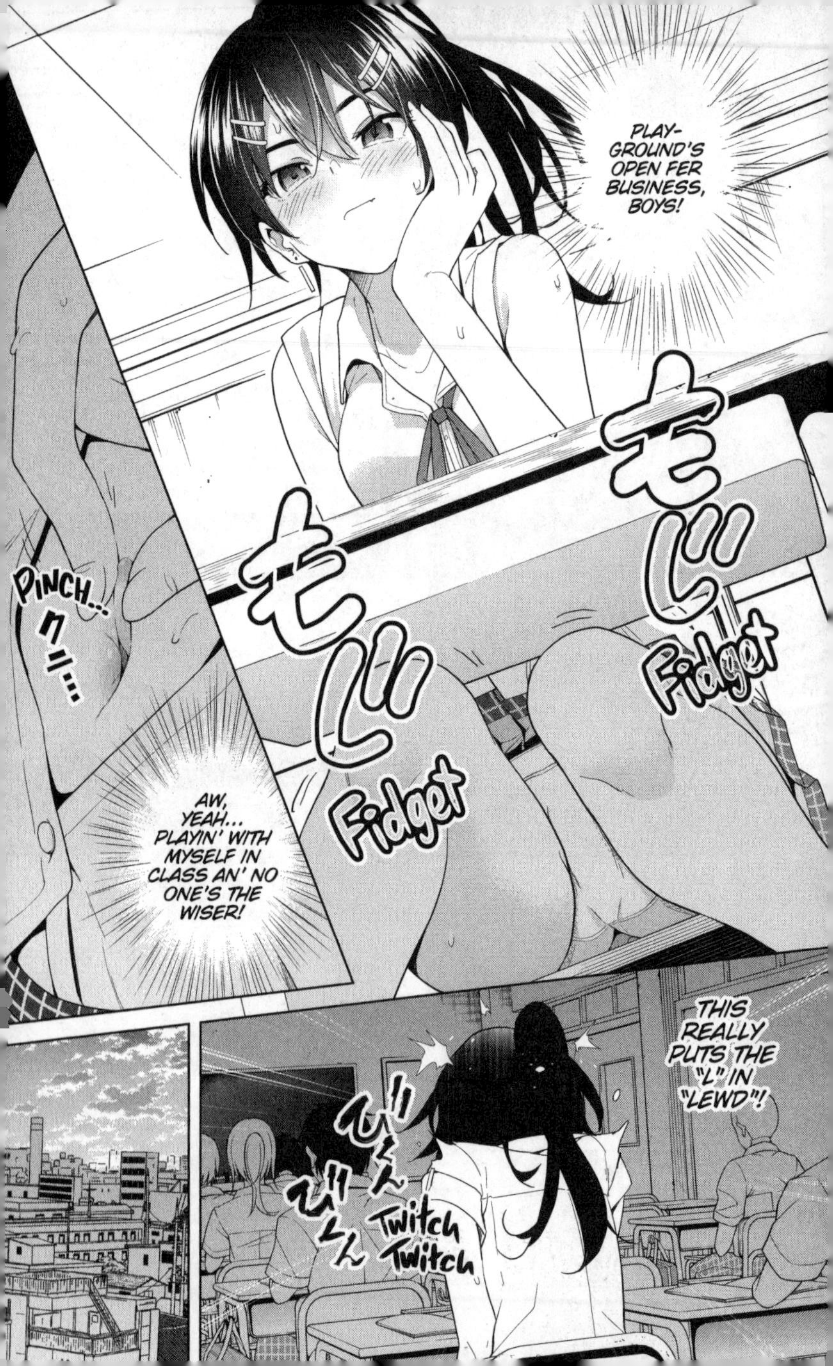
PLAY-GROUND'S OPEN FER BUSINESS, BOYS!
もじ
Fidget
もじ
Fidget
PINCH... クニ...
AW, YEAH... PLAYIN' WITH MYSELF IN CLASS AN' NO ONE'S THE WISER!
THIS REALLY PUTS THE "L" IN "LEWD"!
ぴくん ぴくん
Twitch Twitch

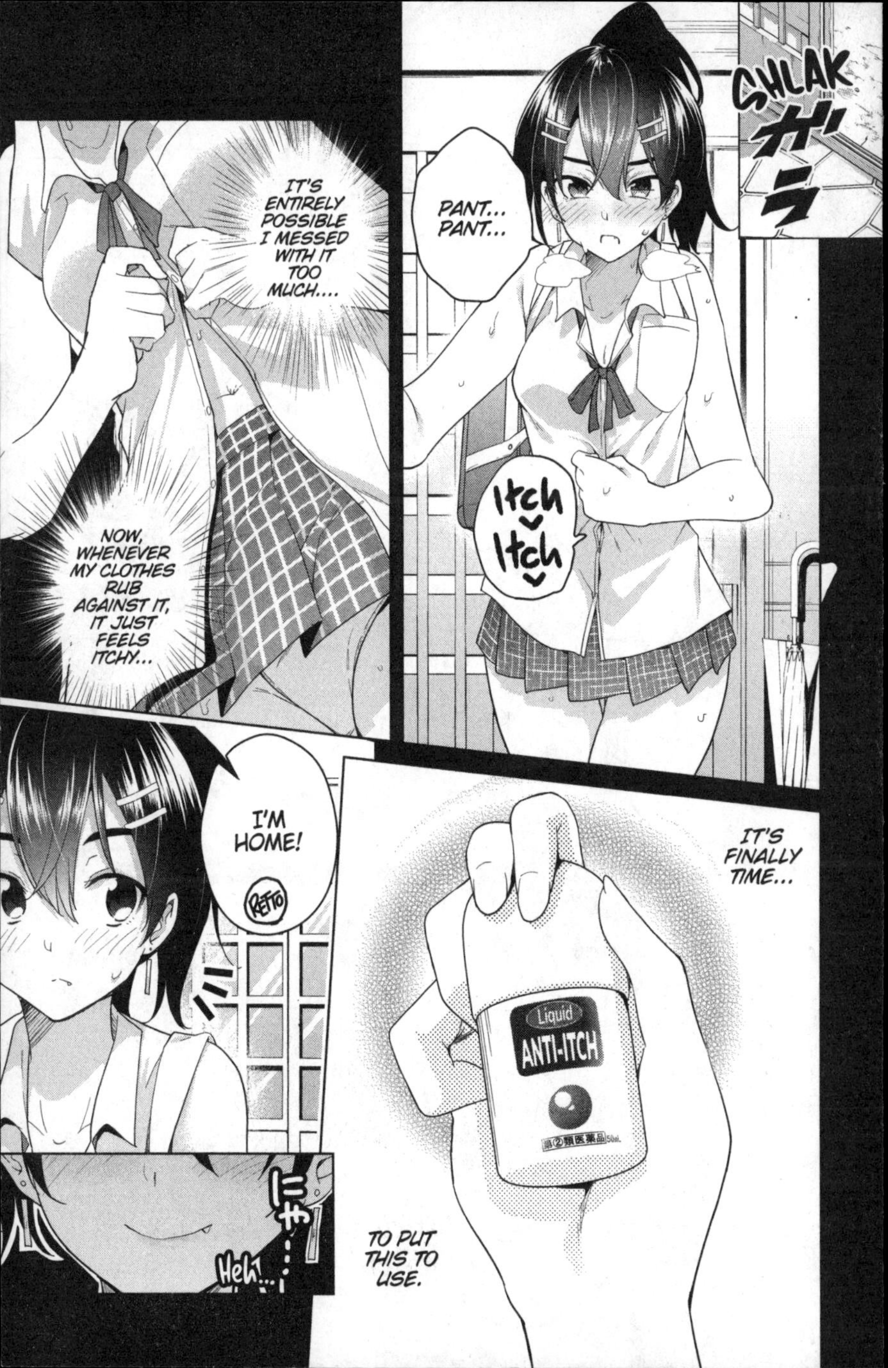

SHLAK
ガラ
PANT... PANT...
Itch Itch
IT'S ENTIRELY POSSIBLE I MESSED WITH IT TOO MUCH....
NOW, WHENEVER MY CLOTHES RUB AGAINST IT, IT JUST FEELS ITCHY...
IT'S FINALLY TIME...
Liquid
ANTI-ITCH
第②類医薬品
TO PUT THIS TO USE.
I'M HOME!
にや…
Heh!...

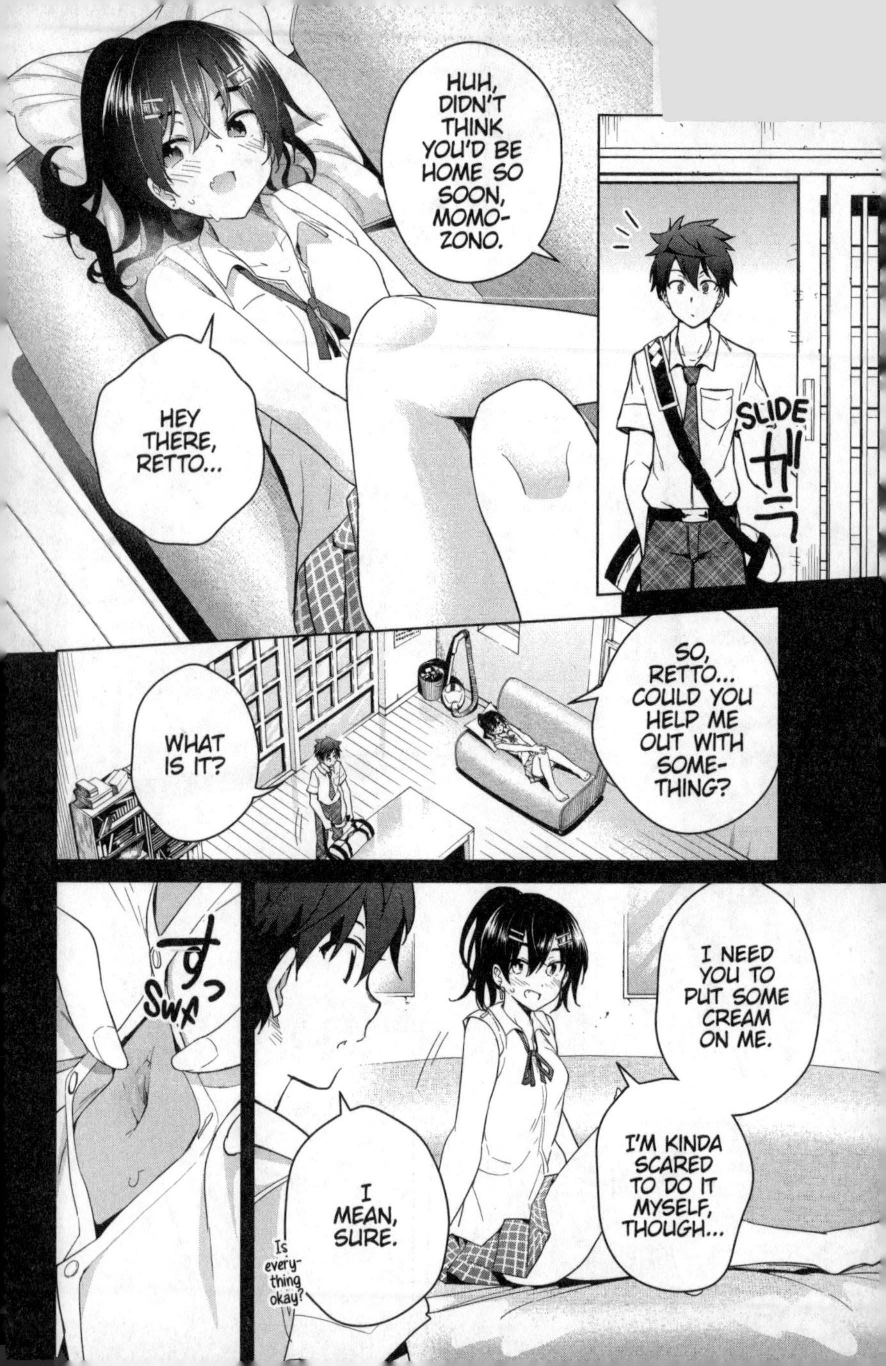
SLIDE
ガラ
HUH, DIDN'T THINK YOU'D BE HOME SO SOON, MOMO-ZONO.
HEY THERE, RETTO...
SO, RETTO... COULD YOU HELP ME OUT WITH SOME-THING?
WHAT IS IT?
I NEED YOU TO PUT SOME CREAM ON ME.
I'M KINDA SCARED TO DO IT MYSELF, THOUGH...
I MEAN, SURE.
Is every-thing okay?
すっ
SWX

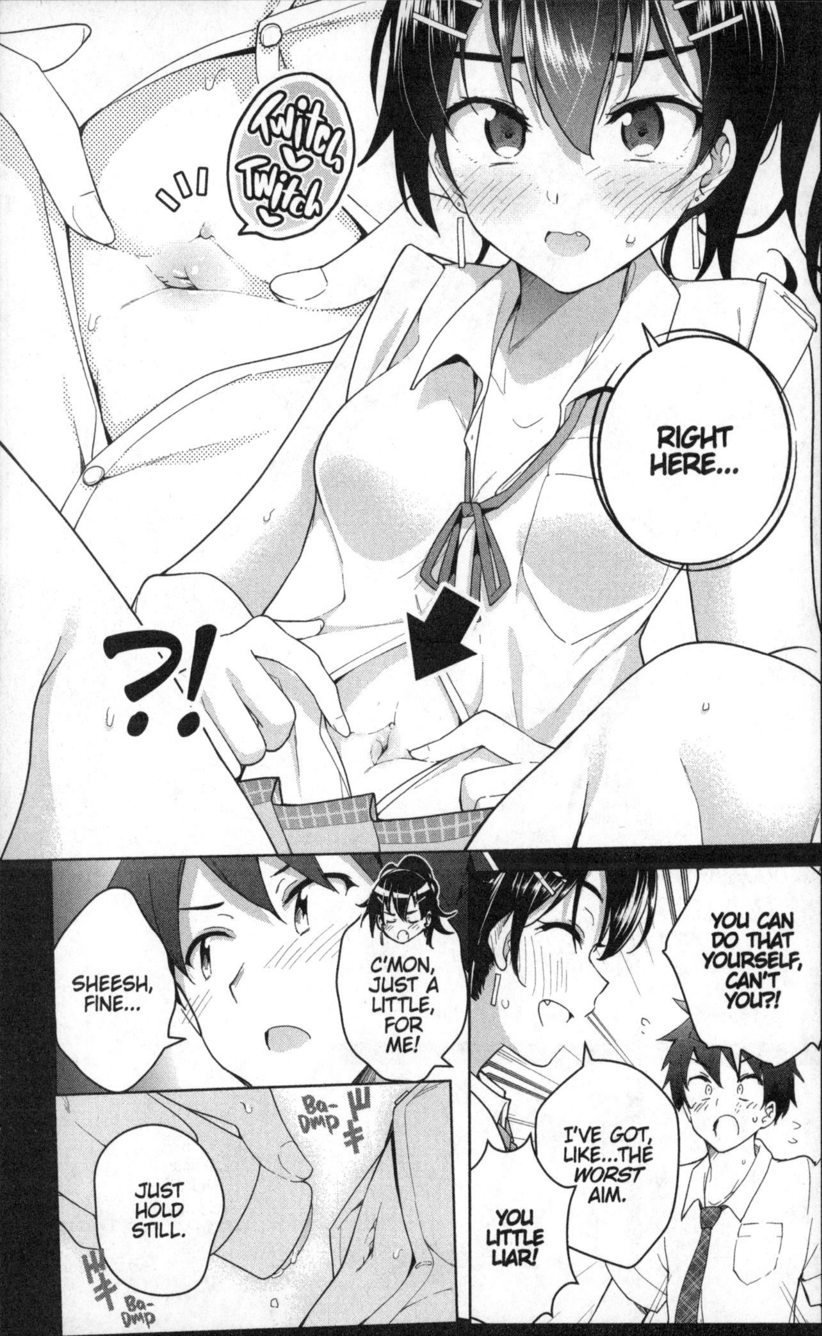
Twitch Twitch
RIGHT HERE...
?!
YOU CAN DO THAT YOURSELF, CAN'T YOU?!
I'VE GOT, LIKE...THE WORST AIM.
YOU LITTLE LIAR!
C'MON, JUST A LITTLE, FOR ME!
SHEESH, FINE...
Ba-Dmp
JUST HOLD STILL.
Ba-Dmp

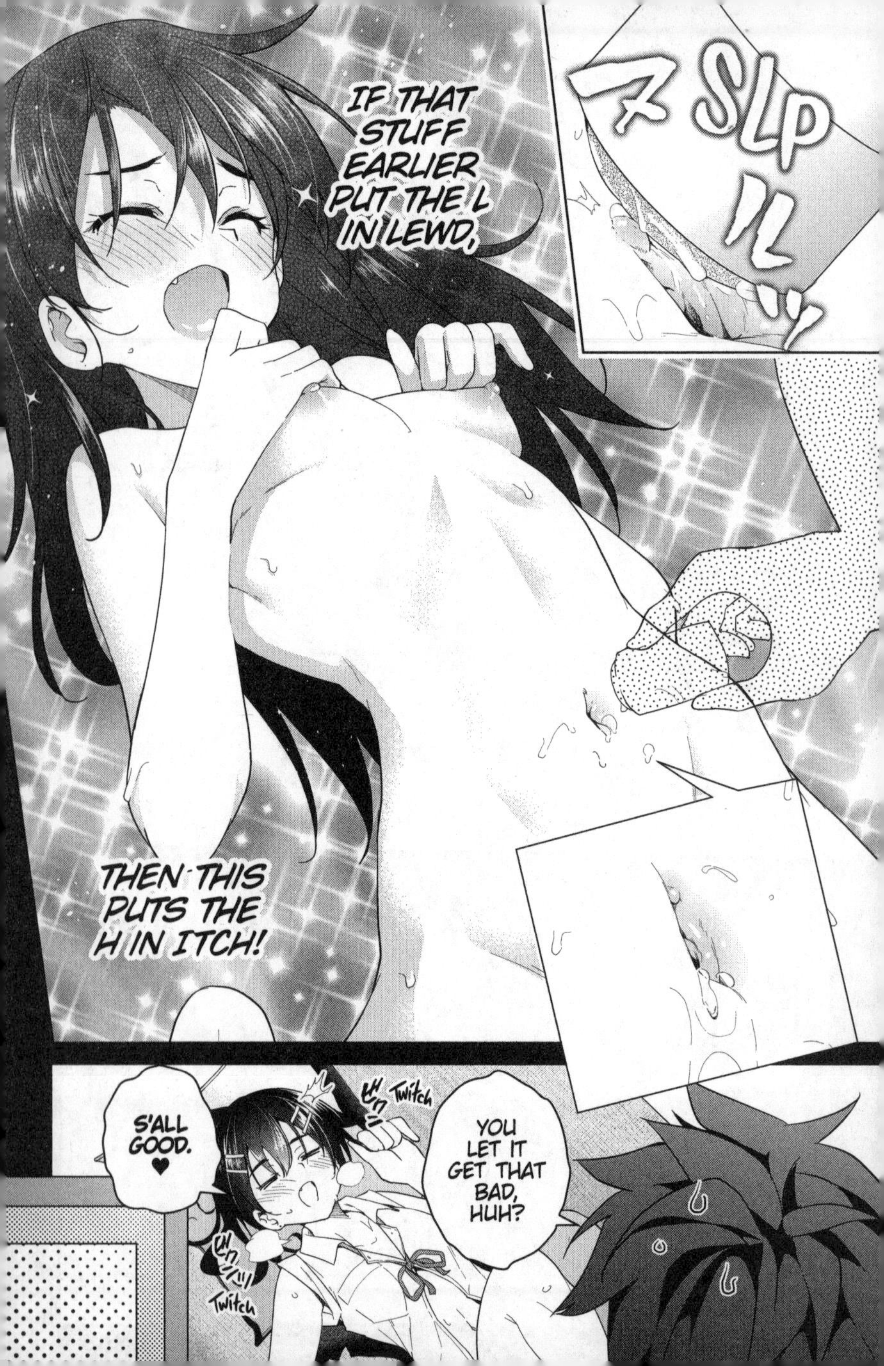
SLIP
IF THAT STUFF EARLIER PUT THE L IN LEWD,
THEN THIS PUTS THE H IN ITCH!
YOU LET IT GET THAT BAD, HUH?
Twitch
S'ALL GOOD. ♥
Twitch

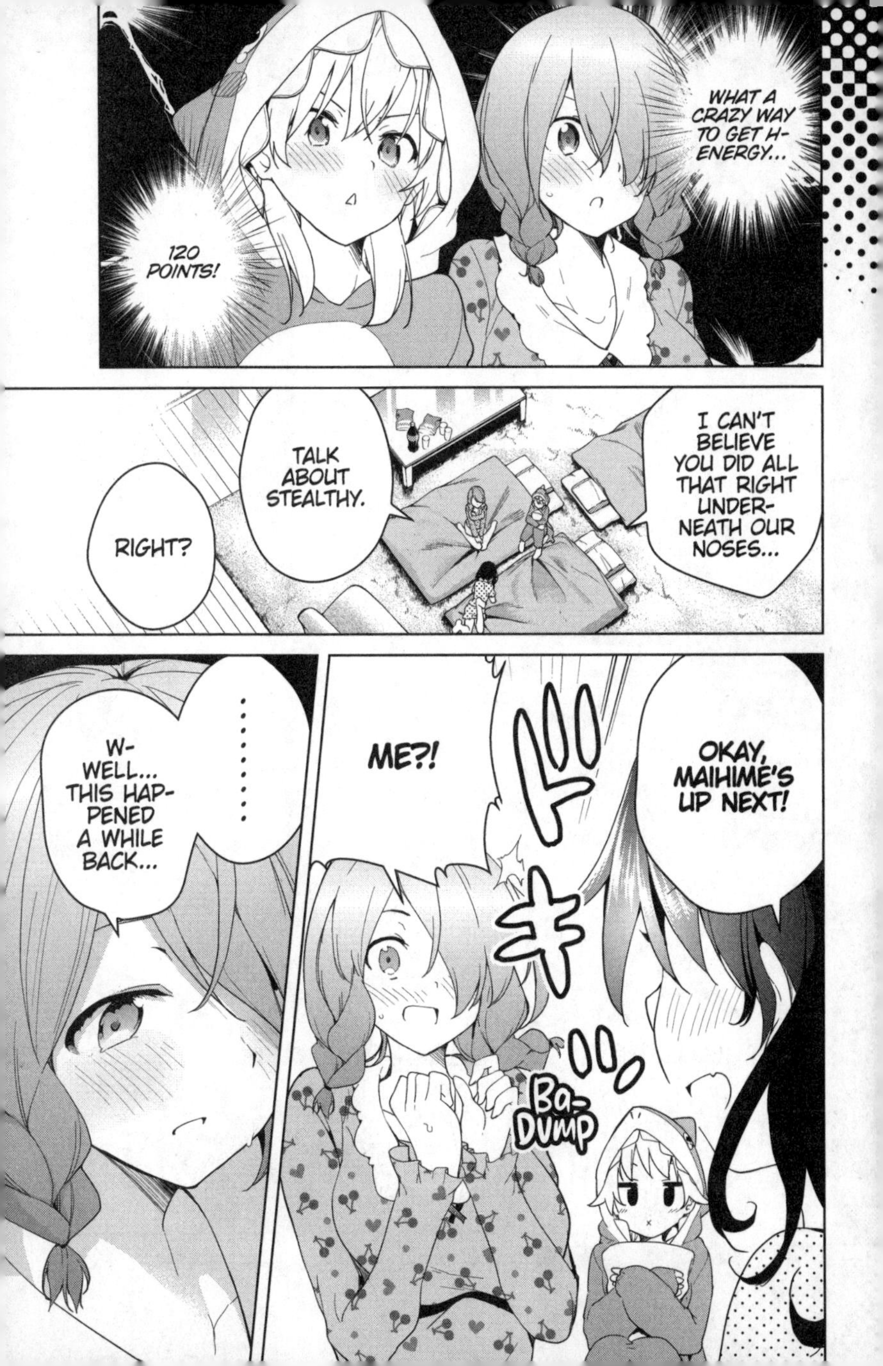
WHAT A CRAZY WAY TO GET H-ENERGY...
120 POINTS!
I CAN'T BELIEVE YOU DID ALL THAT RIGHT UNDER-NEATH OUR NOSES...
TALK ABOUT STEALTHY.
RIGHT?
OKAY, MAIHIME'S UP NEXT!
Ba-Dump
ME?!
....
W-WELL... THIS HAP-PENED A WHILE BACK...

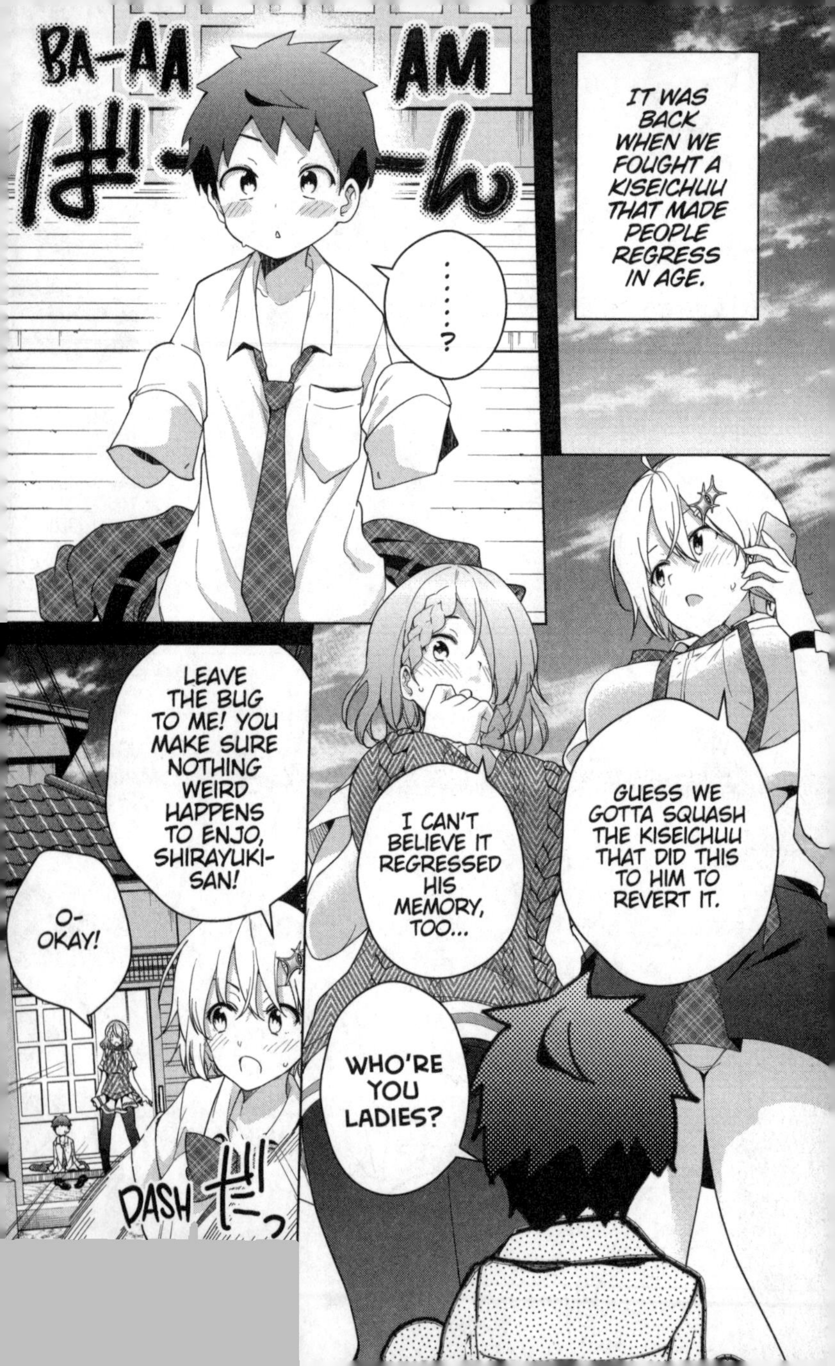
IT WAS BACK WHEN WE FOUGHT A KISEICHUU THAT MADE PEOPLE REGRESS IN AGE.
BA-AAAM
......?
GUESS WE GOTTA SQUASH THE KISEICHUU THAT DID THIS TO HIM TO REVERT IT.
I CAN'T BELIEVE IT REGRESSED HIS MEMORY, TOO...
WHO'RE YOU LADIES?
LEAVE THE BUG TO ME! YOU MAKE SURE NOTHING WEIRD HAPPENS TO ENJO, SHIRAYUKI-SAN!
O-OKAY!
DASH

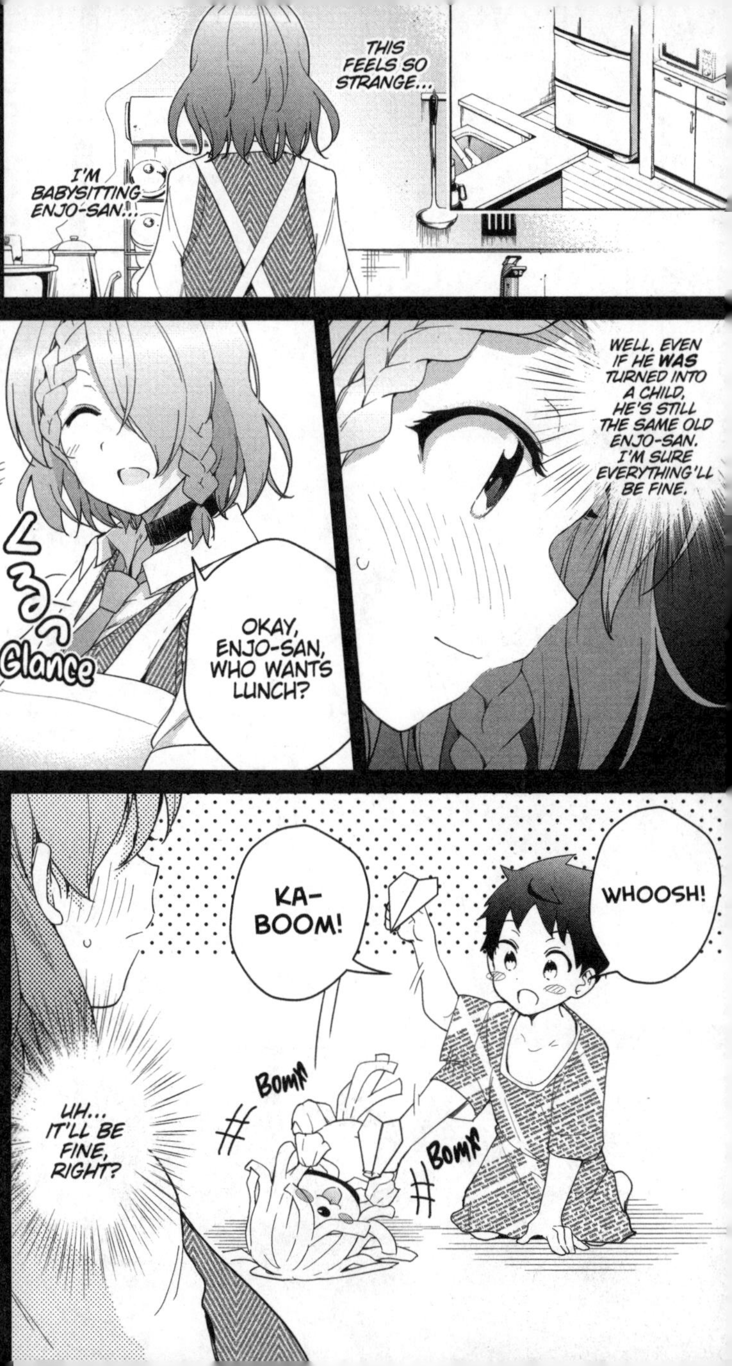
THIS FEELS SO STRANGE...
I'M BABYSITTING ENJO-SAN...
WELL, EVEN IF HE **WAS** TURNED INTO A CHILD, HE'S STILL THE SAME OLD ENJO-SAN. I'M SURE EVERYTHING'LL BE FINE.
くるっ
Glance
OKAY, ENJO-SAN, WHO WANTS LUNCH?
WHOOSH!
KA-BOOM!
Bomf
Bomf
UH... IT'LL BE FINE, RIGHT?

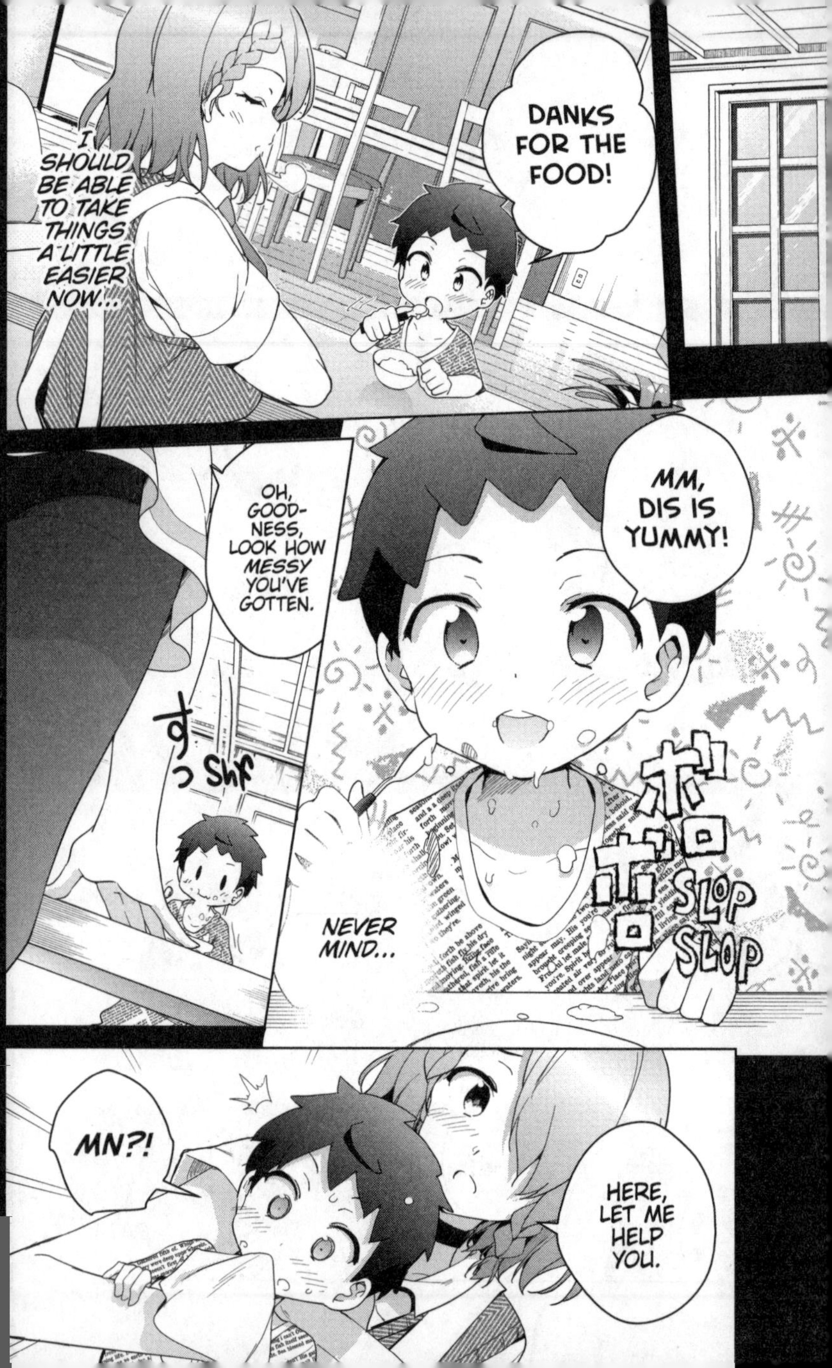
DANKS FOR THE FOOD!
I SHOULD BE ABLE TO TAKE THINGS A LITTLE EASIER NOW...
MM, DIS IS YUMMY!
ボロボロ SLOP SLOP
NEVER MIND...
OH, GOOD-NESS, LOOK HOW MESSY YOU'VE GOTTEN.
すっ SHF
HERE, LET ME HELP YOU.
MN?!

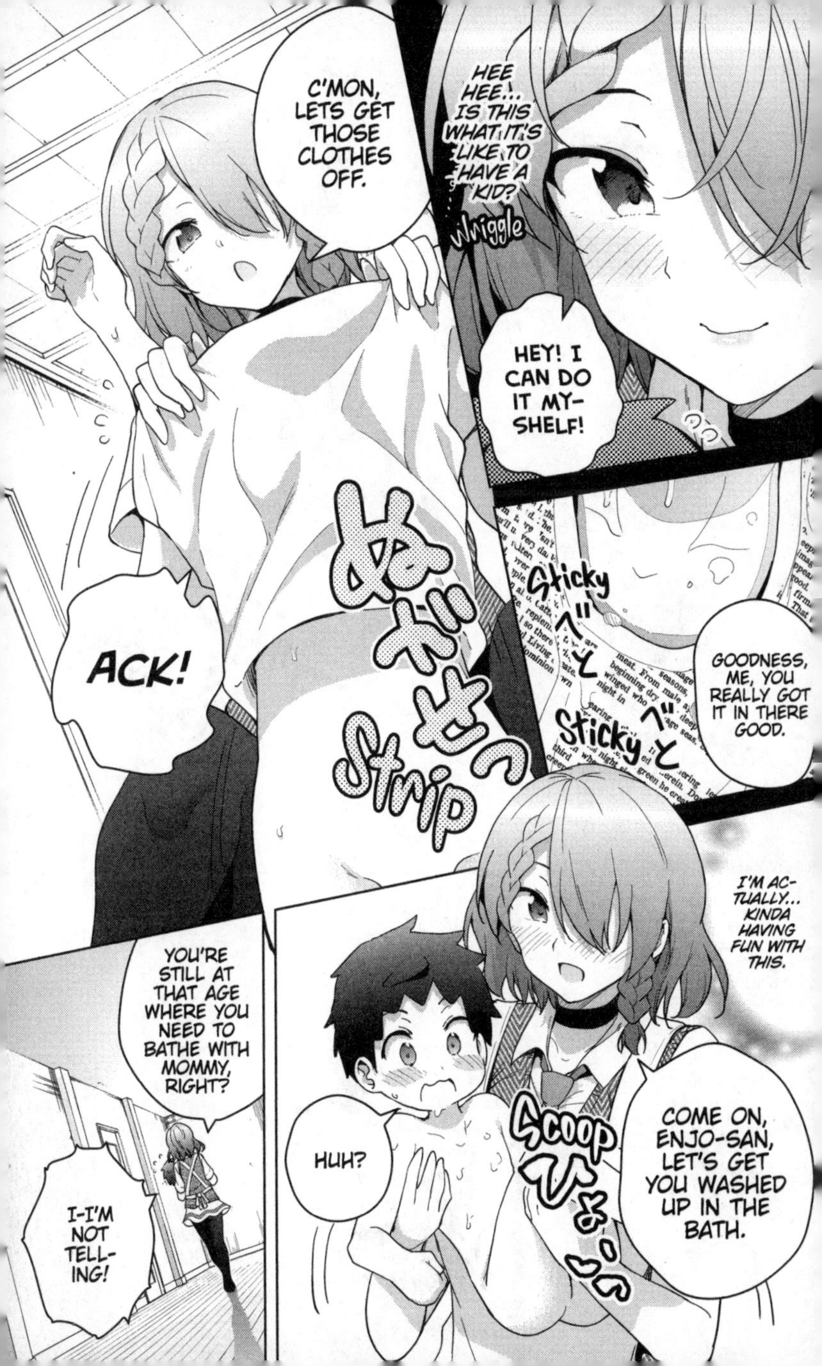

HEE HEE... IS THIS WHAT IT'S LIKE TO HAVE A KID?
Wriggle
HEY! I CAN DO IT MY-SHELF!
GOODNESS, ME, YOU REALLY GOT IT IN THERE GOOD.
Sticky べとべと
Sticky べとべと
C'MON, LETS GET THOSE CLOTHES OFF.
ACK!
ぬがせっ Strip
I'M ACTUALLY... KINDA HAVING FUN WITH THIS.
COME ON, ENJO-SAN, LET'S GET YOU WASHED UP IN THE BATH.
Scoop ひょいっ
HUH?
YOU'RE STILL AT THAT AGE WHERE YOU NEED TO BATHE WITH MOMMY, RIGHT?
I-I'M NOT TELL-ING!

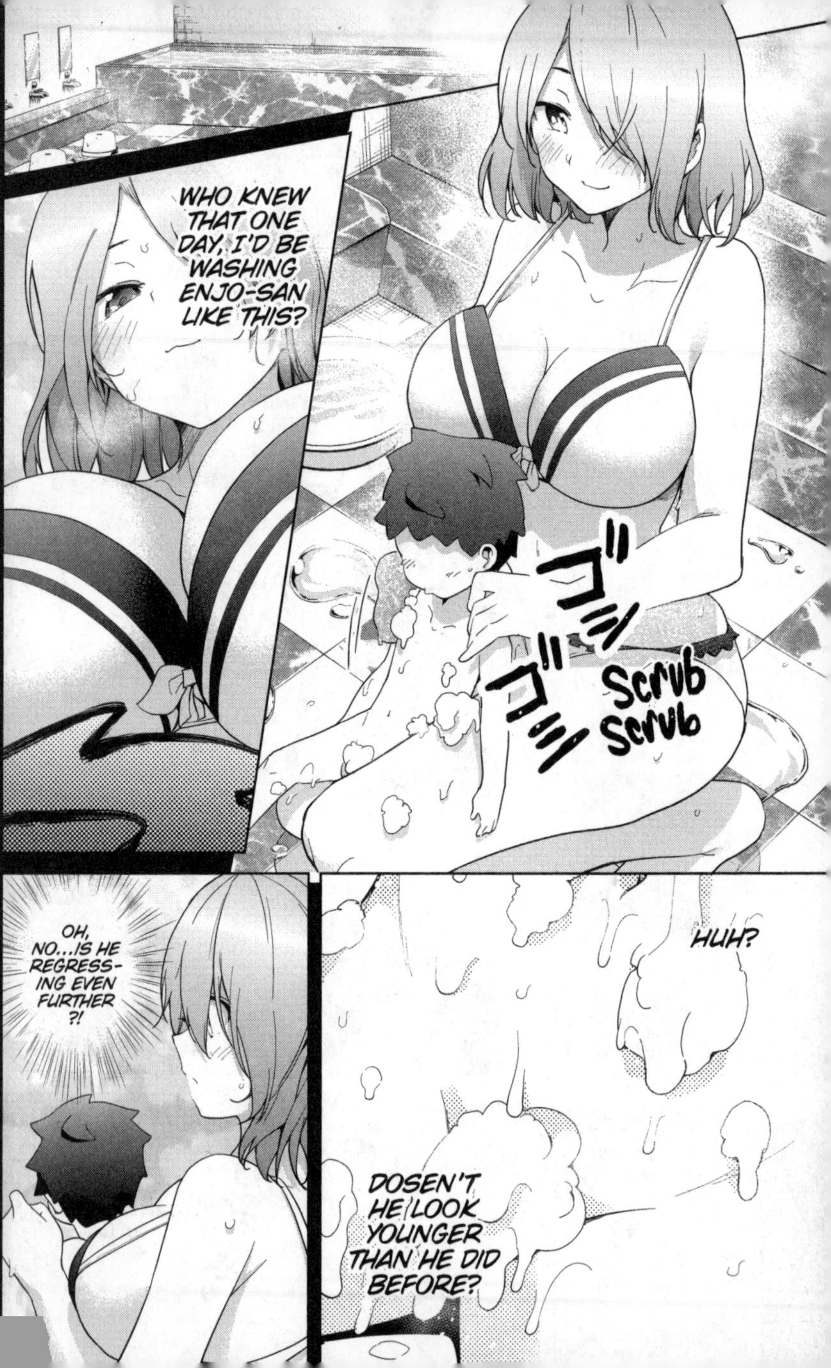
ゴシ
ゴシ
Scrub
Scrub
WHO KNEW THAT ONE DAY, I'D BE WASHING ENJO-SAN LIKE THIS?
HUH?
DOSEN'T HE LOOK YOUNGER THAN HE DID BEFORE?
OH, NO...IS HE REGRESS-ING EVEN FURTHER ?!

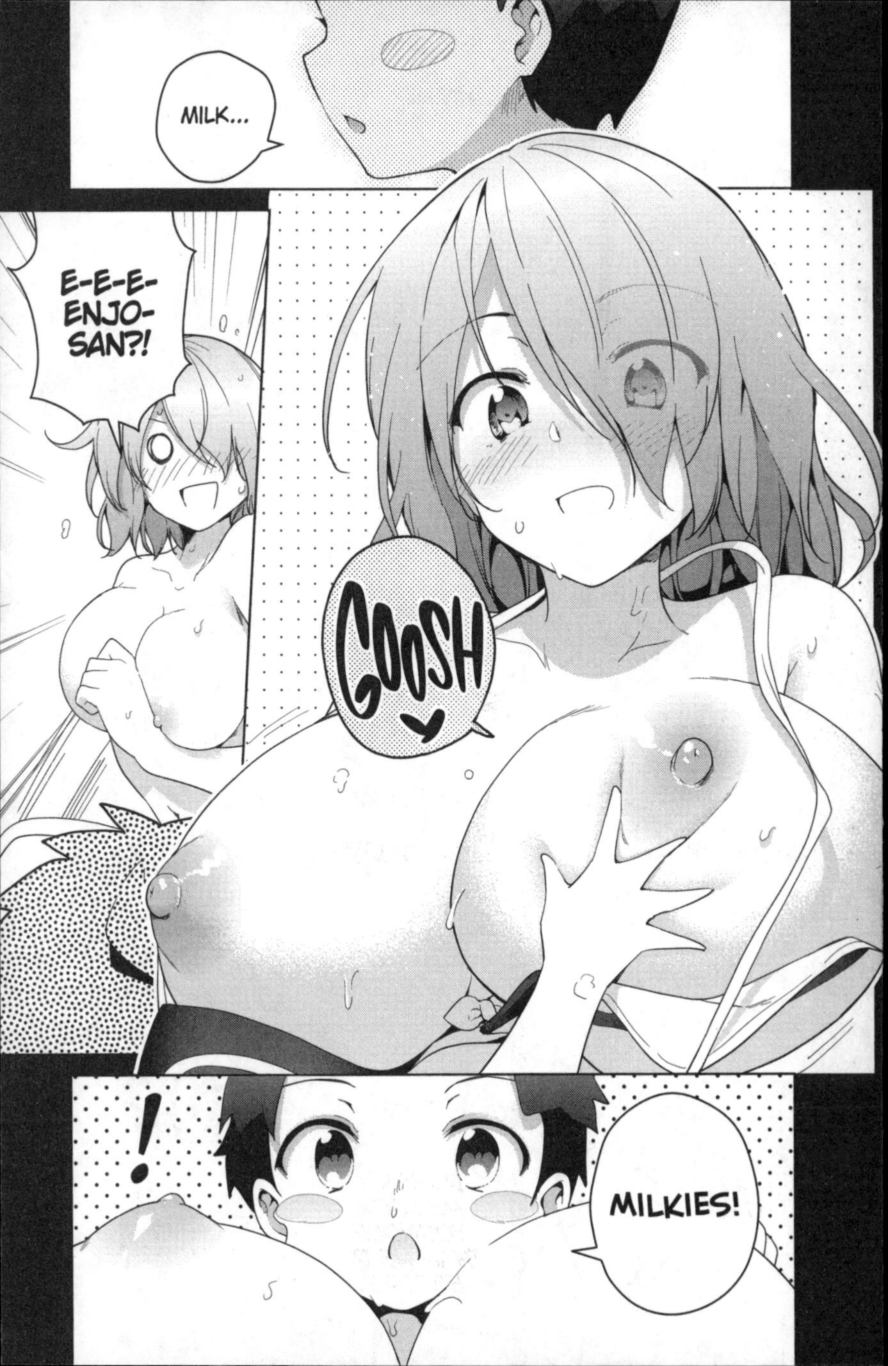
MILK...
GOOSH
E-E-E-ENJO-SAN?!
!
MILKIES!

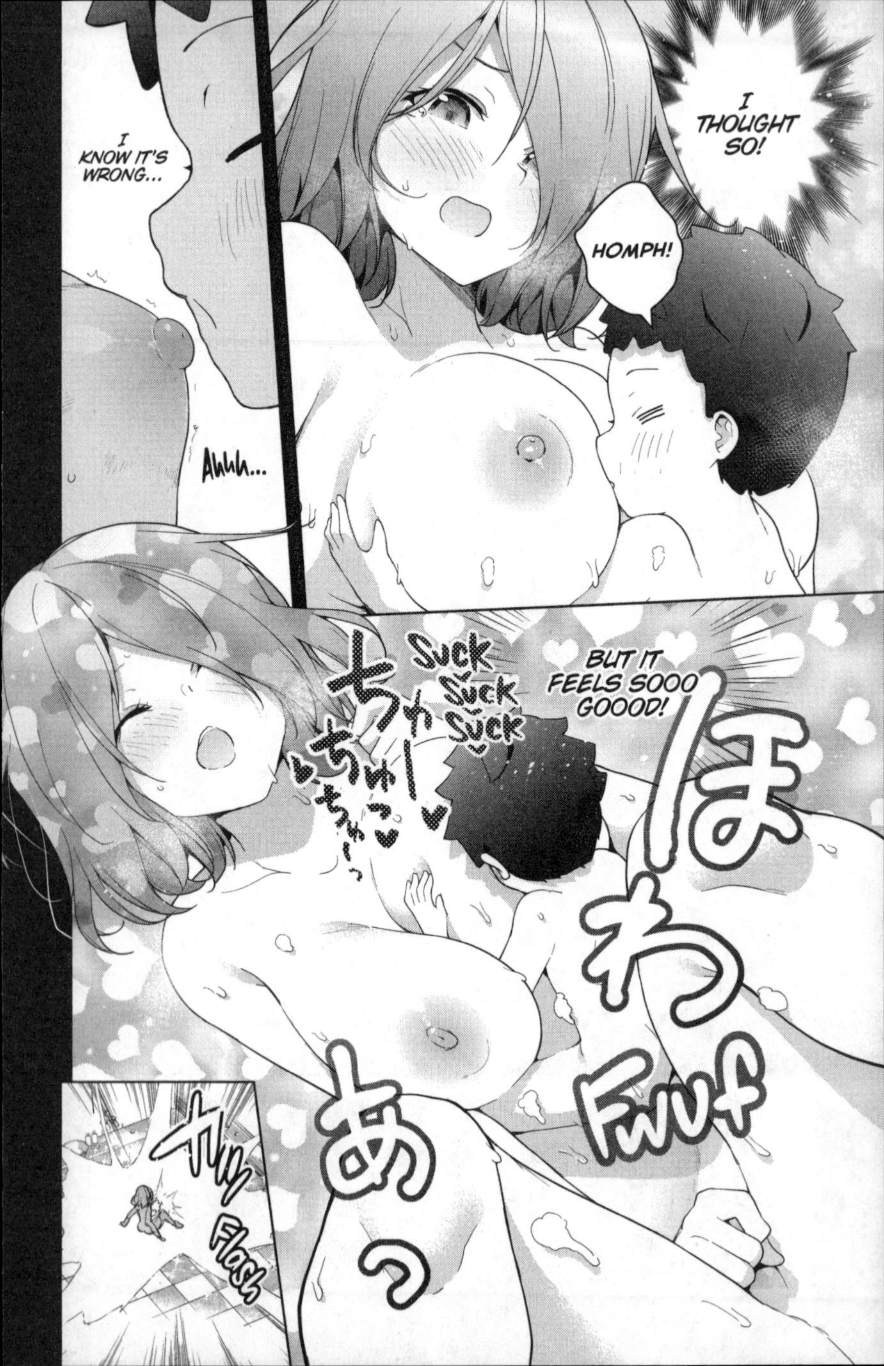
I THOUGHT SO!
HOMPH!
I KNOW IT'S WRONG...
Ahhh...
BUT IT FEELS SOOO GOOOD!
ほわっ
Fwuf
Suck Suck Suck
あっ
Flash

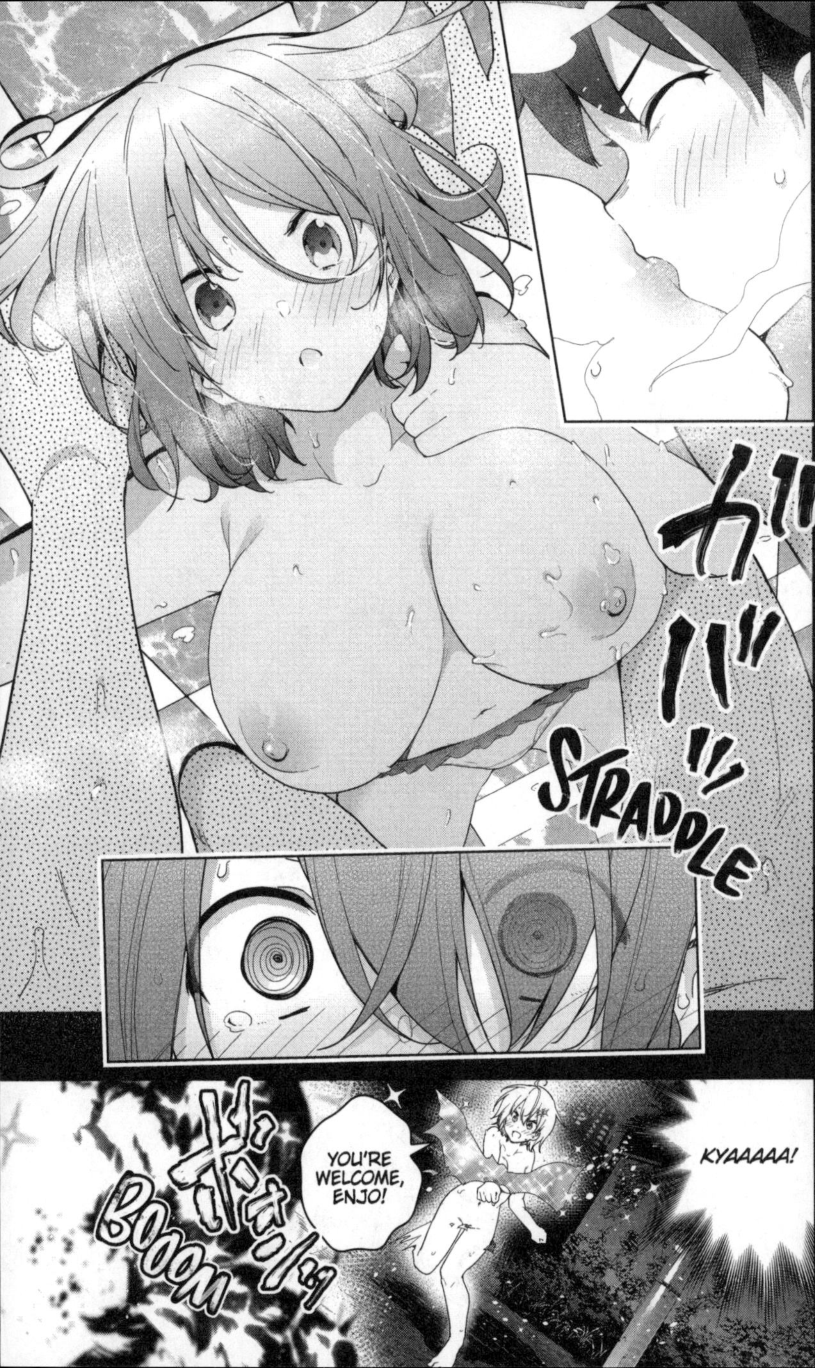
がバ!!
STRADDLE
KYAAAAA!
YOU'RE WELCOME, ENJO!
BOOOM

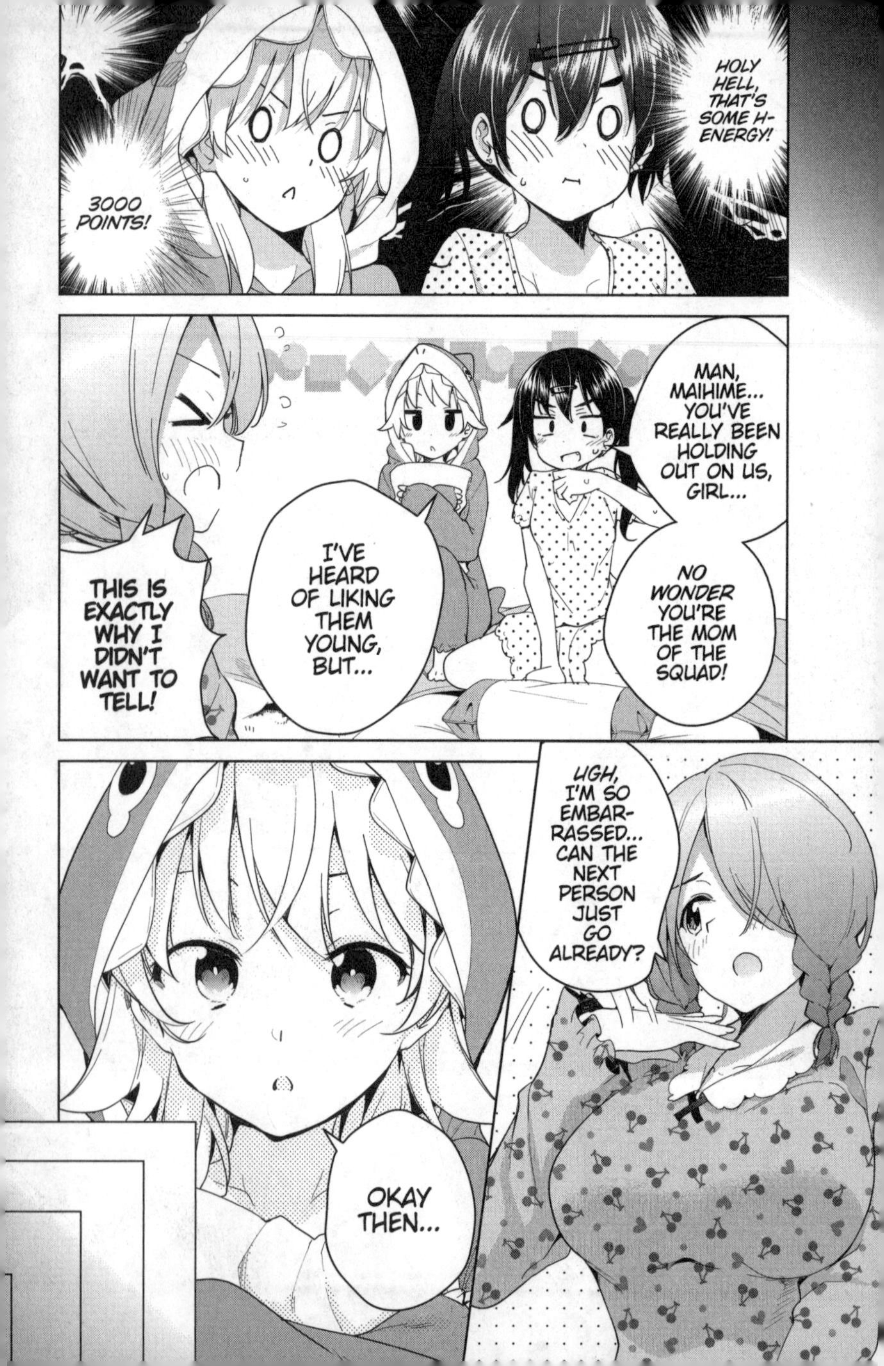
HOLY HELL, THAT'S SOME H-ENERGY!
3000 POINTS!
MAN, MAIHIME... YOU'VE REALLY BEEN HOLDING OUT ON US, GIRL...
NO WONDER YOU'RE THE MOM OF THE SQUAD!
I'VE HEARD OF LIKING THEM YOUNG, BUT...
THIS IS EXACTLY WHY I DIDN'T WANT TO TELL!
UGH, I'M SO EMBAR-RASSED... CAN THE NEXT PERSON JUST GO ALREADY?
OKAY THEN...

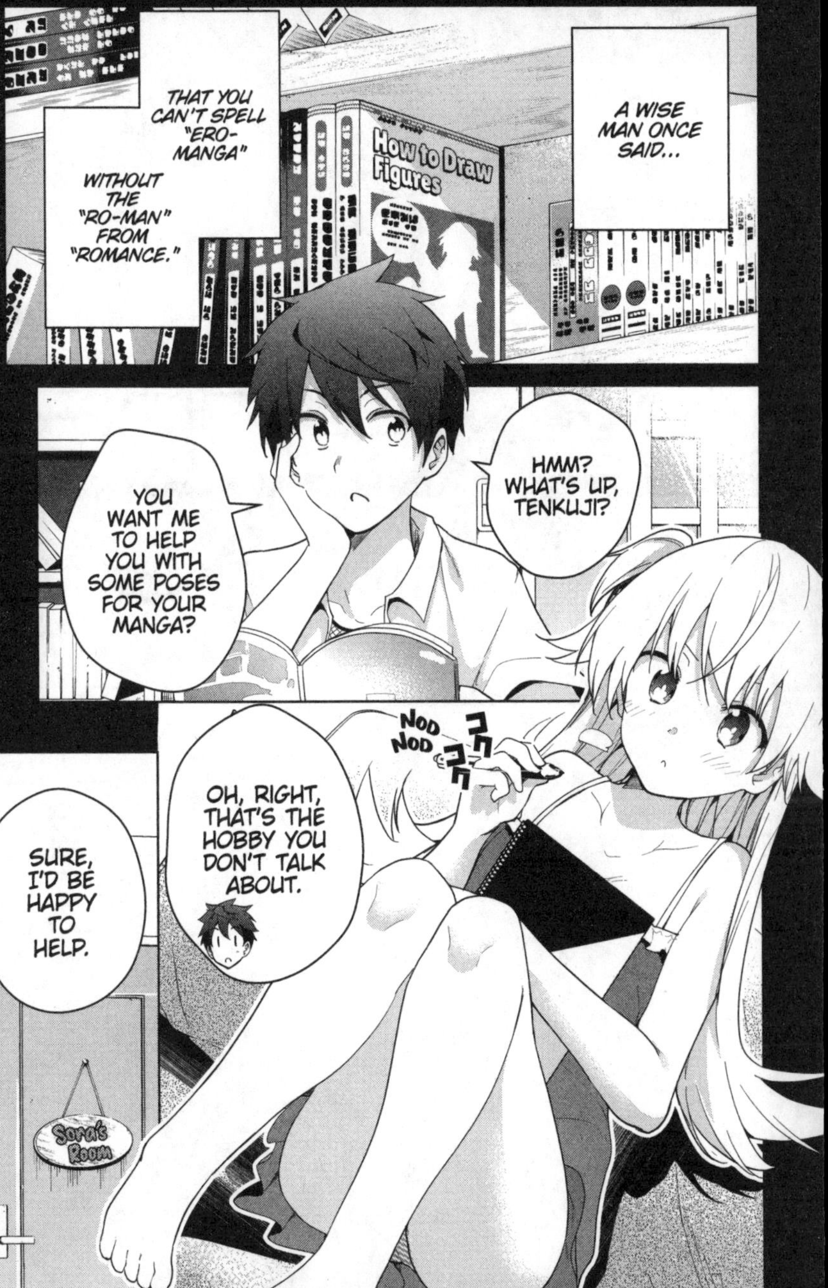
A WISE MAN ONCE SAID...
THAT YOU CAN'T SPELL "ERO-MANGA"
WITHOUT THE "RO-MAN" FROM "ROMANCE."
How to Draw Figures
HMM? WHAT'S UP, TENKUJI?
YOU WANT ME TO HELP YOU WITH SOME POSES FOR YOUR MANGA?
NOD NOD
OH, RIGHT, THAT'S THE HOBBY YOU DON'T TALK ABOUT.
SURE, I'D BE HAPPY TO HELP.
Sora's Room

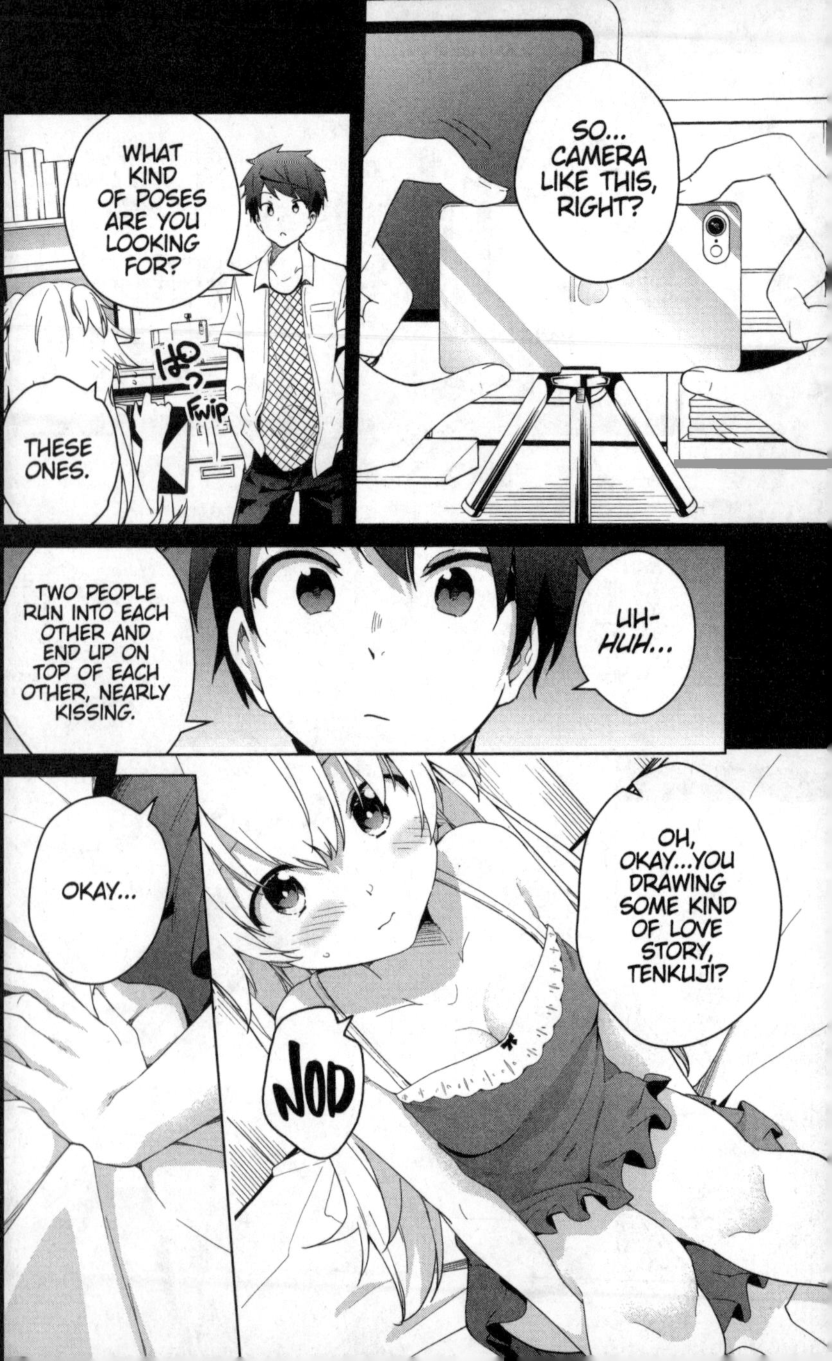
SO... CAMERA LIKE THIS, RIGHT?
WHAT KIND OF POSES ARE YOU LOOKING FOR?
はっ
Fwip
THESE ONES.
UH-HUH...
TWO PEOPLE RUN INTO EACH OTHER AND END UP ON TOP OF EACH OTHER, NEARLY KISSING.
OH, OKAY...YOU DRAWING SOME KIND OF LOVE STORY, TENKUJI?
NOD
OKAY...

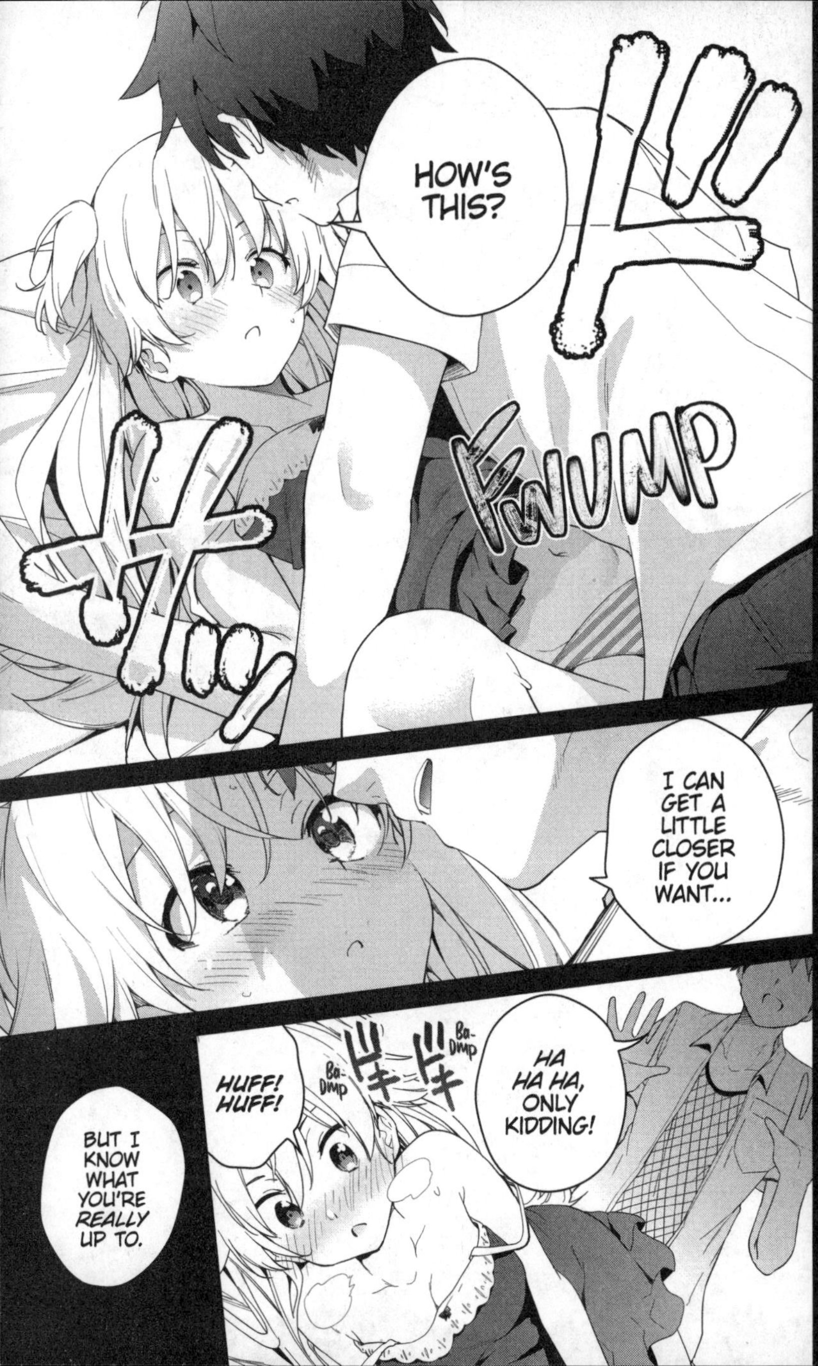
HOW'S THIS?
FWUMP
I CAN GET A LITTLE CLOSER IF YOU WANT...
HA HA HA, ONLY KIDDING!
Ba-Dmp
ドキドキ
Ba-Dmp
HUFF! HUFF!
BUT I KNOW WHAT YOU'RE *REALLY* UP TO.

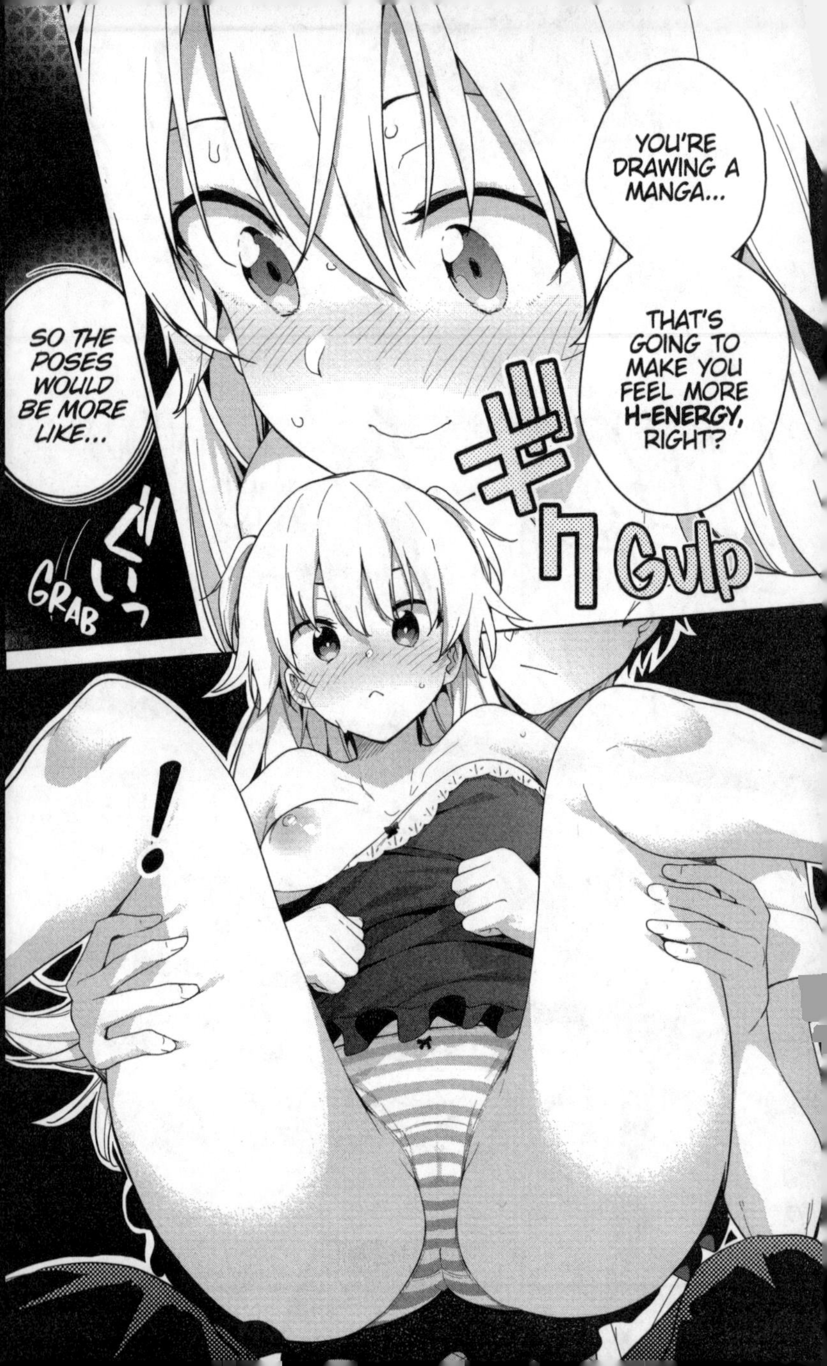
YOU'RE DRAWING A MANGA...
THAT'S GOING TO MAKE YOU FEEL MORE H-ENERGY, RIGHT?
ギク
Gulp
SO THE POSES WOULD BE MORE LIKE...
ぐいっ
GRAB
!

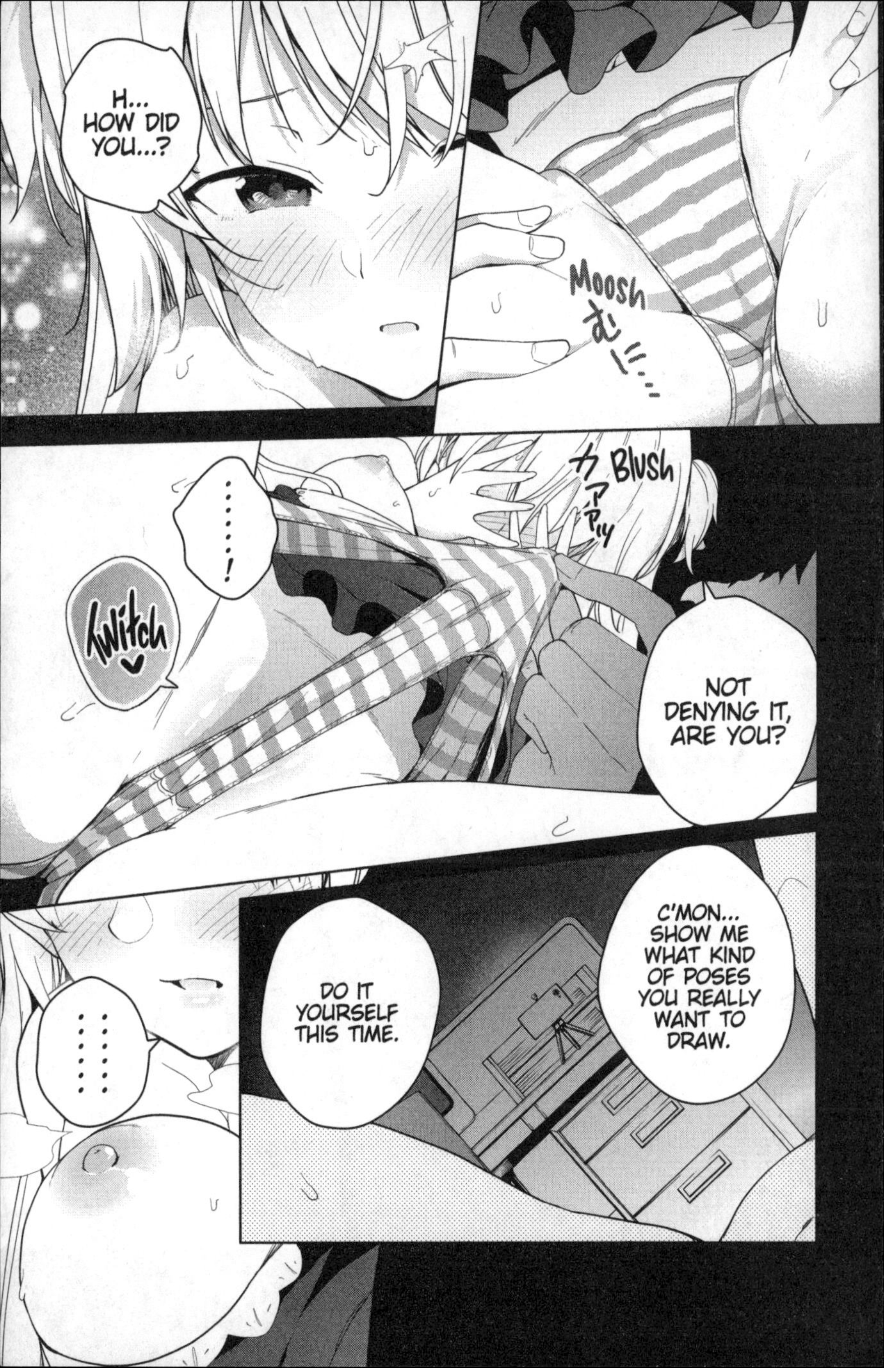
Moosh
むに…
H... HOW DID YOU...?
Blush
カァアッ
NOT DENYING IT, ARE YOU?
......!
Twitch
C'MON... SHOW ME WHAT KIND OF POSES YOU REALLY WANT TO DRAW.
DO IT YOURSELF THIS TIME.
......
......

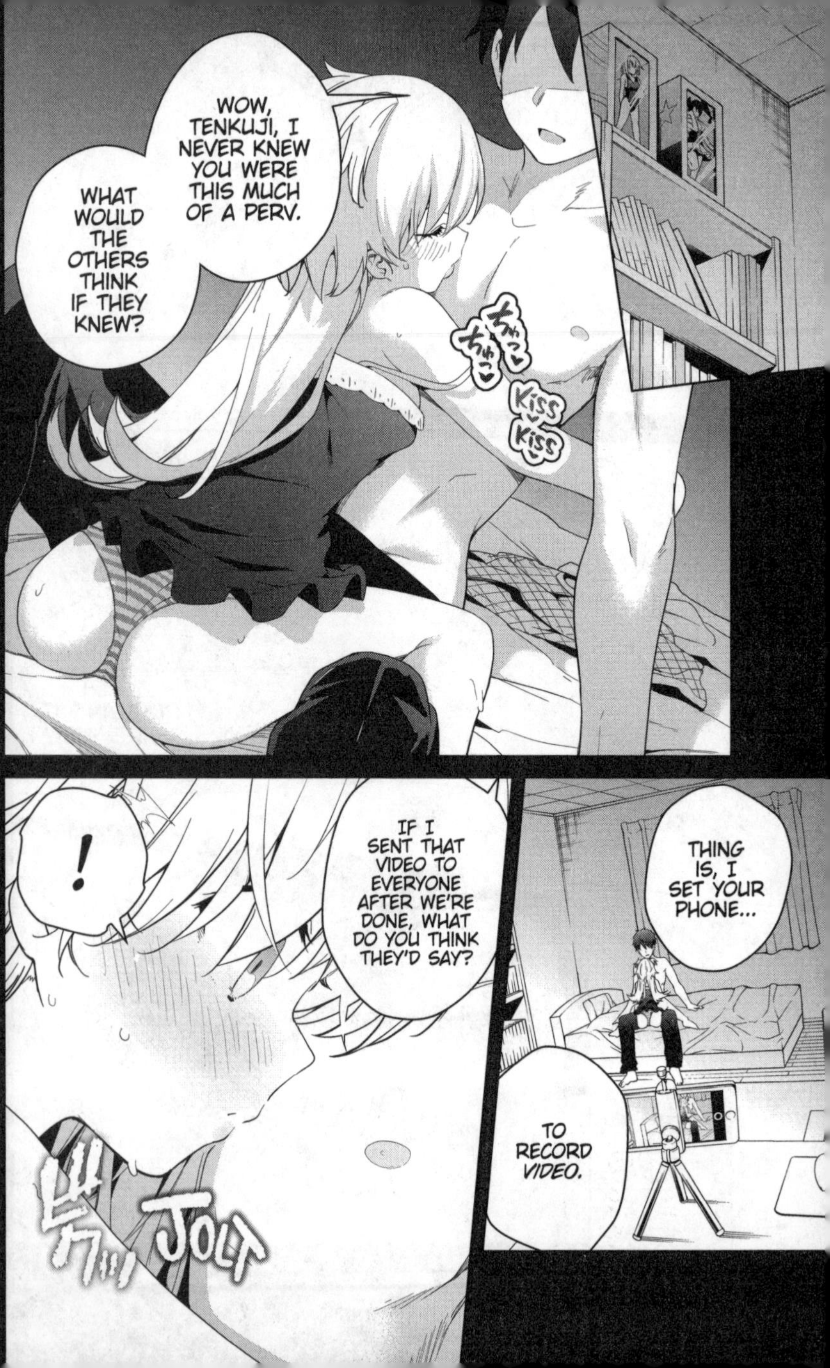
WOW, TENKUJI, I NEVER KNEW YOU WERE THIS MUCH OF A PERV.
WHAT WOULD THE OTHERS THINK IF THEY KNEW?
ちゅっ♥ちゅっ♥
KISS♥KISS♥
THING IS, I SET YOUR PHONE...
TO RECORD VIDEO.
IF I SENT THAT VIDEO TO EVERYONE AFTER WE'RE DONE, WHAT DO YOU THINK THEY'D SAY?
!
ビクッ
JOLT

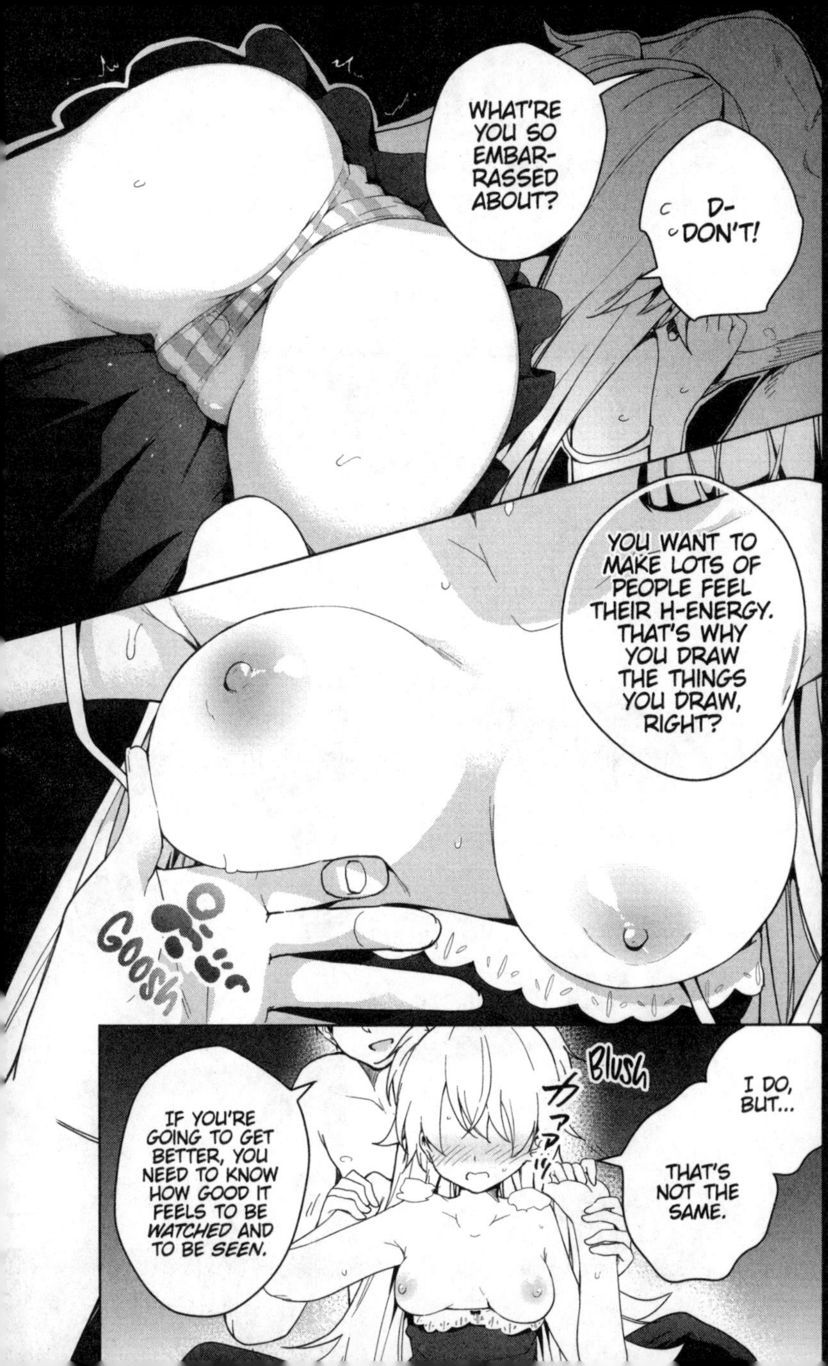
D-DON'T!
WHAT'RE YOU SO EMBARRASSED ABOUT?
YOU WANT TO MAKE LOTS OF PEOPLE FEEL THEIR H-ENERGY. THAT'S WHY YOU DRAW THE THINGS YOU DRAW, RIGHT?
GOOSH
I DO, BUT...
THAT'S NOT THE SAME.
Blush
IF YOU'RE GOING TO GET BETTER, YOU NEED TO KNOW HOW GOOD IT FEELS TO BE WATCHED AND TO BE SEEN.

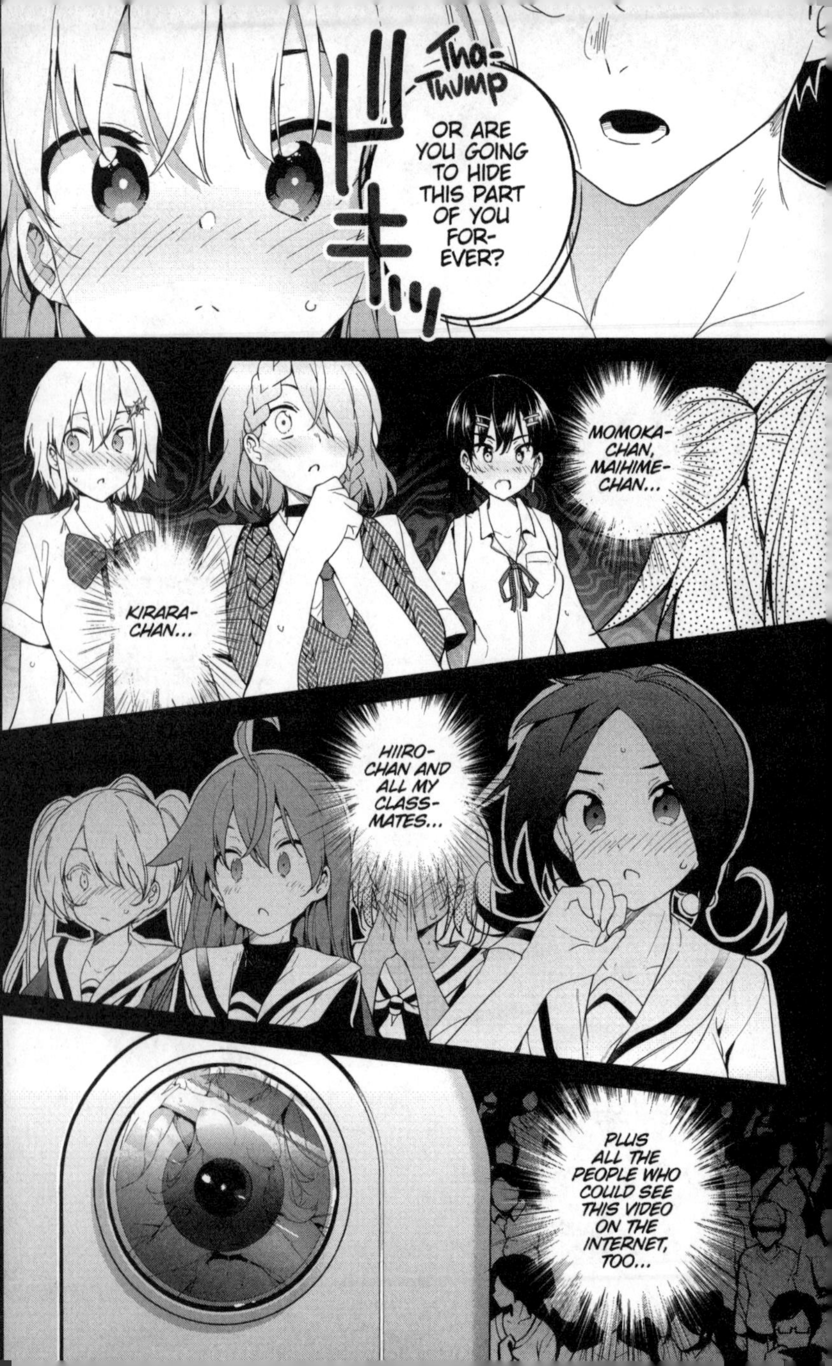
Tha-Thump
OR ARE YOU GOING TO HIDE THIS PART OF YOU FOR-EVER?
MOMOKA-CHAN, MAIHIME-CHAN...
KIRARA-CHAN...
HIIRO-CHAN AND ALL MY CLASS-MATES...
PLUS ALL THE PEOPLE WHO COULD SEE THIS VIDEO ON THE INTERNET, TOO...

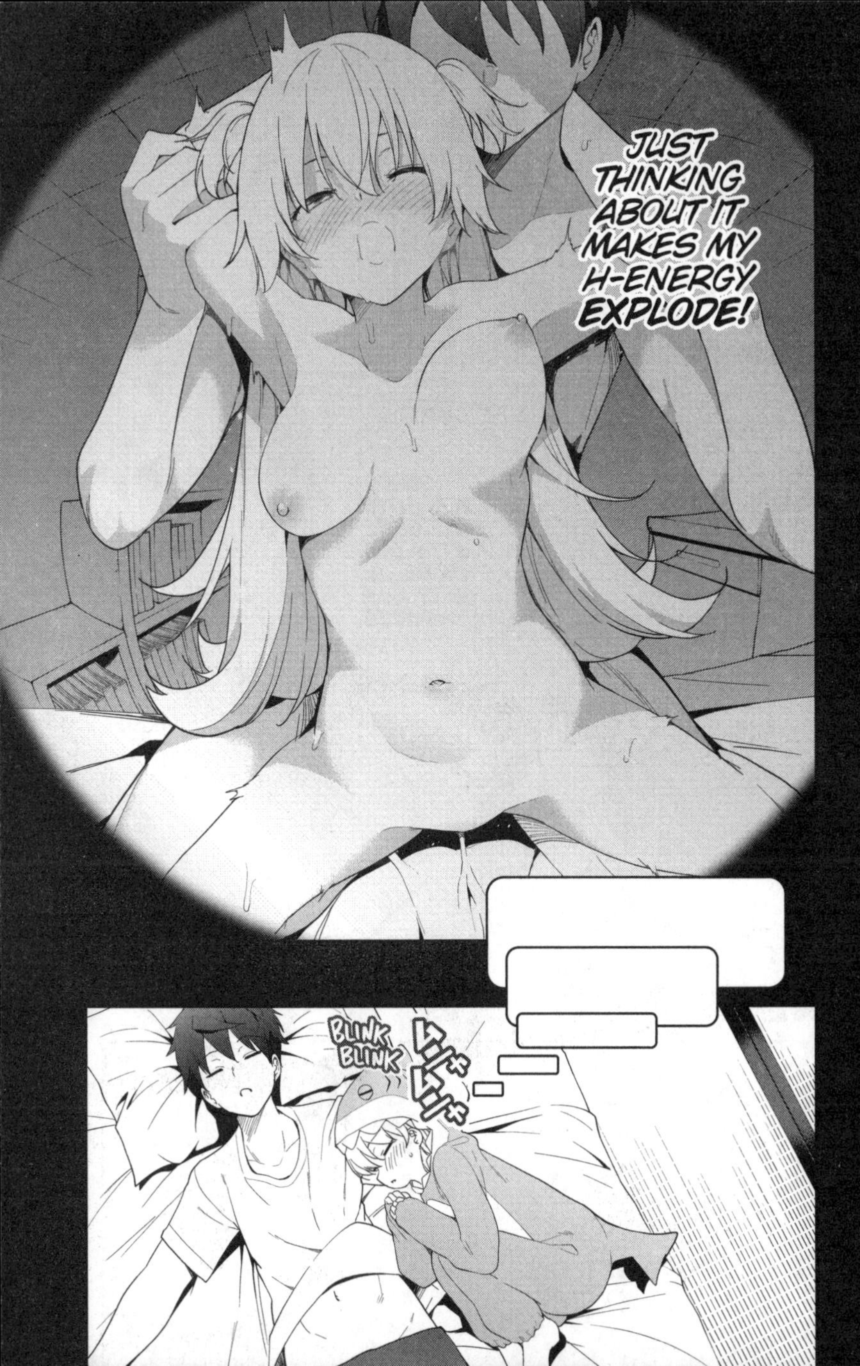
JUST THINKING ABOUT IT MAKES MY H-ENERGY EXPLODE!
BLINK BLINK

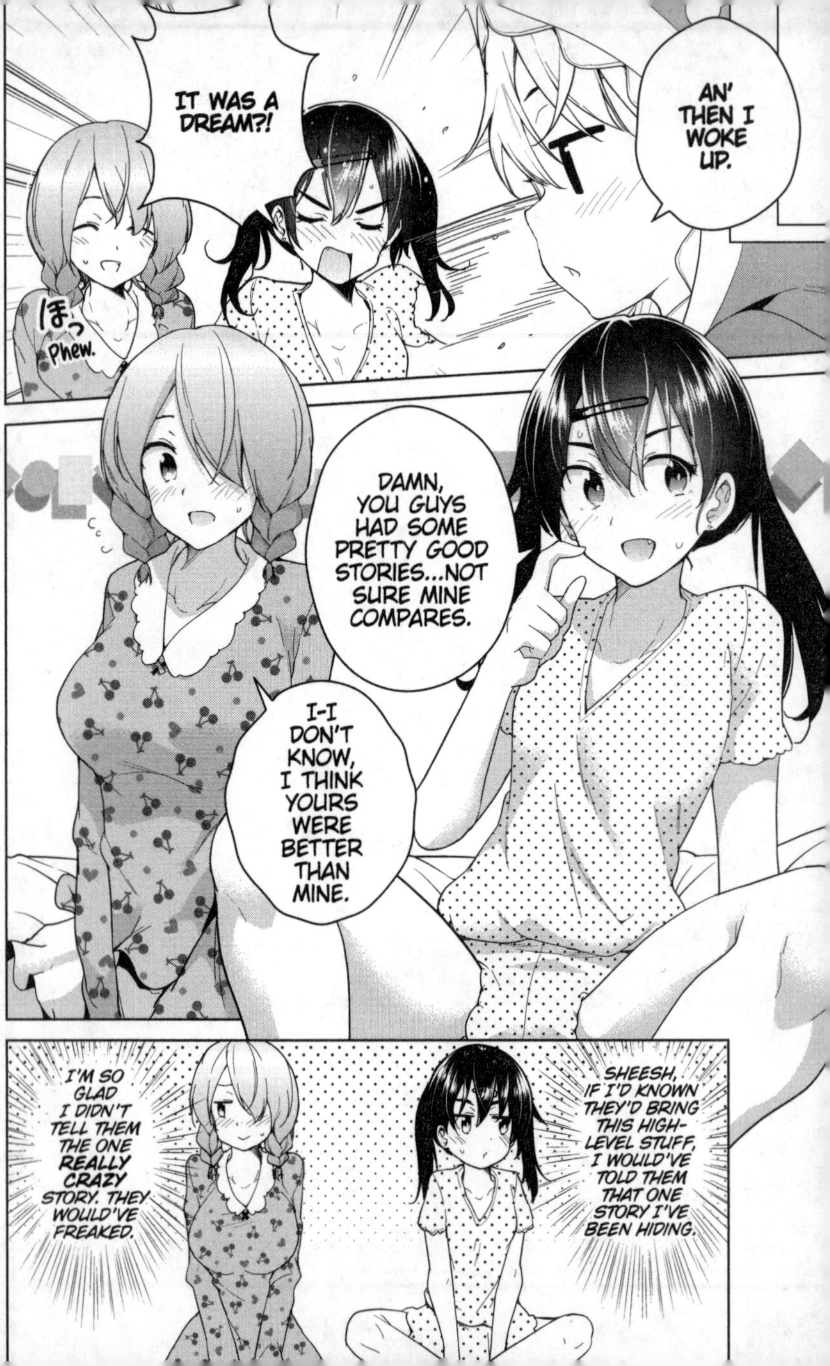
AN' THEN I WOKE UP.
IT WAS A DREAM?!
ほっ
Phew.
DAMN, YOU GUYS HAD SOME PRETTY GOOD STORIES...NOT SURE MINE COMPARES.
I-I DON'T KNOW, I THINK YOURS WERE BETTER THAN MINE.
SHEESH, IF I'D KNOWN THEY'D BRING THIS HIGH-LEVEL STUFF, I WOULD'VE TOLD THEM THAT ONE STORY I'VE BEEN HIDING.
I'M SO GLAD I DIDN'T TELL THEM THE ONE REALLY CRAZY STORY. THEY WOULD'VE FREAKED.

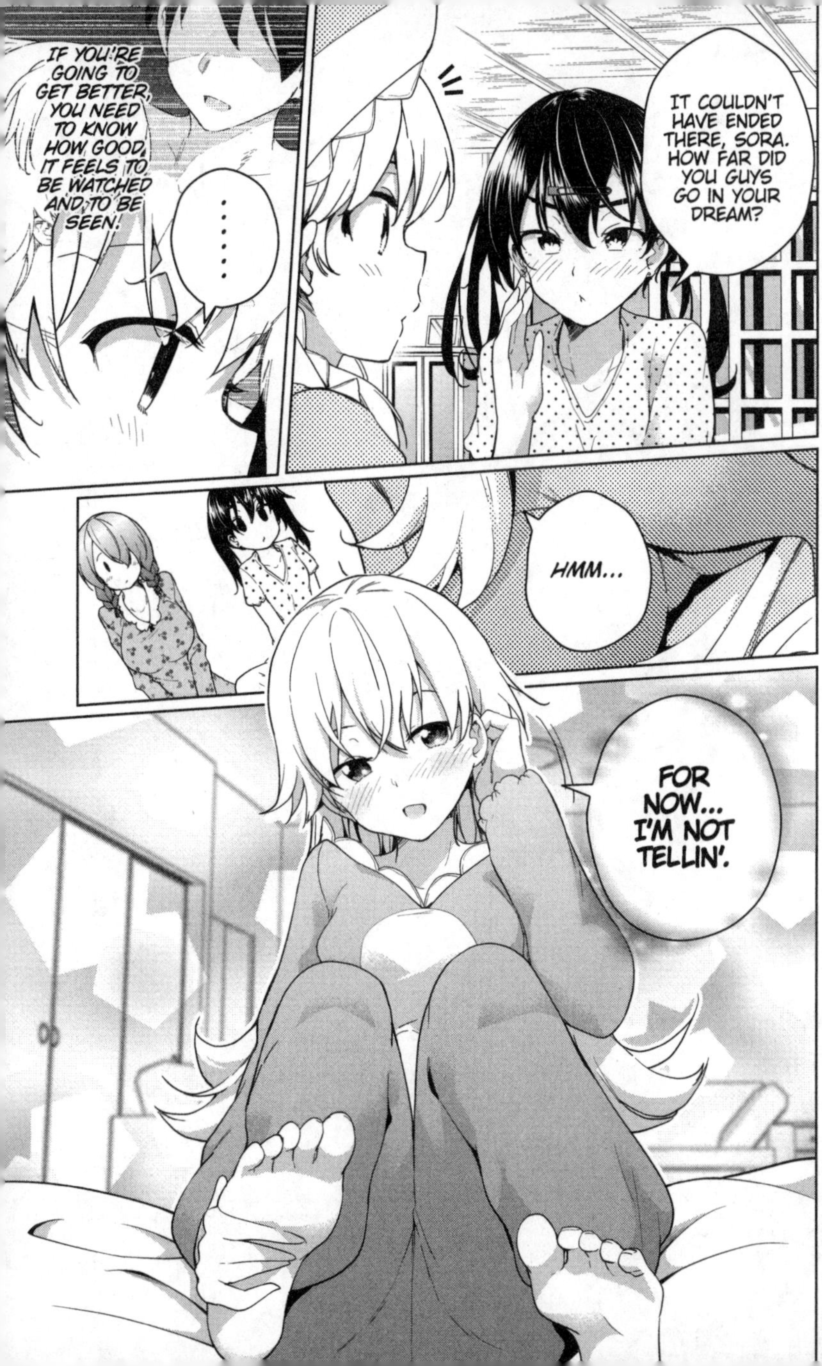
IT COULDN'T HAVE ENDED THERE, SORA. HOW FAR DID YOU GUYS GO IN YOUR DREAM?
IF YOU'RE GOING TO GET BETTER, YOU NEED TO KNOW HOW GOOD IT FEELS TO BE WATCHED AND TO BE SEEN!
......
HMM...
FOR NOW... I'M NOT TELLIN'.

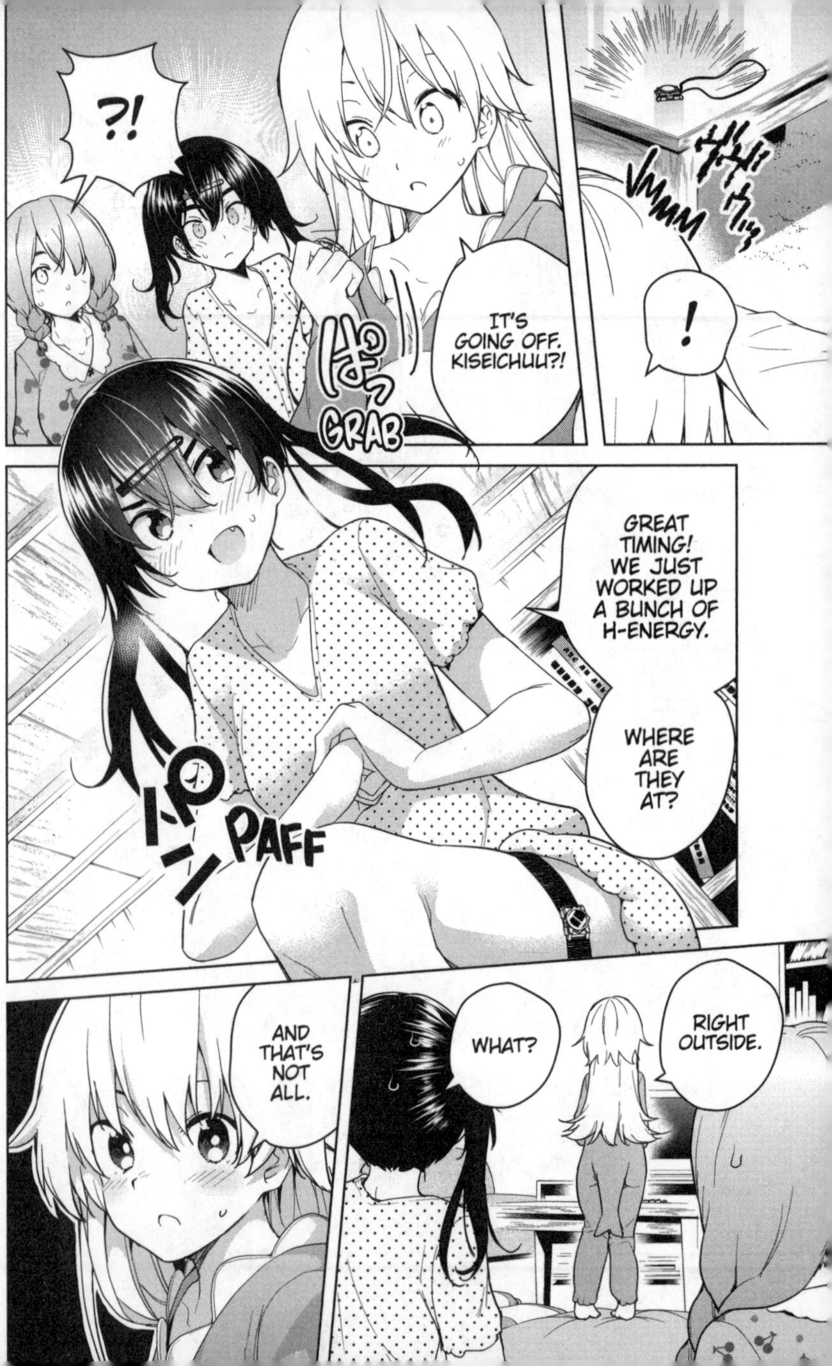
VMMM
!
IT'S GOING OFF. KISEICHUU?!
?!
ぱっ
GRAB
GREAT TIMING! WE JUST WORKED UP A BUNCH OF H-ENERGY.
WHERE ARE THEY AT?
PAFF
RIGHT OUTSIDE.
WHAT?
AND THAT'S NOT ALL.

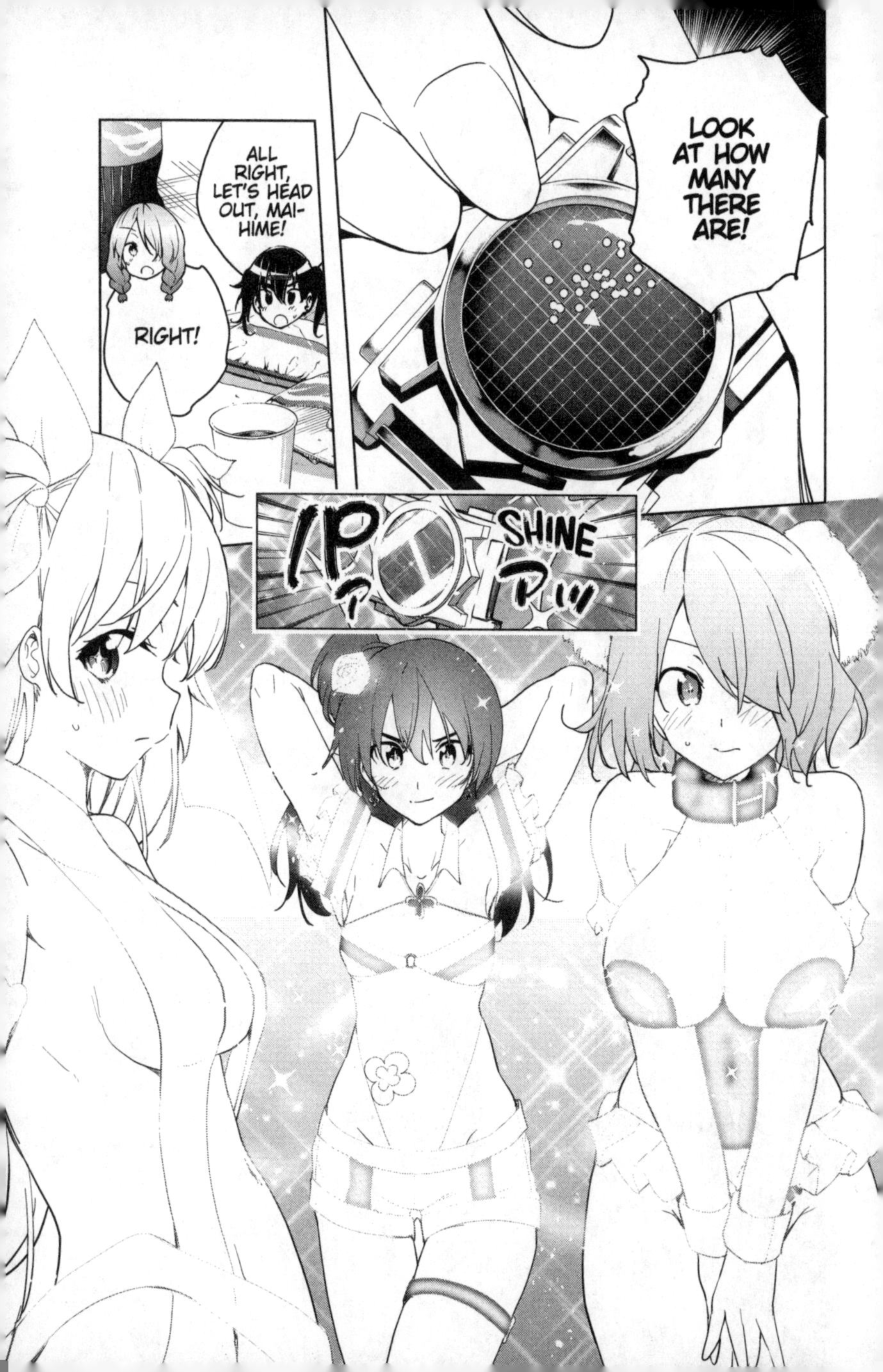
LOOK AT HOW MANY THERE ARE!
ALL RIGHT, LET'S HEAD OUT, MAI-HIME!
RIGHT!
SHINE

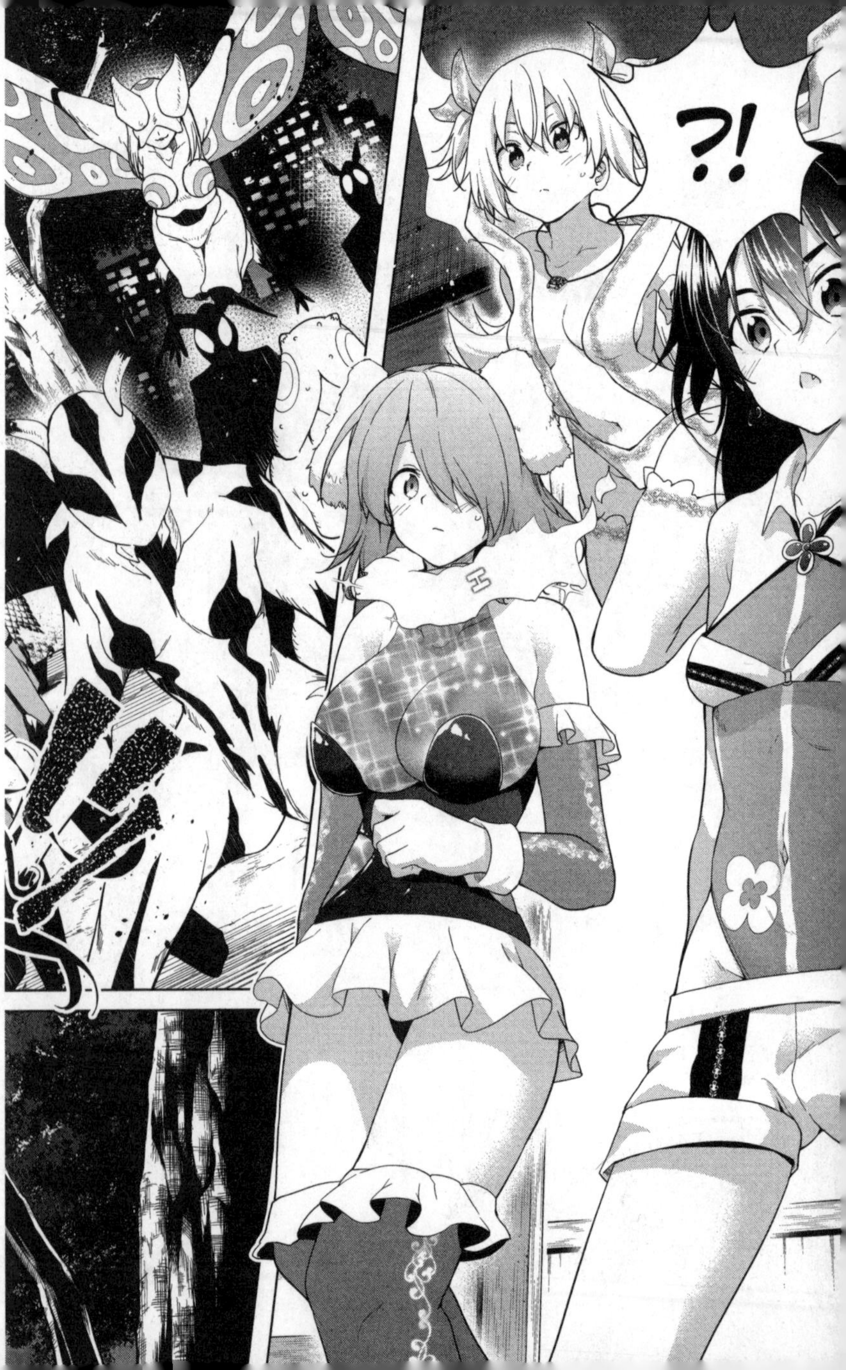
?!

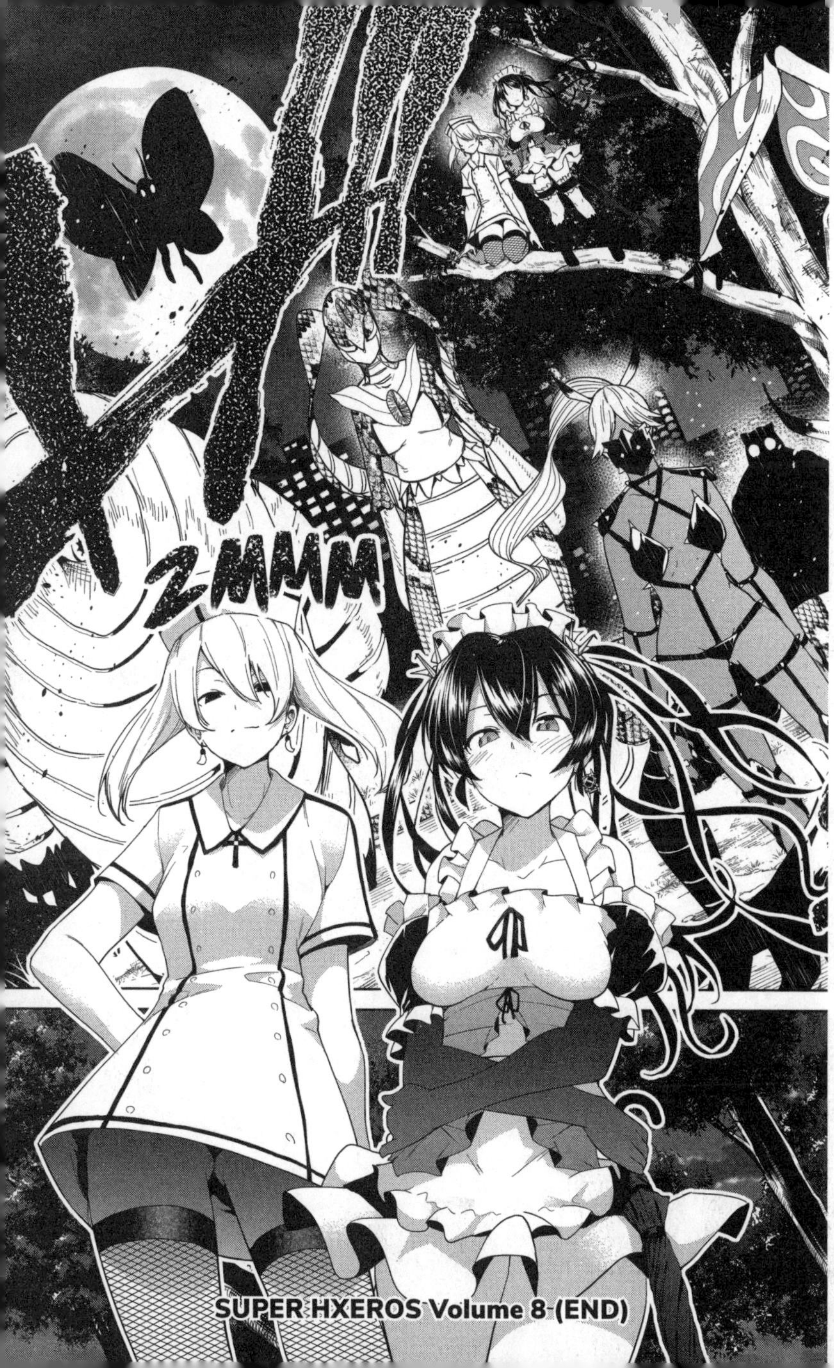
ZMMM
SUPER HXEROS Volume 8 (END)

SUPER

H×EROS

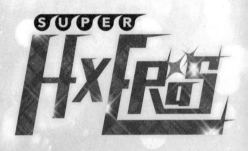

SUPER HxEROS

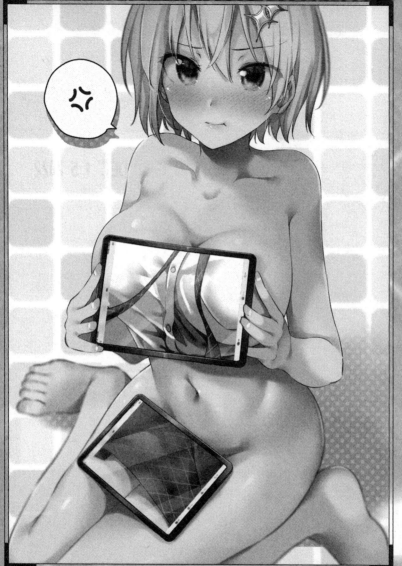

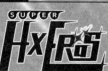

Extra Gallery

SEVEN SEAS ENTERTAINMENT PRESENTS

SUPER HXEROS

story and art by **RYOMA KITADA**

VOLUME 8

TRANSLATION
Katrina Leonoudakis

ADAPTATION
David Lumsdon

LETTERING AND RETOUCH
Joven Voon

COVER DESIGN
Nicky Lim

PROOFREADER
Danielle King

EDITOR
J.P. Sullivan

PREPRESS TECHNICIAN
Melanie Ujimori

PRINT MANAGER
Rhiannon Rasmussen–Silverstein

PRODUCTION DESIGNER
George Panella

PRODUCTION MANAGER
Lissa Pattillo

EDITOR-IN-CHIEF
Julie Davis

ASSOCIATE PUBLISHER
Adam Arnold

PUBLISHER
Jason DeAngelis

SUPER HXEROS -"H"EROES SAVE THE WORLD
DOKYU HENTAI EGUZEROSU © 2017 by Ryoma Kitada
All rights reserved.
First published in Japan in 2017 by SHUEISHA Inc., Tokyo.
English translation rights arranged by SHUEISHA Inc.
through TOHAN CORPORATION, Tokyo.

DEC 1 5 2022

Seven Seas press and purchase enquiries can be sent to Marketing Manager Lianne
Sentar at press@gomanga.com. Information regarding the distribution and purchase of
digital editions is available from Digital Manager CK Russell at digital@gomanga.com.

Seven Seas and the Seven Seas logo are trademarks of
Seven Seas Entertainment

ISBN: 978-1-63858-3
Printed in Canada
First Printing: July 202
10 9 8 7 6 5 4 3

12-13-22
NEVER
0

RE

This book reads from *right to left*,
Japanese style. If this is your first time
reading manga, you start reading from
the top right panel on each page and
take it from there. If you get lost, just
follow the numbered diagram here.
It may seem backwards at first,
but you'll get the hang of it! Have fun!!

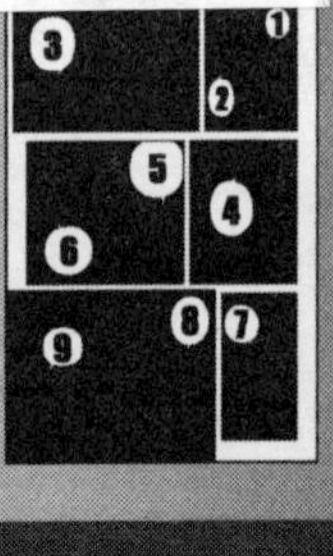